D0803433

Jewish Politics in Vienna,
1918–1938

The Modern Jewish Experience

Paula Hyman and Deborah Dash Moore, *Editors*

Jewish Politics in Vienna

1918–1938

HARRIET PASS FREIDENREICH

Indiana University Press

BLOOMINGTON & INDIANAPOLIS

©1991 by Harriet Pass Freidenreich

All rights reserved

No part of this book may be reproduced or utilized in any form or by any means, electronic or mechanical, including photocopying and recording, or by any information storage and retrieval system, without permission in writing from the publisher. The Association of American University Presses' Resolution on Permissions constitutes the only exception to this prohibition.

The paper used in this publication meets the minimum requirements of American National Standard for Information Sciences—Permanence of Paper for Printed Library Materials, ANSI Z39.48-1984.

Manufactured in the United States of America

Library of Congress Cataloging-in-Publication Data

Freidenreich, Harriet Pass.

Jewish politics in Vienna, 1918–1938 / Harriet Pass Freidenreich

p. cm. — (The Modern Jewish experience)

Includes bibliographical references (p.) and index.

ISBN 0-253-32475-0 (alk. paper)

1. Jews—Austria—Vienna—Politics and government.
2. Jews—Austria—Vienna—History—20th century.
3. Austria—History—1918-1938.
4. Vienna (Austria)—Ethnic relations.
I. Title. II. Series: Modern Jewish experience (Bloomington, Ind.)

DS135.A92V523   1991

943.6'13004924—dc20   90-4767

1 2 3 4 5 95 94 93 92 91

CONTENTS

ACKNOWLEDGMENTS   vii

1. **Introduction: Jews, Politics, and Vienna**   1
   Austrian Politics and the Jewish Question   6
   Jewish Political Options   9
   The Jewish Electorate   12
   Postwar Problems   14
   The Kultusgemeinde   18

2. **The Liberals**   22
   The Union of Austrian Jews   23
   Political Activities   29
   Controlling the Kultusgemeinde   36

3. **The Jewish Nationalists**   48
   Diaspora Nationalists and Zionists   49
   Landespolitik   59
   Conquering the Community   72

4. **The Socialists**   84
   Jewish Voters and the Social Democratic Party   86
   Jewish Socialists and Labor Zionists   91
   Socialist Jews and the Kultusgemeinde   96

5. **The Orthodox**   115
   Orthodoxy and the Kultusgemeinde   118
   The Hungarian Orthodox   125
   The Galician Orthodox   138

6. **Continuity and Disunity**   147
   Financial Constraints and Shifting Priorities   151
   Orthodox Secession Attempts   158
   Filling the Vacancies   164
   The 1936 Elections   172

7. Confronting Antisemitism 180

Kultusgemeinde Defense Activities 181

In the Austrian Corporate State 186

Defense Efforts in the Thirties 190

Austrian Jews and the Fatherland Front 195

Separate but Not Equal 198

Epilogue: After the *Anschluss* 204

ABBREVIATIONS 211

TABLES 213

NOTES 225

SELECTED BIBLIOGRAPHY 259

INDEX 265

Acknowledgments

Over the many years I have been studying Viennese Jewry, I have incurred debts of gratitude to numerous individuals and institutions, which I acknowledge with great pleasure. For financial support of this project, I am indebted to the American Council of Learned Societies, the Memorial Foundation for Jewish Culture, and Temple University. For their invaluable assistance in my research, I wish to thank the archivists and librarians of the Central Archives for the History of the Jewish People, the Central Zionist Archives, and the Jewish National and University Library in Jerusalem; the Austrian General Government Archives, the Archives of the City of Vienna, the Austrian National Library, and the University Library in Vienna; and the Leo Baeck Institute and the Joint Distribution Committee Archives in New York. I am also very grateful to the staff of Temple University's Paley Library, especially its Interlibrary Loan division. In addition, I want to thank the Viennese Jews and their children who shared precious insights with me about life in the Austrian capital.

My most heartfelt gratitude goes to Marsha Rozenblit and Paula Hyman, who carefully read various drafts of this manuscript and provided me with constructive criticism and helpful guidelines for its revision. I also want to thank David Good, Alan Zuckerman, and Vivian Felsen for reading earlier versions of this study and offering valuable comments. I am indebted to my colleagues in the History Department of Temple University for their encouragement of my research and their practical suggestions.

To my family and friends I wish to express my appreciation for their moral support and the interest they have shown in my work. I must add a special word of thanks to my neighbors in Bet Ha-Kerem, Jerusalem, and my cousin, Jane Helmchen, in Germany, who enabled me to complete the initial stages of my research while my children were still very young. I also want to credit Rochelle Lecke with helping me keep my writing in perspective. Lastly, but certainly not least, I am grateful beyond words to my husband, Phil Freidenreich, for his patience, his willingness to listen, and his much-valued advice.

This book is dedicated to our sons, David and Aron, who have grown up alongside it, bringing us much joy; they approach adolescence as this endeavor finally reaches maturity.

Jewish Politics in Vienna, 1918–1938

1

INTRODUCTION

Jews, Politics, and Vienna

Jewish political behavior in the twentieth century reflects the diversity and complexity of the modern Jewish experience. Do Jews constitute a nation or a religious group? Should Jews in the diaspora create separate political parties or lobbies to ensure group survival, or does participation of Jews as individuals in existing parties of the Right, Center, or Left better serve Jewish interests? To what extent do class and antisemitism determine Jewish voting patterns? Such questions have arisen in many different historical and geographic contexts but have yet to be answered.

As members of a minority, Jews often support different political parties than their fellow citizens of the same economic class. Jews vote for what they perceive to be their political interests, which do not necessarily coincide with their pocketbooks. Since Jews rarely constitute a homogeneous group, however, they do not always agree on their political priorities and hence tend not to vote as a unified bloc. Multiple factors influence Jewish political choices, including national identity, ideological commitment, religious observance, degree of assimilation, and place of origin, as well as economic concerns. External considerations, particularly antisemitism, may seriously proscribe Jewish options in general elections. Jews participate in the modern political system both as party activists and as voters. Whereas activists are generally attracted to a particular party for positive reasons, voters may well cast their ballots on negative grounds. Jews may also "split their tickets" and support different parties in various types of elections, depending on circumstances.

Vienna provides us with a microcosm of twentieth-century Jewish politics. The Jewish communal structure as well as the parliamentary system in Austria closely resembled that of Germany, Poland, and the other successor states of post–World War I Europe. Austria's political organization, both Jewish and general, also bears striking similarities to the system which was later incorporated into the State of Israel. Austrian politics had a very strong impact on Jewish politics in interwar Vienna, but Jewish political behavior in the Austrian capital paralleled the political trends of their fellow Jews elsewhere rather than the pattern of their fellow Austrian citizens.

This book seeks to explain the seeming paradoxes of Jewish politics in interwar Vienna, where Liberal, Jewish Nationalist, Socialist, and Orthodox factions competed with one another and attempted to devise strategies for coping with an increasingly hostile environment. In municipal and national elections, a majority of the predominantly middle-class Viennese Jews voted for the Marxist, working-class Austrian Social Democratic Party, which viewed both religion and nationalism with disfavor. Yet in communal elections, Jewish Nationalists eventually succeeded in wresting control of the Jewish community out of the hands of Liberals. What prompted Jewish voters to shift their allegiance from Liberals to Socialists in some elections and to Jewish Nationalists in others?

Like Jews all over the world, Viennese Jews were searching for constructive solutions to the critical economic, social, and political problems which plagued them in the twentieth century. During the interwar years they experienced serious demographic and economic crises, exacerbated by escalating antisemitism. They could seek to improve their difficult situation either through the general political process or within their own community. Whereas antisemitism clearly demanded external resolution, assimilation and growing impoverishment posed internal dilemmas. The Liberals devoted much of their efforts to combating discrimination, whereas the Jewish Nationalists and the Orthodox appeared most concerned with preventing assimilation and the Socialists focused their attention on ameliorating the social welfare needs of the less fortunate.

Viennese Jewry comprised an extremely heterogeneous group. They differed significantly among themselves with respect to wealth, culture, and religion, as well as politics and place of origin. By economic bracket they ranged from a tiny aristocratic elite of ennobled bankers and industrialists to middle-class businessmen and professionals to destitute Galician refugees. Among the Orthodox, we find both Yiddish-speaking Hasidim with caftans and earlocks and strictly observant Hungarians who spoke German and wore Western garb. Modern Orthodox Polish Jews who emphasized decorum in the synagogue coexisted alongside traditional Jews who frequented disorderly prayerhouses. At the other end of the spectrum, we discover atheistic Socialists and secularized intellectual trend-setters who epitomized Viennese cultural brilliance. In between, we encounter Austrian citizens of the Jewish faith who attended dignified Liberal services with

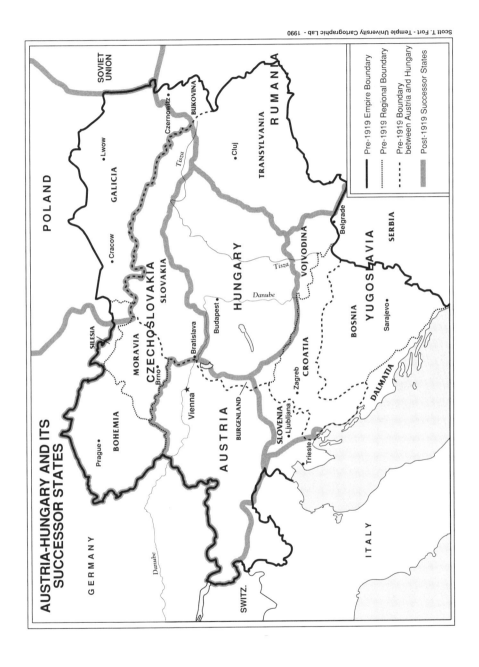

AUSTRIA-HUNGARY AND ITS SUCCESSOR STATES

GERMANY

POLAND

SOVIET UNION

BOHEMIA
• Prague

MORAVIA
• Brno

SILESIA

CZECHOSLOVAKIA

SLOVAKIA
• Bratislava

• Cracow

GALICIA

• Lwow

• Czernowitz

BUKOVINA

Tisza

TRANSYLVANIA

• Cluj

R U M A N I A

HUNGARY

Tisza

• Budapest

Danube

VOIVODINA

Belgrade

SERBIA

★ Vienna

AUSTRIA

BURGENLAND

SLOVENIA
• Ljubljana

Trieste

CROATIA
• Zagreb

BOSNIA

YUGOSLAVIA

• Sarajevo

DALMATIA

Danube

SWITZ.

ITALY

Pre-1919 Empire Boundary

Pre-1919 Regional Boundary

Pre-1919 Boundary between Austria and Hungary

Post-1919 Successor States

Scott T. Fort - Temple University Cartographic Lab - 1990

German sermons mainly on the High Holydays and Zionists who defined themselves as Jews by nationality.

This is a comparative study in Jewish ethnopolitics on communal, local, and national levels. While it deals with all persons identified as Jews, including assimilated Jews and even those who officially opted out of the Jewish community, it focuses primarily on those who consciously identified themselves as Jews, especially those involved in the organized Jewish community. By examining communal politics as well as Jewish involvement in municipal and parliamentary politics, we can better understand the complex nature of Jewish political identity and the tactics available to Jewish activists and voters in different contexts.

As in interwar East Central Europe and in Israel, Jewish political groups proliferated in Vienna, each with its own preferred strategy for Jewish survival, whether as individuals or as a group. The spectrum stretched from Socialists on the Left to Orthodox on the Right, with Liberals and Jewish Nationalists in the Center. The major dichotomy within Jewish political life, however, lay not between the Marxists and the Liberals or the Orthodox and the non-Orthodox, but between the Jewish Nationalists and the opponents of Jewish Nationalism.

In Vienna the foes of Jewish Nationalism, also classified as non- or anti-Zionists, included Social Democrats, Liberals, and the ultra-Orthodox Agudat Israel. Despite their disparate religious and ideological orientations, they could all agree that Jews constituted primarily a religious community whose rights could best be protected by civic equality and freedom of religion for all individuals within the state. The non-nationalist camp tended to support existing political parties in municipal and national elections and, since they defined Jews as members of a religious denomination, they wished to restrict the scope of communal activities largely to the religious sphere.

The Jewish Nationalists, virtually all of whom were also Zionists in interwar Vienna, split into numerous factions. Some felt they should devote their efforts entirely to rebuilding the Jewish homeland in Palestine, while others also engaged in political activities in the diaspora, including fighting for national minority rights for Jews. Middle-of-the-road General Zionists provided the strongest support for involvement in diaspora politics, whether within the Jewish community or in general elections. They created a separate Jewish party to run in municipal and parliamentary races. Labor Zionists, whether adherents of the Marxist Poale Zion or non-Marxist Hitachdut, wavered in their support for diaspora Jewish politics but retained their commitment to creating a Socialist-based Jewish society in the Land of Israel. The Religious Zionists, known as the Mizrachi, restricted their political activities in Vienna to the communal sphere. Despite their differing agendas, all Jewish Nationalists agreed on one basic premise, namely that Jews constitute a separate nation and deserve recognition as such, whether as a majority in their own state or as a minority in the diaspora. They also wanted to democratize the governing body of the Jewish community and broaden its range of activity.

The Austrian capital served as a magnet attracting both Western and Eastern-type Jews from various parts of the Habsburg Empire. On the eve of World War I, Vienna's 175,000 Jews constituted 8.6 percent of its population. (See Table 1.) Roughly a fifth of these Jews were native Viennese. Slightly over a quarter of the Jewish migrants to this Central European mecca had come from the Czech lands and a little less than one-quarter from the Hungarian lands, mainly western Slovakia and the Burgenland. These Westernized Jews from Hungary, Bohemia, and Moravia had streamed into Vienna in the mid- to late nineteenth century. They integrated readily into Viennese culture, since they already spoke German and usually identified themselves as Jews by religion but Germans by nationality. Jews from Hungary and Bohemia tended to be non-Zionists, especially Liberals, as in Germany or interwar Hungary. While some Moravian Jews also belonged to the non-Zionist camp, others gravitated toward Jewish Nationalism, as they did in interwar Czechoslovakia. Yiddish-speaking Eastern Jews, mainly from Galicia, arrived nearer the turn of the century or later and hence had less time to assimilate. They often brought their Jewish national identity and Orthodox religious practices with them. By World War I these Easterners from Galicia or neighboring Bukovina made up approximately one-fifth of Viennese Jewry. As in interwar Poland, Galicians in the Austrian capital tended toward Zionism in its various forms.[1]

In Vienna as elsewhere, Galician Jews, pejoratively referred to as *Ostjuden* or Eastern Jews, found themselves relegated to the bottom of the informal European Jewish pecking order.[2] During the interwar period, members of this group, including their Viennese-born children, continued to be referred to collectively as "foreigners," despite the fact that their residency and citizenship status in many cases did not differ significantly from the more Westernized Jews who considered themselves "natives." This split between the more assimilated Western-type Jews, who constituted a majority of the Viennese Jewish population, and the culturally less integrated Eastern-type Jews, who comprised an increasingly significant minority, plays a crucial role in our understanding of Jewish politics during the interwar years.

Vienna provides a particularly interesting example of the factionalism and coalition-building across the political spectrum that characterize Jewish politics both in Eastern Europe and in Israel. The most enduring barriers separated not Left from Right or observant from non-observant but "Westerners" from "Easterners." Given the relative ethnic homogeneity of the overwhelmingly German Austrian Republic, one might expect Jewish political behavior in Vienna to mirror that of Jews in Germany or Hungary during the interwar period. While the non-Zionists indeed followed these Western examples, the Jewish Nationalists pursued more Eastern political strategies reminiscent of multiethnic Poland and Czechoslovakia.[3]

Austrian Politics and the Jewish Question

The external pressures of their milieu, especially antisemitism, strongly influenced Jewish political behavior in Vienna. In the mid-nineteenth century, only a few thousand Jews resided in the Austrian capital and antisemitism had not yet surfaced as a significant problem.[4] In 1867, Austrian Jews achieved civic emancipation under the auspices of the Liberals, with whom they soon became closely identified. The Liberal heyday lasted until the 1880s. By then roughly 75,000 Jews were living in Vienna, most of them having been born in Hungary, Bohemia, or Moravia. German Liberals and Westernized Jews appeared to be natural allies, since both supported equality of opportunity for all citizens regardless of religion yet favored restricted suffrage based on wealth and property.[5]

The late nineteenth century witnessed the decline of Austrian Liberalism, the rise of modern antisemitism, and the unfolding of what Carl Schorske has labeled "politics in a new key." Out of the old Liberalism emerged three new Austrian political camps, the Clericals, the German Nationalists, and the Socialists, as well as one specifically Jewish camp, the Zionists or Jewish Nationalists.[6] Both the Clerical Christian Socials, led by Karl Lueger, and the Pan-German Nationalists, led by Georg von Schönerer, quickly adopted overtly antisemitic platforms. After the Christian Socials, the party of lower-middle-class Catholics, wrested control of the Viennese municipal council from the Liberals, Lueger became mayor of Vienna in 1897.[7] The Christian Socials maintained their hold over the capital only until World War I, but with backing from former aristocrats as well as peasants in the provinces, they dominated Austrian national politics throughout the interwar years.

Austrian politics operated on a Central European multiparty system with proportional representation by party lists. Whereas before the war electoral curia had existed, based on wealth and class, thereafter a more democratic system eliminated the separate curia and extended voting rights to all Austrian citizens, women as well as men. Since no single party ever gained an absolute electoral majority in the Austrian parliament during the interwar years, the government functioned through coalitions.

The major dichotomy on the Austrian political scene in the twentieth century lay between the Marxists and the anti-Marxists. With the introduction of universal suffrage, the Social Democratic Party began to assume much greater importance in Viennese and Austrian politics and challenged the supremacy of the Christian Socials. In 1919, with the overwhelming support of the Viennese workers, the Socialists succeeded in capturing city hall. They ruled the municipality until 1934, thereby creating the image of "Red Vienna," a Socialist island in the midst of a Christian Social sea. Although the Socialists, with their militantly Marxist rhetoric, generally received over forty percent of the vote in parliamentary elections and even gained a slight plurality in the first postwar national contest in 1919 and again in the last held in 1930, they participated only briefly in a national coalition government with the Christian Socials.

After 1920, the conservative Christian Socials controlled the national scene, in conjunction with the various German Nationalist groups who held the balance of power. In 1933, parliamentary democracy came to an end in Austria, and by the following year, the Austrian Social Democratic Party as well as the Austrian Nazi Party had been outlawed. All political parties were officially dissolved and replaced by the Fatherland Front, led by the Christian Socials together with the paramilitary Austrian nationalist Heimwehr. The Austrian Republic had transformed into a Christian authoritarian corporate state, which lasted until the German *Anschluss*, or annexation, in March 1938.

Already before World War I, antisemitism had developed into an endemic disease in Vienna.[8] The virus infected the entire right-wing spectrum in Austrian politics and even the Liberals and the Socialists were not entirely immune. With the loss of the war and the collapse of the Austro-Hungarian Monarchy, Vienna emerged as a bloated metropolis, the capital of a truncated German Austrian Republic which did not really want to exist. Jews became convenient scapegoats upon which to blame the many ills of society.

The ruling Christian Social Party remained avowedly antisemitic, although not explicitly racist. Its 1918 electoral program referred to the "corruption and love of power of Jewish circles" and the need for defense against the "Jewish danger." It recognized Jews as a separate nation and was willing to grant them self-determination, but insisted that they should "not be allowed to be masters of the German *Volk*."[9] Subsequent party platforms emphasized the need to combat the "predominance of destructive Jewish influence in intellectual and economic fields."[10]

The leading Christian Social spokesman during the twenties, Monsignor Ignaz Seipel, never openly adopted a racist version of antisemitism. He criticized Jews ostensibly on Christian religious grounds and attacked them as vehicles of Socialism and Communism instead. Like Lueger, his predecessor, he was willing to accept the money of Jewish bankers, but his attitude toward baptized Jews was ambivalent.[11] Seipel supported a Jewish homeland in Palestine and the recognition of a Jewish nation, as did many Christian Social leaders.[12] However, Leopold Kunschak, head of the Christian Workers' Movement, and other prominent Catholic politicians regularly delivered crassly antisemitic speeches which were much less diplomatic than those of the statesmanlike Seipel.

Even further to the Right, the blatant antisemitism of the German Nationalist camp, comprised mainly of the Pan-German People's Party and the Austrian Nazis, proved consistently racist and extremely vituperative. The 1920 Salzburg Program of the People's Party harangued at great length against Jews as aliens and a threat to the inner unity of the German *Volk*. It condemned Jewish morality and castigated Jews for representing "dangerous individualism," including Liberalism and Marxism. Jews, it claimed, hate work and engage only in trade and cheating; they are parasites who get others to do their work for them. According to the disciples of Georg von Schönerer, Jewish power had increased during the war and resulted in the weakening of the state.[13] These themes were echoed repeatedly in numerous speeches, pamphlets, and other publications emanating from the entire range of right-wing groups, including not only Pan-Germans but also Christian Socials and the Austrian nationalist Heimwehr, an ostensibly non-partisan defense force which operated primarily in the provinces.

In 1919, members of these different factions joined together to form an Austrian Antisemitic League, which lasted until the mid-twenties. This organization sponsored rallies and demonstrations against Jews in Vienna and elsewhere, with speakers demanding the expulsion of all *Ostjuden* and the introduction of a numerus clausus or quota for Jewish students, as well as economic restrictions. These gatherings often led to physical violence against Jews, particularly in heavily Jewish neighborhoods.[14] Meanwhile antisemitic outbreaks had become rampant at Viennese institutions of higher learning. Although such manifestations seemed to be on the decline in the late twenties, with the economic and political crises of the thirties, antisemitism revived with even greater force. The Austrian Nazis replaced the Pan-Germans as the most vocal proponents of the elimination of Jews from the universities and the marketplace, while the Christian Socials and Heimwehr also supported these goals.

As the Liberal party declined and fragmented, it sought to distance itself from Jewish candidates and to find new allies among the German Nationalists in the vain hope of regaining middle-class voters and counteracting the Christian Socials and the Social Democrats. During the interwar period, although most members of the Liberal splinter groups were not themselves antisemites, by and large their political partners were.

Since the tiny Austrian Communist Party played a negligible role during the interwar years, the Austrian Social Democratic Party became the only major party which neither allied itself with antisemites nor contained an antisemitic plank in its platform.[15] But the Socialists also engaged in antisemitic stereotyping, both in their press and the speeches of their leaders, including those of Jewish origin. Like the Liberals, they assiduously avoided denouncing antisemitism openly or publicly defending Jewish interests for fear of being branded as a Jewish security force. In addition, they refrained from supporting Zionism and Jewish minority rights. As Marxists and protectors of workers' rights, the Social Democrats adopted an economic policy in Vienna which often proved disadvantageous to the predominantly middle-class Jewish population. Their definition of religion as an entirely private matter de facto meant that the Jewish community and its institutions received little or no municipal funding. Thus, while the Austrian Social Democratic Party certainly could not be considered antisemitic, it could scarcely be labeled "philosemitic" either.[16]

Jewish Political Options

The Jewish electorate seemed to resemble the general electorate in the Austrian capital, at least superficially. It also divided into three broad segments, with the Clericals, i.e., the Orthodox, constituting the right wing, the Liberals and the Jewish Nationalists in the Center, and the Socialists on the Left. But given the prevalence of antisemitism, Jewish voters could not vote like their German counterparts. Lower-middle-class Orthodox Jews could not easily support the Clerical Christian Socials, the party of lower-middle-class Catholics. Middle-class Jewish Nationalists and Liberals most assuredly could not vote for increasingly right-wing German Nationalist candidates, as did many middle-class German voters. Working-class Jews might indeed vote in clear conscience for the Austrian Social Democratic Party, as did the overwhelming majority of Viennese workers, but relatively few Viennese Jews were workers. Austrian Jews therefore had to develop a different voting pattern than Austrian Germans.

In national and municipal elections, Viennese Jewish voters had relatively limited freedom of choice. Supporting the radical antisemitic German Nationalist camp was virtually out of the question for any Jew and, except for a small group of wealthy bankers and industrialists who gave their financial backing to the conservative Christian Social Party and the Heimwehr, few Jews could actively support the Clerical camp either. Viennese Jews thus were left with three possible alternatives, each with its own drawbacks. They could continue to support the Liberals; they could switch their allegiance to the Social Democrats; or they could create a separate party of their own. The available options raised different questions for each of the major Jewish groups in Vienna, the Liberals, the Jewish Nationalists, the Socialists, and the Orthodox; in subsequent chapters we shall explore their responses.

Orthodox Jews faced a very difficult choice in Austrian and Viennese elections. Unlike in Germany, where Orthodox Jewish voters sometimes cast their ballots for the Catholic Center Party,[17] the Austrian Christian Socials held little electoral appeal, even for more traditional religious Jews. The Orthodox did not view the Liberal parties as a viable alternative either, while they opposed the Social Democrats on religious grounds. They might vote for a Jewish party, but that was likely to be secular and nationalist and not all the Orthodox belonged to the Zionist camp. What party, then, would the Orthodox voter choose?

Liberal Jewish voters would clearly prefer to cast their ballots for a Liberal party, as they had done in the past. But if the Austrian Liberals were in the process of disappearing and joining hands with German Nationalists, would this prevent Jews from voting for them? Were there any circumstances under which Jewish Liberals would vote for a Jewish party? Or would they shift their support to the Social Democrats? Maybe they should abstain from voting altogether.

As for the Jewish Nationalists, who advocated minority status for Jews, their preference by and large lay in creating a separate Jewish party, but was this a realistic option in Austrian politics? Would such a party help combat antisemitism or would it make the already precarious situation of Viennese Jewry even worse? Perhaps some Zionists would prefer not to engage in local politics at all but focus their attention on rebuilding the Jewish national homeland in Palestine. Others, especially those on the Left, might choose to give their political support to the Social Democrats.

Jewish Socialists, particularly the committed Marxists among them, undoubtedly had the easiest choice of all. They could vote for the Austrian Social Democratic Party with very few reservations. But what about the Labor Zionists? To what extent were they torn between the goals of Austrian Social Democracy and Jewish Nationalism?

The upsurge of right-wing antisemitism and the demise of Liberalism decisively shaped Jewish voting patterns in interwar Vienna. Despite the valiant efforts of stalwart Liberals and determined Jewish Nationalists, a majority of Viennese Jews came to vote for the Austrian Social Democratic Party, many of them by default rather than out of ideological conviction. But would voting Socialist, even with a Social Democratic administration ensconced in city hall, assuage the effects of antisemitism or mitigate the serious demographic and economic problems that confronted Viennese Jewry?

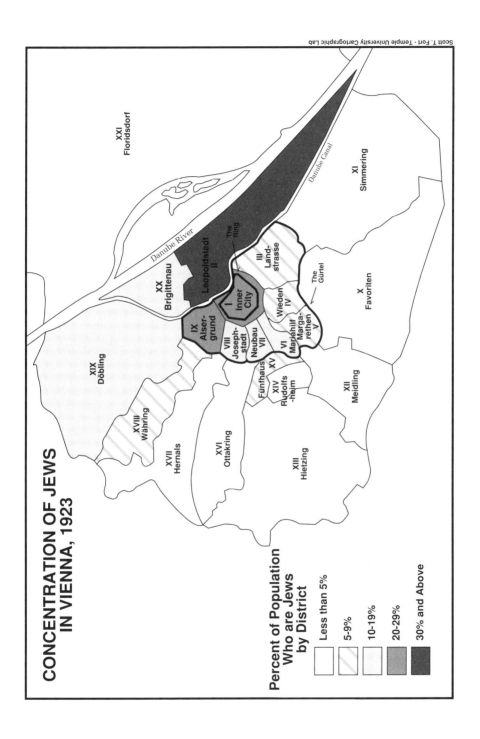

CONCENTRATION OF JEWS
IN VIENNA, 1923

Percent of Population
Who are Jews
by District

Less than 5%

5-9%

10-19%

20-29%

30% and Above

Scott T. Fort - Temple University Cartographic Lab

The Jewish Electorate

By voting Social Democratic in municipal and national elections, were middle-class Jews actually voting against their own economic interests? To what extent could the Jewish electorate affect the outcome in Viennese and Austrian elections? In order for a Jewish vote to have much significance, Jews had to be citizens with suffrage and live compactly enough to influence political races in at least certain electoral districts. A brief survey of Jewish citizenship status, as well as occupational and residential distribution, demonstrates the potential importance of Viennese Jewish voters.

Many Jews in Vienna before the war, including children who had been born there, had not yet received legal residency rights in the capital which would make them eligible to vote in local elections. In the postwar period, those who had not already acquired such permits had to become naturalized citizens of the new Austrian Republic or else be considered foreigners and face a precarious existence. Immediately after the war, acquiring citizenship was relatively simple for those who had arrived in the city before 1914. Soon the process became much more difficult, especially for war refugees.[18]

According to the Treaty of St. Germain, Jews should have been able to opt for Austrian citizenship by claiming German as their mother tongue.[19] Nevertheless, a narrow interpretation of the treaty's "option clause" along racial rather than linguistic lines prevented Jews from becoming naturalized in 1920 and 1921. Thereafter, even Jews who had lived in Vienna more than ten years could obtain citizenship only after a very lengthy and cumbersome application procedure.[20] By the mid-twenties, however, the vast majority of Jews remaining in Vienna had finally acquired the requisite Austrian documents and the right to vote.

Viennese Jewry represented a heavily bourgeois constituency, at least with respect to occupational classification and residency patterns, if not actual wealth. Although considerable Jewish poverty existed in Vienna, most Jews belonged to the lower middle class, while a significant minority can be classified as solidly middle or upper middle class. Unlike the Viennese population as a whole, few Jews were workers.

A disproportionate number of Viennese Jews were involved in commerce, both as self-employed businessmen and as their salaried employees, while relatively few earned their living in industry, especially heavy industry. Jews were much more likely than other Viennese to be active in the free professions, but far less likely to be civil servants.[21] In the thirties, among Jews who could afford to pay communal taxes, roughly 40 percent engaged in commerce; 10 percent were industrialists or artisans; 30 percent were salaried employees or wage earners; 10 percent belonged to the professional class, while the rest were retired or had other sources of income.[22] Jews too poor to be on the communal tax rolls undoubtedly included some workers but many more were petty traders, impoverished white collar employees, and unemployed.

This largely middle-class occupational distribution and the prevalence of self-employment among Jews caused many Viennese Jews during the interwar period to prefer either the bourgeois Liberals or the Jewish Nationalists, but the growing impoverishment of Viennese Jewry and increasing numbers of salaried employees convinced many other Jewish voters to gravitate toward the Socialists. Therefore only some, but not all, middle-class Jews who decided to vote Socialist were voting against their personal economic interests.

Vienna's Jews tended to live, study, and work together and, most conspicuously, they socialized primarily among themselves. As Marsha Rozenblit has convincingly demonstrated, when Jews tried to assimilate into their Viennese milieu, they did so in the company of other Jews.[23] Although Jews constituted only about 3 percent of the population of interwar Austria, since over 90 percent of Austrian Jewry lived in the capital, they comprised approximately 10 percent of the Viennese electorate. In some districts with high Jewish residential density, however, their proportion of voters was significantly higher. Like Jews in other cities, Jews in Vienna tended to concentrate residentially in certain of the capital's twenty-one districts and avoid others.[24] By and large they chose to live in predominantly middle-class districts among other Jews.[25] (See Table 2 and Map 2.)

Leopoldstadt (District II), nicknamed the "Matzah Island," served as the "Jewish ghetto." Located on an island between the Danube Canal and the River Danube, it housed almost one third of Vienna's Jews during the interwar period and they made up nearly forty percent of its total population. Both rich and poor Jews lived in the Second District, albeit on different streets. Most of Vienna's Orthodox Jews lived here, along with many of the recent Galician immigrants, but less traditional Jews with longer residence in the Austrian capital, including those from Moravia and Hungary, could be found here as well.[26]

Brigittenau (XX), formerly part of Leopoldstadt and adjoining it to the northwest, was a heavily working-class district which contained many of the city's poorest Jews, including a large share of the Galician war refugees. Here housing conditions were extremely congested, with six or more persons often occupying a single room.[27] Amid such deplorable circumstances, about 9 percent of Viennese Jewry had established their homes, making up 18 percent of the overall population of the Twentieth District. Vienna's working-class Jews tended to live in Brigittenau or else in Leopoldstadt, not in the predominantly working-class outer suburbs.

Jews clustered in some middle-class districts, especially those along the Ringstrasse, but not in others, particularly those in the outlying suburbs. Alsergrund (IX), bordering Leopoldstadt to the west, provided housing for 12 percent of Viennese Jewry. The Ninth District, where Sigmund Freud lived and the university was located, attracted many Jewish intellectuals and white collar employees. Less well-to-do Jews resided here as well. Like the nearby "Jewish ghetto," Alsergrund, whose population was one-quarter Jewish, was by no means socioeconomically homogeneous.

The Inner City (I), the financial and commercial, as well as government, hub, provided a more prestigious address for Jews, especially professionals and successful businessmen. As in Leopoldstadt and Alsergrund, Jews living in the Inner City tended to cluster on certain streets which were adjacent to one another. Indeed, the heavily Jewish neighborhoods in these three districts were contiguous with each other, on both sides of the Danube Canal. Although only 5 percent of Vienna's Jews lived in the Inner City, they accounted for a quarter of its inhabitants and carried more political weight than their numbers would indicate. Jewish residential concentration, especially in Leopoldstadt, Alsergrund, and the Inner City, boosted the proportion of the Jewish electorate in those voting districts well above the city-wide average and made the Jewish electorate well worth pursuing, especially in municipal but also in national campaigns.

Postwar Problems

Jewish voters attempted to pursue political strategies aimed at improving their socioeconomic situation. Before World War I, Vienna's Jews already experienced difficulties due to discrimination, poverty, and assimilation. As a result of wartime dislocations and the postwar economic crisis, their predicament increased alarmingly. After the war, problems arose regarding Galician war refugees, economic hardships beset middle-class Jews, and the Jewish population began to shrink due to a combination of expulsions, natural decrease, and apostasy. Even before the *Anschluss* the prognosis for the future of the Viennese Jewish community did not look very bright.

In the aftermath of the war, the Austrian economy faced utter chaos. By the end of 1918, the new republic found itself cut off from its sources of raw materials for both food and fuel. Starvation threatened the country, especially its capital, where bread and flour were rationed drastically and milk and meat had become practically unavailable. As soldiers returned home, massive unemployment ensued, along with serious housing shortages.[28] Inflation ran amok, wiping out life savings and investments. Whereas in November 1918 the American dollar was worth 14.3 Austrian crowns, by August 1922 there were 74,450 crowns to the dollar![29] Austrian currency had become almost worthless. The cost of living had risen meteorically and salaries simply could not keep up with the rampant inflationary spiral.[30]

Jews shared this suffering together with other Viennese inhabitants.[31] Jewish war refugees faced the most desperate straits of all and bore the brunt of the blame for the postwar housing, food, and fuel shortages. During the war a massive wave of refugees had escaped from war-torn Galicia and flooded into Vienna. According to official statistics, Jews accounted for 77,000 of the 137,000 impoverished souls who found refuge in the imperial capital.[32] After hostilities ceased many war refugees left Austria voluntarily; others were forcibly repatriated back to Poland between 1919 and 1922.[33] Less than half succeeded in remaining in Vienna.

These refugees had little cushion to protect them from utter destitution. Meyer Gillis, an emissary from the American Jewish Joint Distribution Committee, depicted their dire need and misery in his reports. "No human being can paint a complete picture of the bitter and horrible condition of the places they occupy," wrote Gillis.[34] The novelist Josef Roth also graphically described their dismal plight in his book *Juden auf der Wanderschaft*. He portrayed them as proletarians, not workers but peddlers and street hawkers, living in Leopoldstadt near the Prater amusement park or the North Station, on the verge of starvation. Some dwelt in tiny hovels with six persons in a room, others slept on the floor in small shelters accommodating fifty to sixty people, while the homeless slept on park benches in the Prater. According to Roth, the Viennese population despised the *Ostjuden*, and even their wealthier cousins and coreligionists did not accept them. Politically they were outcasts as well. "For the Christian Socials they are Jews. For the German Nationalists they are Semites. For the Social Democrats they are unproductive elements."[35]

Galician refugees were by no means the only Jews to face serious economic difficulties and discrimination after the war. The Viennese middle class as a whole encountered a significant degree of pauperization.[36] Jewish civil servants and bank officials, in some cases prematurely pensioned off, found themselves among the masses of chronically unemployed. By 1921, roughly 300 Jewish communal employees, including rabbis and other functionaries, were receiving monthly salaries which were the equivalent of less than $5 (U.S.), hence insufficient to support their families.[37]

With the signing of the Geneva Protocols in October 1922, Austria entered a period of economic reconstruction and currency stabilization. The Christian Social national government implemented severe austerity measures, including further rises in food prices, drastically increased indirect taxation, and higher interest rates.[38] These policies exacerbated the economic problems of Vienna's middle-class citizens, and unemployment rates surged.[39] Among those hardest hit by this crisis were Jewish white collar workers who formed an unemployed "commercial proletariat," while many small Jewish-owned businesses and private industries collapsed under the pressures of an unfavorable tariff system, a heavy tax burden, and lack of credit.[40]

Legislation initiated by the Social Democrats helped protect the interests of industrial workers but did not alleviate the economic woes of salaried employees, let alone other middle-class elements. Unemployment and health benefits, together with the eight-hour day, clearly improved the lot of wage earners, as did rent control.[41] The crowning achievement of Austrian Social Democracy was undoubtedly the 60,000 units of municipal housing constructed in Vienna between 1923 and 1933. Since Viennese Jews were not blue-collar workers and tended not to live in working-class districts, very few were eligible to live in the new housing developments. These vast projects, located mainly in the outer ring of industrial suburbs, greatly assisted workers but did not ease the housing shortage for the lower middle class. Meanwhile, the middle class paid for these ambitious Socialist programs through a "housing construction tax" garnered from higher rents and other taxes on property, real estate, and luxury goods. Middle-class Jews contributed a sizable share toward these special taxes, as well as other assessments levied against employers and private businesses. Primarily renters rather than property owners, Jews benefited somewhat from rent control, but generally not from other Socialist measures.[42]

Austria was one of the countries most devastated by the depression, and its recovery proved unusually slow.[43] For Jews, intensified antisemitism further aggravated an already difficult situation. The 1931 collapse of the Rothschild bank, the *Creditanstalt,* and related banks and insurance companies put many Jewish employees out on the street.[44] Even before the official introduction of the Austrian corporate state in 1934, the civil service had officially closed its doors to Jews, and Jewish doctors were systematically dismissed from their positions in municipal hospitals.[45] New regulations prevented Jews from entering certain trades, while economic boycotts became increasingly effective, resulting in the ruin of many Jewish businessmen and professionals.[46] By 1935, Jews had been largely excluded from the cultural realm as well, including the theater, music, and much of the press.[47] Due to their occupational distribution, most Jews out of work could not claim unemployment compensation. Chances of finding new employment were extremely slim, since few companies would hire

Jews.[48] By 1937, more than a third of the Viennese Jewish working population had joined the ranks of the unemployed.[49]

Along with economic hardships and anti-Jewish discrimination, Vienna's Jewish community experienced a steady decrease in size during the interwar years due to a combination of natural decrease and apostasy, as well as the emigration of noncitizens. Whereas the 1923 census recorded 201,513 Jews in the Austrian capital, by 1934, only 176,034 individuals in Vienna identified themselves as Jews by religion. (See Table 1.)

Some Jews attempted to escape from their Jewish roots through apostasy or intermarriage. Already before World War I, Vienna had the highest conversion rate in Europe, due at least in part to the technical difficulties involved in intermarriage. Austrian law prohibited marriages between Jews and Christians unless one partner converted to the other religion before marriage or else either the bride or the groom officially declared her- or himself as *konfessionslos* or without religion. Most converts were young and single. By and large, they had become estranged from, or else indifferent to, the religion of their birth and expected that by converting they would be able to assimilate more completely into Viennese society. While many of the men converted for economic reasons, hoping thereby to achieve a better job, especially in the civil service, most of the women appear to have converted for marriage purposes.[50]

The rate of conversion from Judaism remained very high in Vienna. Between 1907 and 1918, an average of 568 apostasies per year occurred in the Austrian capital. Between 1919 and 1937, nearly 17,000 individuals, or almost 800 per year on the average, officially opted out of Judaism, but the numbers of apostates, after peaking in 1919, declined fairly steadily until 1935.[51] Before the war, about half of the converts were baptized as Roman Catholics, a quarter adopted Protestantism, and almost as many became *konfessionslos*; after the war, a much higher percentage of those leaving Judaism (83% in 1929) chose to be "without religious affiliation."[52] In the postwar era, a baptismal certificate no longer assured one any kind of professional advancement, given the high rate of unemployment, especially among civil servants, coupled with the spread of racial antisemitism. In the years leading up to the *Anschluss*, apostasy had become less attractive as a possible solution to the problems facing assimilated Viennese Jews.

Meanwhile, conversions to (or back to) Judaism also increased somewhat during the interwar period. Between 1907 and 1918, almost 1,700 individuals (about three-quarters of them women) voluntarily joined the Jewish community; between 1919 and 1937, nearly 7,000 persons did so. Many of these "Jews by choice" (in some years almost half) were returning to the fold; others were women converting to Judaism for the purpose of marrying Jewish men. In the traumatic year 1938, the number of apostates skyrocketed to 4,756, while the number of conversions (or reentries) climbed to 1,232.[53] While many were desperately attempting to escape from the onslaught of Nazism through baptism, others had come to realize that one could not escape from being Jewish.

Viennese Jewry during the interwar period clearly faced a demographic crisis. Once large-scale immigration had halted due to the political and economic situation in the Austrian Republic, the Jewish community started to dwindle in size. It had begun rather early to demonstrate many of the characteristics of a highly urbanized and increasingly middle-class Western Jewish community in the twentieth century: delayed marriage, a trend toward small nuclear families with only one or two children, a steadily aging population, and increasing assimilation, which at times manifested itself in the form of intermarriage, often involving conversion. An extremely low birth rate posed even more danger to Jewish survival than did apostasy. Between 1919 and 1938, deaths exceeded births by roughly 20,000, whereas apostasies exceeded conversions to Judaism by about 10,000. The birth rate had continued to decline during the thirties, while the apostasy rate had slowed down considerably before 1938. Both factors combined, however, amounted to a population loss of approximately one percent per year over the entire period.[54]

The problems confronting Viennese Jewry, resulting from discrimination, economic decline, and assimilation, defied the solutions available in the broader political arena. Neither voting for a Socialist party that was itself not overtly antisemitic nor backing Jewish Nationalist candidates in municipal or national elections could stem the growing tide of antisemitism or improve the economic plight of the middle classes. Perhaps the organized Jewish community could accomplish more on behalf of its members and help to alleviate their predicament.

The Kultusgemeinde

The *Israelitische Kultusgemeinde Wien* (or Israelite Religious Community of Vienna) provided the central address for Vienna's Jews, with its offices located on Seitenstettengasse in the Inner City. It served as the official body for legislating and implementing measures to try to improve the Jewish situation and at the same time afforded a forum for debating the different strategies for Jewish group survival. The governing board of the Kultusgemeinde consisted of thirty-six men elected by communal taxpayers. The board chose its own executive committee, including a president, two vice-presidents, and eight other members. This group ran the daily affairs of the Jewish community with the help of the communal bureaucracy.[55]

The electoral system within the Kultusgemeinde reflected strong influences of the Austrian milieu in which it functioned. After the war, the communal body, like the Viennese municipality, abandoned the separate curia for its higher taxpayers and adopted the system of proportional representation by party list, with the entire Austrian capital serving as a single electoral district. The board proved reluctant to introduce universal suffrage, however, since the incumbent Liberal leadership feared that further democratization, especially granting the vote to the recently arrived Galician Jews, would threaten their control over the Jewish community. The more traditional board members also opposed allowing women to participate fully in communal affairs. This same Central European multiparty model, including provisions for universal suffrage, had previously been borrowed by the World Zionist Organization which had made Vienna its home in its early years under Herzl's leadership and was later adopted for the Israeli Knesset, so that the electoral system in the modern Jewish State bears a striking resemblance to that of the Israelitische Kultusgemeinde Wien during the interwar era.

According to its official statutes, the primary tasks of the Kultusgemeinde were religious and educational, involving supervision of synagogues and other ritual activities and the religious instruction of Jewish youth. Its other responsibilities included maintaining birth, marriage, death, and conversion registries for the state. In addition, the Kultusgemeinde had to provide for the needy, the sick, and the elderly within the community to the best of its ability. Along with its assigned tasks, the Kultusgemeinde acted as the spokesman for Jewish interests before the state authorities and attempted to combat antisemitism both publicly and behind the scenes.

The various political factions competing for dominance within the communal board differed markedly in their goals and priorities. The Liberals wanted to perpetuate the Kultusgemeinde as a primarily religious body, supporting existing communal synagogues and institutions as well as religious education for Jewish youth. Similarly, the Orthodox concerned themselves largely with providing for the religious needs of the more traditionally observant Jews in Vienna. By contrast, the Jewish Nationalists aimed at combating both assimilation and Jewish poverty and wanted to broaden the sphere of activity of the Kultusgemeinde, especially in the areas of social welfare, education and Jewish culture, transforming it into a *Volksgemeinde* or people's community based on universal suffrage. Likewise the Socialists devoted their efforts to modernizing the welfare system, improving the conditions for communal employees and creating a more egalitarian community.

The Austrian government recognized Jews as a religious, rather than a national, group and required all Jews to belong to their local Jewish community, unless they officially opted out or converted to another religion. Whereas over 80 percent of Viennese residents were Catholics, Jews comprised the largest religious minority and made up roughly 10 percent of the city's inhabitants during the interwar years. (See Table 1.) The Protestant component in the population amounted to roughly half that of the Jews, while the percentage of *konfessionslos* (unaffiliated) grew from a negligible 0.2 percent in 1910 to 4 percent by 1934, including mainly ex-Catholic Social Democratic workers but also many individuals formerly registered as Jews.[56] Although both the Catholics and the Protestants received substantial state subsidies, the Israelitische Kultusgemeinde had to fund itself and got only a token subvention for educational purposes.

The Kultusgemeinde suffered greatly from the economic woes of the interwar years. Inflation wiped out the value of its prewar bequests and endowments and caused it serious difficulties in paying viable salaries to its employees, especially in the early twenties.[57] Although it charged fees for many of its services, it derived much of its revenues from the collection of taxes. All Jews above a certain income level were expected to pay annual communal taxes which were assessed by special district commissions according to wealth. The vast majority of taxpayers fell into the minimum tax bracket, while very few were included in the maximum range.[58] The Kultusgemeinde's income was never sufficient to cover the steadily mounting social welfare and other needs of its members.

Viennese Jews generally turned to the organized Jewish community for assistance in times of personal difficulty. In carrying out its social welfare obligations, the Kultusgemeinde maintained a communal hospital and old age home, as well as a variety of other institutions, and provided subsidies for a broad range of philanthropic societies, while trying to coordinate relief efforts.

Before World War I, about fifteen percent of Vienna's Jewish inhabitants received some form of communal assistance.[59] After 1914, the Jewish community rallied to help the Galician war refugees. During the war years, the Austrian government had provided at least meager food rations for Jewish refugees, but after the war ended, they became *personae non gratae* and were entirely dependent upon aid from their fellow Jews.[60] Fortunately, the American Jewish Joint Distribution Committee came to the rescue and between 1919 and 1922 supplied monetary assistance to as many as 25,000 Jewish war refugees and students and opened up large soup kitchens which fed 4,000 children and 800 adults daily. It also provided food packages and meals, as well as clothing and medical services, for needy Jewish professionals and intellectuals, including rabbis and other communal employees.[61]

Communal relief declined considerably during the twenties, but it burgeoned dramatically as a result of the depression. By 1936, the Kultusgemeinde welfare bureau's case load had increased to 23,000 households encompassing roughly 60,000 persons or more than one-third of Vienna's Jewish population. To supplement its regular budgetary allocation for social welfare purposes, the Kultusgemeinde ran an annual Winter Relief Campaign, whose proceeds went for coal and clothing for needy Jews, as well as food packages and soup kitchens.[62]

Although escalating welfare demands threatened to swamp the Kultusgemeinde by the end of the interwar period, the communal board did not abandon its religious and educational mission nor did it cease fighting against antisemitism. However, its tactics could not succeed in ensuring the viability of the Jewish community, given the severe political and economic constraints of the day.

Nineteen thirty-three provides a watershed in the saga of Jewish politics in interwar Vienna, since in that year the Jewish Nationalists took over control of the Israelitische Kultusgemeinde Wien from the Liberals and, coincidentally, the Christian corporate state replaced the democratic Austrian republic. The next four chapters will explore the strategies for Jewish individual and group survival of the four major factions, the Liberals, the Jewish Nationalists, the Socialists, and the Orthodox, up until 1933. Each chapter will analyze the political behavior of one bloc, comparing its involvement in national and municipal affairs with its activities on the Jewish communal scene. Chapter 6 will focus on the internal developments within the Kultusgemeinde after 1933, while chapter 7 will examine communal efforts to combat antisemitism and deal with the authoritarian regime prior to 1938. A brief epilogue will trace the demise of the Jewish community of Vienna after the *Anschluss*.

THE LIBERALS

Liberalism had become the dominant political creed among Central European Jewry in the second half of the nineteenth century. In Vienna, Liberals controlled the Israelitische Kultusgemeinde, while their defense organization, the Austrian Israelite Union, claimed to speak for Jewish interests in the general political sphere as well. Before World War I, Liberals unquestionably formed the Viennese Jewish Establishment; during the interwar years they struggled to maintain their hegemony but failed.

Liberalism held great attraction for Westernized Jews, especially of the middle and upper middle classes, in late nineteenth and early twentieth century Vienna. Jewish businessmen, industrialists, and professionals shared many common goals with the German Liberals who had helped bring about their emancipation. Both groups favored civil equality for all individuals and opposed corporate privilege in politics and in the economy and clerical influence over the state and public education. They wished to create a society based on individual achievement and eliminate discrimination on the basis of religion.[1]

With the decline and fragmentation of Austrian Liberalism and the attempts of various splinter parties to forge alliances with antisemitic German Nationalist groups, the relationship between Jewish and German Liberals became increasingly problematic. As the Liberal parties moved further to the Right, Jewish Liberals slowly gravitated toward the Left in municipal and national politics. But since they could not find a comfortable home in the new Nationalist, Clerical, or Socialist camps, many members of the Viennese Jewish elite determinedly clung to their Liberal beliefs long after Liberalism had gone out of fashion.[2]

Whereas in general Viennese and Austrian politics the Jewish Liberals generally allied themselves with the left wing of the Liberal spectrum, supporting the more progressive Democrats, Social Politicals, and eventually the Social Democrats, within the Jewish community the Liberals acted as moderate conservatives, not radical reformers. Nineteenth century Viennese Liberals had not been religious conservatives by nature, but had adopted a more traditionalist posture in the interest of maintaining communal unity and in response to strong forces of religious traditionalism among the Orthodox.[3] By the twentieth century, however, the Liberals had become guardians of the undemocratic communal status quo in order to combat the threat of Jewish Nationalism.

The Liberals regarded the Israelitische Kultusgemeinde as a purely religious body, which should devote itself primarily to ritual affairs and religious education and secondarily to charitable endeavors. They vehemently opposed the idea of transforming it into a *Volksgemeinde*, a more all-encompassing national community which would orient itself toward a broader range of Jewish cultural, educational, and social welfare activities. The Liberals might form temporary alliances with non-Zionist Orthodox or Socialist factions, but they treated the Jewish Nationalists with utmost suspicion.

Viennese Jewish Liberals prided themselves on being patriotic Austrian citizens of the Jewish faith. Although relatively few were natives of Vienna, for the most part they were "Western" in origin, having migrated from either Czech or Hungarian lands, rather than from Galicia. They vociferously denied that they belonged to a separate Jewish nation or that such a nation even existed in their day; they considered themselves Jews by religion only and not by nationality. Since they were German in language and culture, they regarded themselves as part of the German nation among whom they lived. When this notion was challenged by antisemites or Jewish Nationalists, the Liberals merely reiterated their position with increasing firmness. They desperately feared that classification of Jews as a national minority would endanger their status as equal citizens within the Austrian state.

The Union of Austrian Jews

The Austrian Israelite Union, established in 1886, embodied the philosophy of the Viennese Jewish Liberals, determined their program of action, and provided most of their leadership both on the local political scene and within the Kultusgemeinde. After World War I the organization changed its name to the Union of German-Austrian Jews, while in 1931 it officially became the Union of Austrian Jews. Just as its name underwent minor modifications to keep up with the terminology of the day, so too the Union tacked with the wind and adapted its tactics to the times, but it never really altered its approach or strategy. Indeed, on its fiftieth anniversary in 1936, the association congratulated itself that it had retained its tradition faithfully, and resolved to continue on the same path.[4]

The Union was the first Jewish defense organization created in

Central Europe.[5] In its orientation and activities it closely resembled its German counterpart, the Central Association of German Citizens of the Jewish Faith (commonly known as the Centralverein), which was formed seven years later, and the two associations maintained strong ties with each other.[6] Like the Centralverein, but unlike the French Alliance Israélite Universelle or the Austrian Israelitische Allianz, the Union primarily dealt with problems facing Jews within the territorial boundaries of its own state rather than providing aid for needy Jews wherever they were experiencing difficulties.[7]

Dr. Josef Samuel Bloch founded the Union in order to combat what he considered the two most dangerous enemies of Jews, antisemitism and assimilation. This Galician-born rabbi of Floridsdorf, an outlying suburb of Vienna, had attracted attention in the early 1880s for his courageous and successful court battle against the antisemite August Rohling, author of *Der Talmudjude*. He felt that the Jews should be Austrians pure and simple and remain outside the nationality conflict altogether, neither attempting to be Germans, Poles, Hungarians, or Czechs nor demanding national recognition for Jews. Although the older Viennese Jewish Establishment initially opposed Bloch's organization, the association soon gained the adherence of younger members of the Liberal elite who recognized the need for Jewish self-esteem as well as defense against antisemitism. By the turn of the century, the Union had assumed a leading role in Viennese Jewish political life.[8]

From its very beginnings, the Union exhibited a strong sense of Jewish pride and a positive orientation toward Judaism. According to its original statutes, the objective of the Union was "to raise interest in Jewish knowledge and concern for Judaism among Austrian Jews, to clarify and eliminate widespread errors and prejudices against Judaism, and, lastly, to fight against efforts directed toward intensifying religious and racial antagonisms." In order to achieve these aims, the Union decided to publicize pertinent issues in Jewish history and scholarship through lectures and newspapers, to debate all affairs of Jewish concern being deliberated upon in the Austrian parliament, and to take a public stand on questions of importance to Jews through petitions and resolutions.[9]

The Union remained committed to public instruction and the raising of Jewish consciousness, especially with respect to the dangers of antisemitism. The central board and its branches in various districts of Vienna regularly sponsored lectures and discussion evenings addressing a wide spectrum of issues of Jewish interest. In addition to holding annual general meetings, the Union published its own paper, which served to inform its membership and sympathizers of its activities and concerns. After the war, it acquired control over *Die Wahrheit*, a biweekly with a Liberal outlook, which had already been reporting on Jewish communal affairs for some thirty-five years. *Die Wahrheit* soon became a weekly, appearing every Friday and recording the events of the week both within and outside the Jewish community.

Like the Liberals it represented, the party organ was progressive politically and culturally, but rather traditional with regard to religion. It espoused the position that the roots of Judaism, and hence of Jews, lay in religion and it opposed Socialism because of its denial of religion. It also condemned what it considered to be the excesses of Jewish nationalism, since it felt that the Jews were a people unlike other peoples. However, it did claim sympathy for the rebuilding of Palestine as a homeland for persecuted Jews. Following the guidelines of its owners, *Die Wahrheit* declared its most important task to be fighting antisemitism and defending the legal rights of Austrian Jewry.[10]

Over the years, defense activities assumed an increasingly prominent place within the Union's program. Already in 1897 the organization had established a legal rights bureau to provide aid for Jews who suffered discrimination of any kind. Before World War I, this office was actively involved in combating Jew-baiting in the press, protesting against forced conversions, and contesting ritual murder accusations in the courts.[11] During the war, the Union dominated an organization called the Austrian Central Committee for the Protection of the Civil Rights of the Jewish Population in the Eastern War Zone and also assumed the role of protector of the rights of the thousands of Galician Jews who had sought refuge in Vienna. At the same time, it was engaged in defending Jews against charges of shirking military duty and profiteering on the black market.[12]

As antisemitic incidents proliferated in Vienna in the twenties and thirties, the Union's leaders frequently lodged protests with the authorities concerning outbreaks of violence against Jewish students or anti-Jewish street demonstrations. They also sought to suppress certain theater performances and various forms of antisemitic literature, including pamphlets and placards inciting economic boycotts and other actions against Jews. In 1928 the Union submitted to the government a draft press reform bill which would have facilitated the prosecution of antisemitic libel charges. This proposal was never adopted, however, and it remained extremely difficult to get antisemites convicted in the courts.[13]

By the interwar period, the Union saw itself as the spokesman for all those "Austrian citizens of the Jewish faith, who reject any civil, national, or other kind of special status for Jews." The organization had broadened its original goals to encompass "the energetic defense of the constitutional rights of Austrian Jews as citizens of the state with complete rights and equal obligations," as well as "the protection of the general and political rights of each individual Jew."[14] It consistently fought against minority rights for Jews and the recognition of

Jews as a separate nationality for census or other purposes, because it felt that such measures would lead to discrimination against Jews and denial of their equality. The legal rights bureau intervened on behalf of hundreds of Jews facing difficulties in gaining Viennese residency or Austrian citizenship, especially after World War I. The Union vehemently objected to the illegality of a racial interpretation of the "option clause" in the Treaty of St. Germain, claiming that by law Jews were a religious, not a racial or national, group.[15] It condemned the proposed introduction of a numerus clausus limiting the numbers of Jewish students and professors at the university or any regulation that would segregate Jewish students from the mainstream of the student body as a whole.[16] Similarly, it opposed separate classes or schools for Jewish pupils on an elementary or secondary level, except for the purpose of purely religious education.[17] The Union regularly took action against vacation resorts that excluded Jews. It published annual lists of places with this restriction, sought to have such practices declared illegal, and intervened with the Austrian Tourist Bureau to ban "Only for Aryans" advertisements.[18]

While the Union continued its efforts to battle discrimination of all kinds, by the 1930s it was becoming increasingly concerned with the dire economic plight of Viennese Jewry, which was greatly exacerbated by antisemitism. Repeatedly it attempted to thwart economic boycotts against Jewish businesses and protested against the requirement of a baptismal certificate as proof of "German origin" for candidates for public office. In addition, the organization decided for the first time to participate in endeavors to further the economic interests of Austrian Jews, including vocational rehabilitation and the creation of credit bureaus for artisans and small businessmen.[19]

The tactics employed by the Union to deal with antisemitism largely resembled those of the Centralverein in Germany, namely legal defense in the courts, publication of information to counter antisemitic charges, and intercession with the authorities behind the scenes. The defense strategy of these Jewish Liberals continued to be based on the belief that through the use of the legal system, support of political candidates sympathetic to their views, and personal meetings with, and resolutions and protests submitted to, government officials the growing tide of antisemitism could be effectively stemmed. While in some instances the Union did manage to achieve minor victories, the nature and magnitude of the problem of antisemitism far exceeded their capability to cope with it.[20]

The Union consisted of a central board of directors, elected at an annual general meeting and headed by a ten-person executive committee, with branch affiliates in the various districts of Vienna and in provincial cities as well.[21] On the eve of World War I, the organization claimed roughly 7,900 dues-paying members, many of whom lived in

Bohemia and Moravia.[22] During and after the war membership declined significantly due to the difficult circumstances and the loss of former Austrian territories.[23] In 1923, the Union reported a total enrollment of 5,500.[24] Despite frequent appeals for new members and the formation of separate divisions for women, students, and youth, the Union's ranks contracted further as the interwar years progressed. In 1938, the Union of Austrian Jews, including the Union Women's Club, the Union Youth and four provincial groups, had a membership conservatively estimated at 3,000 individuals.[25] The numerical decline reflects a decline in both the attraction and the influence of the Union and its ideology, although the importance of this elite Liberal organization continued to outstrip its actual membership size. Unlike the Centralverein in Germany, however, by the thirties the Union had clearly lost its dominant position in the Viennese Jewish community.

Membership in the Union was open to Jewish citizens of Austria, male or female, over the age of twenty-one who were willing to pay annual dues and adhere to the goals of the association.[26] The citizenship prerequisite provided a vital component of the Union's image of its members and supporters as "natives" and patriotic Austrians. In actuality, a great many members of the organization, including most of its leadership, were not born in Vienna or even within the frontiers of the post–World War I Austrian Republic, but came from elsewhere in the former Austro-Hungarian Empire and thereafter received Viennese residency status. Among the Union candidates in the 1928 Kultusgemeinde elections, for example, slightly more than one quarter were Viennese by birth, whereas another quarter were born in Hungary (including Slovakia and Burgenland) and roughly a third came from the Czech lands of Bohemia and Moravia, while only about 10 percent hailed from Galicia.[27] (See Table 3.) An organization made up primarily of Western-type Jews, the Union had little justification for stigmatizing Eastern Jews as "foreigners," when in many cases the ink on their own naturalization papers had only dried relatively recently.

Before the first decade of the twentieth century, women were excluded from Union membership, since Austrian law prohibited women from belonging to political organizations. After this regulation was rescinded, women became eligible to join the Union's ranks,[28] but how many did so remains unclear. No woman was ever elected to the board of directors, nor did women serve in a visibly active capacity within the organization itself. In attempting to expand the base of its support among women, the Union established a link with the Federation of Jewish Women of German-Austria, a women's charitable and cultural association that shared many of the Union's views.[29] In 1931, the Union formed its own women's auxiliary, the Union Women's Club, which along with philanthropic activities sponsored lectures, discussions, courses, and social events, often together with the men's Union

Club.[30] Despite various efforts to attract women sympathizers within the Union framework, the Union itself, especially its leadership, remained an exclusively male preserve, involving women occasionally in its cultural activities but never in its political sphere.

The Union's leaders, and the bulk of its members as well, were upper-middle-class and middle-class males who were likely to be well educated and hold high-salaried positions or be self-employed. While businessmen made up more than half the Union's supporters and almost two-fifths of its leadership, professionals, especially lawyers, carried a disproportionate weight in its highest leadership ranks. Whereas only 13 percent of the men who signed the 1928 Union communal election platform had university degrees, roughly three times as many board members held doctorates.[31] Much more than its membership, the leadership of the Union constituted an economic and intellectual elite who voluntarily chose to involve themselves in Jewish affairs.

The president of the Union during nearly the entire interwar period, Jakob Ornstein, was a remarkably active older gentleman, a man of considerable intelligence and deep commitment to Jewish causes. A Vienna University–trained lawyer, Ornstein was born in 1858 in a small town in Moravia. He joined the Union in 1907; within four years he was elected vice-president, and in 1919, at the age of sixty-one, he became president. He held that office for fifteen years, until his resignation at the age of seventy-five. Meanwhile, in 1923 he was initiated into B'nai B'rith Lodge "Wien" and the following year was elected to the Israelitische Kultusgemeinde, where he filled a vice-presidency for ten years; he was simultaneously vice-president of the Israelitische Allianz and was elevated to the presidency of the latter organization from 1933 to 1937. In addition, he headed numerous other Jewish cultural and charitable endeavors.[32] Ornstein was not the only example of this dedicated breed of communal activists.

A heavily interlocking Jewish Liberal Establishment prevailed within the most prestigious Jewish organizations in interwar Vienna. A striking overlap existed between Liberals elected to the Kultusgemeinde, serving on the boards of directors of the Union and the Allianz, and belonging to B'nai B'rith. Of the eighty-three Liberals who served on the Kultusgemeinde between 1912 and 1938, twenty were Union board members, sixteen were on the Allianz board, and sixteen were B'nai B'rith members.[33] Of these, seven, including Ornstein and his successor as Union president, the banker Hermann Oppenheim, were associated with all of these bodies simultaneously.

Leadership positions within the Union were generally held by men over fifty years of age. Occasionally individuals might reach board rank in their forties, but an officer under forty was a rarity. The organization did attempt to attract younger members by creating a lower dues category for eighteen- to twenty-five-year-olds.[34] It also set up separate youth and student affiliates. These efforts at recruiting younger Jews seem to have enjoyed very limited success.[35] During the interwar period the Union was clearly an organization of the older, not the younger, generation. Liberalism had become passé. It no longer held great appeal for Viennese Jewish youth in the twentieth century, losing out in popularity to Socialism or Zionism, especially among university students.

Political Activities

The Union was fighting an uphill battle for the survival of Liberalism in Vienna. It fulfilled the function of a Jewish Liberal political club, participating in election campaigns for Austrian and Viennese public representative bodies, as well as for Jewish communal institutions. These Jewish Liberals never regarded as an anomaly the fact that Jews, whom they considered merely a religious group, needed a separate association to represent their political interests. The Union actively engaged in political activities because its leadership understood that the antisemitic environment required such involvement. Such realism proved a sign of political maturity. But the association's determination to support Liberal candidates in general elections despite all odds resulted in an exercise in futility.

By the turn of the century, Austrian Liberals had lost their position of power in both the national parliament and the Viennese municipal council and were faced with the prospect of even further decline due to the expansion of voting rights. Although the mainstream Liberal party was becoming increasingly dependent on the support of middle-class Jewish voters in Vienna, it nevertheless demonstrated a growing reluctance to run Jewish candidates, even in heavily Jewish districts, and to admit Jewish members into its leading circle, the Progressive Club. The party also attempted to build alliances with various antisemitic German Nationalist groups and consistently refused to defend Jews publicly against antisemitic attacks in the vain hope of avoiding the epithet "*Judenliberalen.*"[36]

The Union served as the official representative of the Jewish Liberals with the right to send delegates to the Liberal Central Committee which nominated party candidates for elections.[37] Its political strategy aimed at the public defense of Jewish rights in the face of antisemitism. The organization was eager to endorse candidates who shared its views and were willing to fight openly for Jewish interests. It also campaigned actively against the election of antisemites whenever possible. But what policy should the Union adopt concerning Liberals, Jewish or not, who were reluctant to speak out on behalf of Jews?

The memoirs of Sigmund Mayer, a textile merchant with legal training who was elected to the Viennese municipal council in the 1880s and later became president of the Union, provide prescient insights into the predicament facing Jewish Liberals by the turn of the century. Mayer, a highly assimilated Jew whose son converted to Christianity to advance his career in the civil service, claimed to have almost forgotten his Jewish origins until reminded of the unfortunate accident of his birth by antisemites. Like his fellow Jewish deputies in city hall, he had been chosen not as a Jew but as a leading Liberal party activist. Yet despite party guidelines to ignore such provocations, he felt that he personally could not remain silent in the face of antisemitism.[38]

As early as the late 1880s, Mayer began to realize that the Liberal party was neither willing nor able to stem the flood of antisemitism. He observed that even in a district like Leopoldstadt, with a 30 percent Jewish electorate, it was difficult for the Liberals to maintain a majority, since nearly all middle-class Christians had switched their allegiance to the Christian Socials. He became convinced that as long as such an antisemitic party existed, it would be impossible for a bourgeois Liberal party to win over the population. He also came to believe that a German party could only remain Liberal as long as it was powerful, but if threatened, the Nationalist principle would win out over the Liberal principle and the party would turn out to be more German than Liberal.[39]

At a party conference held on Union premises in 1894, Mayer proposed that the Liberals should demand that the government take action against the antisemitic movement. The authorities should come out publicly in defense of the Jews, name Jewish judges, freely accept Jews in the civil service, and set clear guidelines for public officials concerning the proper response to antisemitic agitation. When his proposal was rejected, Mayer decided that it was incumbent upon the Union to try to persuade Jewish voters that it was no longer in their interest to support the mainstream German Liberals. Instead Jews should back the small left-wing social reform faction of the party, known as the Social Politicals, and, if that failed, they should turn as a last resort to the Social Democratic Party.[40]

The Union's attempt to shift Jewish support to Left Liberals mirrors the actions of the Centralverein in Germany.[41] In 1896 Sigmund Mayer, along with Chief Rabbi Moritz Güdemann and several other prominent Jews, served as members of the nominating committee for the newly created Social Political party. On behalf of the Union, Mayer entered into negotiations with the party leadership, assuring them the support of Jewish voters in the wealthy Inner City district in exchange for their agreeing to fight openly against antisemitism. Mayer, however, was unable to make good his promise, since Union endorsement could not ensure the delivery of the Jewish voters, many of whom continued to vote for mainstream Liberal candidates as in the past. Nonetheless, several Social Politicals did manage to get elected to the provincial assembly and subsequently to other legislative bodies as well and they continued to receive a considerable amount of Jewish backing, especially from the Union.[42]

One of the most prominent figures among the Social Politicals was Julius Ofner. Born of Jewish parentage in 1845 in Bohemia, Ofner trained as a lawyer in Prague and Vienna. Finding the academic path closed to him, he pursued his career in the legal profession with great fervor, dedicating himself to helping oppressed humanity. Ofner was first elected to the provincial assembly in 1896 and then served as deputy in the Austrian parliament from 1901 to 1919, representing the Inner City district until 1907 and thereafter his home district, Leopoldstadt. As a democrat and social reformer, Ofner fought for many years on behalf of universal suffrage and often defended unpopular causes, such as civil marriage and rights for women and workers. Despite the fact that he depended almost entirely on the support of the Jewish voters in his constituency, he never championed any specifically Jewish program, since he denied that this was necessary.[43] Julius Ofner formally remained a Jew, but he identified himself first and foremost as a human being and secondarily as a German by nationality.

The Union did not always favor overtly Jewish candidates over Liberals who were Jews by origin only. In the parliamentary election of 1907, three Jewish candidates entered the running in the electoral district which included Leopoldstadt. One was Isidor Schalit, a Jewish Nationalist; the second was Gustav Kohn, a vice-president of the Kultusgemeinde, running on the Liberal German Progressive ticket; and the third was Julius Ofner. Kohn and Ofner represented virtually identical Liberal viewpoints, except that Kohn was actively involved in Jewish affairs and Ofner was not. At first the Union came out strongly in support of Kohn, whom it had in fact helped to nominate, but in the end, it switched its backing to Ofner. Instead of standing behind an inside Jewish Liberal candidate, the Union chose to endorse a politically more experienced outsider, who happened to be a Jew. Similarly, in the Inner City district, the Union started out advocating the candidacy of Wilhelm Anninger, who twice served as its president, but eventually endorsed the German Progressive candidate Kamillo Kuranda.[44] In Alsergrund, it lent its support to Baron Hock, the son of a convert to Christianity, who, along with Ofner, sat on the left of the Liberal spectrum. Ofner, Kuranda, and Hock all won election in their heavily Jewish constituencies; none of them ever spoke out in parliament on behalf of Jews per se.[45]

Shortly after the 1907 election, a minor scandal erupted within the Liberal ranks in Vienna. Ofner, Kuranda, and Hock, the only three Liberal deputies from the capital, did not receive invitations to a preliminary conference called by the Progressive Club for the purpose of forging a united party out of the various German Liberal, Nationalist, Agrarian, and Radical factions. Perhaps Ofner and Hock might have been excluded because of their leftist orientation, but Kuranda was a moderate who had just been elected on a Progressive ticket. To the Union, this incident smacked of antisemitism within the Progressive camp itself. The Jewish political club accused the Progressive Club of abandoning its Liberal principles and declared that this party no longer promised any hope for the Jews. Meanwhile, the Liberal factions failed to unite and the Viennese Jewish deputies were still unwelcome in the Liberal parliamentary club.[46]

But such incidents did not result in the Union—or Viennese Jews—renouncing their support of political Liberalism. The fact remained that few other palatable alternatives lay open to middle-class Jews. The Union continued to campaign on behalf of Liberal candidates whenever possible, as long as they were not converts or antisemites. But even before World War I Liberal Jewish newspapers in Vienna, including *Die Wahrheit* and Bloch's *Oesterreichische Wochenschrift*, were beginning to advocate voting for certain Social Democratic candidates in order to defeat Christian Socials or German Nationalists. In the 1911 parliamentary elections, the Union once again gave Kuranda and Ofner its solid backing in the Inner City and Leopoldstadt districts respectively, thereby helping to assure their victory.[47] During the municipal elections the following year, while continuing to advocate the support of Liberal candidates in the most heavily Jewish districts, *Die Wahrheit* recommended that the Jews in one wealthy outer district vote for the Social Democratic rather than the Liberal German Democratic candidate in order to prevent a run-off between the Christian Social and the German Nationalist.[48] With the fragmentation of the Liberals into at least three factions on the eve of the war, apathy had begun to set in among middle-class Jews who were unable to vote for Christian Socials or German Nationalists because of their antisemitism and unwilling to vote for Social Democrats, given their economic program. The Union kept a low profile during those years, refraining from holding public political meetings for fear of being disturbed by antisemitic heckling.[49]

At least one representative of the Israelitische Kultusgemeinde Wien generally sat on the Viennese municipal council before World War I and acted as the spokesman for Jewish interests on that body. During the war, the Kultusgemeinde decided to coopt the Liberal municipal deputy, Rudolf Schwarz-Hiller, as a member of their board.[50] Schwarz-Hiller, who represented the Jewish district of Leopoldstadt in city hall from 1910 to 1923, began his political career as a close associate of Julius Ofner. Unlike the more senior Ofner, however, Schwarz-Hiller became actively involved in defending the rights of Jews. Soon after the outbreak of the war he helped organize a refugee bureau, which provided aid for thousands of needy, predominantly Jewish war refugees fleeing from Galicia. Although he did not like to participate in "Jewish debates" on the council floor, both during and after the war he publicly defended the Jewish refugees against such charges as causing the housing shortage and remaining illegally in the capital. After the war Schwarz-Hiller and Ofner, the two most prominent Jewish Liberal politicians, competed for the nomination of the newly formed Democratic Party to represent Leopoldstadt.[51]

The Viennese Liberals had declined from a position of power in the early 1890s to a relatively minor party beset by factionalism on the eve of World War I, and during the interwar years they dwindled even further, becoming almost a political nonentity, except for their continuing role in the bureaucracy, industry, and the press.[52] In the 1920 elections, they received less than 5 percent of the popular vote in Vienna; by 1930 their share had fallen to 0.5 percent. Liberal parties tended to do best in middle-class districts with a high concentration of Jewish voters, but even here they encountered serious setbacks. In the wealthy Inner City with a quarter of its population Jewish, the Liberal factions won roughly a quarter of the vote in the 1920 parliamentary election, but only 5 percent in 1927. In middle-class Alsergrund, also with 25 percent of its inhabitants Jews, their percentage of the vote fell from 10 to less than 3. According to Walter Simon's calculations, the Liberal vote declined fastest in districts with comparatively few Jews and slowest in those districts where proportions of Jews were the highest.[53] Clearly, Jews continued to provide the basis of whatever limited supported remained for the Liberal camp. Upper middle-class Jews clung to their nineteenth century post-emancipation Liberal *Weltanschauung* because they felt they had no other political home.

Liberal representation in the Austrian parliament and the Viennese municipal council declined precipitously after the war. Before 1919, the Inner City had elected four Liberal parliamentary deputies, all of whom had been Jews; between 1920 and 1923 only one Liberal remained in parliament, a non-Jew, Ottokar Czernin; thereafter no Liberal candidates gained election at all.[54] In the 1919 contest in the Northeast constituency which encompassed Leopoldstadt, Ofner lost his parliamentary seat to Robert Stricker, a Jewish Nationalist.[55] Schwarz-Hiller, who sympathized with the Jewish Nationalists and was often willing to work with them, managed to win reelection to the municipal council in 1919 but lost in 1923. Whereas in his previous terms in office Schwarz-Hiller had been joined by as many as eight other Jewish Liberal colleagues, in his final four years the Leopoldstadt deputy was the last lonely Liberal in city hall.[56]

Reluctant to abandon the Liberal cause no matter how hopeless it might seem, the Union continued backing Liberal office-seekers whenever feasible. In December 1918 the Union called its first postwar meeting to discuss the topic "German-Austria and the upcoming elections." The featured speaker of the evening, Julius Ofner, appealed for Jewish unity and support for democracy. He expressed his deep regret at the internal division within the Liberal bourgeoisie and within Viennese Jewry, since in a proportional system only the larger and stronger parties would win election. Because of growing antisemitism, he declared, it was of greatest importance for the Jews to have at least one representative in the Constituent Assembly, not in order to conduct Jewish debates but to ward them off. Jewish voters must present a unified front in order to defend their position in the state, society, and economy. Ofner condemned the Jewish Nationalists for introducing an atmosphere of hatred within Jewry and for making Jews aliens in their own homeland by demanding recognition as a separate nationality.[57] In the early postwar elections the Union was not willing to lend its support to Jewish Nationalist candidates, but preferred to back Liberals, like Ofner and Schwarz-Hiller, or indeed anyone else who was not antisemitic.[58]

After Ottokar Czernin won election to the National Assembly in 1920, the Union failed in its attempts to sensitize him on the issue of antisemitism. Not only did this sole Liberal in parliament remain silent during the debates over option rights, the definition of nationality in the census, and the introduction of a numerus clausus or quota system at the university, he actually gave a speech before the assembly in which he claimed that Jews comprised 99 percent of the Communists and an overwhelming majority of the war profiteers as well! In light of this and the fact that Czernin sought a bourgeois unity front with Christian Socials and German Nationalists, the Union could scarcely continue to endorse his candidacy in 1923.

About one month before election day, albeit without great enthusiasm, the Union entered into a coalition with the Jewish Nationalists on the condition that the latter not press for the recognition of a Jewish nationality in Austria. Both sides agreed on a joint list of candidates, headed by Rudolf Schwarz-Hiller and Robert Stricker, and a fairly bland electoral platform emphasizing defense of Jewish rights against antisemites, loyalty to Austria, and support for the rebuilding of its economy.[59] Campaign posters bore the signatures of the leaders of both the Union and the Austrian Zionist Federation and the same appeals to voters appeared in both the Zionist *Wiener Morgenzeitung* and the Liberal *Die Wahrheit*. For a brief period, harmony prevailed between the two major Jewish political camps.

This electoral coalition undoubtedly helped to bring about the defeat of Czernin, but it did not succeed in achieving a victory for itself. Overall the Jewish coalition did somewhat better at the polls than did the Liberals, winning almost 25,000 votes as compared to fewer than

19,000. In this election, at least, more Jews voted "Jewish" than Liberal, but neither a Jewish nor a Liberal representative was elected to the National Assembly. The Jewish list did manage to retain a single mandate on the municipal council, the only seat not held by either Social Democrats or Christian Socials.[60]

From the Union's perspective, the coalition proved a failure. The combined Jewish list received only about one-quarter of the total Jewish vote. Quite a few Union supporters undoubtedly cast their ballots for Czernin, despite the leadership's attempts to dissuade them from doing so; many middle-class Jews probably did not exercise their right to vote at all, while most Jews voted Social Democratic.[61] The coalition did not succeed in electing a deputy who would represent the Union's interests in parliament or even in city hall.

By the time the next election rolled around four years later, the Union leadership had become disillusioned with its coalition partner and decided to return to its former practice of actively endorsing the Liberal Democratic list.[62] Although the results of this policy proved disastrous, with the Union's party receiving only 5 percent of the vote in its strongest district, the Inner City, and a total of fewer than 15,000 votes (1.3%) in all the capital, nevertheless the Union persisted in lending its backing in 1930 to the tiny Democratic Center Party. The Union and the Liberal Democrats would have liked to join the middle-class Economic bloc headed by Johann Schober, a former Liberal who as municipal police chief had often protected Jewish lives, but the Schober party had allied itself with antisemites and would not accept Jews. The Union and its Democratic partners thus found themselves once more out on a limb, fighting a futile battle to regain lost Jewish votes.[63] By 1932, the Liberals had given up hope and for the first time they refrained from running any candidates in the municipal election. The Union advised its supporters to follow the dictates of their conscience and vote Social Democratic, if they could, or else not vote at all.[64] By this time, the Union had made its peace with the Social Democrats, since it realized that there were no other possible allies left to defend Jewish equality in the public forum.

While the Union was willing to join forces with the Jewish Nationalists in the mid-twenties and then with the Social Democrats in the early thirties, under no circumstances would it give its support to a political alliance with antisemites. When necessary, it would deal with antisemites in power, but it never voluntarily helped to put them there. This policy remained axiomatic. Individual Jews, especially among the wealthier elements, cast their votes for the Schober bloc and even the Christian Socials in the early thirties and some apparently gave their financial support to the Heimwehr as well,[65] but the Union never put its imprimatur on such behavior.

Jewish Liberals faced a serious dilemma in interwar Vienna. What remained of the old Liberal party was extremely weak and fragmented, with ever-lessening chances of its candidates' winning elections. Voting for a Liberal nominee thus essentially meant wasting one's vote. Much the same prognosis could be made for backing a Jewish list, which in any case most Liberals were reluctant to support since they opposed the idea of a separate Jewish party and minority status of any kind. The other parties which basically shared the Liberals' economic views, the Christian Socials and the German Nationalists, were both avowedly antisemitic. Supporting either of them would therefore definitely not meet the economic or political needs of most Jews. All other possibilities having been eliminated, the average middle-class or upper-middle-class Jewish voter who rejected Jewish nationalism was left with two choices: to vote Social Democratic or not to vote at all. Most chose the former option, despite the Social Democratic economic policy and the party's unwillingness to combat antisemitism openly. The rest simply abstained from voting altogether, given the apparent hopelessness of their political situation.

While voter turnout in Vienna was very high in most interwar elections, generally amounting to roughly 90 percent or better, electoral participation was consistently lowest in the former Jewish Liberal stronghold, the Inner City, where it fell to 85 percent in 1923 and 1927 and as low as 78 percent in the 1932 municipal elections when no Liberal candidates were running.[66] Such evidence suggests that many Jewish Liberals did not bother to cast their ballots because they considered the process futile. Some observers have even gone so far as to claim that a majority of the Jewish bourgeoisie in Vienna, not only some famous intellectuals among them, abandoned politics entirely in the twentieth century and turned to art and culture as a means of escape from the political and social realities of their day.[67]

Controlling the Kultusgemeinde

Since Liberalism had clearly failed as a political option in Austria even before World War I, the continued efforts of the Union to bolster Liberal candidates in national and municipal elections were inevitably doomed to failure. But participation in the broader Viennese political arena was by no means the main focus of Union activity during the interwar years. The Union was becoming increasingly involved in the affairs of the Kultusgemeinde, where the Liberals retained their ascendancy considerably longer. The Union fought some of its hardest battles trying to hold on to its remaining bastion of power.

Before World War I, the Liberals dominated the Kultusgemeinde board completely, although the Jewish Nationalists had already begun to present a challenge. Two Zionists had been included on the official electoral list in 1912, but Liberals held the remaining thirty-four seats on the communal council on the eve of the war. Many of these individuals, especially the top leadership, were well over sixty years of age. The president upon reelection in 1912 was in his eighties, while the two vice-presidents were in their seventies. Sixteen of these gentlemen died before the next election was held in 1920.[68] The Liberals liked to refer to the Kultusgemeinde as a "venerable" institution and it certainly was.

Control over the prewar Viennese Kultusgemeinde lay almost totally in the hands of one man, its president, Alfred Stern. Stern was born in 1831 to a leading Jewish family who had come to Vienna from the Hungarian community of Pressburg (or Bratislava, Slovakia) as "tolerated Jews" in the 1770s. He received his doctor of laws degree from the University of Vienna.[69] A fighter by nature and a formidable opponent, he is described by friend and foe alike as a man with a will of iron and a spirit of steel.[70] From 1888 to 1900 Stern served as a Liberal Progressive deputy representing Leopoldstadt on the municipal council and in 1889 he was elected to the Kultusgemeinde board.[71] He fought unsuccessfully against the introduction of a separate curia for the highest taxpayers in communal elections, but once he had assumed the presidency in 1903 he upheld the undemocratic status quo. Stern strongly supported the Union and actively defended Jewish rights against antisemitic attacks both as a city councilor and as president of the Jewish community. Unlike most Liberals, Stern believed that the Kultusgemeinde board should represent Jewish interests in the political as well as religious arena and should take a stand on any matter affecting Jews. He was instrumental in the creation of a communal federation which unfortunately never managed to encompass all Jewish communities in prewar Austria and existed for the most part on paper only.[72]

Stern was deeply committed to improving the lot of his fellow Jews both at home and abroad. He became prominently involved in the Israelitische Allianz and held office as its president from 1913 to 1918. He also served on committees to aid Galician Jewry during the war. Within the Kultusgemeinde he worked on behalf of a Jewish children's hospital, as well as a new communal synagogue and administrative quarters, and a new Jewish cemetery. He was able to put the community on a sound financial footing and raise large amounts in philanthropic endowments, but many of his pet projects were interrupted by the outbreak of the war.[73]

Alfred Stern was an upright and pious Jew who attended synagogue regularly in his later years, sprinkled his speech generously with biblical quotations, and dreamed of visiting the Holy Land in his old age. He advocated strengthening religious education and financial support for the Old Yishuv in Palestine, but he demonstrated little understanding of the younger generation and even less sympathy for the Zionist cause.[74]

Stern ran the Jewish community autocratically. He held meetings of the Kultusgemeinde board in secret session and when he was out of town for four months each year, no board meetings took place at all. When, on several occasions before the war, serious opposition to his wishes arose, he threatened to resign.[75] To the last, he was not a man who compromised his principles.

The era of Liberal complacency within the communal council came to an abrupt end in the immediate aftermath of World War I with the forced abdication of Stern in November 1918. In the midst of the revolutionary turmoil in Vienna which surrounded the armistice and the dissolution of the Empire, a Jewish National Council for German-Austria emerged, demanding recognition for Jews as a nationality and democratization of the Kultusgemeinde. With the threat of physical violence on the Seitenstettengasse where communal administrative offices were located, Jewish Nationalist representatives reached an agreement with the Liberal board members whereby the president would submit his resignation and a special commission composed of three Jewish Nationalists and three Liberals would be established to revise the voting statutes in preparation for communal elections. Fearing bloodshed, Stern reluctantly capitulated, although he strenuously objected to legitimizing the Jewish National Council. Alfred Stern left office at the age of 87; he died less than a month later.[76]

After the war the Liberals continued to control the Kultusgemeinde for another fourteen years, but they increasingly had to share their power with members of the opposition. A new generation of Liberal leaders served on the communal council but the old Liberal philosophy remained largely intact. These men were somewhat younger than their predecessors, but the top leadership positions generally remained in the hands of Liberals over sixty. Six men, including five continuing on from the previous administration, served as board members for more than twelve years, while two Liberals participated in Kultusgemeinde affairs throughout the period 1920 to 1938.[77]

By occupation the Liberals who served on the communal board between 1912 and 1938 can be fairly evenly divided into three categories: self-employed businessmen, including bankers and manufacturers; professionals; and managerial employees. Within this leadership group professionals were clearly overrepresented and businessmen underrepresented as compared with the Viennese Jewish population as a whole, but the general trend toward increased salaried employment in private enterprises is clearly reflected among the Liberals on the communal board.[78] The few ennobled Jews, including Baron Louis Rothschild and Rudolf Ritter von Schwarz-

Hiller, who had participated in Kultusgemeinde affairs before or during the war disappeared from the rolls thereafter. The Liberals on the Kultusgemeinde board exhibited a high level of education, with more than 40 percent both before and after the war bearing the prestigious title of doctor. As one would expect, these Liberal Kultusgemeinde board members constituted an affluent intellectual elite. (See Table 4.)

A dramatic rise in Union activists within the Kultusgemeinde leadership after World War I clearly demonstrated the growing activism of the Union in communal affairs. One-quarter of all Liberals elected to the communal council between 1912 and 1938 also served on the Union board. Whereas before 1920 only 16 percent of the Liberals on the communal board were prominent within the Union, by the mid-twenties nearly half the men elected on the Union ticket were also Union leaders, and after 1932 over 90 percent of the Liberals on the communal council were simultaneously on the Union board.[79] By the end of the interwar period, the Liberal faction in the Kultusgemeinde and the Union leadership who nominated the slate had become virtually identical. The Union of Austrian Jews had completely shifted the focus of its aspirations from general politics to Jewish communal politics.

The office of president of the Kultusgemeinde lost much of its power after Alfred Stern left the scene in late 1918. From 1920 to 1932, Alois Pick, who was affiliated with the Union but never a member of its board, served as the last Liberal president of the Viennese Jewish community. Born in 1859 near Prague in Bohemia, Pick received a medical education and then joined the military. In the 1890s he headed the gastrointestinal department at the Vienna General Hospital and was later appointed professor at the University of Vienna. During World War I he achieved the top rank of major-general in the army medical corps. For a Jew within Austrian society it is difficult to conceive of a much more impressive-sounding title than that of Professor Doktor Alois Pick, General Oberstabsarzt. Pick only became actively involved in Jewish affairs at sixty years of age, following his retirement from military service and after having already succeeded in attaining prestigious professional status.[80]

Pick strongly identified with the Union and sympathized with its views. Immediately after the war he signed a proclamation of German-Austrian Jews against the Jewish National Council[81] and led a protest by a group of military doctors who were being prevented from taking an oath of allegiance on the basis of their being Jews, not Germans, by nationality. He proudly proclaimed that, after thirty-one years of service to his country, no one could deny that he was a true German and a true German-Austrian![82] Pick never became prominent within the Union, nor was he active in the Israelitische Allianz. He had not previously served on the communal board and did not join B'nai B'rith

Lodge "Wien" until 1919.[83] He may therefore be considered an "outsider" and not really part of the Liberal Jewish Establishment before his election to the presidency of the Kultusgemeinde as the head of the "non-Nationalist" list in 1920. Pick was evidently chosen for this position because of his professional prestige and personality, not because of any prior experience or demonstration of Jewish commitment. He provides a classic example of a "leader from the periphery."[84]

Few people could have contrasted more in temperament than Alois Pick and his predecessor Alfred Stern. Whereas Stern had been autocratic and strong-minded, Pick was conciliatory and kind-hearted. Pick was primarily interested in the health and welfare institutions of the Jewish community and evinced less concern for religious and educational affairs. He nevertheless espoused Stern's philosophy of maintaining the Kultusgemeinde as an essentially religious body, committed to traditional Jewish values. Pick adopted a nonpartisan approach as president and dealt fairly and sympathetically with the Zionist faction.[85] Under his genial leadership, the Liberals and the Jewish Nationalists reached their highest degree of cooperation within the community.

Throughout the interwar period the goals of the Viennese Jewish Liberals remained essentially conservative: to retain their control over the Kultusgemeinde and to preserve the status quo as much as possible. In order to achieve these objectives they needed to prevent the introduction of universal suffrage, which was a major demand of their Jewish Nationalist and, later, their Socialist opponents. Universal suffrage would mean the enfranchisement of poorer Jews who could not afford to pay communal taxes, including recent Galician immigrants, who would be much more likely to cast their ballots in favor of Jewish Nationalist, Socialist, or Orthodox factions rather than Liberals. The Liberals had already suffered defeat due to democratization in general politics and hence were in no mood to jeopardize their dominant position within the Jewish community in the name of democracy.

After lengthy negotiations within the electoral commission, the Liberals succeeded in maintaining a minimum tax requirement for voter eligibility in communal elections, but they were forced to make some major concessions with regard to the elimination of the special curia for the highest taxpayers, the acceptance of proportional representation by party list, and the granting of franchise to tax-paying women. Women and communal employees were still not permitted to run for office. The most important, although temporary, gain for the Liberals in 1919 was the creation of a citizenship prerequisite for voters in Kultusgemeinde elections.[86]

As a result of this new stipulation, which affected all newcomers to Vienna since 1912 as well as any noncitizens who had not voted before that date, the composition of the Jewish communal electorate changed very little between 1912 and 1920. Although the number of Jews had increased by more than 10 percent in that interval, the number of eligible voters had grown by less than 4 percent and their distribution remained unevenly weighted in favor of the more affluent.[87] Out of more than 34,000 taxpayers, only 19,303 were declared eligible to vote. (See Table 5.) It is therefore not surprising that in the first postwar election the Liberals managed to stay in power with little difficulty.

In June 1920, after a relatively subdued campaign against Jewish Nationalist and Orthodox challengers and with a fairly respectable 55 percent voter turnout, the "non-Jewish Nationalist" slate, as the Liberals styled themselves, won 5,912 out of a total of 10,553 votes. Since the Liberals obtained only 56 percent of the ballots cast by the heavily middle-class Austrian citizens who voted, these results indicated that serious trouble might lie ahead for them. But with a clear majority in hand, the Liberals occupied twenty out of the thirty-six seats on the communal council. (See Table 6.) Pick, who headed the Liberal list, assumed the office of president and, for an interim period, the Liberals held both vice-presidencies and all seats on the executive council. After an agreement, roughly based on proportional representation, was worked out with the Jewish Nationalists in January 1921, the Liberals retained one vice-presidency and only half the seats on the executive, but they continued to chair nearly all of the eleven major committees.[88] Because the Liberals realized that owing to drastically changed circumstances they needed help in running the Kultusgemeinde, they began to share some of their power with the burgeoning Jewish Nationalist opposition. The two groups worked together fairly amicably, trying to overcome the severe financial crisis that faced Vienna and its Jewish community in the aftermath of the war.

In response to considerable pressure from the Jewish Nationalists and in partial repayment for their cooperation, the Liberals agreed to further electoral reforms on the eve of the 1924 communal elections. The board rescinded the citizenship requirement for voter eligibility, although it remained in effect for those running for office. Communal employees, an increasingly vocal group, became eligible to vote, even if they paid no taxes, but certain categories among them remained ineligible for election.[89] By then there were almost 53,000 taxpayers on the communal rolls, of whom 35,628 had paid their taxes in the previous two years and hence were permitted to vote. This amounted to an 85 percent increase in eligible voters since 1920.[90] (See Table 5.) With the changing complexion of the electorate, especially with large numbers of Galician Jews gaining franchise for the first time, the Liberals feared that their supremacy within the Kultusgemeinde might be at risk.

In order to assure their retention of power, the Liberals decided to enter into a coalition with both the Jewish Nationalists and the anti-Zionist Orthodox Agudah group. They justified maintaining the status quo in light of the continuing economic crisis and in the hope of avoiding an expensive and time-consuming election campaign. This arrangement was in keeping with the general good will which had prevailed for several years within the communal council and also with the pact made between the Liberals and the Jewish Nationalists to run a joint Jewish list in the national and municipal elections the previous fall. In order to enter this alliance, the Liberals had to make certain concessions to their partners, especially the Jewish Nationalists. While no mention was made of a *Volksgemeinde* or minority rights for Jews, the platform of the "United Jewish Parties" did embrace the idea of the Kultusgemeinde as the sole authority capable of fulfilling "all religious, cultural, and other" needs of the Jewish population, including the rebuilding of Palestine. It also recognized the right of the Kultus-gemeinde, as the general representative of Viennese Jewry, to intervene in defense of Jewish equality as guaranteed by the constitution. This compromise formula upheld the status quo for religious and social welfare institutions but pledged to reform religious instruction in order to imbue the youth with "Jewish spirit and communal awareness." In response to Orthodox demands, the program promised continued support for prayer-house associations (or minyanim) and private Jewish supplementary schools, while at the same time emphasizing communal unity.[91]

The results of the 1924 election proved very disappointing for the Liberals. Instead of an uncontested election as they had hoped, the coalition encountered opposition from a newly created Socialist Alliance, as well as two religious lists, one Mizrachi (Religious Zionist) and the other independent Orthodox. While the United Jewish Parties received a very substantial 75 percent of the vote (11,205 out of the 14,865 ballots cast) and hence a total of twenty-eight out of the thirty-six seats on the communal board, after these seats were distributed among the coalition partners, the Liberals ended up with only fifteen seats, five less than they had previously held.[92] (See Table 6.) Their electoral strategy had backfired; in effect, they now no longer constituted a majority within the Kultusgemeinde on their own. Nevertheless, Pick won reelection as president and Jakob Ornstein, president of the Union and one of the main architects of the coalition, assumed a vice-presidency. Liberals constituted four out of the eight members of the expanded executive council and also retained nearly all the committee chairmanships.[93]

Like the Liberal–Jewish Nationalist coalition in general politics, the coalition within the Kultusgemeinde survived only one election. Relations between the two major partners steadily deteriorated. The

Liberals did not take kindly to being outvoted on occasion by the Jewish Nationalists and the Socialists, and they continued to view themselves as the indisputable leaders of the Kultusgemeinde, even though the tide had begun to turn against them.

By 1928, the Liberal–Jewish Nationalist coalition had collapsed. The Liberals maintained their electoral alliance with the Orthodox Agudah faction, however, since the two groups, while differing considerably in the degree of their religious conservatism, shared their opposition to Jewish nationalism and the desire to preserve the Kultusgemeinde as a primarily religious body. During the 1928 campaign, the Liberals drew up a detailed platform that provided a comprehensive formulation of the Union's program regarding communal affairs. Once again the Liberals reiterated their commitment to adhere to the Austrian law of 1890 that obligated the Kultusgemeinde to satisfy the religious needs of the Jewish community in the spheres of ritual, religious education, and social welfare. They insisted that "politics" had no place whatsoever within the communal boardroom. Since they considered the essence of Judaism to lie in the ancient sacred religion, they vehemently opposed the transformation of the religious community into a national community or *Volksgemeinde*. Furthermore, they felt it their duty as citizens of the state to repudiate all efforts to replace religious bonds by tribal, ethnic, or national allegiance. They upheld the unity of the community in which all religious orientations must be freely able to participate.[94]

According to the Liberals and their Agudah allies, only persons who loved the "venerable" community and were devoted to the "old tradition" should have any say in its governance. Therefore, only those who were willing to pay an annual tax of a very minimal amount deserved the right to vote. Suffrage should not be granted to those who refused to contribute or who wanted to use the communal board primarily as a base for expanding their sphere of power and their political influence. Class struggle must not be introduced into the Kultusgemeinde arena and hence they rejected the demands by Jewish Nationalists and Socialists for further electoral reform.[95] Although inability to pay taxes might have had little to do with love for the Jewish community, expanding the franchise would most likely have benefited all the other factions and caused most serious harm to the Liberals, who were determined to prevent any encroachment on their preserve.

The Liberals wanted the communal board to devote special attention to religious affairs and the "ethical-religious" education of the youth in order to train them as "true citizens" and "good Jews." Religious instruction should provide the youth with a knowledge of the high moral principles of Judaism, Jewish history and literature and enable them to take part in worship services and understand the Holy Scriptures and prayers.[96]

The platform clearly articulated the Union's non-Zionist position on Palestine. It affirmed that the Kultusgemeinde should support efforts to create a new home in "the land of our fathers" for all those coreligionists who could not, or did not wish to, remain in their homelands, but it implicitly rejected any claim to Jewish statehood. The Liberal campaign statement concluded with a promise of maximum economy in finances and the assurance that only their candidates could provide the character, sense of obligation, and abilities necessary for effective communal leadership, as if to imply that their opponents were all spendthrifts and unreliable upstarts.[97]

After a bitterly fought election campaign, the slate which called itself the "Jewish Union/United Parties for the Purpose of Excluding any Politics from the Communal Boardroom" received 9,068 (or 46.9 percent) of the 19,348 votes cast. The Union received its strongest support in the wealthier districts, like the Inner City, where the voter turnout was lowest, and its weakest backing in the poorest districts, like Brigittenau, with higher levels of voter participation. Overall, slightly more than 50 percent of the 37,557 eligible voters participated in this election.[98] (See Table 5.) As more Jews became eligible to vote in communal elections, these new voters, often poorer and Eastern in origin, chose not to vote Liberal.

Since the Union list received roughly 47 percent of the vote overall, the Liberals together with the Agudists were allocated exactly half or eighteen out of the thirty-six seats on the communal board, with the Union and the Agudah retaining the same number of mandates as before, i.e., fifteen and three respectively.[99] (See Table 6.) With the Jewish Nationalists now formally in the opposition, the situation had become extremely precarious and it was unclear whether the Kultusgemeinde could continue to function.

The problem manifested itself very clearly at the first board meeting, when officers were elected. The Liberals had expected the Jewish Nationalists to support the Union candidates for president, vice-president, and the executive committee, in return for a vice-presidency and proportional representation on the executive, as in the past. But the Jewish Nationalists were no longer in the mood to cooperate with their erstwhile allies, and adopted obstructionist tactics. While Pick was reelected president by a majority vote, none of the remaining Union candidates received more than eighteen ballots in their favor. The Jewish Nationalist and Socialist candidates could not muster an absolute majority either. When the Jewish Nationalists refused to accept the validity of a lottery as an alternate means of election to overcome the tied votes, the Liberals declared the entire Union slate of officers to be elected with eighteen votes each.[100] This was a hollow victory, however, since they faced a stalemate unless they could win over the opposition. The Union threatened to resign their mandates and call a new election if the Jewish Nationalists did not agree to a modus vivendi.

After a lengthy stand-off, the Jewish Nationalists eventually succumbed to the Liberals' demands in order to permit the Kultusgemeinde to operate. Jakob Ornstein and Josef Löwenherz, the Zionist nominee, were both reelected vice-presidents, while the Liberal-Agudah coalition lost one place on the executive and the Jewish Nationalists gained one. Now, instead of five out of the eight seats (four Liberals and one Orthodox) on this council, the coalition occupied only four and depended on the one Socialist vote in order to attain a majority. In 1930, however, they managed to form an alliance with the Socialist incumbent on the executive. The Liberals were forced to give up several important chairmanships to the Jewish Nationalists, but they succeeded in maintaining a six to five majority on all the major committees.[101] They were still holding onto the reins of power, but their grasp was none too secure.

On the eve of the 1932 communal elections, the Liberals dissolved their eight-year-old partnership with the Orthodox Agudists and entered into a new coalition with another of their former adversaries, the Socialists. This step was in keeping with the Union policy adopted for the first time that same year of officially backing Social Democratic candidates in the municipal elections. While such an alliance between the capitalist Liberal bourgeoisie and the Marxist Socialist "proletarians" might seem incongruous, according to one Union spokesman at least, the gap between the two had narrowed considerably as a result of Socialist municipal economic legislation coupled with the depression. Middle-class Jews, having lost their political clout as Liberals and much of their economic security as well, accommodated themselves to the realities of the day, whether they approved Socialist economic policies or not. For a number of years the Union leadership had included some Social Democrats within its ranks and the two groups which shared a common opposition to Zionism had been working together in relative harmony on the Kultusgemeinde board since around 1930.[102]

The sole purpose of this marriage of convenience was to win enough votes to prevent a Jewish Nationalist takeover of the community. Their joint campaign propaganda warned that a Jewish Nationalist victory would mean the total ruin of the Viennese Kultusgemeinde and Austrian Jewry would be handed over to its antisemitic enemies. They compared their opponents to Nazis and predicted that if the community fell into Zionist hands, hundreds of millions of schillings would be taken from the Kultusgemeinde coffers and given as subventions for the building of Palestine or else used by the Nationalists for their own selfish purposes.[103]

Undoubtedly the Union decided to ally itself with the Socialists and thereby risk offending the Orthodox and perhaps some Liberals as well because they realized that the ultra-Orthodox Agudists were already becoming increasingly alienated from the Kultusgemeinde and that many Liberals did not bother to vote anyway; they clearly felt it necessary to try to attract some of the considerable pool of Jewish Social Democratic voters to their side.

Although the Liberals had successfully prevented the introduction of universal suffrage into the Kultusgemeinde, just before the 1932 election they made a significant concession regarding the interpretation of the existing voter legislation. Eligibility to vote would still be restricted to taxpayers, but instead of payment in the two years immediately prior to the election, it was deemed sufficient for a person to have paid taxes in two out of the preceding three years.[104] While the total number of taxpayers had declined by more than 10 percent from 58,690 in 1928 to 51,813 in 1932, owing primarily to the impact of the depression, surprisingly enough the number of eligible voters increased during the same period by roughly one-third, from 37,557 to 49,929, including 10,449 women heads of households. (See Table 5.) By 1932, 28.5 percent of all Viennese Jews had the right to vote in communal elections, as compared to roughly 18 percent four years previously.[105] The electoral system was becoming much more equitable, although full democracy had by no means been attained. This trend did not bode well for the Liberals, unless they could manage to gain the support of at least some of the newly eligible voters who were outside their normal middle- or upper-middle-class constituency.

Once again the Liberals' electoral strategy did not work. Although they received 11 percent more votes than in the last election, their share of the vote fell sharply from 47 percent to 39 percent. The "Non-Nationalist List of the Jewish-Democratic Bloc" won a total of fifteen seats on the communal board, of which eleven went to the Liberals and four to their Socialist partners. (See Table 6.) Although the Socialists registered a net gain, the Liberals had de facto lost four seats, while their former Agudist allies no longer had any representation at all. Even though the Liberal-Socialist coalition had won the most votes and most seats for any single list competing in this election, they were clearly outnumbered by the alliance of the various Zionist factions which coalesced after the election and held the remaining twenty-one mandates.[106] The Liberals had encountered a major defeat and after more than half a century in power had to give up their control over the Kultusgemeinde.

It is difficult to assess the effectiveness of the Liberals in implementing their program and running the Kultusgemeinde before 1933 or even the significance of their loss of power to the Jewish Nationalists in terms of its actual effect on the community. The Liberals represented the conservative Establishment which was intent on preserving the status quo as much as possible. Since one can demonstrate that very little change took place in the policies of the Kultusgemeinde during the interwar years, one might be justified in concluding that the Liberals were successful in carrying out their goals, even though the economic status of the community as a whole steadily deteriorated and their opponents, the Jewish Nationalists and the Jewish Socialists, claimed that the real needs of Viennese Jewry were not being met. However, one might also admit that the financial difficulties facing the Kultusgemeinde throughout the period were so great as to preclude funding major new projects without seriously curtailing the support of basic commitments. Because of the severe economic crisis, communal priorities did shift, even under Liberal management, and these same trends, which we shall explore in chapter 6, largely continued after the Liberals left office.

By 1932, Viennese Jewish Liberals faced a serious crisis. They had finally come to accept the fact that Liberal candidates were no longer viable in municipal or national elections. Instead of focusing its efforts on the general political scene, the Union concentrated on combating Austrian antisemitism and retaining its hold over the Jewish community. But the Liberals no longer enjoyed a dominant role within the Kultusgemeinde. Their day had passed here too, even though they refused to concede the point.

By the early thirties, the older generation of Liberal leaders, men like Alois Pick and Jakob Ornstein, were beginning to fade from the active communal scene and hand over their positions to a slightly younger generation of leaders like Josef Ticho, Hermann Oppenheim, and Ernst Feldsberg, men in their fifties, sometimes even their forties. But even though the faces were gradually changing and new leaders were working their way up to the top ranks, Liberal policies and ideology were becoming even more rigid. While Pick and Ornstein tended toward moderation and conciliation with their Jewish Nationalist opponents, Ticho, Oppenheim and Feldsberg tended to be hard-line anti-Zionists.

The Liberals had become anachronistic in the twentieth century, outflanked by their opponents in attracting new blood. Socialism and Zionism were attracting Jewish youth away from joining the Liberal Establishment, which they viewed as conservative or even reactionary. The Union of Austrian Jews, while still an important organization on the Viennese Jewish scene, lost its vibrancy and growth potential and instead became a holding operation. The Liberals had to give way to the Social Democrats on the municipal and national political scene and to the Jewish Nationalists within the Kultusgemeinde. A younger generation with different ideas as to the nature of organized Jewish life had come to replace the Liberal Old Guard.

3

THE JEWISH NATIONALISTS

The Jewish Nationalists rejected Liberalism as a solution to the problems of modern Jewry. While the Liberals concentrated on achieving complete civil equality for all Jews as individuals within the state, the Jewish Nationalists focused on obtaining minority rights for Jews as a national group in the diaspora, in addition to striving for sovereignty for the Jewish nation in its ancestral homeland. As a modern movement emerging in the late nineteenth century, Jewish Nationalism redefined Jewish identity in primarily secular terms. Although Jewish Nationalists did not entirely reject the religious aspect of the Jewish experience and many remained traditionally observant, they emphasized the national or ethnic component of Jewish peoplehood.

The dichotomy between nationalists and religionists became a universal phenomenon in twentieth century Jewish life, whether in Europe, America, or Palestine/Israel. It split the entire political spectrum from left to right, dividing Jewish working-class and ideological leftists into Labor Zionists and Social Democrats or Communists, middle-class Jews into General Zionists and Liberals, and Orthodox Jews, who were mainly lower-middle-class, into Religious Zionist Mizrachists and anti-Zionist Agudists. The Jewish community thus splintered into two distinct and often hostile camps, differing significantly in self-perception and strategies for survival.

Geographic origins and degree of integration into the host society influenced, but did not always determine, this division. Emancipated, more assimilated German or Hungarian-speaking Jews tended to be non-nationalists. In Vienna, this group included Hungarian and Czech Jews, as well as some Galicians, who arrived in the capital before the 1880s and quickly identified with its German culture. Modernizing Jews of Eastern origin, usually from multiethnic, predominantly Slavic-speaking areas, often gravitated toward Jewish Nationalism. Thus Jews who came to Vienna after the 1880s, especially from Galicia but also from Moravia, were more likely to join the Jewish Nationalist camp. Although most middle-class and lower-middle-class Jewish

Nationalists, like upper-middle-class Liberals, spoke fluent German and were by no means immune to Viennese culture, they felt less at home in Vienna and their primary identity remained Jewish, rather than Austrian. Whereas Galician newcomers supplied the support for the Jewish Nationalists, Moravians provided much of their top leadership, as they had done for the Liberals as well.

The German-Austrian Republic comprised an ethnically relatively homogeneous nation state, much like interwar France, Germany, or Hungary, where Liberals retained control over the Jewish community and Zionists did not become very heavily involved in diaspora politics. The odds against Jews gaining recognition as a national, rather than religious, group remained much greater in Austria than in multinational states, such as the Soviet Union, Poland, Czechoslovakia, or Yugoslavia. Yet the Jewish Nationalists in Vienna persisted in pursuing policies that more closely resembled those of their Polish, Czech, or Yugoslav counterparts than those of German or Hungarian Jews. They succeeded in taking over control of their local community, as did Jewish Nationalists in parts of Czechoslovakia and Yugoslavia, and they ran candidates in general elections, as in Poland and Czechoslovakia, but in Vienna, as elsewhere in East Central Europe, their efforts at effectively representing Jewish interests in the larger political arena failed owing to lack of sufficient Jewish votes and an inhospitable environment.[1]

This chapter will focus on the middle-of-the-road General Zionists as the main opposition force to the Liberals within the Viennese Jewish community. We shall concern ourselves with the Labor Zionists in the next chapter on the Socialists and with the Religious Zionists in the following section on the Orthodox. Here we shall investigate Jewish Nationalist involvement in diaspora politics, first analyzing their unsuccessful forays into general politics and then charting their progress in wresting control of the community away from the Liberal Establishment.

Diaspora Nationalists and Zionists

Jewish Nationalists in East Central Europe often subdivided into two discrete types: diaspora nationalists, who concerned themselves with the short-term objective of gaining Jewish national autonomy in the states in which they were living, and Zionists, whose primary goal was to rebuild a Jewish homeland, and ultimately create a Jewish state, in Palestine. The idea of national autonomy made sense within the large multinational Habsburg Empire, especially in areas of strong Jewish concentration such as Galicia. Before World War I, separate diaspora nationalist groups coexisted alongside Zionist groups in the Austrian capital and some diaspora nationalists rejected Zionism in

favor of autonomism.[2] In interwar Vienna, the two categories largely
overlapped, unlike in Poland and Yugoslavia where some diaspora
nationalists maintained a separate existence from the Zionists.[3] Nearly
all leading Viennese Zionists favored some form of Jewish Nationalist
involvement in diaspora politics, especially within the Kultusgemeinde, alongside their commitment to creating a Jewish homeland
in Palestine. Although diaspora nationalist political organizations were
often distinct from Zionist bodies in Vienna, for the most part the same
individuals provided the leadership for both. The term "Jewish
Nationalist" can thus be used almost interchangeably with the term
"Zionist" and designates the supporters of both agendas combined,
but especially those who emphasized diaspora affairs.

The first Jewish Nationalist association in Vienna was Kadimah, a
university fraternity formed in 1883 by a group of Eastern European
students for the dual purpose of strengthening Jewish national identity and supporting Jewish colonization in Palestine. Kadimah paved
the way for the advent of Theodor Herzl on the Viennese scene, and its
alumni filled many of the leadership positions within the World Zionist
Organization during its early years. The various Jewish Nationalist
student fraternities, modeled after Kadimah, continued to provide a
valuable training ground for Viennese Zionist leaders in the twentieth
century.[4]

Even though Herzlian political Zionism, with its headquarters in
Vienna until 1905, concentrated almost exclusively on gaining a
charter for a Jewish homeland, preferably in Palestine, from the outset
the local Viennese Zionists by no means limited their activities to
endeavors on behalf of this single objective. In 1898, the Second Zionist
Congress adopted the doctrine of *Gegenwartsarbeit*, which literally
translates as "working in the present," but in practice meant engaging
in local Jewish affairs with the intent of arousing Jewish national
consciousness and "capturing the community." While this concept was
contrary to Herzl's own basic approach,[5] it was quickly adopted by his
Viennese followers, perhaps because of its compatibility with the
Jewish Nationalist student background shared by many of them. As
early as 1900, Zionists began competing in Kultusgemeinde elections
with the ultimate goal of taking over what was essentially defined as
a religious community and transforming it into a *Volksgemeinde*, a
"people's community" based on Jewish Nationalist principles.
Throughout the period up until World War II, virtually all Viennese
Zionists retained their commitment to active involvement in communal
politics.

After the 1906 Austrian Zionist conference in Cracow officially
endorsed the idea of *Landespolitik*, meaning participation in national,
as well as municipal, politics for the purpose of representing Jewish
interests and gaining recognition and rights for Jews as a national

minority, Zionists took over control of the existing diaspora nationalist Jewish People's Party and transformed it into the Jewish Nationalist Party. While some prominent diaspora nationalist figures, including former Zionists such as S. R. Landau and Nathan Birnbaum, remained outside the Zionist framework, by and large Jewish Nationalist politics had become a Zionist preserve in Austria even before World War I.[6]

During the war, Viennese and Galician Zionist leaders together presented an extensive list of Jewish Nationalist demands to the Austrian government, clearly outlining their position. They based their memorandum on the principle that Austria, as a multinational state, must guarantee all national groups the right of free cultural, political and economic development. Nationalities must be recognized by public law and granted autonomous rights, while membership in any nation must not affect eligibility for citizenship.

The Jewish Nationalists made seven specific demands. First, the Jewish nationality must be recognized and its free acknowledgment must be protected. Language must not be used as the criterion for nationality, since the Jews constitute a nation, despite their use of many different languages. Nevertheless, the free usage of Yiddish and Hebrew as vernaculars must be protected. Second, the Jews have a right to their own schools in order to educate their children in the Jewish spirit. These Jewish schools must be supported by public funds, wherever there is a need. They should be supervised under the state school law, but be administered by Jews. Third, Jews must be represented in the national parliament, provincial diets, and municipal governments in accordance with their numbers and achievements through the creation of Jewish curia and the introduction of a proportional voting system. Fourth, Jews must be represented in the imperial government through a minister or a secretary of state. In addition, a Jewish administrator must be appointed in all central offices which deal with Jewish affairs, such as the Ministries of Religion, Education, and Social Welfare. Fifth, civil equality for Jews as guaranteed by the constitution must be implemented immediately. To date Jews had de facto been barred from certain public service branches, including various ministries, central offices, provincial administration, and the higher judiciary, as well as military, political, and diplomatic service. All these areas must be made accessible to Jewish candidates. In particular, the system which made baptism a job requirement and favored converts must be abolished. The law must take into account the requirements of the Jewish religion, for example allowing Sabbath rest on Saturday instead of Sunday. The Jewish confession must be allotted a proportional share of the state budget for confessional purposes. Sixth, the Jewish nation must be legitimized through the creation of an imperial federation or a chamber of nationalities elected on the basis of equal, secret, and direct suffrage. Finally, Jewish religious institutions must be legally strengthened by the establishment of an imperial federation of Jewish communities.[7]

The Jewish Nationalists formulated their proposal at a time when the dissolution of the Austrian Empire was not yet regarded as inevitable; hence they based it on the assumption that Austria would remain a large, multinational entity.[8] By the end of 1918, the war was over and a small, overwhelmingly German, Austrian republic had come into existence. The Jewish Nationalists, however, did not feel the need to change their policy significantly in the light of this new reality. Perhaps this represented short-sightedness or a lack of realism on their part, but logically they could not strongly advocate *Landespolitik* without basing it on a demand for national minority rights for Jews, if not complete national autonomy.

After the war, Jewish National Councils under Zionist auspices sprang up in the successor states of East Central Europe.[9] In November 1918, Austrian Zionists established the Jewish National Council for German-Austria to defend the national and political interests of the Jews in their new state. They proclaimed the dawning of a new era of (freeedom, wheen for the first time in two millennia JJews would take) charge of their own fate aand not remain passive and defenselless, depeendent onn the goodwill of others. They demanded a Jewish national home in Palestine and the acceptance of Jews within the League of Nations, predicated on the recognition of the Jewish nation as a member of the family of nations with equal rights. Within Austria, they also demanded recognition as a nation and assurance of national minority rights, as well as complete political and civi! equality for Jews as for all citizens of the state, so that Jews might live in peaceful and friendly coexistence with the German majority. They wanted proportional representation in the Austrian constituent assembly and in all legislative and executive bodies. In addition they called for a Jewish constituent national assembly to be elected by universal suffrage and demanded the right to administer their own affairs autonomously in the context of a democratic *Volksgemeinde.*[10]

In the euphoric days of revolutionary upheaval in the immediate aftermath of the war, the Jewish Nationalists experienced a ground swell of popular support and some early triumphs. The Council succeeded in forcing the resignation of Alfred Stern as president of the Kultusgemeinde, and three Zionist leaders were coopted onto the communal board for the purpose of helping revise the electoral statutes along more democratic lines. The Kultusgemeinde board, overwhelmingly Liberal in composition, reluctantly capitulated to the demands of the Jewish National Council, fearing possible violence within the community if this clamorous minority were not accommodated.[11]

The creation of the Council naturally caused a great deal of consternation among the Liberals, who feared that any demand for national minority status might endanger their civil equality. The Union published a statement, accompanied by an impressive list of signatures, challenging the right of the Jewish National Council to speak on behalf of all Austrian Jewry, since, they maintained, a majority considered Jews to constitute an exclusively confessional, rather than a national, group. In response, the Council issued a clarification of its position. It affirmed that it only spoke in the name of those Jews who felt themselves part of the Jewish people and regarded world Jewry as a national entity. It declared as a fundamental principle of Jewish Nationalist politics in Austria that each Jew must be free to acknowledge the Jewish nation. Any Jews who rejected this identification would not be represented by the Council, but by representatives of that nation to which they ascribed themselves instead. Belonging to the Jewish nation, the statement reiterated, should not conflict with either the fulfilling of civic duties or the enjoyment of civil rights.[12]

Indeed, the most difficult task confronting the Jewish National Council was attempting to achieve its national goals without jeopardizing Jewish civil equality. Immediately after the war, the Council intervened with the state authorities to protect the rights of Jewish soldiers. It wanted assurances that Jews would be able to take an oath of allegiance to the new Austrian army which would not discriminate against them on the basis of nationality, but it also wanted to create a Jewish division within the army and allow Jewish soldiers to wear a special blue and white insignia.[13] With the dissolution of the old army, the Council managed to form a defense force made up of demobilized Jewish soldiers. Subsidized by the Kultusgemeinde, a Jewish troop of about 300 men within the Viennese municipal guard protected heavily Jewish neighborhoods, especially during elections and antisemitic demonstrations.[14] Similarly, the Council negotiated with the authorities in order that the self-acknowledgment of Jewish nationality would not adversely affect Jewish civil servants, including railroad and postal officials and military doctors, who indeed encountered obstacles in taking their new oaths of office.[15]

The Jewish National Council fought behind the scenes to prevent, or at least postpone, a mass expulsion of Galician refugees from Vienna. When these efforts proved only partially effective, the Council sought to alleviate the plight of those hapless individuals who were evicted from the capital by helping to arrange their transportation and ensure their safety on their way back to Poland.[16] The Council attempted to protect the rights of Jews to opt for Austrian citizenship by fighting against an interpretation of the option clause of the peace treaty which would have limited citizenship to persons of German nationality or race. In addition, it vigorously opposed the introduction of any sort of numerus clausus for Jewish students at Austrian universities.[17] In such efforts, the activities of the Jewish National Council paralleled those of the Union of German-Austrian Jews.

It was very difficult to maintain the delicate balance between striving for beneficial minority rights for Jews in the now relatively homogeneous Austrian republic and avoiding a special status advocated by antisemites which would have been detrimental to Jewish interests.[18] Ultimately, the Jewish National Council failed to achieve its primary political goal, since recognition as a separate nationality was denied to the Jews in Austria, but ironically this very failure made it somewhat easier for the Jewish Nationalists, as well as the Liberals and the Social Democrats, to protect the civil rights which the Jews already had and prevent the adoption of specifically anti-Jewish legislation, including official quotas at universities.

Another urgent problem confronting the Jewish National Council was the desperate economic situation facing Austria and its Jews in the immediate aftermath of the war. In December 1918, the Council subscribed 100,000 crowns toward the Austrian state loan as an expression of support and confidence in the new state; at the same time, it appealed to the Zionist Organizations of America, England, and Western Europe to influence their countries to come to the aid of the newly founded republic, which appeared on the verge of political and economic collapse.[19]

The Council set up its own social welfare bureau which provided aid for destitute Jews, especially war refugees, and sent more than six thousand children abroad by mid-1920.[20] It also established a bureau for vocational advancement, which worked together with the Vienna Palestine Office to promote occupational rehabilitation and productivization among younger Jews. Training in manual labor, including agriculture and construction, was intended as preparation for diaspora as well as Palestinian needs, although the bureau admitted that it was generally difficult for Jews to find employment in such fields in Austria.[21] The Jewish National Council thus attempted to combine a Palestine orientation with its efforts to alleviate the economic woes of Viennese Jewry.

In the field of Jewish education, the Council had its own education bureau which helped to create a Hebrew Teachers' Institute and a Jewish high school in Vienna, thus spreading its secular values to the younger generation. The Teachers' Institute, which lasted until 1931, offered a five-year training program for Hebrew and kindergarten teachers and also prepared elementary and middle school instructors for teaching Hebrew and general subjects. The high school, later known as the Chajes Realgymnasium, provided quality Jewish and secular education, mainly for children of the Jewish poor.[22] A Jewish elementary school, although under discussion, did not materialize for more than a decade.

Originally, the Jewish National Council had hoped to broaden its appeal to encompass not only Zionists but all Jewish parties, including the Orthodox and Jewish Social Democrats, if not Liberals as well, so that it could speak on behalf of Austrian Jewry as a whole. It had also planned for a Jewish national assembly to be elected on the basis of universal and equal suffrage by all members of the Jewish people.[23] These aspirations were never achieved, however, since none of the non-nationalist groups agreed to join and democratic elections never took place. Therefore, the Council remained a self-selected and exclusively Zionist body. Indeed, after the Labor Zionist Poale Zion seceded from the Council in 1919, it became virtually identical to the Austrian Zionist Federation, which was predominantly General Zionist in composition.[24] In the early twenties, the Jewish National Council gradually faded out of existence, while the Federation assumed full charge over all aspects of *Gegenwartsarbeit.*

The General Zionists dominated Jewish Nationalist politics in interwar Vienna. This middle-of-the-road, pragmatic brand of Zionism, which combined political and practical approaches and favored the gradual upbuilding of a Jewish home in Palestine with international Jewish support, appealed largely to middle- and lower-middle-class Jews of the Austrian capital, especially those who had arrived more recently from ethnically diverse Galicia or Moravia and did not feel comfortable identifying themselves as Germans by nationality and Jews merely by religion.

The General Zionists in Vienna, as elsewhere, did not remain a cohesive bloc but eventually split into several groups, including A and B factions. By the thirties, the General Zionists A, often referred to as the Radical or Democratic faction, became closely linked with Chaim Weizmann, president of the World Zionist Organization, and sometimes allied themselves with Labor Zionist factions. The General Zionists B Group, the stronger element in Vienna, had broken with Weizmann over a variety of tactical issues and moved further to the right. The dominant General Zionist B faction, and the Radicals as well, lost some of their supporters in the thirties to the Revisionists and the Jewish State Party, even more hard-line groups on the right wing of the Zionist spectrum which backed a maximalist program of creating a sovereign state in Palestine, based on mass Jewish immigration, as soon as possible.

This splintering among Viennese Zionists resulted in the proliferation of the Austrian Zionist press by the late twenties. From 1919 to 1927 Vienna boasted the only Zionist daily in Central Europe, the *Wiener Morgenzeitung,* published by Robert Stricker. After receiving subsidies from the World Zionist Organization for several years, the newspaper foundered financially and was replaced by a weekly *Die Neue Welt*, also published by Stricker, who had joined the Radical faction. In 1928, the National Zionist Committee, controlled by General Zionist B group supporters, created another weekly of its own, *Die Stimme*. Once *Die Neue Welt* adopted Stricker's Revisionist platform (later that of the Jewish State Party), the Radicals began to issue another weekly, *Der jüdische Weg*, in 1932. The Labor Zionists and the Religious Zionists also had their own party organs which appeared intermittently. All the Zionist papers engaged in lively disputes with one another.[25]

Factionalism was endemic to the Zionist movement in the twentieth century and Vienna proved no exception to the general rule.[26] The results of elections for the biennial World Zionist Congresses, as well as the multiplication of Zionist lists in Kultusgemeinde elections, reflect the increasing fragmentation within Viennese Zionism. (See Tables 6 and 7.) Often the controversy revolved around expanding the Jewish Agency for Palestine and working together with non-Zionists; sometimes it centered on supporting or rejecting *Landespolitik*, while at other times it assumed the form of Left vs. Right. But all these issues were really interconnected and ideological disputes were further complicated by personality conflicts.

Only one individual actively involved in Zionist affairs after 1918 managed to remain above parties and factions, namely Vienna's Chief Rabbi, Hirsch (Zvi) Perez Chajes. Chajes was both a strong supporter of Palestine and a proponent of minority rights in the diaspora. A spokesman for Jewish national pride, he was also a voice for Jewish harmony and conciliation. Chajes, with his charismatic personality and superb leadership qualities, provided spiritual guidance for Viennese Jewry and a guiding light for the Jewish Nationalists. His premature death in 1927 at the age of fifty-one left a void which no one else could fill. This meant a particularly critical loss for Viennese Zionists who desperately needed such a distinguished yet nonpartisan figure in the decade that followed.[27]

How many Jewish Nationalists were there in Vienna, and who provided their leadership? How did the Jewish Nationalists compare with their Liberal opponents with regard to age, sex, geographic origins, place of residence, occupation, and education? Jewish Nationalists resembled their non-nationalist Jewish neighbors in many respects and were fairly evenly distributed among the various Viennese districts. But by and large, they were younger than Liberals, more likely to have been born in Galicia, and more likely to be professionals. Moreover, women, students, and teenagers tended to become more actively involved in Zionist affairs than in Liberal-sponsored activities.

Membership in the various Zionist organizations fluctuated considerably in interwar Vienna. It ranged from roughly 10,000 in the mid-twenties to almost 16,000 a decade later.[28] Much of this membership did not become actively involved in Zionist affairs but limited themselves to payment of their shekel dues, especially in the alternate years when shekel-payers were eligible to vote in elections for the World Zionist Congress. The hotbeds of Zionist activity in Vienna were located in Leopoldstadt and neighboring Brigittenau. The Zionist organization tended to be relatively weak in most other districts, especially the Inner City where Zionist headquarters were located, although Jewish Nationalist voters in both Zionist Congress and Kultusgemeinde elections, unlike the activists, were on the whole fairly evenly distributed throughout the city.

The Jewish Nationalists, like most Jews in Vienna, generally chose to live among other Jews, but not necessarily among fellow Jewish Nationalists. This pattern seems to apply particularly to the top Jewish Nationalist leaders who served on the Kultusgemeinde board. Of the thirty-six individuals elected to the communal council on the Zionist ticket during the interwar period, almost 40 percent reported their residency in the prestigious Inner City district. A higher percentage of Jewish Nationalist Kultusgemeinde leaders were concentrated in the Inner City district than their Liberal counterparts, of whom less than 20 percent were to be found there. Zionist leaders were also more likely than Liberals to be living in Leopoldstadt. Two-thirds of the leading Zionist figures in Vienna, as opposed to fewer than half of the Liberal elite, lived in these two central districts; the remainder were scattered in various other districts, but not a single elected individual resided in lower-class Brigittenau, where so many of the rank-and-file Zionists made their home.[29] (See Table 4.)

While the residential distribution of Zionist supporters did not greatly differ from that of Viennese Jewry as a whole, the same did not generally hold true for their geographic origins. Jewish Nationalists were more likely to hail from Galicia and Moravia, rather than Hungary, Bohemia, or Vienna itself, as compared to the Viennese Jewish population at large. Among the Zionists elected to the Kultusgemeinde during the interwar years for whom place of birth is known, more than 40 percent hailed from Galicia, roughly a third were from Moravia, and 16 percent were from Austria proper. Among the Liberals on the Kultusgemeinde board, by comparison, a third each hailed from Hungary and the Czech lands, less than a quarter from Vienna, and a mere 9 percent from Galicia.[30] (See Table 4.) Whereas the Liberals were overwhelmingly Westerners, a majority among the Jewish Nationalists were undoubtedly Easterners by origin.

The Liberals frequently accused the Zionists of deriving their support from among the *Ostjuden*, whom they labeled "foreigners," since many of them had come as refugees during the war. To some degree this charge has validity, although most Zionists had resided in Vienna since before the war and those who had not yet become citizens were subsequently naturalized or else expelled from the capital after the war. Most of the top Jewish Nationalist communal leaders, including Robert Stricker, Jakob Ehrlich, and Desider Friedmann, were Moravians by birth, and Leopold Plaschkes, although born in Lower Austria, had Moravian-born parents, but a few, like Josef Löwenherz, were in fact Galicians of recent vintage. Like the Liberals and the majority of Viennese Jews, relatively few Zionists were "native" Viennese. Although the stigma of being associated with the "East" continued to cling to them, the Jewish Nationalists were as Western in their occupations and education, as well as their language and dress, as the majority of Viennese Jewry of which they formed an integral and almost indistinguishable part.

Indeed, the occupational distribution among Zionists resembled that of local Jewry at large. A list of 587 signatories on the Zionist Electoral Committee for the 1928 Kultusgemeinde elections contained a slightly lower percentage of businessmen, manufacturers, and artisans and roughly the same percentage of white collar employees as compared with a Union list for the same year. The Zionist signatories, however, reflected twice as high a percentage of professionals within their ranks as did the Liberals. Among these professionals, more than a third were lawyers. As might be expected given this high degree of professionalization, the Zionist supporters proved twice as likely to hold academic degrees as did their Liberal counterparts.[31] (See Table 8.)

It is scarcely surprising that Zionist activists should exhibit an unusually high level of advanced education, since the universities, and the gymnasia as well, provided an important training ground for Jewish Nationalist leadership. During the interwar years, Jewish high school and university students gravitated toward Zionist, or else Socialist, groups, but not toward the Liberals. Youth movements and student societies contributed a reservoir of support for the Zionist cause and helped to guarantee the Jewish Nationalists a much lower age profile than their non-nationalist opponents. Some Jewish young people, especially students, became alienated from mainstream Austrian Zionism during the interwar years, however, owing to the focus of many of the older generation on *Landespolitik* rather than Palestine.[32]

Not only were Zionist supporters as a rule younger than non-Zionists, but Zionist leadership proved younger as well, especially in the top ranks. The first three Zionists to enter the Kultusgemeinde boardroom were all men in their thirties when they took their seats, while the two Jewish Nationalists who served as communal vice-presidents in the twenties had barely reached forty when each assumed office. Given the gerontocracy of the Liberals, for whom seventieth and eightieth birthdays and death while in office were not uncommon, the Jewish Nationalists represented a younger generation of Jewish communal leaders. Unlike in the case of their rivals, it tended to be the younger, rather than the older, Zionists who served multiple terms and held high positions within the Jewish communal hierarchy.[33]

The Zionists not only managed to attract younger people into their ranks, both as members and as leaders, but as a more egalitarian group they also encouraged greater participation by women than did the Liberals. The Zionist National Committee usually included at least one woman, most often in charge of women's Zionist affairs, and in the thirties a woman was repeatedly elected as one of the two vice-presidents of this body. Prominent Zionist women, including Anitta Müller-Cohen, a philanthropist and social activist, and Erna Patak, a social worker, ran as candidates on the Jewish Nationalist ticket in early postwar parliamentary and municipal campaigns, although none won election, and several women served as delegates to Zionist Congresses in the thirties.[34] These women, together with the male Zionist leadership, fought unsuccessfully to gain equal suffrage for women within the Kultusgemeinde.[35] Women did not play an equal role to men in Zionist affairs, but they were seriously involved, especially in the separate women's Zionist sphere.

Austrian Zionists preached egalitarianism but did not always practice it. The Organization of Zionist Women of Austria helped organize the first International Conference of Jewish Women, which took place in Vienna in May 1923. At that time, the leading Viennese Zionist women, including Erna Patak and Anitta Müller-Cohen, acknowledged that Zionism had provided new opportunities for Jewish women to assume the role of organizers, speakers, educators, and activists alongside men, but they recognized that their special concerns as women regarding children, health, and welfare might conflict with other Zionist priorities.[36] Indeed, Zionism did offer a new avenue for women's involvement in the community, alongside the traditional charitable network, but women's Zionist activities remained circumscribed by broader, male-dominated Zionist goals; women tended to engage in the cultural and humanitarian aspects of Zionism rather than in the more strictly political dimensions of Jewish Nationalism so important in interwar Vienna.

Landespolitik

The most striking feature of Austrian Zionism in the early twentieth century was the strong commitment to *Landespolitik* shared by most of its top leadership, if not always its membership, especially women and youth. The Viennese Zionists formulated their policy of support for involvement in diaspora politics before and during World War I, while Vienna still served as the hub of the multiethnic Austro-Hungarian Monarchy, and they retained it largely intact thereafter, despite the fact that they now found themselves operating in the capital of a small German-Austrian republic. This faithful continuity with the past undoubtedly reflects the Galician and Moravian origins of the Viennese Zionist leadership, who defined themselves as Jews by nationality and demanded recognition as such. The borders might have changed drastically, but the proposed Jewish Nationalist solutions remained much the same in postwar as in prewar Austria, although some Zionists began to question the prudence of perpetuating such a course of action.

One of the main goals of *Landespolitik* was to elect Jewish Nationalist representatives to the Austrian parliament and the Viennese municipal council. In the aftermath of the 1907 election, four Jewish Nationalists constituted the first Jewish Club within the Austrian parliament. All these deputies represented constituencies in Galicia or Bukovina.[37] In the same election, Isidor Schalit, a leading Zionist, campaigned unsuccessfully against Julius Ofner for a seat in Leopoldstadt, receiving only 529 votes or roughly 6 percent of the ballots cast in the most heavily Jewish district in Vienna.[38] In the 1911 and 1919 elections, Robert Stricker challenged Ofner for his parliamentary seat; he lost the last prewar election but managed to win a victory in the first postwar campaign. In all subsequent National Assembly elections, Stricker was defeated.[39] Although Schalit eventually abandoned *Landespolitik*, Stricker never did.

Schalit, born in 1871 in the Ukraine but raised and educated in Vienna, had been actively involved in Kadimah in the 1890s and was an early supporter of Herzl. A dentist by profession, he helped organize the First Zionist Congress and ran the Zionist Office in Vienna until Herzl's death. He headed the Austrian Zionist organization before World War I and after the war continued to act as vice-president of the Zionist National Committee for Austria until 1923.[40] In 1920, Schalit was elected to the Kultusgemeinde board on the Zionist list, but served for only one term. This pattern of sustained involvement within the Austrian Zionist Federation but not within the communal board proves typical for many prominent General Zionist leaders who were not "Westerners" by birth.

Schalit started out as a strong advocate of *Landespolitik*. In 1906, he presented the Austrian government with a request on the part of Austrian Zionists for Jewish national autonomy, proportional representation, and a separate voting curia.[41] By 1925, however, Schalit had given up these demands as futile. In the Zionist Congress election of that year, he headed a list of dissidents, calling themselves the Free Zionist Association, who were opposed to diaspora nationalist politics.

Their main goal was to eliminate Jewish Nationalist candidates in Austrian general elections and allow all individuals to vote in national and municipal politics according to their own personal convictions. This would enable Zionists to vote for the Austrian Social Democratic Party if they so desired, rather than being bound by Zionist "party discipline" to vote Jewish Nationalist. Although Schalit's slate won a plurality of the votes cast, renunciation of *Landespolitik* was rejected by the Zionist National Committee and, in particular, by Robert Stricker.[42]

Without a doubt, Stricker was the most colorful and controversial personality within Viennese Zionist circles during the interwar years. As Siegfried Graubart, one of his Revisionist colleagues on the Kultusgemeinde board in the thirties, later wrote, "If any Jew in Austria had been asked who was the most beloved of the 250,000 [sic] Jews in Austria; who had the greatest number of enemies, both among Jews and among Gentiles; who was the most respected by the Gentile world, feared by our enemies, and hated by the assimilated or baptized Capitalists and Socialists alike—in every case, he would have replied unhesitatingly—'Stricker, of course.'" Graubart went on to say, "He was not a good administrator either of his personal affairs or of those of such a great community, and he valued money and finance very little, but he was a born leader of the masses and ruthless in attack."[43]

Robert Stricker was born in Brno, Moravia, in 1879 and after receiving an engineering degree worked as a surveyor for the Austrian State Railways. He became a Zionist while still a student and soon began writing and editing for the Zionist press. After moving to Vienna in the early 1900s, he edited and published a series of Zionist newspapers, which served as vehicles for his passionately held ideas.[44] A secular Jew, Stricker first won election to the Kultusgemeinde in 1912 and served on the communal board throughout most of the interwar period, including several brief stints as vice-president and member of its executive committee.

Louis Lipsky, the American Zionist leader, described Stricker as a Vienna café politician: "You thought of him—mindless of the time of day—sitting at a table in a café surrounded by motley characters, talking volubly about foreign affairs, about the quarrels of newspapers, what was going on in the theatre, and about the politics of the Jewish community." Lipsky recalled him as "a well-built man whose black beard fanned from his face, then was clipped short and trimmed and his voice was loud and raucous. But he was a powerful orator, capable of reaching heights of amazing denunciation. . . . He had all the good manners of a Viennese; but he loved the boisterous and the unruly."[45]

Stricker had an abiding commitment to two goals, a Jewish state in Palestine and a strong Jewish party to represent Jewish interests in Austria. At first he was part of the Zionist mainstream, but then he left to join the opposition. In 1913 he was elected to the Greater Zionist Actions Committee of the World Zionist Organization and in 1921 hc assumed the vice-presidency of that body. In 1924, however, he resigned his position over the issue of Jewish statehood and the expansion of the Jewish Agency for Palestine to include non-Zionists; soon thereafter he helped found the Radical Zionist faction. By 1931, he had left to join the Revisionists, but a few years later he abandoned them and affiliated with the Jewish State Party.[46] Such behavior appeared fickle and alienated many people, but Stricker retained a loyal following who continued to support him on his journey toward the Zionist right wing. Robert Stricker was clearly the most popular Zionist politician in Vienna and the one who could "get out the vote" most often, regardless of the list he was running on. (See Table 7.)

Stricker may be seen as the personal embodiment of the idea of *Landespolitik* in Austria. During his unsuccessful 1911 campaign Stricker outlined his basic philosophy.[47] Jews must vote for the Jewish Nationalist Party in order to guarantee Austrian Jewry parliamentary representation, which he considered their strongest weapon in fighting political and economic battles. Jews were faced with three problem areas: the "Jewish question," the nationality question, and the economic situation. With regard to antisemitism, the German Liberals and the Social Democrats were identical, Stricker claimed, since neither supported Jews per se. Jew-hatred must be combated by deeds, not phrases. The Liberals were led by antisemites and Jewish Liberals were only lackeys who needed special permission to speak out. Likewise, the Social Democrats did not respond to Jewish misery, since they did not want to be considered a "Jewish defense troop." But Jews *needed* their own defense troop to protect their interests and only the Jewish Nationalist Party provided the answer by advocating national autonomy and the equality of all peoples of Austria.

In the economic sphere, Stricker maintained that the Social Democrats concerned themselves entirely with wage-earners and not with the middle class, white collar employees, or members of the free professions, whereas the Liberals were not interested in the little man, but only in large-scale capitalists, especially industrialists and bankers. The Jewish Nationalist Party, however, represented a party for all Jews, regardless of class. Its economic program covered a broad spectrum, including complete freedom of trade, support for industry and export, far-reaching protection for workers and the creation of a state social security system for all occupational groups. In sum, according to Stricker, only a Jewish party could truly meet Jewish political and economic needs.

The Austrian electoral system, although based on proportional representation, strongly favored large parties, rather than smaller political factions. In the earliest postwar parliamentary elections, in order to stand a chance at winning a victory in any voting district, the Jewish Nationalists had to arrange surplus vote agreements with the various Liberal groups. Thereafter, the electoral geometry was altered so that no small party could realistically expect to achieve even a single parliamentary mandate, even if suitable pre-election deals could be made.

In the February 1919 elections for the Constituent National Assembly, the Jewish Nationalist Party ran its own list, headed by Stricker, in the Vienna Northeast constituency, which included Leopoldstadt and Brigittenau. In all other voting districts, it endorsed the candidates of the Liberal Democratic Middle Class Party, as opposed to the heavily Jewish Liberal Democratic Party. Stricker's ticket received 7,760 votes, which was slightly more than the two Liberal tickets combined, but well under the voting key of 15,000 required for election. However, since the Jewish Nationalist Party had officially coupled with the Liberal lists, Stricker narrowly managed to win a seat. In parliamentary elections the following year, the Jewish Nationalist Party ran separate lists in all Viennese districts and did not enter a surplus vote agreement with the Liberals. Although the Jewish list received 9,725 votes in the Northeast constituency, 20 percent more than in the last round, this total by itself was not enough to return Stricker to office.[48]

The Jewish Nationalist voting record in the 1919 and 1920 parliamentary elections was not particularly impressive. Both men and women could now vote, but noncitizens were ineligible. Many of the Jewish Nationalists' supporters were fairly recent newcomers, especially from Galicia, who had not yet acquired official Austrian residency, and they were disqualified from participating. Only about one in four Jewish voters in heavily Jewish Leopoldstadt chose the Jewish Nationalist Party, whereas in Brigittenau, the poorest Jewish district, more than half of the relatively small Jewish electorate voted for the Jewish list. In other voting districts, the Jewish Nationalist vote was much lower. In Alsergrund, roughly one in five Jewish voters supported the Jewish list; in the Inner City, less than one in eight Jews did so. All told, the Jewish Nationalists received 18,358 votes in Vienna in 1920, slightly under 2 percent of the total vote, while Vienna's 200,000 Jews accounted for 10.8 percent of the capital's population.[49]

In its campaigns the Jewish Nationalist Party tried to persuade Jewish voters that neither the Social Democrats nor the Liberals could meet their real needs and that a vote for the Jewish Nationalist Party would not go to waste or lead to the election of antisemites. The party's program proclaimed the right of the Jews to nationhood, but did not emphasize this point. Instead, it promised to protect the political equality of Jewish citizens and to fight constantly against antisemitism which threatened the existence of Jews as individuals and the honor of the Jewish people. It sought to promote greater understanding with non-Jewish citizens through open and dignified discussions. It also advocated improving the health and strength of the Jewish community through nationalist education and vocational rehabilitation which would transform the youth into more committed Jews and make them more employable and "productive." Its economic policy was one of class reconciliation, supporting free trade and rights for workers, as well as fair taxation of all occupational groups according to their ability to contribute. The cornerstone of its foreign policy was the acceptance of Austria into the League of Nations and political neutrality. While it claimed to favor the "self-determination of the German people," it stressed the need for establishing friendly relations with the neighboring successor states and building bridges between East and West.[50]

The Jewish Nationalist Party tried to appeal to a wide spectrum of Jewish voters, including women. Second from the top of the list, after Stricker, came Anitta Müller-Cohen, who especially during the war years had played a very active role in public life, working tirelessly on behalf of refugees, children, and women's rights.[51] Nevertheless, slightly fewer women than men voted for the Jewish Nationalist Party in all Viennese electoral districts, except for the Northeast.[52] Despite all the campaign rhetoric, the majority of Jewish voters remained unconvinced that the Jewish Nationalists offered a viable solution to their problems or merited their support in parliamentary elections. Evidently many Jews, after realistically assessing the political situation, decided that voting for any small party, whether Jewish Nationalist or Liberal, essentially meant throwing away their vote.

When Robert Stricker won his seat in the Constituent National Assembly in 1919, the Zionist press hailed this victory as a landmark in the history of Austrian Jewry,[53] but Stricker's brief career as a parliamentary deputy illustrates the serious limitations inherent in being the lone spokesman for a minority viewpoint. The Jewish Nationalist deputy courageously, if not always wisely, stood up for whatever he felt was right, not only for Jews but for Austria as a whole. In his maiden speech, he criticized the idea of *Anschluss* with Germany as not being in the interest of either Austria or Germany, and he cast the sole dissenting vote against unification.[54] In other parliamentary speeches, Stricker often related issues to Jews and Jewish pride, sometimes in a rather unusual fashion. In a debate over taxing name changes for individuals, he maintained that 95 percent of all such cases, which were especially prevalent among Jews, were due to shame and character weakness. In theory, he posited, since prostitution was not subject to tax, this should not be either, but in practice, if one were going to tax it anyway, name changes should be taxed to the hilt, since those Jews who wanted to hide their origin could, he claimed, generally afford to pay![55] Along more conventional lines, he raised an inquiry into the matter of foreign Jews being prevented from enrolling in

Austrian universities.[56] He also appealed for Austrian support of Zionist endeavors in Palestine, on the grounds that Austria could thereby help itself by helping some of its Jews find a place to go and at the same time aid in the transformation of the entire Jewish people.[57]

In accordance with his party's program, Stricker spoke out on behalf of the recognition of Jews as a nationality on the one hand and in defense of the equality of Jews as citizens on the other. During a debate on resettlement of war veterans, he opposed limiting beneficiaries to persons of German nationality, arguing that no state should tolerate more than one category of citizenship and individuals who admitted to being Jewish nationals, rather than Germans, must not be discriminated against.[58] The most heated discussion over Jewish nationality arose during a debate concerning a special postwar census. Stricker objected to the use of language as the criterion for nationality, since although Jews might speak German, this fact did not necessarily make them Germans by nationality. He demanded the opportunity for Jews freely to acknowledge their nationality as Jewish, if they so desired. It was up to the Jews, not the state, he claimed, to decided whether a Jewish nationality existed and he wanted nation to replace language on the census form, with Jews having the right to enter "Jewish" under that rubric.[59] The Social Democratic parliamentary leadership strongly objected to Stricker's proposal on the grounds that officially Jews were recognized only as a religious group and that they themselves were divided as to whether or not they indeed constituted a nation. Despite support from outspoken antisemites, the motion to recognize Jews as a separate nationality for census purposes went down to defeat.[60]

In one of his last speeches before the National Assembly, during the 1920 budget debate, Stricker voiced his opposition to the Austrian electoral system, which, he asserted, through the division of the country into small voting districts rather than a single unit resulted in the disenfranchisement of minorities. Jews should not be artificially fragmented, he felt, but instead deserved representation according to their overall numbers.[61] Once again, this voice was like a cry in the wilderness, evoking little or no response or sympathy. Instead of improving, the electoral geometry deteriorated still further, so that Stricker's chances for reelection diminished with each subsequent election. This did not deter him from running, however.

While the Jewish Nationalists managed to elect only one deputy to the Austrian parliament for a single term lasting one and a half years, they proved slightly more successful in their bids for municipal council seats in the early postwar years. In the May 1919 elections for city hall, the Jewish Nationalist Party ran candidates in five selected districts and garnered 13,075 votes all told, winning three seats. Two of these mandates came from Leopoldstadt, where the Jewish list earned 6,854 votes, which amounted to approximately one out of every three Jewish votes. The third seat, which came as a surprise, was won in Alsergrund with 2,719 votes, roughly a third of the Jewish vote here as well.[62] The two Leopoldstadt seats went to Leopold Plaschkes and Jakob Ehrlich, both Jewish Nationalists of long standing, while the one from Alsergrund went to Bruno Pollack von Parnau, a newcomer on the Jewish Nationalist scene.

Plaschkes, whose parents originated in Moravia, was born in the Austrian provincial town of St. Pölten in 1884, but grew up in Vienna. He first became involved in Jewish Nationalist affairs while a law student at the University of Vienna, beginning as a diaspora nationalist and only gradually becoming attracted to Zionism. Until the mid-twenties, his main concern remained *Landespolitik*; only after 1925 did he adopt a somewhat more Palestine-centered approach.[63]

For many years, Plaschkes was a very close ally of Robert Stricker. He was a staunch democrat who, once appointed to the Kultusgemeinde board to serve on its electoral commission in 1918, fought long and hard for universal suffrage within the community. Unlike Stricker, Plaschkes remained moderately leftist, considering himself a Socialist, although he opposed Marxism and Social Democracy in its Austrian form. While both men joined the Zionist opposition by 1928, Plaschkes remained in the Radical-Democratic faction and weakened his ties with his erstwhile friend when Stricker became a Revisionist.[64]

Plaschkes was an ardent defender of Jews, not only on the municipal council, but also in the courtroom, where he served as lawyer in a number of prominent cases. He successfully defended an editor of the Zionist *Wiener Morgenzeitung* against a libel accusation by the Liberal politician Ottokar Czernin and managed to get the volatile Stricker acquitted from a charge of incitement against a judicial decision.[65]

Jakob Ehrlich, Plaschkes's fellow city councilman from Leopoldstadt, was likewise a lawyer and an effective speaker, who was born in 1877 in Moravia and became a Zionist as a high school student. Before the war, he was involved in the leadership of the Viennese Jewish Nationalist Association and in 1912, along with Stricker, was elected to the communal board, on which he served as head of the Zionist Club or faction continuously until 1938. Ehrlich remained a committed General Zionist within the B group, hence part of the Viennese Zionist mainstream, throughout the period. On several occasions, he occupied the presidency of the Austrian Zionist Federation.[66]

By contrast, Bruno Pollack von Parnau, a wealthy industrialist bearing a title of nobility, was a former Liberal and vice-president of the Austrian Israelite Union, elected in 1913 and reelected in 1916. Near the end of the war, Pollack-Parnau underwent a change of heart and adopted Jewish Nationalism. Once he became a member of the executive of the Jewish National Council, he was ousted from his Union office.[67] Unlike most other Jewish Nationalist leaders of the postwar era, Pollack-Parnau never served on the Kultusgemeinde board or the Zionist National Committee, but he continued to be a Jewish Nationalist candidate for elections and campaigned on their behalf. Pollack von Parnau rarely participated in city council debates during his single term as deputy, but his colleagues, Ehrlich and Plaschkes, regularly spoke up on behalf of Jewish interests.

The 1919 municipal election, with universal suffrage in effect, marked the ascension of the Social Democrats to power in Vienna for the first time, since they won 100 out of the 165 seats on the municipal council.[68] The three Jewish Nationalists voted with the Social Democratic majority on most issues, although they criticized the city administration for not combating antisemitism vigorously enough, not treating Jewish refugees and noncitizens fairly, not subsidizing Jewish educational, sports, and cultural institutions, and not hiring Jews as civil servants. Most often, their speeches dealt with antisemitism and the need to protect Jewish civil rights. They condemned Christian Social and German Nationalist demands for the introduction of quotas for students and instructors at the universities and the exclusion of Jews from tourist clubs and other associations, and insisted that the city not grant financial support to any group which propagated hatred and persecution of Jews.[69]

Shortly before the 1923 elections were to be held, the city council passed a new electoral reform reducing its number of seats from 165 to 120, thereby strengthening the larger parties, the Social Democrats and Christian Socials, at the expense of the smaller ones, like the Jewish Nationalists and the Liberal factions. The Jewish Nationalist deputies protested, but to no avail.[70] Their only hope for reelection lay in forming an alliance with the Jewish Liberals and creating a united Jewish front. As a result of pragmatic rather than ideological considerations, the Austrian Zionist Federation and the Union of German-Austrian Jews entered an agreement to create the "Jewish Electoral Partnership" which would run a joint list, headed by Robert Stricker and Rudolf Schwarz-Hiller, in the upcoming parliamentary and municipal elections. Their program was necessarily rather vague, playing down Jewish national minority status and emphasizing civil rights and constitutional equality. The partnership promised to fight antisemitism and defend Jewish honor, unlike other parties, such as the Liberal splinter groups and the Social Democrats, who depended on Jewish voters at election time, but ignored their interests thereafter.[71] While this coalition essentially linked Jewish Nationalists and Liberals, it tried to attract the support of Orthodox and Jewish Socialist voters as well. Despite vigorous campaigning and innumerable meetings, sponsored mainly by the Jewish Nationalists, these efforts at preventing fragmentation of the Jewish vote did not meet with great success.[72]

The Jewish Electoral Partnership ran candidates in all districts in Vienna and received a total of 24,784 votes, almost twice as many as in the 1919 municipal elections, but despite this increase in overall votes they lost two of their three seats. While the coalition with the Liberals helped the Jewish Nationalists gain votes in wealthier districts, such as the Inner City, the alliance did not prove a big asset in less affluent Alsergrund or Leopoldstadt. In the working-class district of Brigittenau, support for the Jewish list declined significantly, undoubtedly due in large measure to the antagonism of poorer Jews against the Liberals. Whereas roughly one out of every four Viennese Jewish voters cast their ballots for the Jewish list in the 1923 elections, those living in the better-off inner districts, including Inner City, Leopoldstadt, and Alsergrund, generally exceeded this ratio, while in the poorer outer districts, such as Brigittenau, only about one out of six Jews chose their own slate.[73] The partnership thus gained some middle-class votes at the expense of the Liberal faction but lost working-class votes to the Social Democrats.

The broader distribution of votes among various districts, together with the revised electoral regulations reducing the number of deputies, spelled defeat for the combined Jewish list. As in the previous election, the Jewish slate won no seats in the National Assembly, and it retained only a single seat in the municipal council. Leopold Plaschkes became the sole representative of Jewish interests in city hall. This election marked a major political defeat for the Jewish Nationalists from which they never fully recovered. It proved to be the last time a Jewish list would win any mandates in a general election in Austria.

The 1923 electoral setback necessitated a reevaluation of Jewish Nationalist political tactics and the role of *Landespolitik* within the Austrian Zionist Federation. Clearly the Jewish Liberals had very limited usefulness as allies and the Social Democratic Party remained the only real contender for Jewish votes and hence the most serious competitor for the Jewish Nationalists in the general political arena. During his second term in city hall, Plaschkes adopted a more strident tone in his criticisms of the Social Democratic majority. He devoted much of his annual speech during budget hearings to attacks on Social Democrats, rather than Christian Socials, German Nationalists or Nazis, since, he claimed, antisemitism "with a red carnation" (i.e., on the Left) was even more dangerous than the "white" or right-wing variety. From 1924 on, he voted with the opposition against the budget, even though he personally objected to being classified with the Right, considering himself a man of the Left.[74] Not all Jewish Nationalists agreed, however, that such a strategy was either prudent or desirable.

Within Zionist ranks, antagonism toward *Landespolitik* was growing. By late 1925, a group had formed which explicitly rejected Jewish Nationalist participation in inner Austrian politics. The Free Zionist Association, led by Isidor Schalit, maintained that all Zionists should be free to take part in political life according to their own personal convictions. This faction issued a statement accusing the top Zionist leadership of neglecting the rebuilding of Palestine due to their exclusive concentration on Austrian affairs. It claimed that achieving mandates in local public bodies was useless for Zionism, since postwar Austria played a very subordinate role in international politics and it was not possible to elect very many deputies to parliament in the first place. By joining in a coalition with the Union in 1923, it asserted, the Zionist leadership had abandoned its true support for Jewish Nationalist politics in Austria.[75]

Nevertheless, the Zionist National Committee continued to endorse *Landespolitik* as an integral part of the Austrian Zionist program. At a party conference soon after the 1923 election, its president, Desider Friedmann, insisted that Austrian Zionists must continue to take an active position regarding political events in Austria in order to counter escalating antisemitism and threats to the economic and civil well-being of Jews.[76] By 1926, the coalition with the Liberals had collapsed and the Jewish Nationalists renewed their demands for national recognition and minority rights, along with representation in public bodies. At a Zionist conference held that year, Friedmann reiterated this official commitment to diaspora politics on the grounds that renunciation of *Landespolitik* would mean an abdication of Zionist responsibilities. The only question remaining, in Friedmann's opinion, was to what degree members of the Austrian Zionist Federation, including the dissidents of the Free Zionist Association, should be obligated to uphold this policy.[77]

In 1927 a party council of the Zionist Federation voted unanimously to enter another electoral campaign, but this time no longer in conjunction with the Liberals. An appeal to voters to support this separate Jewish list cited dangers from both the Right and the Left.[78] It argued that the two major parties did not concern themselves with Jewish interests. The Christian Socials were basically antisemitic, both in theory and in practice, while the Social Democrats, although attracting many Jewish votes and lacking an anti-Jewish statement in their platform, were imbued with the antisemitic instincts of the masses. Their press made fun of anything Jewish, and their representatives, especially the Jews among them, did everything possible to avoid being friendly to Jews. The Jews, therefore, suffered on all sides.

The Jewish Nationalist campaign literature enumerated a long litany of grievances. Jews were hired by neither the Christian Social state civil service nor the Social Democratic municipal civil service. It was very difficult for them to obtain licenses and concessions. Taxation policy deliberately discriminated against Jews. In schools, Jewish youth were persecuted and it was harder for them to gain access to higher education. Naturalization was denied to Jews and they were subject to expulsion. Jews were threatened and criticized at public meetings, in newspapers and on placards, but even when their death was demanded, officials did nothing. They were not even able to enjoy the rights guaranteed them in the peace treaty and under Austrian law. Jewish institutions should be eligible for state and municipal tax money for education and social welfare, as well as religious purposes, but this too was denied. For these reasons, the Jewish Nationalists insisted, all Jews must vote for the Jewish list. On behalf of all minority factions, they demanded democratization of the electoral laws which promoted a two-party system.[79]

The 1927 election results proved disastrous. Following behind-the-scenes negotiations between the Zionist and Social Democratic leaders, the Jewish Nationalists had agreed to run candidates only in selected districts, including Leopoldstadt, Alsergrund, and Brigittenau. Their total vote was officially recorded at 7,234.[80] Plaschkes's seat on the municipal council disappeared so that the Jewish Nationalists no longer had any elected representatives. The Jewish Nationalists seem to have exhausted whatever limited appeal they had for Jewish voters.

On the eve of the next parliamentary election in 1930, the Austrian Zionist Federation convened a meeting of the party council to decide whether or not to put forth their own candidates once more. A majority, including most General Zionists and the Hitachdut Labor faction, voted not to run a Zionist-sponsored list. Stricker and the Revisionists opposed this motion, while Plaschkes's Democrats abstained from voting. Support for nonparticipation was based more on practical grounds than on principle. A Jewish Nationalist candidacy would have absolutely no hope of victory, given the existing electoral regulations whereby more than 25,000 votes would be needed in a single electoral district. The Zionists lacked inner political cohesiveness and the means to conduct an effective campaign. They realized that the undertaking would be doomed from the outset and might damage any future chances of success.[81]

Despite this resolution, Stricker and his most loyal followers were determined to run an independent Jewish list, since, they insisted, no other party could or would represent Jewish interests and Jewish honor had to be defended.[82] Lacking even official Zionist support, an election debacle in 1930 was entirely predictable; Stricker's list received a minuscule 2,134 votes in all of Vienna.[83] In the municipal elections of 1932, for the first time since 1907, no Zionist candidates entered the race.[84]

The decision of the Austrian Zionist Federation no longer to participate formally in national or municipal elections implied its tacit endorsement of the Social Democrats on the one hand and its abandonment of *Landespolitik* on the other. At a Zionist party conference in 1930, Robert Stricker had introduced a resolution demanding the active political involvement of all Zionists in *Landespolitik* and the exclusion from Zionist ranks of anyone who belonged to "another political organization," i.e., the Social Democratic Party. While this proposal met with approval among Revisionists and Radicals/Democrats, it was rejected by the remaining General Zionists and the moderate left-wing Hitachdut.[85] In 1931, after the embarrassing parliamentary defeat, a special Zionist conference was convened to discuss the issue further. The veteran Jewish Nationalist politician Jakob Ehrlich pointed out that the trend everywhere within Zionism was away from *Landespolitik* as a tactical move. There had always been some opposition within the Zionist organization to involvement in Austrian politics, especially in the provinces, and many Zionists, he acknowledged, were actively involved in other political parties. It was not possible, he claimed, to exclude them from Zionist ranks, nor was it desirable. One could no longer close one's eyes to realities and engage in self-deception. *Landespolitik* in its existing form was no longer practical in Austria. Over the protests of the Revisionists and the Democrats, the motion to exclude it from the Federation's agenda was adopted by a 37 to 26 vote. Thereafter, Kultusgemeinde politics was the only form of *Gegenwartsarbeit* within the purview of the Austrian Zionist Federation.[86]

This official bifurcation of Zionism and diaspora nationalism did not quite signal the end of *Landespolitik* in Austria, however. Even before this resolution was adopted, Robert Stricker and Leopold Plaschkes had applied to the authorities to grant recognition to a revived "Jewish People's Association," which evolved into the "Jewish People's Party." The stated purpose of this organization was to strengthen Jewish national consciousness, protect and further Jewish nationalist aspirations, and assert the rights and interests of Austrian Jewry in political, cultural, and economic spheres.[87] Although the People's Party announced that it would not compete in the 1932 municipal campaign, it set as its task to "raise once again the flag of nationally conscious Jewry" and promised to run again in the next election (which was never to take place). It denounced the Austrian Zionist Establishment for renouncing *Landespolitik* and accused them of forging ties with the Social Democratic Party, a move which the People's Party considered shameful and humiliating to Jewry. Since it did not consider any other party worthy of Jewish support, it refused to grant any endorsements. By implication, the Jewish People's Party was advocating that, in the absence of a Jewish list, Jewish voters should abstain from voting altogether.[88]

Landespolitik had failed as a political strategy in interwar Austria. By 1932 the Jewish Nationalists, like the Liberals, had finally come to accept the futility of their continued involvement on the general political scene and instead devoted their attention almost entirely to the Kultusgemeinde, where they achieved considerably greater success.

Conquering the Community

Jewish Nationalists began competing in communal elections as early as 1900. While the Zionist list never won any mandates on its own before World War I, one Zionist managed to gain a seat on the official list in 1904 and two more, Robert Stricker and Jakob Ehrlich, were included on the Liberal list in 1912 in order to prevent a contested election. Considering the limited voter eligibility due to communal tax requirements, the Jewish Nationalists did remarkably well in prewar elections, however. In 1902, they received almost 30 percent of the vote, and in 1906, they increased their share to 44 percent. In 1908, the Zionist vote declined significantly as a result of a tightening up of tax payment regulations, which reduced the number of their supporters entitled to vote. Nevertheless, in 1910 the opposition vote climbed once again to 35 percent. Although voter turnout was extremely low, it had already become clear that Zionist sympathizers were likely to vote whenever possible. In 1912, when the new restrictions were lifted and the number of eligible voters rose from 12,060 to 18,632, with 1,134 in the wealthiest bracket, the Liberals preferred to reach an agreement with the Jewish Nationalists rather than face another challenge to their leadership monopoly.[89]

Electoral reform stood at the top of the Jewish Nationalist communal program. The Zionists wanted to eliminate the privileged curia of higher taxpayers and to institute universal suffrage, as well as a proportional system of election so that groups which did not receive a majority of the votes would also have representation.[90] In November 1918, an accord between the Jewish National Council and the Kultusgemeinde board created a special commission composed of three Jewish Nationalists and three Liberals to devise new electoral procedures. The draft proposal which the Jewish Nationalists submitted included equal voting rights for all members of the Jewish community, regardless of sex, citizenship, and tax status, and eligibility of women and communal employees for election to office.[91] The Jewish Nationalists fully realized that by increasing the size of the communal electorate they would increase their chances of assuming control over the Jewish community and implementing their program.

Among the Liberals then serving on the Kultusgemeinde board, only a very few, such as Rudolf Schwarz-Hiller, sympathized with the Jewish Nationalists' egalitarian demands. The most heated debates in the dispute over electoral reform centered on the issues of votes for women and noncitizens. The Jewish Nationalists insisted that women be eligible to run, as well as vote, in communal elections, since they already had gained that right in municipal and national elections and they deserved recognition for their valuable services to the community, especially during the war. They denied that there were serious grounds for objection and claimed that the issue of women's participation was simply a matter of prejudices and taste. One of the more traditional members of the board, however, argued that the proper role for the Jewish woman was to meet her lofty obligations to her household and her family and that it would be impossible for her to participate in public affairs and board meetings without detracting from her other duties. Another asserted that a woman had her place in the home and also in charitable activities, but not in the religious domain. The Liberal majority had adopted the traditionalist religious arguments against women's rights generally espoused by Orthodox spokesmen, who were not represented on the board at the time. They made sure that, while a female head of household who paid a minimum of 20 Austrian crowns in communal taxes could exercise the right to vote just like a male head of household, she could not herself run for office.[92]

With regard to voting rights for noncitizens, the Jewish Nationalists argued that the Kultusgemeinde should be democratic and not distinguish among Jews, stamping Galician newcomers as inferior people. They emphasized the importance for the Kultusgemeinde of having the largest possible electorate in order to give it the right to speak for all Jews. They pointed out that all communal taxpayers had been eligible to vote before the war regardless of citizenship and that all Germans were allowed to vote for the national, provincial, and municipal assemblies in postwar Austria regardless of citizenship. As one Jewish Nationalist commented, "If that is good enough for the Christian Socials, it should be good enough for us." As the central institution of the community, the Kultusgemeinde had to take Galician Jews into account, especially if it viewed itself primarily as a religious organization. If they paid taxes, they should certainly have voting rights.

One of the Liberals, however, piously replied that since the Kultusgemeinde functioned as a state institution with a certain amount of autonomy, only citizens should be allowed to participate in its governance. Another Liberal candidly admitted that the majority opposed admission of the recently arrived Galicians into the electorate for fear of strengthening the Jewish Nationalists. Therefore the Liberal majority on the board decided that noncitizens who had been eligible to vote in 1912 could continue to be registered voters, but all others who had not yet been naturalized could not vote. The Jewish Nationalists managed to achieve some significant victories in the elimination of the special curia for highest taxpayers and the introduction of a proportional system of elections which allowed representation to minority slates according to their percentage of the overall vote, but they did not succeed in their basic aim of democratizing the community by expanding its voting base.[93]

The Jewish Nationalist communal program, like that of the Liberals, changed very little from the prewar to the postwar era. The 1920 electoral platform closely resembled that of 1912 and underwent only minor modifications in subsequent years.[94] Its basic premise stated that the Jewish people everywhere constituted an indivisible national entity and that the Kultusgemeinde should be transformed into a *Volksgemeinde*, a community of the people, with the goal of reviving the Jewish people in religious, cultural, social, and other spheres, especially through the rebuilding of Palestine. The new *Volksgemeinde* would encompass all Jewish men and women and would represent their interests to the outside world and protect their constitutional rights, including minority rights in accordance with the peace treaty. All Jewish communities in Austria should join together and establish a federation recognized by public law.

In addition to democratic electoral reforms, the Zionist program demanded wide-ranging administrative changes. It advocated the adoption of the public principle, with open board meetings and an agenda issued in advance. The Kultusgemeinde should publish a detailed annual report, including a list of all "deserters," i.e., all those who had officially opted out of the community. The board should reorganize itself and create standing committees for religious affairs, administrative reform, financial affairs, welfare activities, education, social policy and health affairs, and technical affairs, all of which would utilize specialists from among the members of the community. The district commissions which assessed communal taxes should be restructured into effective working bodies with greater autonomy.

With respect to fiscal reforms, communal taxation should become progressive, a percentage of total income based on state income tax returns. Registry fees and other encumbrances should be eliminated. The Kultusgemeinde should pay its officials and teachers no less than state employees in similar categories and protect them by modern contracts, but all perquisites should be eliminated. The treasury must collect all fees and dues directly and no communal employee should demand or accept money or valuables in return for services. Purchasing methods also needed reform. The community should allocate supply and work contracts for its institutions through open competitions and wherever possible give them to a communal member rather than a non-Jew.

In the religious sphere, the Jewish Nationalists, not wanting to alienate more traditional Jews, expressed a commitment to strengthening the religious institutions of the community and assuring the freedom of all religious orientations within it. They wanted to preserve communal unity and the use of the Hebrew language in synagogue liturgy. Among their cultural demands, the Jewish Nationalists emphasized the need to imbue Jewish youth with a Jewish spirit and consciousness and create appropriate Jewish schools with intensive instruction in Hebrew as a living language, teaching about both the Jewish past and the present. They advocated the reform of religious instruction and the setting up of Jewish kindergartens, schools, and teacher training institutes, as well as broader facilities for adult education. Finally, they supported the erection of a new community building which would house the administration, the communal library, a Jewish museum, archives, and other central institutions. While their religious program remained relatively neutral, their educational and cultural goals tended to play down the religious aspects and accentuate their nationalist secular orientation.

The Zionists ran a vigorous campaign for the 1920 elections, competing primarily against the Liberals, who called themselves the "Non-Jewish Nationalist Parties," but also against the "United Orthodox Jewry" list, which essentially represented the anti-Zionist Agudat Israel. The various Zionists groups, including the Religious Zionist Mizrachists, ran together, attempting to attract votes from across the political spectrum. They accused the Liberals of moral bankruptcy for allowing the Kultusgemeinde to degenerate into merely an administrative apparatus. They cited a strike by religious teachers as a shameful example of modern social consciousness. The well-heeled burghers who sat in the communal boardroom were not concerned with the hunger of their employees, they charged. The services provided by the Kultusgemeinde had been reduced to a minimum and no longer met Jewish needs, especially in the fields of education and social welfare. The economic crisis was merely an excuse, they maintained, since proper financial management was indeed possible.[95]

On the eve of the election, in a final appeal for electoral support, the Jewish Nationalists direly predicted that the fate of the community was about to be decided: it was a choice between life or death, democracy or German Nationalist reactionaries! They denounced their opponents as enemies of both Judaism and the Jewish people. They charged them with stirring up antisemitism by accusing Zionists of being unpatriotic and spreading hatred of *Ostjuden*. They tried to tar the Orthodox Agudah-dominated list with the same brush, criticizing them for siding with the Liberals against the Jewish Nationalists.[96]

The 1920 Kultusgemeinde election brought out 10,553 voters to the polls, 55 percent of those eligible. Of these, 3,714, or 35 percent, cast their ballots for the Zionists. (See Table 6.) Although in absolute terms the Zionist vote had more than doubled since the last contested election in 1910, their share of the vote remained roughly the same, due to a significantly higher voter turnout and the exclusion of noncitizens from voting. Thanks to proportional representation, the Zionists won a total of thirteen seats, instead of none in 1910 and the two seats they had been allocated in 1912.[97] This represented a significant step forward for the Jewish Nationalists, since they now constituted the official opposition and were clearly a group to be reckoned with within the Kultusgemeinde.

The immediate question facing the Zionist Club was whether to cooperate with the Liberal majority and try to help resolve the desperate postwar economic crisis confronting the community or to act as an obstructionist oppositional force until the Liberals agreed to meet their demands for electoral reform. At the constituent meeting of the communal council in September 1920, the Zionist deputies abstained from voting for leadership positions. When a majority vote nonetheless elected a prominent Jewish Nationalist, Desider Friedmann, as second vice-president, he declined the honor, claiming that according to the numerical strength of his party and on the basis of proportional representation, the Jewish Nationalists should by right have the first vice-presidency, an office which the Liberals were reluctant to grant them. The Zionist minority therefore decided to participate in the work of the community but to leave responsibility for direction of its affairs to the majority.[98]

By January 1921, after lengthy negotiations, the Jewish Nationalists and the Liberals reached a compromise whereby the two vice-presidents would be of equal rank. New elections resulted in Friedmann assuming a vice-presidency and three Zionists joining the executive committee, which also included four Liberals and one Orthodox representative.[99] But in the spring, Friedmann once again resigned from the presidium in protest over the majority's refusal to consider introducing universal suffrage. The vice-presidency remained temporarily vacant until Friedmann returned to occupy it after accepting reelection the following year.[100]

The community was indeed in dire financial straits, tottering on the verge of fiscal collapse. The 1921 budget revealed a deficit of 30 million crowns and, with inflation, this debt had increased to 6.5 billion by the following year. Important branches of communal activity had to be drastically curtailed. The Kultusgemeinde had to limit further admissions to both its old age home and the Rothschild hospital, which was only filled to one-third capacity. It greatly reduced its welfare budget, with no new allocations to social services, youth, or education. The salaries of communal employees were so low as to threaten starvation and yet there was the possibility that the Kultusgemeinde might not be able to meet its payroll. The Liberals could surely not be held responsible for this situation, which went far beyond their control, but they needed all the assistance they could muster to help bring about a recovery. A $10,000 contribution from the Joint Distribution Committee helped tide the community over a particularly difficult juncture.[101]

Despite their initial obstructionism, the Jewish Nationalists agreed to work together with the Liberals to overcome the crisis. They managed to implement some of the more practical recommendations in their electoral program. The board organized within itself a dozen standing committees, which included religious and ritual affairs, school and educational affairs, cemetery and burial matters, financial and administrative affairs, welfare, hospital, and old age home, as well as other subcommittees dealing with the library, minyanim, kosher meat, and a historical commission. The Kultusgemeinde set up a personnel arbitration committee with equal representation for the board and communal employees. By 1922, communal employees had achieved the same salary scale as municipal workers. The community also made attempts at centralization of its social services. It instituted some tax reforms but the state refused to allow the Kultusgemeinde access to income tax records upon which to base its assessments. The system was progressive with a very nominal minimum sum, which was paid by the majority of taxpayers, while the maximum, contributed by only a handful of individuals, increased from 20,000 Austrian crowns in 1913 to 30,000,000 by 1924, the last year of the rampant inflationary spiral. Some sessions of the communal board became open to the public and in 1924 the Kultusgemeinde published a summary report of its activities over a twelve-year period.[102]

Limited democratization took place prior to the 1924 elections but universal suffrage continued to be denied and a minimal tax payment remained a precondition for voting, except for communal employees who were now allowed to vote, regardless of whether or not they could afford to pay taxes. However, like women, certain categories of employees were still not considered eligible to run for election. The board rescinded the citizenship requirement for voter eligibility, but reintroduced the prerequisite of actual payment of taxes in the two years prior to an election.[103] The Zionists thus had again won some victories, but they lost most of their major battles for electoral reform.

Having worked together with the Liberals for several years in trying to solve the community's economic difficulties and after running on a joint list with them in the general elections the previous year, the Zionists decided to enter into a coalition with their former rivals, the Liberals and the Agudists, on the eve of the 1924 Kultusgemeinde elections. They all hoped to maintain the status quo and avoid an expensive and divisive campaign at a time when the financial situation still remained bleak. While claiming not to abandon their original platform, the Zionists agreed to a compromise program that included a commitment to the upbuilding of Palestine but played down most other nationalist goals.[104] Their strategy of averting a contested election failed, however, when three opposition slates presented themselves, one Socialist and two Orthodox.[105]

The 1924 elections resulted in a slight loss of representation for the Zionists but an overall gain in terms of clout. The coalition won an impressive 75 percent of the vote and twenty-eight out of the thirty-six seats on the communal council. Of these, the Jewish Nationalists received ten places, instead of the thirteen they had held previously. But a Religious Zionist slate had won 6 percent of the vote and two seats, raising the actual Zionist total to twelve. In addition, the Jewish Nationalists could count on the support of the five Socialists and the lone independent Orthodox deputy on most issues, for a combined total of eighteen. The fifteen Liberals, together with three Agudists, no longer enjoyed a majority on the board. The Zionists continued to hold one vice-presidency, with Josef Löwenherz as the incumbent, but they lost one of their three seats on the executive committee to a Socialist. While Liberals served as chairmen of nearly all the committees, Zionists generally acted as alternate chairmen and participated actively in all aspects of communal affairs. The Liberals still held the power, but they were forced to depend on support from their Zionist coalition partners in order to run the community effectively.[106]

Just as the Jewish Nationalist–Liberal alliance did not survive more than one general election, so too their coalition within the Kultusgemeinde did not prove of lengthy duration. In 1925, while the partnership still functioned, the Zionists managed to achieve an important victory of at least a symbolic nature when the communal board voted unanimously to contribute 20,000 Austrian schillings to Keren Hayessod, the Palestine Foundation Fund, on the occasion of the opening of the Hebrew University in Jerusalem. This represented the first in a series of annual donations to various funds for Palestine, with Keren Hayessod receiving the largest share.[107] By the following year, however, the Liberals and the Agudists were already objecting to sending communal money abroad when the needs at home remained so great.[108]

In 1926, a Zionist party council adopted a resolution that rendered the coalition agreement meaningless. It instructed the Zionist deputies in the Kultusgemeinde to defend with all their energy the goals of the original Jewish Nationalist program, especially the demand for cooperation in the reconstruction of Palestine and the practical implementation of minority rights, as guaranteed to the Jews by the peace treaty and by the constitution.[109] Soon thereafter, the Jewish Nationalists voted against a budget proposed by its coalition partners because it did not include funds for Palestine. A group of Radical Zionists led by Stricker and Plaschkes called for a formal dissolution of the pact and a declaration of open warfare against the Liberals for not upholding their side of the coalition agreement. After considerable negotiation, the board grudgingly approved a special budget allocation for Palestine.[110] The following year, when the Liberals rejected a renewed Zionist request for universal suffrage, the Radicals again demanded that the Jewish Nationalists formally pull out of the coalition and join the pure opposition. When their colleagues refused to agree to this, Stricker and Plaschkes both resigned their seats on the board in protest, denouncing their fellow Zionists for betraying their democratic principles.[111]

The Jewish Nationalist party leadership contended that they had not abandoned their program but were merely adopting necessary tactics in order to implement it. They continued to insist that the Kultusgemeinde must change its priorities and expand its activities to cover all Jewish needs. They emphasized cultural as well as social tasks and the necessity of educating the Jewish people as a whole. Since sufficient funds could not be raised through communal taxation, the Zionist leaders felt that the Kultusgemeinde must go to the state and municipal governments and demand the subsidies which rightfully belonged to it according to the peace treaty.[112]

In 1928, the Zionists decided to run their own list in communal elections instead of renewing their coalition with the Liberals. Their electoral platform for the first time openly advocated the creation of communal elementary schools and also urged widespread economic activities on the part of the Kultusgemeinde, including the establishment of a communal savings and loan fund, as well as vocational training and rehabilitation. The Zionists continued to emphasize the need for a *Volksgemeinde* and the kinship of all Jews around the world.[113]

The Jewish Nationalists' campaign literature vehemently denied the Union's claims that equality and minority rights were mutually contradictory and that the latter would lead to anti-Jewish quotas. They warned the voters not to be led astray by that "meaningless Viennese association," i.e., the Union of German-Austrian Jews, which was responsible for the decline of the Kultusgemeinde and a betrayal of local Jewry. They described the Union program as a little bit of religion, with ritual and charity thrown in, but a rejection of all else. The Zionists vowed to change the Kultusgemeinde from a lifeless bureaucratic apparatus to a true center of Jewish life, which would be involved not only with registering one's birth and one's burial, but with one's entire life and sustenance. They attempted to wage a vigorous campaign on two fronts, against their Liberal former allies and also against their Socialist opponents.[114]

The November 1928 elections resulted in a complete deadlock, with eighteen seats going to the Liberals and their Agudah coalition partners and eighteen to the opposition: eleven General Zionists, five Socialists (including three Labor Zionists), one Religious Zionist, and one "Apolitical," an Orthodox independent. The mainstream Jewish Nationalist list received 5,834 votes or 30 percent of the vote, 5 percent less than in the 1920 elections, but the separate Mizrachi list attracted an additional 4 percent, which made up most of the difference. All in all, the Jewish Nationalists did not do better in this election than previously. Although they gained one seat more than they had received as part of the 1924 coalition, the Religious Zionists lost one, which still left them with a total of twelve, one short of the thirteen they had following the 1920 election. (See Table 6.) Nevertheless, the four parties outside the coalition controlled exactly half of the seats on the communal council and together they could bring the Kultusgemeinde to a standstill if they so desired.[115]

At first the Jewish Nationalists renewed their old obstructionist tactics and refused to cooperate with the Liberals. By the end of January 1929, however, the Zionists and the Liberals had again hammered out an agreement. The Liberals retained control over the executive committee and enjoyed a majority on the various subcommittees, thereby continuing to dominate the decision-making process of the community, but the opposition forced them to give up several important committee chairmanships, including social welfare and personnel, as well as religious affairs. Josef Löwenherz resumed his vice-presidency, while three Zionists again won election to the executive committee.[116] The Jewish Nationalists once more worked together with the Liberals, but with ever-lessening enthusiasm. The tide had already begun to turn in their favor and they seemed to be biding their time until they could take over the Kultusgemeinde and run it their own way.

The major turning point for the Jewish Nationalists came as a result of the 1932 elections, when they finally succeeded in "conquering the community." Nine different slates, including four separate Zionist lists, competed in this election. The General Zionist B group led by Desider Friedmann ran together with Stricker's Revisionists as the official slate of the Zionist Federation. Campaigning on their usual platform, they directed most of their attacks against the Non-Nationalist Union–Working Class coalition, which they referred to disparagingly as the "Capitalist/Socialist-Free-thinker/Orthodox mish-mash party."[117] A Democratic list, representing the Association of Radical Zionists (General Zionist A group), headed by Leopold Plaschkes, ran with a similar program, but placed greater emphasis on universal suffrage, especially rights for women.[118] Once again, a Mizrachi list competed for the religious vote, and for the first time a separate Socialist Zionist list also appeared on the scene.[119]

All four Zionist lists combined received 13,961 votes or 53 percent of all the ballots cast. Of these, 34 percent went to the General Zionist/Revisionist list, 11 percent to the Socialists, 5 percent to the Democrats, and 3 percent to Mizrachi. As a result of this election, the official Zionist list obtained fourteen mandates, the Labor Zionists four, and the Democrats and Mizrachi one each, for a total of twenty altogether, while the non-nationalist list got fifteen places and the "Apolitical" independent Orthodox list had one seat, which was again occupied by a Zionist sympathizer.[120] With twenty-one out of thirty-six deputies on their side, the Jewish Nationalists of all shades had gained a clear majority on the board and had achieved a momentous victory.

The upsurge in support for the various Zionist parties which resulted in this electoral triumph can be attributed to a number of factors. First, a reinterpretation of the requirements for voter eligibility resulted in the enfranchisement of many more individuals, raising the percentage of eligible voters among communal taxpayers from 64 to 96 percent, which in turn led to a dramatic increase in the number of voters who participated in the election. (See Table 5.) Many of these first-time voters, especially the Galicians among them, clearly preferred Jewish Nationalists over non-nationalists. Second, general disillusionment with the performance of the previous Liberal administration had begun to spread and this disenchantment was undoubtedly exacerbated by their split with the Agudah and their somewhat incongruous alliance with the Social Democrats. Third, Socialist voters overwhelmingly chose to vote for the Labor Zionist slate rather than for bourgeois Liberals. Finally, the economic and political situation had become so desperate that many voters decided that the Kultusgemeinde needed a radical change and that Zionists of one shade or another offered the only real alternative. The Liberals had failed to alleviate the serious problems facing the Viennese Jewish community. With antisemitism ever on the increase and the even more alarming rise of Nazism, especially in Germany but also in Austria, a majority of the voters turned in frustration to the Jewish Nationalists.[121]

The 1932 Zionist victory was the result of the immediate crisis facing Viennese Jewry, but also a sign of the beginning of a realignment of Jewish attitudes. Conditions in Vienna, especially the continued burgeoning of antisemitism, called into question the self-definition of Jews as merely a religious group and seemingly legitimized the idea of Jews constituting a separate nation. Galician Jews were gradually gaining acceptance among their fellow Jews in Vienna, while the Liberals were becoming increasingly defensive. The 1936 communal election, which we shall discuss in chapter 6, further consolidated the

Jewish Nationalists' gains and reaffirmed the shift away from the Liberals toward the Zionists.

The Jewish Nationalists had conquered the community and could now begin the process of transforming it into a *Volksgemeinde.* Over the years, the Zionists had become *the* force to be reckoned with within the Viennese Jewish community. Not only did they attract the support of many nonobservant, fairly assimilated middle-class Jews, they split the Orthodox and made inroads among the Socialists as well. By 1932, Jewish Nationalists had replaced Liberals as the official representatives of Viennese Jewry.

The Jewish Nationalists exemplified a younger generation of Jewish leadership taking over the Kultusgemeinde. As a rule, they were not the children of their Liberal rivals but instead constituted a new cohort of late nineteenth and early twentieth century migrants to the Austrian capital. Many of the top General Zionist leaders were "Westerners," especially from Moravia, but most of the activists and supporters undoubtedly were "Easterners" from Galicia. The General Zionists became acceptable candidates for leadership of the Viennese Jewish community due to their high level of secular education, their professional occupations, and their residency in very respectable neighborhoods. Despite the Eastern origins and lower-class status of many within their ranks, the Jewish Nationalist spokesmen enjoyed a middle-class Viennese or "Westernized" life style and socioeconomic status similar to the bourgeois Liberals. Their electoral backing came from all over the city, crossing virtually all geographic and economic boundaries.

The Jewish Nationalists, while predominantly General Zionists, only came to power with the help of their Labor Zionist and Religious Zionist colleagues. Running on separate lists and disagreeing ideologically among themselves, whether differing on class or religious lines, the various Zionist groups managed to form a working coalition within the Kultusgemeinde, if not within the Zionist Federation. The 1932 election thus constituted an across-the-board Jewish Nationalist victory over their non-nationalist counterparts, the Liberals, the Social Democrats, and the Agudists.

While the Jewish Nationalists managed to seize control over the Jewish community from the Liberals, they did not succeed in implementing their demands for minority rights for Austrian Jewry. National minority status for Jews was simply not a realistic option in an ethnically homogeneous state like Austria. Unlike in Czechoslovakia or Yugoslavia, in Austria the Christian Social authorities, who were generally not racists, had no reason to encourage Jews to identify themselves as Jews by nationality, instead of as Germans. With Jews comprising less than 3 percent of the Austrian population and roughly

10 percent of the inhabitants of the capital, one could scarcely expect Jewish Nationalist representatives in the national parliament or the municipal council to make significant contributions to Jewish welfare, even if they occasionally managed to win seats. Unlike Poland, Austria lacked a significant minority bloc with which Jews might align themselves. Despite all the time and effort spent on its behalf, Jewish Nationalist diaspora politics outside the sphere of the Kultusgemeinde was doomed to failure in interwar Vienna from the very beginning.

Whereas a majority of tax-paying heads of households voted for Jewish Nationalist slates in communal elections by the thirties, an even higher percentage of Viennese Jewish voters, both male and female Austrian citizens, cast their ballots for Social Democratic candidates in interwar parliamentary and city council elections. The next chapter will attempt to reconcile this seeming paradox.

THE SOCIALISTS

During the interwar years the Austrian capital became famous throughout the world as "Red Vienna," an exemplary model of a large metropolis with a Socialist city administration. Just as a majority of Viennese citizens voted Social Democratic in municipal and national elections, so too did an overwhelming majority of Viennese Jews, albeit often for different reasons than other voters. A great many Jews voted for the Social Democratic Party simply because it was the only major party in Austria which did not include an antisemitic plank in its program and did not form electoral alliances with any party which did. Some Jews supported the Socialist ticket for pragmatic personal reasons, hoping thereby to improve their chances of obtaining a job, a contract, or perhaps an apartment. Others ardently backed the party because they genuinely sympathized with its humanitarian ideals of social justice and equality.

Following the demise of the Liberal Center, intense polarization between the Left and the Right characterized Austrian politics. The forces of the Right, the Christian Socials and the German Nationalists, despised both Jews and Socialists, often equating the two. As Austrian right-wing antisemitism became increasingly vicious, Viennese Jewry had little choice but to turn to the Left for succor. The Austrian Social Democratic Party, which was Marxist and working-class in its ideological orientation, radical in its rhetoric but reformist in practice, attracted many Jews to its ranks, and individuals of Jewish origin played an extremely important role within its leadership elite. The Austrian Communist Party, which remained tiny and almost insignificant during the interwar years, also included Jews in its cadres.[1] Although there were very few Jewish industrial workers in Vienna, middle-class Jewish intellectuals and professionals, lower-middle-class salaried employees, and small businessmen contributed to the strength of Austro-Marxism as members, activists, and leaders of the Social Democratic Party, as well as voters and fellow-travelers.

Even more than in Weimar Germany, Social Democracy served as the ideological heir to Liberalism among the Jews in the Austrian

Republic.[2] The Social Democratic Party provided a strongly secular, anticlerical force, which was also non-nationalist and egalitarian. Instead of civil equality which would primarily benefit the bourgeoisie, it advocated social and economic equality for the working classes. Like the Liberals, the Socialists preferred to define Jews as a religious group, rather than a separate nationality, and most viewed assimilation within the context of a Socialist society as the ultimate solution to the "Jewish question." The Jewish Socialists were to some extent the biological descendants of the Jewish Liberals as well. The more assimilated, Viennese-born Jews of middle-class parentage, especially the children of Liberals from the Czech lands, often found the Left more attractive than the Jewish Nationalists during their student years and thereafter.

The Jewish Socialists in interwar Vienna did not constitute a homogeneous group. Although they all supported the Austrian Social Democratic Party and could agree on certain basic socioeconomic principles, they differed in their attitudes toward the Jewish community and Zionism. One can divide them into two broad categories: Jewish Socialists, who were Jews by birth but Socialists by conviction and did not generally involve themselves in Jewish affairs, and Socialist Jews, who remained involved in Jewish life as committed Socialists. Like the rest of the Viennese Jewish population, the Socialists split rather unevenly into two further subclassifications, Zionists and non-Zionists. The vast majority of Jewish Socialists were non-Zionists, but among the Socialist Jews many were committed Labor Zionists. At one end of the range we find universalist, atheistic Socialists of Jewish origin who spurned virtually all Jewish concerns as parochial. Not only did they reject Jewish Nationalism, but some renounced their association with Judaism as well. While most rank-and-file Jewish Socialists only retained a nominal affiliation within the Kultusgemeinde, some Socialist Jews, including both Zionists and non-Zionists, became actively involved in communal affairs, especially within its social service sphere. While secularists, who were areligious or antireligious, made up the vast majority of Jewish Socialists, at the opposite end of the Socialist spectrum some Socialist Jews continued to adhere to traditional Jewish religious observances.

Among the Labor Zionists, who combined Socialism with Jewish Nationalism, Poale Zion (the Workers of Zion) constituted the left wing and the Zionist Labor Party Hitachdut (Union), the right wing. These factions, like other Zionist groups in Vienna, were offshoots of larger international organizations within the framework of the World Zionist Organization.[3] Soon after World War I, an extremist branch of Poale Zion merged with the newly formed Austrian Communist Party. Thereafter, a reconstituted Poale Zion, which remained outside the mainstream Austrian Zionist Federation, closely allied itself with the

Austrian Social Democratic Party. During the twenties, while maintaining its strong commitment to the development of a model socialist
society in Palestine, this group participated in Jewish communal
elections in partnership with non-Zionist Social Democrats. The more
moderate, non-Marxist Hitachdut, which remained part of the
Austrian Zionist Federation until the early thirties when it officially
merged with Poale Zion, strongly opposed the adherence of the General
Zionist leadership to *Landespolitik,* preferring to allow its supporters
to vote Social Democratic without violating Zionist party discipline.
Hitachdut did not engage actively in Kultusgemeinde politics in the
twenties, but in the thirties its adherents became more involved in
communal affairs. Labor Zionism attracted as its adherents mainly
younger, lower-middle-class Jews of Galician origin.

Unlike in Poland, a diaspora nationalist strain of Jewish Socialism
never developed much strength in Austria. The Federation of Jewish
Workers, known as the Bund, had emerged in Tsarist Russia in the
late nineteenth century but had remained relatively weak in pre–World
War I Galicia.[4] While a very small Bundist organization did exist in
interwar Vienna, it never achieved political significance and played
absolutely no role within the Kultusgemeinde. Vienna, which lacked a
substantial Jewish working class, provided a very inhospitable environment for a separate anti-Zionist Jewish workers' party which
emphasized the importance of Yiddish and national cultural autonomy
for diaspora Jewry. The capital of German-Austria, unlike Warsaw,
Paris, or New York, possessed a constellation of factors that rendered
the Bundist program largely irrelevant. In this German cultural mecca,
Yiddish was ignored as a separate language, while the Zionists ardently
espoused national minority rights and the powerful Social Democratic
Party freely admitted Jews into its ranks.[5]

This chapter will delve into the complex relationship between the
Austrian Social Democratic Party and Viennese Jewry, both as voters
and as active Socialists. Since we are primarily concerned here with
Jewish survivalist politics rather than integrationist tactics, we shall
concentrate more on committed Socialist Jews than on Socialists of
Jewish origin. We shall also analyze the involvement of Socialists in
Kultusgemeinde activities, comparing the role of non-Zionists and
Labor Zionists. By investigating the strong Jewish support for the
Social Democrats in general politics but weak backing for Socialists
within the Jewish community in interwar Vienna, we hope to uncover
more clues which will enhance our understanding of Jewish political
behavior.

Jewish Voters and the Social Democratic Party

An overwhelming majority of Viennese Jewish voters supported the

Social Democratic Party in both municipal and national elections during the interwar period. Among the electorate as a whole, the Socialist share of the vote in municipal elections ranged from 54 to 60 percent, whereas at least three-quarters of the Jews regularly voted Socialist, with the proportion increasing steadily as the years progressed.[6] As George Clare (Klaar) wrote in his memoirs of his assimilated middle-class Jewish family, "We were, of course, all Social Democrats. What other party could a Jew vote for? The Social Democrats were, at least officially, not antisemitic, and many of their leaders were Jews." However, he added, "Most of the Klaars were merely Social Democratic voters. Their socialist convictions could easily have been knocked down with the feather of liberalism, had a worthwhile Liberal Party still been in existence."[7] This same observation undoubtedly held true for many other middle-class Jews as well. In Germany, where the Democratic and Center parties remained more viable options for Jewish voters, less than 30 percent of the Jews voted Social Democratic in the twenties, but that percentage doubled in the thirties with increased polarization between the Left and the Right.[8]

Voting for a Marxist party could scarcely have been in the economic interest of more affluent middle-class Viennese Jews; certainly their non-Jewish economic counterparts did not follow their example, but voted heavily for Christian Socials or German Nationalists instead. The municipal taxation program, referred to by its opponents as tax sadism, targeted self-employed businessmen and entrepreneurs, a group which encompassed a considerable number of Jews. Direct taxes on employers, luxuries, high rents, and real estate helped finance the building of more than 60,000 apartments for workers.[9] Jews were for the most part not property owners; they rented apartments, generally in more respectable neighborhoods rather than in working-class districts. Many middle-class Jews were undoubtedly adversely affected by the economic policies of the Socialist municipality, although less well-to-do lower-middle-class Jews, including salaried employees, probably benefited somewhat.

Jews in Vienna, as elsewhere, did not cast their votes purely in accordance with their own class position. Even before World War I, some Jews had begun to shift their support from the Liberals to the Social Democrats and this trend accelerated during the interwar years. Although the Socialists received their strongest overall support in the heavily working-class outlying districts which, except for Brigittenau, had very few Jewish residents, middle-class districts with large concentrations of Jews demonstrated higher Socialist voting trends than comparable districts with fewer Jews. From 1923 to 1932 Socialist vote increases occurred in precisely those middle class districts with comparatively large proportions of Jews.[10] In the affluent Inner City, the Socialist vote climbed from 26 percent in 1923 to 44 percent nine years later; in predominantly middle-class Alsergrund, it went from 45 to 54 percent; and in mixed-class Leopoldstadt, the "Jewish quarter," it increased from 53 to 65 percent. Brigittenau, which was the poorest Jewish district but ranked only sixth in working-class composition, registered a record 71.4 percent Socialist vote, the highest in the city.[11] The Jewish vote thus provided a crucial ingredient in the Social Democratic electoral victories that produced and maintained "Red Vienna."

As antisemitic outbreaks increased in the Austrian capital after World War I, Jewish voters turned to the Left to protect them against possible pogroms from the Right and to prevent the introduction of official quotas, especially at universities. But the Social Democrats were reluctant to defend Jews publicly against antisemitic attacks, since, like the Liberals before them, they did not want to be considered a "Jewish defense force." Formally they tried to maintain a "neutral" stance on antisemitism, claiming that "philosemitism" was almost as bad.[12]

The Social Democratic leaders themselves, including those of Jewish origin, were not above antisemitic stereotyping. Their party organ, the *Arbeiterzeitung*, frequently published cartoons depicting hook-nosed Jews as exploiters and capitalists, sometimes even equating their Jewish Nationalist rivals with Nazis.[13] As Leopold Plaschkes, the Jewish Nationalist deputy, wryly pointed out, it was easy to identify the posters of the various parties by the type of Jew they portrayed: Social Democrats featured Jewish bankers; Christian Socialists, Jewish artisans; and Pan-Germans, Jewish usurers.[14] Social Democratic spokesmen frequently made deprecatory remarks about wealthy Jews which could easily be interpreted as antisemitic, rather than merely anticapitalist. Stung by the Christian Social charge that they were a Jewish-led party, the Social Democrats retorted that the Christian Socials catered to Jewish industrialists and depended on their money.[15] In attempting to deflect the stigma of Jewish connections from themselves to their opponents, the Social Democrats did not combat antisemitism as effectively as their Jewish supporters might have hoped. While the Socialists campaigned vigorously for Jewish votes, they made few concessions to Jewish interests for fear of alienating the non-Jewish electorate.

Social Democratic administrators tended to be equivocal in their treatment of Jews. Not only did the Social Democrats regularly direct their attacks against rich Jews, they also made it more difficult for many destitute Jewish war refugees to remain in Vienna. A Social Democratic provincial government official issued a decree in 1919 expelling some 40,000 refugees from the capital due to the acute housing and employment shortage.[16] When Socialist municipal administrators processed applications for naturalization in the early twenties, Jews complained of arbitrariness, divided families, and a needless prolongation of the process.[17] However, those Galicians who were allowed to become citizens eventually benefited from the Social Democratic regime in Vienna and, judging by the voting records in Leopoldstadt and Brigittenau where most of them clustered, they certainly gave it their unreserved support.[18] The Social Democrats thus did not defend Jews openly, but sometimes helped individuals behind the scenes; they denied Jews civil service positions, but gave their Jewish backers party jobs.

The Social Democrats figured that they already had the Jewish vote in their pocket, but giving their support to an antireligious Marxist party could not have been an easy choice for more traditional Jews. As Walter Simon has pointed out, "only intellectuals alienated from Judaism could accept socialism without reservations; liberalism permitted continued attachment to Judaism but socialism did not."[19] Jewish communal leaders, both Liberals and Jewish Nationalists, feared the effectiveness of Socialist propaganda in countering whatever impact was made by Jewish religious education, whether in the school or in the home. Jewish youth were particularly susceptible to the lure of Socialism and this often resulted in their loss of interest and participation in Jewish affairs.[20] The strength of Social Democracy in Vienna doubtless helped to increase the rate of assimilation, if not apostasy, in the Austrian capital.[21] Given that adherence to Socialist ideology clearly weakened the fabric of Jewish life, it must have been difficult for many committed Jews to vote Social Democratic, yet they evidently came to do so, albeit probably not with a great deal of enthusiasm.

The Jewish Liberal activists associated with the Union of Austrian Jews disagreed with the Social Democratic economic agenda but agreed with their position in most other areas, with both groups sharing their fundamental opposition to Jewish Nationalism.[22] Although the Liberals supported lists running against the Socialists in all national and municipal elections prior to 1932, their campaigning tended to be rather half-hearted and therefore ineffectual. By 1932 the Jewish Liberals had for all intents and purposes made their peace with their erstwhile adversaries.[23] The Jewish Nationalists, however, especially those on the Zionist right wing, remained very ambivalent in their relationship with the Social Democrats and were inwardly divided as to whether they should fight them or join them. The two groups differed not so much over economic and social welfare policy as over national minority recognition, subsidies for Jewish institutions, and Zionism.

From the outset, the Austrian Social Democratic Party refused to grant Jews minority status or endorse Zionism. Nonetheless, from 1919 to 1923, the representatives of the Jewish Nationalist Party on the Viennese municipal council backed the ruling Socialists.[24] In a

1920 speech, Leopold Plaschkes declared that the worst Social Democrat was far better than any Christian Social. The Jewish Nationalist Party and the Social Democrats had common interests, he asserted; without the Social Democrats, Jews would be subjected to an oppressive Horthyite regime, as in neighboring Hungary. Plaschkes vowed that his party would always vote with the Social Democrats on behalf of social justice.[25]

Minor confrontations occurred between Jewish Nationalist and Social Democratic activists during the 1920 election campaign,[26] but friction between the two parties escalated considerably in 1923. Hostility toward the Jewish Nationalists tended to be greatest among Social Democrats of Jewish origin, who viewed them as their natural competitors.[27] After the Jewish Nationalists formed their electoral alliance with the Jewish Liberals, a group of Jewish communal employees established their own Socialist electoral committee, aimed at undermining the Jewish unity front.[28] The Jewish Nationalists accused Social Democrats of breaking up their electoral meetings[29] and on election day, the Liberal *Neue Freie Presse* reported that the police had arrested several Social Democrats, including two who were armed, for trying to penetrate Jewish Nationalist campaign headquarters in Leopoldstadt and had apprehended fourteen others for giving out false pamphlets, supposedly signed by the Jewish electoral coalition, urging voters to vote Social Democratic.[30] Relations between Jewish Nationalists and Social Democrats approached their nadir soon thereafter; between 1924 and 1926, despite his earlier promise, Plaschkes voted together with the Christian Socials against the Social Democratic budgets.[31]

When the World Zionist Organization held its Fourteenth Congress in Vienna in 1925, Social Democratic Mayor Seitz declined to attend the opening ceremonies, claiming it was a religious gathering, whereas Christian Social government officials and dignitaries were well represented.[32] In 1927, Austrian Zionist leaders decided to attempt a rapprochement with the Social Democrats and arranged for a meeting between their representatives and Mayor Seitz and party chief Otto Bauer to discuss their hostile relations and the possibility of the Social Democratic Party adopting a friendlier attitude toward Zionists in Palestine. Despite these efforts, no leading Social Democrat participated in the Pro-Palestine Committee which was formed soon thereafter.[33] The Austrian Social Democratic Party remained noncommittal on the question of Zionism, largely due to the influence of its Jewish, rather than its non-Jewish, leaders.

If Austrian Social Democrats were officially neutral with regard to Zionism, Austrian Zionists were far from neutral when it came to Social Democracy. During the twenties, the Austrian Zionist Federation endorsed separate Jewish lists to run against Social Democrats in both national and municipal elections, but considerable opposition to this policy developed among the leftists within its ranks, including the Hitachdut faction and the Free Zionist Association, who sympathized with the Socialists and felt Zionists should be allowed to vote according to their own conscience in Austrian elections.[34]

By 1932, the choice before Viennese Jewish voters was basically whether to vote Social Democratic or not to vote at all. The Zionist Radicals and Revisionists and, to some extent, the Liberal Union as well were urging Jews to withhold their votes entirely. The Zionist Federation itself refrained from taking a public stand one way or the other.[35] In contrast, the Labor Zionists, with Poale Zion and Hitachdut having united, called upon all Jews to close ranks behind the Social Democrats as the only possible solution to the desperate political and economic crisis confronting Austria.[36]

The formal decision by the Zionist Federation to abandon *Landespolitik* in 1930 may be seen as a symbolic victory for the Social Democrats. In reality, however, most Zionists, like other Viennese Jews, had already been voting Social Democratic for years. One did not have to consider oneself a Socialist to vote Social Democratic in interwar Vienna. If one was a Jew, whether by religion or by nationality, one had little alternative. With the help of well over 80 percent of the Jewish voters, the Social Democrats handily won the 1932 municipal elections, capturing sixty-six out of one hundred seats on the city council.[37] This was to be the last Social Democratic victory in interwar Austria.

Jewish Socialists and Labor Zionists

The right-wing enemies of Social Democracy in interwar Austria derogatorily referred to their capital as "Red Jewish Vienna" due to the conspicuous presence of Jews in the Socialist administration which ran the city from 1919 to 1934. As elsewhere in Europe, Jews had become actively involved in left-wing politics in Austria by the early twentieth century. Many more Jews joined the Austrian Social Democratic Party, whether out of belief or opportunism, in the years immediately following World War I. What had been essentially a party of industrial workers, led by a small intellectual elite, with roughly 90,000 members in all of Austria before the war ballooned into a party of more than five times that size by 1922, including middle-class elements such as doctors, lawyers, white collar employees, businessmen, and even some small entrepreneurs. In 1924, one out of every five adults in Vienna was a member of the Social Democratic Party; the ratio among Jews might have been considerably higher.[38]

Membership in the party proved particularly attractive to middle-class Jews with higher education. According to Joseph Buttinger,

"Eighty percent of the intellectuals who joined the labor movement in Vienna were Jews. They made up the bulk of the Socialist students' organization, formerly 3,000 strong. The 200 lawyers who were organized Social Democrats, the 400 members of the Socialist Jurists' Association, and the 1,000 members of the Social Democratic physicians' organization in Vienna were almost exclusively Jews."[39]

Jews were very well represented within the party apparatus, especially in its higher echelons. Among the fifty most prominent figures in Austrian Social Democracy in the twentieth century, including both men and women, almost one-third were Jews, at least by birth.[40] Viktor Adler had been the party's founder and its leader until his death in 1918, while Otto Bauer, who served as Austrian Foreign Minister immediately after the war, led the party throughout the interwar years. Friedrich Austerlitz edited the party newspaper, and Julius Deutsch was commander of the *Schutzbund*, the Socialist army. Other prominent Socialists who were Jews by origin included Wilhelm Ellenbogen, who represented Leopoldstadt in the Austrian parliament and Hugo Breitner, the financial wizard on the municipal council elected from the Inner City. The Social Democratic Party offered many more opportunities for Jews within its ranks than any other major Austrian party.[41]

A variety of motives prompted Jews to become card-carrying Social Democrats. Some highly assimilated, secular Jews were trying to overcome their own Jewishness. As Buttinger dramatically phrased it, "This was their real escape from the loathsome ghetto. The charismatic idea of socialism superseded the faith of their fathers."[42] Some abandoned their Jewish affiliations altogether. Viktor Adler, for example, converted to Protestantism and had his son Friedrich baptized, while Wilhelm Ellenbogen, among others, officially declared himself *konfessionslos* or without religion. Most Jewish Socialists, including some of the top leaders, nominally remained Jews and some, like Otto Bauer, even paid their annual Kultusgemeinde taxes, but on the whole they evinced little concern for Jews or Judaism.[43] As Marxists, they generally held religion in low esteem, viewing it at best as a private matter and at worst as the opiate of the masses.

Although Jews were accepted within the party, nevertheless, much to their own dismay, they remained a conspicuous element. Whereas Jewish Socialist leaders were generally well-educated intellectuals with comfortable middle-class backgrounds, their non-Jewish counterparts most often came from poor artisan or working-class homes and worked their way up through the labor unions.[44] In his memoirs, Julius Braunthal recalled that "an air of distinction between Jews and Gentiles was always present . . . the Gentile comrade, while accepting his Jewish comrade as equal in the Socialist community, felt that he was in some way different. Some Jewish comrades would discount such disquieting feelings by emphasizing their indifference toward the Jews at large; some would alter their family names (or adopt a pen-name), so as to conceal their Jewish origin."[45] Simply by joining the labor movement, however, one apparently did not succeed in eradicating one's Jewish identity.

Many Jews undoubtedly joined the Social Democratic Party with loftier purposes in mind and out of a deep-seated commitment to Socialist goals of justice and equality. George Clare depicts the leading Austrian Jewish Socialists as follows: "They were idealists, do-gooders many of them, who devoted their lives to improving the lot of the working classes. Their conscious motives were absolutely sincere, their unconscious ones were guilt and fear. The guilt that drove them was the shame that motivates so many middle-class people today, who, ashamed of their inherited educational and social privileges, turn to the 'progressive' causes, so long as they can form an elite of the Left and enjoy more equality than the others. Their fear was of the antisemitic mob. A party that stood first and foremost for equality obviously could not allow inequality between Austrians who were Jews and those who were not. Hence, every Jewish Social Democrat sensed a protective wall of non-Jewish Social Democrats around him. And an added attraction was the intellectually fascinating challenge of the human engineering needed to create the egalitarian society of the socialist dream."[46]

Other Jews within the party, especially members of its rank and file, had much more mundane interests at heart. As Julius Braunthal described the postwar influx, "Many of the newcomers to the party had joined it because they hoped it would help them to a flat in one of the newly erected municipal housing blocks, or a job in one of the municipal enterprises, or to a loan at low interest for their small business, or to a works contract, or to an engagement as a doctor, teacher, or lawyer."[47] The Social Democratic Party governed the city of Vienna for fifteen years and was the largest builder, employer, and disburser of patronage in town. Jews remained almost entirely excluded from civil service positions and it is unclear to what extent they benefited from municipal housing, which was primarily intended for workers. Nevertheless, without question, belonging to the party improved one's chances of earning a livelihood and having a roof over one's head.

Many Zionists also joined the party during the interwar years. In 1930, Robert Stricker and his right-wing followers attempted to exclude from the ranks of the Zionist Federation all members of the Social Democratic Party, claiming that the two political organizations were mutually exclusive. In response to this overture, Michael Steinberg, a vice-president of the Zionist Federation who belonged to the Hitachdut group, explained their motivation in a highly enlightening article in the

Zionist press. It cannot be disputed, he wrote, that hundreds of Zionists, including even some Radicals and Revisionists, belonged to the Social Democratic Party and, especially in the provinces, many leaders were involved in both. This situation was not new, he claimed, and the number had not increased very much in recent years. Many Zionists joined the Social Democratic Party due to purely personal, material interests. Some wanted to acquire Austrian citizenship; others, a place to live or a job in public service. In light of the great importance of personal political connections for gaining positions and contracts and the tremendous amount of patronage involved, it was only human for Jews to turn to the Social Democratic Party to help solve their problems. By and large, Steinberg maintained, these people were Zionists by conviction and Social Democrats for convenience only. It was therefore not the Zionists who should evict the Socialists, but vice versa. Since the Zionists did not have the ability to meet Jewish economic needs, Jewish employees and workers had no other choice but to join Social Democratic unions, and small businessmen and artisans were often forced to join the party for economic rather than political reasons. No incompatibility existed between Zionist and Social Democratic affiliations, Steinberg claimed.[48]

While Jews as individuals joined the Social Democratic Party for a combination of idealistic and pragmatic reasons and most Jewish Socialists evinced little concern for what they considered particularist Jewish interests, Socialist Jews who combined a belief in Socialism with a commitment to Jewish group survival encountered difficulty furthering their goals within the framework of the party. The Austrian Social Democratic Party, which was both antireligious and antinationalist, defined Jews strictly as a religious denomination, and the Viennese Socialist administration refused to subsidize any Jewish institutions, including secular schools, health and welfare facilities, and sports organizations, because they classified them all as religious.

The party hierarchy rejected Jewish Nationalism in any form. Otto Bauer, in his classic study of the nationality problem in the Habsburg Empire written in 1907, grudgingly acknowledged that the Jews constituted a nationality of sorts, but he refused to grant them any form of national autonomy or minority rights, unlike other national groups in the multiethnic Austro-Hungarian Monarchy. Instead, he recommended that Jews assimilate.[49] Bauer's philosophy determined party policy throughout the interwar years. Only a few prominent Austrian Jewish Socialists, such as Julius Braunthal and Max Adler (unrelated to Viktor), sympathized with the Zionist cause.[50]

Poale Zion, the left-wing Labor Zionist organization which espoused both Social Democracy and Jewish Nationalism, confronted a difficult dilemma in reconciling both sets of its ideals in the Austrian context. Poale Zion supporters were included among the Jewish communal employees who formed the electoral committee of Jewish Social Democrats in opposition to the bourgeois coalition of Jewish Nationalists and Liberals in 1923. They also actively participated in the establishment of the Committee of Jewish Workers which campaigned on behalf of the Social Democratic Party in the 1927 elections.[51] In that year, Poale Zion distributed a statement among Jewish voters defining its position and its demands vis-à-vis the Austrian Social Democratic Party. This four-point credo linked the fate and the vital interests of the working Jews of Austria inextricably with the fate of the working classes and proclaimed it as their absolute duty to vote Social Democratic. It considered as the duty of Social Democrats "not only to uncover the reactionary brotherhood-in-arms between the Christian Socials and the Jewish capitalist bankers, but also to fight against antisemitism on principle as contrary to progress and culture, indeed as inimical to humanity." The Poale Zion credo affirmed the national identity of the Jewish population of Austria and demanded that the Social Democrats not oppose Jewish national aspirations, but instead guarantee the free development of this minority in accordance with the right of national self-determination. Finally, the statement urged Austrian Social Democrats to join other Socialist parties around the world in supporting Jewish efforts in rebuilding Palestine.[52]

Despite serious reservations regarding party policy on antisemitism, Jewish Nationalism, and Zionism, and their inability to bring about any changes in orientation on these matters, Poale Zion continued to regard the Austrian Social Democrats as friends who had been led astray but were deserving of active Jewish support. In 1932, in the midst of the depression, these Jewish Social Democrats expressed hope that their Austrian colleagues would attempt to alleviate the dire situation created by massive Jewish unemployment, especially among the youth. They pointed out the systematic exclusion of Jews from large factories and from nearly all state and municipal enterprises. The Austrian state apparatus was under the control of Christian Socials who were extremely unlikely to alter their hiring practices upon Jewish request, but the Viennese municipality was in the hands of the Social Democrats. The Labor Zionists urged their fellow Socialists to take into account the needs of the Jewish working population and to hire Jews in local government, since plenty of capable candidates were available.[53] These Austrian Labor Zionists remained staunch in their support of the Social Democratic Party but they refused to toe the party line completely when it came to Jewish issues. Their agenda, however, was scarcely realistic, especially given the political and economic situation facing Austria in the thirties.

By 1933, the raging conflict between the Right and the Left in Austrian politics was nearing its climax. The Christian Socials who controlled the national government had become determined to eliminate their Social Democratic and Nazi opponents. In February 1933, Engelbert Dollfuss, the Christian Social chancellor, dissolved the Austrian parliament. In response, the Poale Zion paper, *Der jüdische Arbeiter*, pleaded with both Jewish workers and the Jewish bourgeoisie to continue to defend the interests of the Social Democratic Party and help prevent its dissolution under an authoritarian Christian Social regime. The author of a lead article warned his fellow Jews against engaging in "ostrich politics" by blindly supporting whatever social forces were in power and streaming into the ranks of the patriotic, anti-Marxist Fatherland Front. It might be understandable, he wrote, for Jews to see their fate linked to that of German Austria and look to Dollfuss as the savior of the state, but such attitudes were dangerous and would lead to a dictatorship. Joining the Austrian front would not solve the Jewish question, he prophesied, but merely lead to further implementation of the antisemitic economic program of the Right. Jewish interests therefore lay with the survival of the Social Democratic Party, not with a victory of the Christian Socials and the Nazis who were waiting in the wings.[54]

Committed Jewish Social Democrats, including most Labor Zionists, had little option but to heed such clairvoyant advice and stick to their party until the bitter end following the Civil War of March 1934; many prominent Jewish Socialists found themselves in exile soon thereafter.[55] However, many Jewish Liberals and mainstream Zionists who had previously voted Social Democratic abandoned the sinking ship to which they had never been deeply attached, and some sought entrance into the much less hospitable Fatherland Front.[56]

A great many Viennese Jews gave their support to the Austrian Social Democratic Party, while it was in power, for pragmatic reasons rather than out of firmly rooted convictions. The weakness of the Socialist factions within the Kultusgemeinde demonstrates that most middle-class Viennese Jews were not really Socialists at heart. As a corollary, it also indicates that most Jewish Socialists, aside from Labor Zionists, were not very interested in involving themselves in communal affairs.

Socialist Jews and the Kultusgemeinde

While many Jews as individuals found supporting the Social Democratic Party personally advantageous, the organized Jewish community in interwar Vienna did not benefit greatly from having a Social Democratic municipal government before 1934. The Austrian Social Democratic Party was vehemently anticlerical, which meant not only anti-Catholic, but to some extent anti-Jewish as well. The party's 1926 Linz Program demanded the total separation of church and state and the equality before the law of all world views, religious or otherwise. According to this platform, all religious communities should be treated as private corporations under civil law. They should regulate and administer their own affairs and appoint their own officials without state interference. They should assume full responsibility for the costs of their administration and worship practices, as well as their religious instruction and the training and maintenance of their clergy and religious teachers. No public funds were to be expended for these purposes. In addition, all public education was to be secular; any form of religious instruction was to be left entirely to the various denominations.[57]

This program proved at best a mixed blessing for the Kultusgemeinde. Neither Liberals nor Jewish Nationalists could object to formal equality for all religious groups, a goal for which they had long been striving, or to the separation of church and state, insofar as it signified the disestablishment of Roman Catholicism. But the denial of public funding for all religious purposes, broadly defined, meant the cutting off of what limited support the Jewish community had previously received for religious instruction in the public schools, as well as a refusal to grant subsidies to Jewish-sponsored welfare institutions or even Jewish-related sports and recreational facilities.[58] The Social Democratic administration attempted to eliminate Jewish representation on the municipal school board, claiming it was clerical by nature,[59] while the building that housed the Chajes Realgymnasium, a predominantly secular Jewish high school, was not considered eligible for exemption from property taxes. Such circumstances made Jewish education in the public schools as well as in separate Jewish schools a formidably expensive undertaking.[60] The Social Democrats placed great emphasis on education and social welfare, which was one of the reasons so many Jews were attracted to their ranks, but they put the entire burden for all forms of Jewish educational and social welfare activities on the shoulders of the Kultusgemeinde, which could ill afford to pay for all the services that were needed. The Jewish Nationalist deputies on the municipal council protested against these policies, as did communal leaders, but to no avail. It proved futile for the Kultusgemeinde to apply to the municipality for the subventions for which it considered itself eligible according to the peace treaty and the Austrian constitution.[61]

Jewish Socialists played a much more important role as individuals within the Viennese municipal administration and the Austrian Social Democratic Party than they did as a group within the Jewish community. It might seem odd that Socialists, who were for the most part areligious, if not actually antireligious, would be at all interested in becoming involved in the affairs of the Kultusgemeinde, a body which, officially at least, had primarily religious functions. Their Liberal and Zionist opponents frequently accused the Socialists competing in communal elections of being "godless" and lacking a commitment to

Judaism, as well as a positive Jewish program. Their adversaries also charged them with introducing class-struggle and Social Democratic Party politics into the Kultusgemeinde.[62]

The Austrian Social Democratic Party adhered to an official policy of neutrality on the subject of religion and its most active leaders very rarely entered into the Jewish communal arena. Nearly all of the Socialists who participated in communal elections identified themselves closely with the party, but the party never formally endorsed their activities.[63] While the party considered religion to be strictly a private matter, not all of its supporters personally considered it of merely peripheral concern. One non-Zionist Socialist who was elected twice to the Kultusgemeinde board was described after his death in office as a "religious conservative" with views similar to those of the Liberals. Another was an observant Jew who even served as vice-president of a small private Orthodox prayer-house (or minyan).[64] These two men can scarcely be viewed as "typical" Jewish Socialist activists, but those Socialists who chose to run in communal elections undoubtedly demonstrated a higher level of Jewish commitment than the average Jewish member of the party and generally did not hold very high positions within the Social Democratic hierarchy. Such people we can definitely label "Socialist Jews," with greater emphasis on the noun than the adjective. For the most part, however, Socialists active within the Kultusgemeinde, including virtually all the Labor Zionists among them, were basically secular Jews who were generally willing to leave ritual matters to persons more deeply religious than they, preferring instead to concentrate on democratizing the community and expanding its social welfare services.[65]

Interestingly enough, more Socialists actually appeared on the ballots for communal elections between 1920 and 1936 than Liberals, Zionists, or Orthodox Jews. (See Table 9.) Socialists were much less likely than Zionists or Liberals to put their names up for candidacy repeatedly, perhaps because the chances for election were much slimmer for any Socialist, even if his name appeared near the top of a list. Socialists actively involved within the organized Jewish community were divided among themselves, generally along Zionist, non-Zionist, or dissident lines. Splits occurred within their ranks and on several occasions more than one Socialist list competed in Kultusgemeinde elections, which at least partially accounts for the large overall number of Socialist candidates and the fact that relatively few individuals ever ran on the same slate twice.

The occupational distribution of these Socialists reveals a somewhat surprising profile. Socialist candidates turn out to have been more likely than either Liberals or Zionists to be engaged in business, whereas fewer were professionals or white collar workers. (See Table 9.) For the most part, however, the occupations of the Socialists did not differ very greatly from those of other candidates for communal office. They did not display a particularly high incidence of artisans and virtually no workers appeared among them. Except for a few lawyers and doctors, the level of education appears to have been somewhat lower for the Socialists than for their major rivals.[66] From the impressionistic evidence available on Jewish Social Democratic leadership in Austria one would have expected to find a higher representation of professionals and white collar employees and fewer businessmen and entrepreneurs than indeed proves to be the case among the Socialists competing for seats on the Jewish community council. Whereas Jewish intellectuals appeared very prominently within the Social Democratic Party apparatus in Vienna, such individuals clearly had little interest in becoming involved in Kultusgemeinde affairs. Instead, a somewhat less educated, but more Jewishly committed, "second string" of Socialist Jews presented themselves on the communal scene.

Socialists running for communal office were much more likely than either Liberals or Zionists to live in Leopoldstadt and, to a lesser degree, the outlying working-class districts. They were much less likely than their major rivals to live in the prestigious Inner City, the upper-middle-class inner districts, or the outer "villa districts." (See Table 9.) Overall, Socialist candidates were generally to be found in those areas housing Jews in the middle to lower-middle economic range, presumably where they expected to locate most of their voting support.[67]

With respect to place of birth, the candidates running on the 1928 slate of the "Electoral Alliance of Jewish Workers," which comprised both non-Zionists and Poale Zion members, can be divided into three roughly equal groups: those born in Vienna (31%), in Galicia (also 31%), and elsewhere (38%). Whereas 22 percent hailed from the Czech lands, only 9 percent came from the Hungarian lands. Socialist candidates were more likely than any of their competitors to have been born in Vienna. While they were significantly less likely than the Zionists or the Orthodox to have come from Galicia, three times as many Socialist candidates as Liberals did so. Many of those Socialists who were Viennese natives undoubtedly had Galician-born parents. The likelihood of these Socialists to have been born in the Czech lands was roughly the same as the Zionists, but less than the Liberals, whereas Hungarian Jews were clearly underrepresented among the Socialist candidates as compared to the Liberals and the Orthodox. (See Table 3.) Although impressionistic evidence might lead one to speculate that most of those born in Galicia were probably Labor Zionists, while the native-born Viennese were more likely to be found among the non-Zionists, the data available do not fully bear this out.

Not only were the Socialist candidates more likely than the others to be native Viennese, they also tended to be younger. Indeed, these two characteristics often went hand in hand. The median age for Socialists running for election in 1928 was in the low forties, while for the Zionists it was in the late forties and for the Liberals (and the Orthodox) it was in the early fifties. (See Table 9.) Poale Zion candidates generally proved even younger than non-Zionist Socialist candidates. Judging by age, at least, Socialism, especially its Zionist variant, would appear to have been the wave of the future within the Viennese Kultusgemeinde. In reality, however, a total of eighteen of these Socialist candidates, including ten non-Zionists and eight Zionists, won election to the communal board during the interwar years and most of them served only a single term in office. (See Table 4.) The Socialists never gained much seniority within the Kultusgemeinde, whether judged by age or status, and generally acted as critics of the Viennese Jewish Establishment.

The person who most often headed a Socialist list but with least success was Saul Raphael Landau. Landau can undoubtedly be considered one of the greatest political mavericks on the Viennese Jewish scene. Born in Cracow in 1870, he was one of Herzl's earliest followers in Vienna but he soon became a diaspora nationalist and defender of the Jewish proletariat, constantly finding fault with both Liberals and Zionists.[68] Although clearly on the Left, he does not seem to have maintained formal ties with either Poale Zion or the Austrian Social Democratic Party. In the 1920 communal election, he led a four-person ticket which called itself the "Jewish People's Group" and received a mere forty-nine votes. He also ran unsuccessfully in 1928 and 1932. Landau clearly did not enjoy very much of a personal following and no one ever ran together with him more than once. While Landau completely failed to exert any influence on communal policy and was generally ignored, he did serve as a voice of conscience and as a thorn in the side of the communal leadership, at least at election time. He epitomizes the role of leftist as protester and social critic.

More within the mainstream of Viennese Jewish communal Socialism was the Alliance for Social Action in the Kultusgemeinde, later known as the Alliance of Jewish Workers, which initially included both Labor Zionists and non-Zionists. This group came into being shortly before the 1924 elections for the purpose of combating the Liberal–Jewish Nationalist coalition. While the slate comprised party members exclusively, its program and campaign literature did not refer directly to any formal Social Democratic affiliation.

These Viennese Jewish Socialists, unlike their Bundist counterparts in most other large Jewish centers at the time, decided to enter into Kultusgemeinde politics ostensibly because they felt strong enough to pressure the communal board into introducing universal suffrage without minimum tax-payment for all Jews living in the Austrian capital. The union of the two erstwhile bitter opponents in the bourgeois camp, the Liberals and the Jewish Nationalists, proved a great boon to the Socialists, since it enabled them to usurp much of the old Jewish Nationalist program, with a somewhat greater emphasis on democratization and social welfare reform, while at the same time allowing them to lump the Zionists together with the Liberals and condemn them both for what they considered to be the failures of the previous administration.[69] They issued a harsh critique of the recent attempts at electoral reform, calling the system reactionary and claiming that the new three-year, rather than one-year, tax-payment requirement had disenfranchised tens of thousands of white collar workers and lower-middle-class tradespeople. A communal board elected by such an undemocratic process, they insisted, did not have the right to be considered the true representative of Viennese Jewry as a whole. Thus the Socialists attempted to displace the Jewish Nationalists as the major champions of democracy within the community.[70]

Like the Liberals, most Socialists regarded the Kultusgemeinde as essentially a religious body. While maintaining that religion should be a private matter, they complained about insufficient communal subsidies for private Orthodox prayer-houses and the need for private contributions to cover the repair costs for the Leopoldstadt temple, which had been severely damaged by fire. The Socialists acknowledged that one of the highest obligations of the Kultusgemeinde was to satisfy the religious needs of all of its members to the fullest degree possible and believed that no one should be considered "too pious" for such a community. Moreover, they recommended that a special committee made up of religiously learned individuals have complete autonomy to deal with all matters of a religious or ritual nature. In this way, the Socialists were evidently trying to pacify the Orthodox, while at the same time absolving themselves of direct responsibility in the sphere of religion.[71]

The main area of concern for the Socialists within the Kultusgemeinde, however, was not religion but social welfare. They criticized the administration for neglecting its welfare institutions, including the hospital and old age home, and blamed it for ineffectiveness in dealing with the Jewish poor and orphans. They noted that many abandoned Jewish children had been given over to Christian care and thereby permanently alienated from Judaism, although they neglected to mention that such lamentable conditions were due in large measure to the refusal of the Social Democratic municipal government to support specifically Jewish welfare endeavors, including orphanages. In place of the existing system, which they deemed totally antiquated, the Socialists presented a fairly detailed agenda of welfare reform, which echoed and elaborated upon many ideas also endorsed by the

Jewish Nationalists. Certainly the Jewish Nationalists, and many Liberals as well, were not likely to object to this very ambitious program, if only the funds were available to implement it in an era of spiraling inflation compounded by austerity measures.[72]

The Socialists maintained that the financial woes of the Kultus-gemeinde were primarily caused by its plutocratic taxation system which sacrificed the poor for the wealthy. They regarded the retention of a tax ceiling during the inflationary period as grossly unfair and recommended not raising communal taxes but redistributing them so that the major burden would be on the rich, not those who could least afford it. They asserted that a modernization of the communal tax structure, retaining its progressive basis in modified form but eliminating the tax maximum and simplifying the assessment and collection procedures, would alleviate the economic difficulties and provide sufficient resources for funding their projects.[73] Their "Robin Hood" approach of forcing the rich to pay for the poor bears a close resemblance to the municipal taxation policy introduced by their fellow Jewish Social Democrat, Hugo Breitner.

The Electoral Alliance for Social Action was even more explicit in its desire to model the administrative organization of the Kultusgemeinde on that of the Viennese municipality. The Socialists accused the Kultusgemeinde management of treating its employees as pariahs by denying them the right to run for communal office. They felt that the Jewish community underpaid its staff and discriminated against them with regard to benefits. In the early twenties there had been a great deal of tension and hostility between the Kultusgemeinde leadership and the communal employees, which had manifested itself in the form of several strikes, including one by religious teachers in 1923, on behalf of better wages and more rights. A group of communal employees had actively campaigned on behalf of the Social Democrats, as opposed to the united Jewish list, during the 1923 national and municipal elections. Although some improvements in the situation of Jewish communal employees had already occurred, the Socialists were demanding that the Jewish community guarantee its employees complete equality with municipal workers, not only with respect to salary levels but also other emoluments, including pensions. They wanted the Kultusgemeinde and all its affiliated institutions to conduct themselves democratically, with workers having a say in their management and district tax assessment commissions having more authority over a broader range of functions.[74] Clearly the Socialist Jews believed that what was good for Vienna was also good for its Jewish community.

At the conclusion of their electoral program, the Socialists proposed that the Kultusgemeinde board create a committee made up of all parties which would concern itself with the protection of constitutionally guaranteed rights for Jews and represent the community before the authorities and legislative bodies. They refrained from advocating militant self-defense or any other nontraditional form of fighting antisemitism, even though they acknowledged the seriousness of the problem. Their pre-election platform did not contain any reference to Zionism or Jewish Nationalism, but, in a post-election declaration, the Socialists extended greetings and sympathy to their working friends in Palestine and promised to be on hand wherever and whenever the working class of Palestine needed their help.[75] This statement did not constitute a very strong affirmation of Jewish Nationalism, although it did stray somewhat from the Austrian Social Democratic Party's declared policy of neutrality.

The Liberals, Jewish Nationalists, and Agudists had originally formed their 1924 coalition in an attempt to avoid a costly election campaign during a time of continuing economic difficulties. The coalition partners offered the two competing Orthodox factions a total of three mandates and were willing to concede the same number of seats to the Socialists, if they agreed not to contest the election. All three groups refused to accept this settlement, since they hoped to do better for themselves among the electorate at large. A bitterly fought campaign resulted.[76]

In the 1923 municipal elections, the Jewish list backed by the Jewish Nationalists and the Liberals had received roughly one out of four Jewish votes, while the Social Democrats harvested most of the rest. Within the Kultusgemeinde, however, the Socialists were at a somewhat greater disadvantage than among the Viennese Jewish electorate at large. Many of their most active supporters did not pay communal taxes, whether because they could not actually afford them or because they managed to avoid doing so. Those who did not pay the minimum tax, which was extremely nominal, were not eligible to vote. Although a substantial number of communal taxpayers regularly voted Social Democratic in Austrian and Viennese elections, they were not necessarily committed to voting Socialist in communal elections, since here they had other options which they might well have considered more desirable. If support for the Social Democratic Party in Austrian politics was largely a matter of pragmatism, especially among the Jewish middle and upper middle class, who were most likely to pay their communal taxes and hence be part of the Kultusgemeinde electorate, then a Socialist list would inevitably attract far fewer voters in communal than in municipal or national elections.

After all their vigorous campaign efforts, the Electoral Alliance for Social Action managed to garner 2,266 votes, which amounted to only 15 percent of the total count. The Socialist share of the vote exceeded that of the two separate Orthodox lists by roughly a third, but the United Jewish list won five times as many votes as the Socialists and three times as many as all three protest lists combined.[77] (See Table

6.) While approximately three out of four Jewish voters chose the Social Democratic Party as opposed to the Jewish list in the municipal elections, less than one out of six of those individuals who were eligible to vote in communal elections and bothered to do so balloted for the Socialist slate a year later. This result confirms the fact that relatively few committed Socialists were involved in Jewish communal affairs and that, among those Jews who were interested enough to participate in communal elections, support for the Socialist agenda was very weak.

Nevertheless, despite their small share of the vote, the Socialists were not necessarily the losers in the 1924 elections. According to the proportional system for allocating mandates, the Alliance for Social Action gained five seats on the communal board. For the first time, Socialists had representatives within the Kultusgemeinde and the chairman of their party was elected to serve on the executive committee as well.[78] The Socialists had, temporarily at least, assumed the role formerly held by the Jewish Nationalists as the official opposition within the Jewish community.

The behavior of the Socialist deputies in the Kultusgemeinde during their first term of office was somewhat reminiscent of that of the Jewish Nationalist representation on the municipal council in the mid-twenties. In theory, one might have expected the Socialists to find natural alliees

desire to democratize the community; in practice, however, with the Jewish Nationalists forming part of the governing coalition and after such rancorous campaigning, the two groups emerged as bitter antagonists. As a small minority whose motions could never hope to gain enough support for passage, the Socialists generally limited their participation to lengthy harangues against the administration during the annual budget debate, followed by a negative vote on the budget proposal as a general expression of protest. On occasion exchanges between Socialists and Jewish Nationalists became extremely vituperative, degenerating into heckling and name-calling and resulting in deputies on one side or the other walking out of board meetings in anger.[79] Such highly undignified scenes, which also characterized general Austrian politics, repeated themselves with minor variations over the years.

A situation illustrative of the controversy surrounding the Socialists within the Kultusgemeinde arose with regard to the creation of a communal paper. The Socialist deputies introduced a resolution that the Kultusgemeinde publish its own official organ, to be circulated free of charge to all 50,000 communal taxpayers. The Socialists saw this as an opportunity to establish continuous contact with all members of the Jewish community, which would exert a positive moral influence and awaken interest in the Kultusgemeinde and its activities. Despite some Zionist support for the measure, the resolution went down to

defeat by a close vote of fifteen to thirteen, primarily due to the expense
which would be involved in the project. Instead, the Liberals presented
a motion that the communal council regularly place official announcements in existing Jewish papers, which would help subsidize
their operations. This motion was adopted by majority vote, against
the opposition of the Socialists, who were deeply insulted because their
organ was not included on the list of approved communal papers.[80] As
a result of this disappointment and other frustrations, the five Socialist
deputies decided to resign their positions on all committees at the end
of 1926, feeling that it was no longer possible for them to reach any
kind of understanding with the majority.[81] A year and a half later, the
board gave permission to the Jewish Socialist paper to publish paid
communal announcements, but on the first occasion when it did so,
both the Liberals and the Jewish Nationalists roundly criticized it for
abridging and editing an article on restrictions against Jews at summer
resorts.[82] The Socialist minority could not get their own way, but they
were clearly unwilling to toe the line and agree to the terms set by the
majority.

With the approach of the 1928 communal elections, both the Liberals
and the Jewish Nationalists began to step up their campaigns against
the Socialists, as well as against one another. Both groups found the
Socialists to be convenient scapegoats for the rising tide of apostasy
in the late twenties.[83] The Jewish Socialists vigorously denied any
responsibility for this trend, blaming the Liberal communal leadership
instead.[84]

The appearance of a second Jewish Socialist newspaper accompanied rumors of dissension within their ranks. This new periodical
set out to demonstrate that "Judaism and socialism, true human love
and human obligation are intimately bound to one another." It became
the organ of the Alliance of Jewish Workers but represented the views
of those Socialist Jews who were furthest removed from Labor
Zionism.[85] As tensions mounted between the non-Zionist and Zionist
factions within the Jewish Workers' Alliance, a conference of delegates
from its various district associations took place in the summer of 1928
to try to work out a programmatic formula acceptable to all groups.[86]

The joint statement of purpose which the two factions eventually
hammered out could not have greatly pleased the Poale Zion elements.
The Alliance's two self-assigned tasks were "to convince the working
Jewish population that its fate is closely linked only with that of the
workers and employees of this country and that therefore the Austrian
Social Democratic Party is appointed to represent their political and
economic interests" and "to arouse within the Social Democratic Party
of Austria an understanding of the justified social, economic and
cultural desires and demands of the Jewish working-class population."[87] The Jewish Workers' Alliance was thereby identifying itself

even more explicitly with the Social Democratic Party and muting its overtly Jewish concerns in the process. Its opponents, especially the Liberals, vehemently protested that an organization whose basic goal was to attract more Jews into the Social Democratic ranks did not belong within the confines of the Kultusgemeinde.[88]

By the time communal elections took place in December 1928, the Poale Zion faction and most of the non-Zionist Social Democratic leadership had patched up their differences and formed a joint list, calling itself the Electoral Alliance of Jewish Workers. Among the top dozen candidates, about one-third can be identified with Poale Zion and the rest were non-Zionists. The Socialists campaigned on the basis of much the same program as in 1924[89] and achieved virtually identical results. The Socialist list won a total of 2,899 votes, which amounted to roughly the same 15 percent of the overall vote as before, and held on to the same five seats. (See Table 6.)

After the 1928 elections, the Socialist deputies assumed a new role within the communal council. Instead of serving as a permanent opposition to a Liberal–Jewish Nationalist coalition, they could now become the power-brokers between the Liberal administration and their Zionist opponents. Since the Liberals, together with the Agudah, had won only eighteen seats and did not control a majority on their own, if the five Socialists voted with the eleven Jewish Nationalists and their two Orthodox allies, a deadlock would result. If they abstained or voted with the Liberals, the Liberals would have a majority.

A demonstration of the strategic position of the Socialist Club occurred on the occasion of the constituent meeting of the newly elected Kultusgemeinde board in January 1929. Since the Socialists decided to vote with the Liberals to reelect the genial Alois Pick as president, he won over Desider Friedmann by a margin of 23 to 13. In the voting for the vice-presidents, the Socialists abstained; as a result, two Liberals, Jakob Ornstein and Josef Ticho, gained election with 18 votes each, as against 13 for the Zionist candidate, Josef Löwenherz. In the election of the members of the executive committee, however, the Socialists allied themselves with the Jewish Nationalists and a complete deadlock ensued.[90] Several weeks later, after the Liberals and the Jewish Nationalists negotiated an agreement over a vice-presidency and proportional representation on the executive committee and the various subcommittees, the Socialists once more abstained from voting for vice-president but cast ballots in favor of the other officers. A Labor Zionist won election to the executive committee, while a non-Zionist Socialist became chairman of the personnel committee.[91] Although their numbers had not increased, for the first time the Socialists had the opportunity to play a decisive part in communal affairs.

But the Socialists did not remain a united camp within the Kultusgemeinde. The conflict that had been brewing between Poale Zion and the non-Zionist Social Democrats erupted into the open in the spring of 1929. During the budget debate, a ludicrous spectacle presented itself on the floor of the communal boardroom. A Poale Zion spokesman announced at the end of his long-winded speech that his party would vote against the budget as a whole but would support subventions for Palestine, as in the past. A non-Zionist deputy claimed, however, that his colleague was only expressing his own personal views, not speaking for the entire Socialist Club. Much as they sympathized with Palestine, the non-Zionist Socialist board members could not support such a large contribution for Palestine since, because of the great suffering in Vienna, the money was urgently needed for productive social welfare at home. An argument ensued between two other veteran Socialist representatives, one Labor Zionist and one non-Zionist, in which each lost his self-control, while disavowing the other's right to represent the Socialist position on Palestine subventions.[92]

Soon after, during a Jewish Workers' Alliance conference, the Poale Zion faction exited en masse and the non-Zionists adopted a motion whereby a member of the Alliance could no longer belong to any other Jewish political party. Henceforth, the leaders and deputies representing the Alliance had to be exclusively affiliated with the Social Democratic Party and could no longer be members of any constituent body within the World Zionist Organization.[93] The Poale Zion group promptly convened its own conference, elected its own executive, and adopted the name Association of Socialist Jews.[94] Interestingly enough, the Socialist Alliance succeeded in evicting the Zionists, whereas the Zionist National Committee failed in its attempt to exclude the Social Democrats from its ranks a year later. The status of shekel-paying Zionists within the Austrian Social Democratic Party, however, never seems to have been in jeopardy.

After this split within their party, two non-Zionist and three Zionist Social Democrats remained on the communal board. The non-Zionists decided that they could no longer vote together with the Jewish Nationalist opposition and unofficially joined ranks with the Liberals, giving them a majority of 20 to 16.[95] This action set a precedent for a Liberal-Socialist coalition in the next election. While Socialists on both sides of the fence continued to deliver critical budget addresses, by 1932 only the Poale Zion deputies, now de facto an independent faction within the Kultusgemeinde, were left voting against the budget as a matter of principle.[96]

Having expelled the Zionists from within their midst, the Alliance of Jewish Workers set about clarifying more fully their position vis-à-vis the Social Democratic Party on the one hand and the Kultusgemeinde on the other. Their revised statutes contained the explicit statement: "The organization and activities of the Alliance of Jewish Workers of

Austria follow the guidelines of the Social Democratic Party." The goals of the association included making the Jewish population familiar with the principles and objectives of the Social Democratic Party, representing the interests of the Jewish working-class population in all respects and advancing all efforts of Jewish women in every field of social, economic, and cultural life. Although Jewish women prominently took part in the Austrian Social Democratic Party, they never played a conspicuous role in the exclusively male bastion of Kultusgemeinde politics in interwar Vienna. The main stated purpose of the Alliance, however, was to democratize and reform the communal organization in order to better meet the needs of the Viennese Jewry.[97] These Socialist Jews thus tried to balance their obligations toward the party and toward the Jews whom they wanted to serve, especially workers, employees, and women. These two aspects of their program did not mesh well, however. While the Alliance leaders generally refrained from introducing specifically Social Democratic politics into the communal council, unlike the Labor Zionist Poale Zion they seemed reluctant to intervene with their Social Democratic colleagues on behalf of Jewish interests. Their aims of democratizing the Kultusgemeinde and expanding its social welfare and cultural facilities proved difficult to implement, despite the fact that they shared these basic goals with their Zionist adversaries.

Somewhat surprisingly, given this newly articulated program, shortly before the 1932 communal elections the Alliance decided to enter into an electoral coalition with their former antagonists, the Liberals. This agreement would guarantee the Social Democrats more seats on the board than they might otherwise attain on their own, but it could by no means help to further their cause, since the Liberals continued to be the staunchest opponents of universal suffrage and extensive social reform.[98] The two groups, the Alliance and the Union of Austrian Jews, although normally poles apart on economic issues, had been drawing closer together in recent years due to their common antipathy toward Zionism. Their joining forces was decidedly a risky venture and probably a sign of desperation on both their parts. In the end, it did not prove greatly advantageous to either side.

During the election campaign, three rival left-wing factions put forth their own slates, including a Labor Zionist coalition and two dissident non-Zionist groups. The Labor Zionists, now labeled the Association of Socialist Jews, billed themselves strictly as the true representatives of Socialism in the community, rather than as Jewish Nationalists. They accused the Jewish Workers' Alliance of betraying their democratic principles in allying with the Liberal "plutocrats" and quoted the Social Democratic *Arbeiterzeitung*'s formal announcement that the party endorsed no slate in the communal elections.[99] In all,

Socialist voters within the Kultusgemeinde had four different lists from which to choose.

When the 1932 communal election returns were tallied, the Liberal-Socialist coalition ticket had received 10,194 votes, only 236 more than the Union-Agudah combination had accrued in the previous election. The Liberals' share of the vote, however, had fallen from 47 to 39 percent. Very few Socialists could apparently bring themselves to vote Liberal, while Liberals had little choice but to vote for the coalition or else not vote at all. The Labor Zionist list attracted the support of 2,859 voters, only 40 fewer than the Alliance list had received in 1928. (See Table 6.) These results clearly demonstrate that the Socialist voters in Kultusgemeinde elections were overwhelmingly pro-Zionist in their sympathies. The overall Zionist victory in 1932 was therefore accompanied by a clear-cut Labor Zionist electoral victory within the Socialist camp.[100]

As an outcome of these elections, the number of Socialists serving on the Kultusgemeinde board actually increased from five to eight. The Poale Zion–Hitachdut list had won four seats, one more than the Labor Zionists had previously occupied, while the coalition with the Liberals gained the Jewish Workers' Alliance four places, twice as many as before.[101] (See Table 6.) Two Socialists, one Zionist and one non-Zionist, were elected to the executive committee, and for the first time Socialist board members assumed several committee chairmanships.[102] However, one can visualize the two Socialist groups as pitted against one another on opposite sides of the fence, half Zionists, half non-Zionists, with their votes canceling each other out. Thus, while Socialists controlled more than one-fifth of the mandates and a quarter of the seats on the executive committee, along with roughly proportional representation on subcommittees, their potential strength and ability to influence policy was considerably diluted by their disunity.

Under a Jewish Nationalist administration, Socialists certainly stood a much better chance of implementing at least some of their program than under a regime dominated by the Liberals. The Jewish Nationalist leadership depended on the support of an entire spectrum of Zionist allies in order to maintain their control over the communal council. The four Labor Zionist votes determined whether or not the Jewish Nationalists got a majority on the thirty-six-member board. If they all abstained from voting, a measure could still pass, but if they chose to vote together with the Liberal-Socialist opposition, they could manage to defeat a motion.[103] In theory, the Labor Zionists wielded a certain amount of clout; in practice, they tended to vote as a bloc with their fellow Zionists.

Given the appropriate economic and political circumstances, the Jewish Nationalists, once in power, would have carried out many of the goals which they held in common with the Socialists, including the introduction of universal suffrage and a greatly expanded social welfare program, with an emphasis on productivization of labor. In reality, however, by the thirties the situation was not propitious for the realization of this agenda due to the worsening political climate and the impact of the depression. Although the Socialists criticized the Jewish Nationalists for not bringing to fruition their mutual objectives, in January 1934 the Kultusgemeinde board, including all eight Socialists, unanimously adopted the annual budget.[104] Perhaps this was more a sign of despair than of harmony, but evidently the wind had been taken out of the Socialists' sails.

Two months later, in March 1934, when all Social Democratic groups were outlawed in Austria in the aftermath of the Civil War, all Socialists deputies, including both Zionists and non-Zionists, lost their seats on the communal council.[105] For the remainder of that term of office, no Socialists per se served on the Kultusgemeinde board. The complex ramifications of this event for the Jewish community will be explored in chapter 6.

Surprisingly enough in light of the official proscription of all Socialist activity, the Labor Zionists, unlike their non-Zionist Social Democratic rivals, were allowed to resuscitate themselves under a new name. Poale Zion–Hitachdut had been officially dissolved in 1934, but soon thereafter a group calling itself Binyan Ha'arez (Rebuilding the Land) came into existence.[106] In the 1936 communal elections, the Labor Zionists again put forth their own slate, this time labeled the "Social Task Force—List of Palestine Labor." Doubtless all the people on this list could be identified with the illegal Social Democratic party, yet they competed openly for communal office. Evidently the Austrian government was willing to apply a different set of rules for those Jewish Socialists who were also Zionists than for those who were non-Zionists.

The Labor Zionists ran a very low-key campaign in the 1936 communal elections, leaving most of the mudslinging and name calling to the other Jewish Nationalists and the Liberals. The balloting netted the Labor Palestine list 2,772 votes, 87 fewer than in 1932, but their share of the vote fell from 11 to 9 percent, due to greater voter participation. The absolute number of Socialist voters in communal elections had remained remarkably stable since 1924, especially considering the vicissitudes of Socialist politics in Vienna at large and within the Jewish community itself. (See Table 6.)

Since their overall share of the vote had declined by several percentage points, the Labor Zionists lost one of their four seats on the communal board, but Michael Steinberg, a Hitachdut activist, won election to the Kultusgemeinde board on the official Zionist slate instead. In addition, two non-Zionist Social Democrats, one of them Ernst Feldsberg, a Union board member, were reelected on the Union slate, albeit without a great deal of fanfare. Thus, in 1936, two years after all public Socialist activity had been banned in Austria, at least six ardent Socialist sympathizers had been elected to the Jewish community council, three as Labor Zionists, two as Liberals, and the remaining one as a Jewish Nationalist, but none as a Social Democrat per se.[107] By the mid-thirties, however, there was no longer any question but that those elected on a Union list voted as a bloc, as did the Jewish Nationalists of all shades in nearly every instance. Socialist affinities no longer played a significant role in communal politics.

When trying to evaluate the contributions of the Socialists to the Kultusgemeinde, one must bear in mind that until 1930 they solidly belonged to the opposition, whereas thereafter they were split into two almost equal camps, one supporting the majority in power and the other not. Although these men were often outspoken in their critique of the system, particularly during the annual budget debates, their objectives, especially in the social welfare sphere, could not be readily accomplished. At best they helped the Jewish Nationalists to realize some aspects of their program which the two groups held in common. For the most part, however, the Socialists managed to achieve little during their years of active participation in Jewish communal affairs. Their dreams of an egalitarian community remained ephemeral.

While there were undoubtedly a great many more non-Zionist Socialists than Labor Zionists among Viennese Jewry at large, Labor Zionist supporters clearly outnumbered non-Zionist Socialist voters among the Kultusgemeinde electorate, since the latter were evidently less willing or less able than the former to pay communal taxes. Perhaps the introduction of universal suffrage, long advocated by the Left, might have altered this situation and boosted the total Socialist share of the communal vote above 15 percent, but it seems more likely that non-Zionist Socialists were simply less interested than Zionists in participating in communal affairs. Relatively few Jewish workers lived in Vienna and even fewer became involved in the organized Jewish community. Labor Zionists appear to have voted in communal, as well as Zionist Congress, elections whenever possible, but many non-Zionist Socialists probably did not bother to cast ballots in specifically Jewish elections, even if they were eligible to do so.

A great many of the Labor Zionists in Vienna originated from Galicia, rather than elsewhere in the former Austro-Hungarian Monarchy. The geographic distribution of Galician Jews in Vienna, as well as their lower-middle-class socioeconomic status, corresponded closely with the general characteristics displayed by Labor Zionist voters.[108] As a general rule, Galician Jews, along with Jews of Moravian origin, were more prone to support Zionism than Jews of Hungarian or Bohemian extraction or native-born Viennese. Likewise, many Galicians, along with Czech and Viennese-born Jews, were strongly attracted to Socialism, unlike most Jews of Hungarian origin in Vienna. Although they were to be found in considerable numbers among the rank and file of the General Zionist, Radical, and Revisionist factions, and to a lesser extent among their leadership as well, Galicians played an even more salient role on the Zionist Left in Vienna than in the Center or on the Right. Eastern Jews were often looked down upon as not being truly "Viennese," since many of them had arrived in the capital only in the twentieth century. Perhaps their preponderance among Labor Zionists contributed to the overall weakness of Labor Zionism in the Austrian capital, whether in general politics, within the Kultus-gemeinde or within the Austrian Zionist framework.

Whereas Labor Zionists became relatively strong in interwar Poland and dominated the political scene in Palestine, wielding dispropor-tionate influence within the World Zionist Organization due to allian-ces with Chaim Weizmann and his followers, the Labor Zionists in Vienna never managed to attract the support of more than a quarter of all Zionists and they failed to achieve effective bargaining positions vis-à-vis the General Zionists or the Radicals. They were poles apart from the Revisionist–Jewish State Party not only in terms of ideology but in the popularity of their spokesmen as well. They lacked charis-matic orators, such as Robert Stricker or Leopold Plaschkes, and did not seem to have had efficient administrators of the caliber of Desider Friedmann or Josef Löwenherz. Their leaders could speak at great length criticizing the status quo, but they had no means of implement-ing an alternative program on their own. They remained a small minority, with little or no real power. In the Austrian capital, middle-class General Zionists, rather than lower-middle or working-class Labor Zionists, continued to control both communal and Zionist politics until World War II.

The major reason for the weakness of Jewish Socialism of all varieties in interwar Vienna lay in the strength of the Austrian Social Democratic Party. It is impossible to calculate exactly how many Jews, especially young intellectuals, were attracted to the party's ranks but ironically this very success in winning over significant numbers of Jews to the Socialist cause diluted the strength of the Socialists within the Jewish community and within the Zionist movement in the Austrian capital. The "best and the brightest" Jewish minds seem to have chosen to renounce specifically Jewish interests and join the leadership cadres of the Social Democrats, rather than the much smaller and weaker Alliance of Jewish Workers or Poale Zion. The leadership of these Jewish Socialist groups, while much more Jewishly committed, generally tended to be less gifted and less dynamic, and also less well educated and less ambitious, than their counterparts

higher up in the party apparatus. To some extent they can be considered "second-string" Socialists.

To make matters worse, the Austrian Social Democratic Party often
treated these Socialist Jews as stepchildren, accepting their backing
but refusing openly to endorse their activities within the Kultusgemeinde or to give their support to a Jewish homeland in Palestine.
Because of their ambivalent relationship with the party, the non-
Zionist Socialists active within the Kultusgemeinde had difficulty
articulating a full-blown Jewish Socialist program, comparable to that
of the Bund in Poland. It was surely not easy to be a loyal Austrian
Social Democrat and at the same time to try to justify the need for
separate Jewish welfare institutions which deserved, but did not
receive, municipál subsidies. It must have been even harder being a
Labor Zionist of the Poale Zion variety in Austria, urging others to
support the Social Democratic Party while at the same time opposing
its stand on antisemitism, Jewish Nationalism, and Zionism, as well
as its general indifference to Jewish concerns. Perhaps it was their
affiliation with the Social Democratic Party that inhibited the Austrian
Labor Zionists from developing any strategy of their own for combating
antisemitism. Given the local circumstances, for many Jews of a leftist
bent this particular mixture of Socialism and Zionism probably seemed
self-contradictory, if not absolutely untenable. Far more Viennese
Jews chose either Socialism or Zionism than adopted a combination
of the two. Those Jews who opted for Socialism proved much less likely
than Zionists of any kind to take part in communal affairs.

Viennese Jews, in their overwhelming majority, supported the
Austrian Social Democratic Party in municipal and national elections.
Many if not most of these Jews were certainly not committed Socialists,
but among those who were indeed dedicated Social Democrats only a
small minority participated in any way within the organized Jewish
community. Individual Jews made extremely important contributions
to the development of Austro-Marxism. The Austrian Social
Democratic Party drained a great deal of talent and energy from the
Jewish community but gave back little in return. As a result, while
there were a great many Jewish Socialists in interwar Vienna, Jewish
Socialism as a separate force proved weaker in the Austrian capital
than in other major European Jewish centers during the same era.

Although most Jews, including the Orthodox, voted Social
Democratic in Viennese and Austrian elections, only between 10 and
15 percent of the Jewish communal electorate chose to vote Socialist
in Kultusgemeinde contests. Nevertheless, the Socialist share of the
vote regularly exceeded that of the various Orthodox slates who
competed in the quadrennial elections. Certainly Socialism attracted
a great many more Jews of the younger generation than did traditional

Orthodoxy during the interwar period and undoubtedly many more Jewish Socialists than Orthodox Jews became politically active in the Austrian capital. But how did it come about that Socialist Jews played a more active role, numerically at least, within the confines of the organized Viennese Jewish community than the Orthodox at the opposite end of the religious spectrum? The next chapter will address this question.

5

THE ORTHODOX

The Orthodox proved the weakest Jewish group in interwar Vienna and the least able to unite and mobilize support effectively for political purposes. Orthodox Jews made up approximately twenty percent of the Jewish population of the capital, but no party existed for which they could cast their ballots with a clear conscience in either national or municipal elections. The Social Democratic Party advocated atheistic Marxism, and both the Liberal factions and the Jewish Nationalist Party were also heavily secular in their orientations. In Germany Orthodox Jews could vote for the Catholic Center Party, but in Austria the Christian Socials were too overtly antisemitic to allow for a Clerical option.[1] In interwar Poland many Orthodox rallied around their own traditionalist party, the anti-Zionist Agudat Israel,[2] but the Viennese branch of the Agudah never became actively involved in Austrian politics. Indeed, with respect to the general political scene, the Orthodox in Vienna adopted an almost apolitical stance. Their press might comment occasionally on an upcoming election, but the Orthodox leaders never actually entered the fray. While some Orthodox groups, including the Hasidim, largely remained outside the Kultusgemeinde political arena as well, others decided to compete in communal elections in the aftermath of World War I.

Although ideologically they were poles apart and their concerns differed greatly, the Orthodox shared many of the same problems that the Socialists confronted within the Kultusgemeinde. Heavily concentrated in the poorer sections of Leopoldstadt and Brigittenau, these traditionally observant Jews mainly consisted of lower-middle-class self-employed small businessmen with a much lower socioeconomic profile than most Liberals or Jewish Nationalists. Like the Socialists, many Orthodox Jews could not vote in communal elections, since they were recent immigrants who were too indigent to pay their taxes but received communal relief instead. Almost two-thirds of the more than 36,000 individuals who obtained weekly allocations of kosher meat through the Joint Distribution Committee after the war paid nothing or else a subsidized rate.[3] Roughly one-fifth of the more than 4,000 monthly users of the communal *mikvah* or ritual bath, approximately one-quarter of whom were women observing the laws of family purity, were exempted from paying fees.[4]

The Orthodox suffered from even more deeply rooted internal factionalism than did the Socialists or even the Jewish Nationalists. They divided themselves into modern Orthodox and traditional Orthodox, Hasidim and Mitnagdim, but the fundamental split within Viennese Orthodoxy, as within the Jewish population as a whole, lay between the Zionists and the anti-Zionists. Geographic origin often served as a significant factor in this dichotomy, with the major fissure occurring between the "Poles" or Easterners, who came from Galicia, and the "Hungarians" or Westerners, most of whom originated in western Slovakia or the Burgenland, which formed part of prewar Hungary. The anti-Zionist Agudah represented mainly the Westerners, and the Religious Zionist organization, Mizrachi, the Easterners. Adas Jisroel, known as the Schiffschul, and Beth Israel, which was called the "Polish shul," served as the flagship synagogues for the two major Orthodox camps, the "Hungarians" and the "Poles" respectively. While all Orthodox Jews in the Austrian capital basically shared the same religious beliefs, practices, and requirements, they differed considerably among themselves as to how best to satisfy their particular interests, either within the context of the Kultusgemeinde or outside its framework.

The Hungarian Orthodox differed from both Eastern European Orthodox and German Orthodox with respect to the outward manifestations of their Jewishness. Influenced by their spiritual leaders in Pressburg (Bratislava), the major Orthodox center in western Slovakia, they resisted any form of religious innovation. Yet, unlike the Polish Orthodox, they adopted modified forms of modern, western dress and did not speak Yiddish, but instead used German as their vernacular. Unlike the German Orthodox, they, along with their rabbinical leaders, generally lacked formal advanced secular education.[5] The Hungarian Orthodox in Vienna would have liked to follow the example of their fellow Orthodox in Hungary and Germany, who formed separate communities, independent of the Liberals, but despite several attempts at secession they were compelled by Austrian law to remain within the Kultusgemeinde and pay taxes to it.[6] The less cohesively organized Galician Orthodox, both at home and in Vienna, proved much more willing to work out a modus vivendi with the non-Orthodox, especially the Zionists, which would permit the Jewish community to remain unified in the spirit of "k'lal yisrael" or Jewish unity. The predisposition of religiously conservative Galician Jews to form alliances with the Jewish Nationalists within the Kultusgemeinde sphere in Vienna resembles the electoral partnership between religiously traditional Easterners of Polish origin and the Zionist opposition in prewar Germany.[7]

Several Orthodox factions actively participated in Kultusgemeinde politics during the interwar years but they never formed a united front. The vote for Orthodox lists grew in absolute terms from 878 in 1920 to 2,313 in 1932, but whether one, two, or three such slates ran in a given communal election it did not seem to affect their combined share of the vote, which remained stable at between 8 and 9.5 percent.[8] Like the Socialists, their constituency formed a fixed minority within the communal electorate, many of whom were unwilling or unable to exercise franchise. Perhaps as many as half of Vienna's most strictly observant Jews did not vote at all.

The Orthodox, like the Socialists, diluted their collective strength even further by the fact that the different factions formed separate alliances with other parties on the communal council. The "Hungarians" or the Agudah/Schiffschul faction eventually aligned themselves with the Liberals with whom they shared a strong antipathy toward secular Jewish Nationalism, while the "Poles," whether Mizrachists or "Independents" associated with Beth Israel, normally joined forces with the Jewish Nationalists. Thus the Orthodox, like the non-Orthodox, found themselves split between the Zionist and non-Zionist camps within the communal boardroom.

The Agudah branch which organized in Vienna in 1919 remained consistently anti-Zionist throughout the interwar period, with bitterness and resentment growing as the years passed. Agudat Israel had formally been established in 1912, but actually became active in 1916 in Poland. It comprised a rather curious amalgam of German, Hungarian, and Polish Orthodox rabbis, and thus included both Western and Eastern, neo-Orthodox and traditional, elements. Its major stronghold was in Poland, especially among the Gerer Hasidim of former Congress Poland, but it always remained weak in Galicia, where there was a lack of political solidarity among religious Jews who often supported secularist parties. Most of the Galician Hasidic dynasties, especially the followers of the Belzer rebbe, refused to back the Agudah.[9] As a result, in Vienna as well, relatively few Galician Orthodox Jews belonged to the Agudah, although several Hasidic rabbis were prominently associated with it. Unlike its counterpart in Poland, the Austrian Agudah did not engage in municipal or national politics, but it did become involved in Kultusgemeinde affairs, despite provisions in its statutes to the contrary.[10] Most individuals identified with the Austrian branch of the Agudah also belonged to the Hungarian-dominated Schiffschul community and its related institutions and virtually all the Hungarian Orthodox Jews competing in Kultusgemeinde elections were closely associated with Adas Jisroel/Agudat Israel.

The Orthodox, like the Liberals and the Socialists, defined the Jewish community primarily in religious terms and firmly believed that the most important function of the Kultusgemeinde was to provide for the religious needs of all of its members. Their greatest concern lay in increasing subsidies for Orthodox houses of worship and assuring that communal institutions adhered to rigorous Orthodox standards. Nevertheless, even the Agudists did not deny the national component in Jewish identity; they merely assigned it lesser importance than the religious aspect. The Agudists vehemently opposed Zionism, not because it was a nationalist movement but because of its secularism. They accused the Jewish Nationalists of advocating group assimilation, which they regarded as even more of a threat to the survival of traditional Judaism than the individual assimilation of the Liberals. The Religious Zionist Mizrachists, however, believed that they could successfully reconcile Zionism with a modernized Orthodoxy. They felt that religion and nationalism were intertwined in Jewish life and that traditional culture could be transformed to accommodate modern Jewish Nationalism.[11]

Given their inner divisions and general lack of political experience, how effective were the Orthodox in achieving their goals and preserving their distinctive institutions and lifestyle amid the difficult political, economic, and social climate of interwar Vienna? This chapter will analyze the relationship between Orthodox Jewry and the Kultusgemeinde, comparing the strategies for Orthodox survival of the Hungarians, who generally advocated separatism, with those of the Galicians, who favored communal unity.

Orthodoxy and the Kultusgemeinde

While the large influx of Galician Jews into Vienna in the early twentieth century greatly augmented the number of Orthodox Jews in the Austrian capital as well as the number of Orthodox prayer-houses, the religious antagonisms between the Orthodox and the Liberals externally and the "Hungarians" and the "Poles" internally had emerged well before the end of the nineteenth century and the stage had long since been set for the communal struggles that ensued during the interwar period.

Despite persistent conflicts over the years between the more traditional and the more progressive Viennese Jews, the Kultusgemeinde remained a unified body, not only because Austrian law mandated it in 1890 but also because the Viennese Liberals assumed an essentially conservative stance with respect to public observance. The fairly minor changes which were introduced in the Viennese communal synagogues in the nineteenth century more closely resembled those instituted by the Conservative Jewish Theological Seminary in Breslau and later in New York than the more extensive reforms advocated by the more radical German or American Reformers. The periodic threat of an Orthodox secession served to moderate the Liberals' efforts at religious innovation in Vienna.[12]

The Viennese rite practiced in Liberal communal synagogues in the Austrian capital in the early twentieth century differed little from that introduced by Isak Noa Mannheimer and the noted cantor Salomon Sulzer more than half a century before. Worship services were conducted in a very dignified manner and decorum prevailed. Women sat in separate galleries upstairs and an all-male choir sang with no organ accompaniment. Prayers were recited almost exclusively in Hebrew with few emendations, but petitions for a return to Zion were only said silently and a German sermon remained central. This highly formal and decorous atmosphere involving little congregational participation undoubtedly made more traditional Jews, especially recent arrivals from the provinces, feel distinctly uncomfortable, but very little which took place in a Viennese Liberal synagogue was not in accordance with Jewish law. That the Liberals did not deviate very far from Orthodox norms allowed the Kultusgemeinde to maintain its unified status more easily; that the Liberals modified the service at all resulted in tensions between the Viennese Jewish Establishment and the Orthodox, especially the Hungarian Orthodox, from the very beginning.

Separate Orthodox prayer-houses coexisted alongside the communal synagogue framework, although the Kultusgemeinde board often frowned upon them as unwanted competition. Already by the mid-nineteenth century, distinct Hungarian, Polish, and even Moravian Orthodox congregations had developed in the Austrian capital, each following the customs of their respective places of origin. During the interwar years, Vienna had as many as one hundred and four Jewish houses of worship which received official recognition from the Kultusgemeinde.[13] Of these, seven were communal synagogues, built and maintained by the Kultusgemeinde, and sixteen more were designated associational synagogues, privately constructed but generally communally funded. Some seventy-seven fell into the category of associational prayer-houses, eligible for minimal subsidies, and four more were considered private chapels. Whereas six of the seven communal synagogues and thirteen of the associational synagogues were Liberal "temples," with services held according to Mannheimer's Vienna rite, the remaining eighty-five houses of worship were all Orthodox synagogues or "shtiebels" of one variety or another. At least fourteen of these, including the private chapels, identified themselves with various Galician Hasidic dynasties, and nine others were Religious Zionist in orientation, while six were clearly "Hungarian," five "Polish," and one "Turkish" or Sephardic.[14]

The various classifications of Viennese synagogues reflected differences in size, prestige, and levels of communal support. A disproportionate amount of funding went to the large Liberal establishments, all of which received regular subventions. Nearly all of the Liberal temples featured a communal rabbi, who was authorized to perform weddings and other official functions, and more than one cantor. The communal synagogues, as well as several of the associational temples, also had choir directors and male choirs.

The two main Liberal synagogues, erected in 1826 and 1858, were located on Seitenstettengasse in the Inner City and on Tempelgasse in Leopoldstadt. The other communal synagogues, all constructed before the turn of the century, were situated in four outlying districts. Leopoldstadt had one associational temple in addition to its communal synagogue, while the other thirteen Liberal temple associations were distributed among the remaining districts.

The six communal synagogues had a total seating capacity of about 5,000, as did all thirteen Liberal associational synagogues combined. Worshipers purchased synagogue seats on an annual basis. For the most part, the communal synagogues were "sold out" for the High Holydays, and the Kultusgemeinde had to rent temporary facilities for the overflow crowd. Altogether the nineteen Liberal temples could accommodate less than 10 percent of Viennese Jewish adults, with separate seating for men and women.[15]

The Orthodox houses of worship were on the whole much smaller than the Liberal synagogues and considerably more modest in their accouterments. At least two of them, however, had a large enough membership and were sufficiently well established with their own imposing edifices to be designated associational synagogues. Adas Jisroel, known as the "Schiffschul" because of its location on Grosse Schiffgasse in Leopoldstadt, claimed 700 members, and Beth Israel, or the "Polish shul," had 450. The other Orthodox prayer-houses ranged in size from 60 or fewer members to 350 households.

At the end of World War I, the forty then existing Orthodox synagogues and prayer-houses could hold an estimated 10,000 worshipers, roughly the same number as their Liberal counterparts. During the course of the interwar period, no new Liberal temples were founded, but the number of Orthodox prayer-houses more than doubled. Nearly all the Hasidic "shtiebels" or "kloiser" came into existence during this era, as did the various Zionist congregations. Since most of the new postwar prayer-houses were smaller in size than their prewar counterparts, the seating capacity of Orthodox prayer-houses did not quite double, but nevertheless grew appreciably.

By 1936, the various Jewish houses of worship in Vienna had a combined total of 29,200 seats available on a regular basis, while an additional 22,000 temporary places accommodated the High Holyday overflow.[16] While over 50,000 Viennese Jews, about one out of every two adults, apparently participated in High Holyday religious services, a majority of them undoubtedly did not attend synagogue regularly during the rest of the year. On a daily or even a weekly Sabbath basis, the Orthodox prayer-houses, as well as Adas Jisroel and Beth Israel, tended to attract many more worshipers than did the Liberal temples, except for the two main communal synagogues.

More than half of the eighty-five Orthodox houses of worship in the Austrian capital were located in Leopoldstadt. Twelve Orthodox prayer-houses were to be found in heavily working-class Brigittenau, six were located in Alsergrund, and three in the Inner City, while the remainder were scattered in other districts. Orthodox prayer-houses were reasonably widespread in Vienna and helped to fulfill the religious needs of a fairly broad range of Jews, especially recent migrants from Galicia, who did not necessarily strictly adhere to Orthodox observances in their daily lives but felt more at home praying in an Orthodox setting.

Orthodox prayer-houses were considerably less well off financially than Liberal synagogues in Vienna, not only because their smaller membership was by and large less affluent, but also because they received much less in communal subsidies. In 1932, almost half of the Orthodox congregations did not have rabbis, hardly any had regular cantors, and only one, the modern Orthodox Beth Israel, had a choir director. Small Orthodox prayer-houses did not normally need paid functionaries and in most cases could not afford them. The notable exception to this general rule of impecunious Orthodoxy was Adas Jisroel, which derived much of its revenue from its separate kosher slaughtering activities.[17]

The Schiffschul community generally refused to accept communal subventions but Beth Israel was the regular recipient of sizable communal allocations. Fifty-six Orthodox prayer-houses also received Kultusgemeinde subventions during the interwar years; twenty-nine did not, including the private Hasidic chapels, most of the Zionist congregations, and several Hungarian "shtiebels." Older prayer-houses were more likely to receive communal funding than newer entities. The number of religious associations receiving subsidies almost doubled from the twenties to the mid-thirties, while the amounts allocated climbed tenfold, but the supply of communal funding never approached the perceived needs or demands of the Orthodox. The Orthodox prayer-houses considered themselves to be the poor stepchildren of the Kultusgemeinde.

At least 15 percent of the men elected to the Kultusgemeinde board during the interwar years belonged to Orthodox houses of worship. This percentage is probably less than the Orthodox proportion of the population, but higher than the actual Orthodox vote would seem to warrant. Most Liberal board members, and probably most of the Zionists as well, affiliated with the large communal synagogues, yet several deputies elected to the Kultusgemeinde on non-Orthodox tickets, including at least one Socialist, also served as officers of Orthodox congregations. Twelve individuals, six Agudists, three Mizrachists, and two "independent Orthodox" won election on separate Orthodox tickets or else as part of electoral coalitions during the interwar era. The larger Orthodox synagogues, Adas Jisroel and Beth Israel, had their own spokesmen on the board on a regular basis; the smaller prayer-houses were represented only sporadically. The Hasidim had no presence on the communal council whatsoever. In general, the problem facing the Orthodox was not lack of representation, but lack of sufficient influence.

Orthodox candidates in communal elections were on the whole slightly younger than the Liberals, but older than the Zionists and the Socialists. (See Table 9.) The elder statesman of the Kultusgemeinde from 1920 to 1932 was Wolf Pappenheim, born in 1848, the highest ranking Agudah leader, whereas the youngest Orthodox candidate was Leo Landau, born in 1891, the president of Beth Israel who headed the "Apolitical" list. Like the Liberals and the Social Democrats, the Agudah chose their top communal leaders from among their older members, whereas the Mizrachi and the "Apoliticals," like the Jewish Nationalists, drew their most prominent figures from among younger elements.

Roughly 60 percent of Vienna's Orthodox lived in Leopoldstadt, an estimate borne out by the Orthodox candidates in communal elections. (See Table 9.) The Orthodox were much more likely than any other group of candidates to live in Leopoldstadt and less likely to reside in other more prestigious parts of the city. This probably indicates a lower socioeconomic status for the Orthodox as compared to other communal leadership factions, but some wealthier Orthodox leaders may well have chosen to remain within close walking distance of their religious institutions.

The Orthodox electoral candidates exhibited a somewhat different occupational stratification than did candidates on the various other lists. The Orthodox leaders were very heavily concentrated in commerce. Fully three-quarters of them, as compared to 37 percent of the Liberals, 44 percent of the Zionists, and 52 percent of the Socialists, fell into the category of businessmen. Fewer than 1 percent of the Orthodox were white collar employees, as compared to 24 percent of the Liberals, 19 percent of the Zionists, and 17 percent of the Socialists. They were also much less likely than other candidates to be professionals; only 10 percent of them, nearly all Mizrachists and Independents, can be so classified. (See Table 9.) Less than ten percent—five Mizrachists, four Independents, and two Agudists—bore the title of doctor. As a group, the Orthodox leadership would appear less educated, less affluent, and less upwardly mobile than their Liberal, Zionist, and probably their Socialist counterparts as well.

The split among the Orthodox between the "Hungarians" and the "Poles" can be clearly discerned within their communal leadership cadres. As far as can be ascertained, virtually all individuals associated with Adas Jisroel/Agudat Israel leadership circles originated from former Hungarian territories, especially Slovakia. By contrast, all of the Mizrachi candidates running for communal office in 1928 were Easterners and only one was born in Vienna. Of the eight candidates on the independent "Apolitical" list the same year, all except one had been born in Galicia, while the lone exception was from Rumania. Thus, Westerners and Easterners consistently ran on separate religious lists. The Orthodox, whether leaders or followers, were much less likely than Socialists, Liberals, or even Zionists to be native-born Viennese.[18] (See Table 3.)

Interestingly enough, Moravians by birth never appeared on religious slates, even though individuals such as Josef Ticho and Ernst Feldsberg, both Liberals, Josef Löwy, a Social Democrat, and Desider Friedmann, the Jewish Nationalist, were among the more traditional Kultusgemeinde board members both in background and orientation. The "Hungarians" on the one hand and the "Poles" on the other therefore monopolized Orthodox lay leadership within the Kultusgemeinde, with the former most often siding with their fellow Westerners, the Liberals, and the latter with their fellow Easterners, the Zionists.

World War I marked an important turning point with respect to Orthodox involvement in Kultusgemeinde politics. Before the war, the Orthodox had no formal representation on the communal council; the Hungarian Orthodox had de facto opted out of communal affairs since the 1870s and the more recently arrived Galician Orthodox remained largely disorganized and disenfranchised. During and after the war both the "Hungarians" and the "Poles" began to emerge from their relative isolation, publish their own newspapers, strengthen their own organizations, and consider fielding their own candidates in communal elections. In general, the Westerners proved somewhat more effective than the Easterners in making their voice heard in the cacophony of interwar Viennese Jewish communal politics.

One long-standing bone of contention between the Hungarian Orthodox and the Viennese Jewish Establishment involved recognition of the legitimacy of the communal rabbinate. In 1914, Chief Rabbi Moritz Güdemann, a religious conservative who was already over eighty years of age, indicated to the Kultusgemeinde leadership that he wished to retire from the pulpit.[19] A lengthy quest for a successor resulted in the hiring of Hirsch (Zvi) Perez Chajes, an outstanding candidate, but a somewhat unusual choice for a body then almost wholly composed of Liberals.[20]

Chajes had been born in 1876 into a highly esteemed rabbinic family in Brody in eastern Galicia. He obtained his early education at heder and yeshiva and never attended a gymnasium, instead covering the secular courses on his own with a tutor. In 1894, he began studying at the University of Vienna and the Israelite Theological Seminary, which former Chief Rabbi Adolf Jellinek had established the previous year. Four years later he completed his doctoral dissertation and soon after he became ordained. In 1902 Chajes received an appointment as professor of Bible and Jewish history at the Italian Rabbinical College in Florence, where he also taught Hebrew at the university and published a wide range of scholarly works. In 1911 he became Chief Rabbi of the Jewish community of Trieste. It took a considerable amount of persuasion to convince Chajes to return to Vienna.[21]

Initially, at least, the Orthodox did not object to the newly appointed Chief Rabbi. They had to acknowledge that he was eminently qualified for the job "in most respects" and had an excellent reputation which extended beyond the borders of Austria. A serious scholar and a man of great knowledge, he had made a worthy contribution to Jewish learning. Moreover, as the scion of an eminent rabbinical family he was familiar with "authentic Judaism from a primary source," as one article in the Agudah-oriented press phrased it.[22]

Like Güdemann, Chajes was definitely a conservative in his personal religious practices, and fundamentally opposed to religious reform. His aim was to combat assimilation through a revival of true Jewish religiosity, both in the home and in the synagogue. While he made few changes in the liturgy at the main Seitenstettengasse temple, he did reinstate the Kol Nidre prayer on the Day of Atonement, as well as the repetition of the Amidah or "silent prayer," which included references to a return to Zion. Unlike his predecessors, he wore a flat kipa or skullcap rather than a dome-shaped biretta, and he wrapped himself openly in a traditional *tallit* or prayer shawl. Thus Chajes leaned toward the religious right in his personal observance and scrupulously followed Jewish law. He was also sensitive to the needs of conservative Jews and willing to protect their interests. On this basis, the Orthodox had little real ground for complaint.[23]

But Chajes's outspoken pronouncements of progressive views generated a great deal of controversy among the Orthodox and the Liberals as well. He was a man of great integrity who could not be muzzled. Not only was he an ardent Zionist, he was a democrat to the core and a convinced pacifist.[24] Moreover, Chajes was an electrifying orator. His sermons came from the heart and addressed the problems of the day, be they hunger, antisemitic student riots, or events in Palestine. As he himself once said, "I do not speak what I want to speak but what I must speak, that which my inner being dictates." His sermons drew crowds, including younger congregants who might not normally have attended synagogue.[25] People felt compelled to listen to Chajes, even if they did not always agree with what he said.

The Kultusgemeinde leadership had never attempted to censure Rabbi Güdemann for his anti-Zionist political statements, but they strongly objected to Chajes's Zionist activities. His original contract contained a clause that stated: "It is taken for granted that, in the interest of unity and peace in the community, the rabbi will refrain from any partisan political agitation."[26] Evidently Chajes and the Liberal leadership interpreted these words differently. In October 1918, two months after his arrival, during a private audience with Emperor Karl, Chajes defended the necessity of recreating a Jewish homeland in Palestine, even though a majority of Jews would remain as loyal citizens in the diaspora.[27] This event, along with Chajes's pro-Zionist sermons, generated numerous private and public complaints about the new Chief Rabbi, as well as demands for his resignation.[28]

The Liberal furor eventually calmed down and Chajes continued to express his ideas freely and play a prominent role in Zionist affairs. Some opposition remained, especially among the Hungarian Orthodox camp, which periodically attacked the Chief Rabbi, accusing him of implying that the Torah was no longer sovereign in Israel and that most of the Shulchan Aruch, the seventeenth century authoritative code of Jewish law, was antiquated.[29] Nevertheless, by the time of his sudden death in 1927, Chajes had won the respect, if not the love, of the vast majority of Viennese Jews.

The Hungarian Orthodox

The most vocal segment of Viennese Orthodoxy during the interwar period was to be found within the Hungarian Adas Jisroel or Schiff-schul community, whose leadership became virtually identical with that of the Austrian branch of the international Orthodox anti-Zionist organization Agudat Israel. In 1915, a paper called *Jüdische Korrespondenz* began to appear as a "weekly for Jewish interests," representing the religious viewpoint. After the war it evolved into the official Agudah organ in Vienna and merged with a Slovak Orthodox paper called *Jüdische Presse*, providing political commentary, news of the Agudah and its activities, and a variety of articles appropriate for the religious reader.[30]

In February 1918, *Jüdische Korrespondenz* announced an upcoming conference of Austrian Orthodoxy to be held in Vienna. This would mark the beginning of a new epoch for observant Jews in the monarchy, it declared, and serve as the first outward sign of life of this segment of Austrian Jewry, bringing the fragmented Orthodox community together in order to claim the power of their numbers.[31]

The conference adopted a motion to create an organization made up of all observant Jews living in the Austrian Empire and passed a number of resolutions which shed light on the main concerns of the Orthodox. First, they demanded of the authorities the broadest consideration of Sabbath rest, so that Jewish tradesmen, as well as Jewish employees and workers, who observed the Sabbath should have the opportunity to earn their living on Sunday. Jewish soldiers and those sick in hospitals, as well as prisoners, should have access to kosher food. The Orthodox supported demands for complete equality of Jews in both political and economic spheres, but they also demanded that observant Jews have the opportunity to follow a religious way of life and satisfy their religious needs in accordance with appropriate religious autonomy. In this regard, they demanded that Jewish communities establish all institutions on a strictly religious basis, that appropriate religious instruction be provided for children from observant families, and that the Orthodox have complete freedom to satisfy their religious needs with support from communal funding. Finally, the Orthodox viewed the Jewish settlement of Palestine as a fulfillment of a religious obligation as well as a means of improving Jewish economic life. They wanted to have a decisive influence in building up the Holy Land as a religious spiritual center based on the further growth of the Old Yishuv, the traditional Orthodox community in Palestine, rather than the secular Zionist New Yishuv.[32]

The Hungarian Orthodox press challenged the right of the Jewish Nationalists to speak on behalf of Austrian Jewry. When the Zionists submitted their demands to the Austrian government early in 1918, *Jüdische Korrespondenz* responded adversely, fearing that such efforts would only worsen the problems facing Austrian Jewry as a whole. The Orthodox were ambivalent about the recognition of Jews as a separate nationality. They accepted the national element in Judaism as a given, since they rejected assimilationism, but they considered the religious element as primary. In their minds, a guarantee of religious rights was much more important than the assurance of national rights. The Orthodox, like the Zionists, wanted to eliminate the regulation invalidating the use of Hebrew and Yiddish in legal documents and they acknowledged the need to clarify the issue of whether Hebrew or Yiddish should be recognized as the official Jewish language. From the Orthodox point of view, Hebrew was the holy tongue which should only be revived when all Jews returned to the land of their fathers in messianic times. Therefore, they opted for the right of Eastern Jews to use Yiddish, even though the Hungarian Orthodox in Vienna themselves spoke German. Furthermore, they resisted national education as a substitute for religious training. The education of Jewish youth must be in a strictly religious vein; no watering down would be tolerated. Rabbis who studied at yeshivot or Orthodox rabbinical schools should enjoy the same job opportunities as those with secular education trained at non-Orthodox rabbinical seminaries. Finally, these Orthodox were adamantly opposed to a federation of Jewish communities, and promised to fight it with all their strength. Despite the possible political and economic advantages of such a Jewish umbrella organization, no guarantees were available against majority rule and the Orthodox were unwilling to buy unity at the expense of their religious autonomy.[33]

The Hungarian Orthodox remained consistent in their staunch opposition to the Jewish Nationalists throughout the interwar period and forged political alliances with the Liberals in an attempt to thwart the Zionists from achieving their goals. In the 1919 national and municipal elections, their paper advocated voting for Democratic, rather than Jewish Nationalist, candidates. One rather atypical editorial did recommend that Orthodox voters in the Vienna Northeast district cast their ballots for the National Assembly in favor of the Jewish Nationalist list, headed by Robert Stricker, but it went on to castigate the Jewish National Council for giving dangerous electoral advice with regard to voting only for candidates who supported recognition of a Jewish nation.[34]

The voice of Orthodoxy applauded the election of the Democrat Rudolf Schwarz-Hiller to the city council, but not the victories of three Jewish Nationalists, Jakob Ehrlich, Leopold Plaschkes, and Bruno Pollack von Parnau. The Jewish Nationalist Party had grounds to rejoice at their success, it claimed, but Viennese Jewry as a whole could not receive it with unmixed joy. If 13,000 votes gave legitimacy to the Jewish Nationalists to speak in the name of Viennese Jewry, the lead article went on to say, then the Social Democrats, who surely received many more Jewish votes, were much more justified in claiming to be representatives of the Jewish electorate. The Orthodox press advised the Jewish Nationalists to moderate their rhetoric a bit, since they were still not masters of the Jewish street in Vienna. They had only circumstances to thank for their victory, since no other outspokenly Jewish candidates opposed them.[35] In 1923, despite repeated appeals for Orthodox support, the Agudah refused to endorse the Liberal–Jewish Nationalist electoral coalition.[36]

The Orthodox voter in postwar Vienna confronted the same dilemmas as other Jewish voters in the Austrian capital, only more so. *Jüdische Korrespondenz* readily identified the problem at the outset of the period, but its editors could not suggest a viable solution. On the one hand, Jews had to prevent the Christian Socials from holding on to the reins of power in the city, but on the other, the Socialists posed an economic danger for self-employed small businessmen.[37] As in Poland, the Agudah supporters strongly believed that identification with the Left was contrary to Jewish political interests and might weaken their leverage with the antisemitic Right, which might be more willing to make religious concessions to Jews.[38]

For what party could an Orthodox Jew vote, especially if he or she was unwilling to vote Jewish Nationalist and if voting Liberal essentially meant wasting a vote? Initially some Orthodox undoubtedly followed the advice of *Jüdische Korrespondenz* and voted Liberal, but eventually most Orthodox, like most Viennese Jews, probably came to cast their ballots for the Social Democrats, whether they liked the idea or not. *Jüdische Presse*, the successor to *Jüdische Korrespondenz*, generally refrained from endorsing any party in Austrian elections.[39]

When the Christian Socials outlawed the Social Democratic Party and established a Christian corporate state in February 1934, a most illuminating editorial, entitled "Back to the Religious Homeland," appeared on the front page of the newest mouthpiece for Hungarian Orthodoxy, *Unser Wort*. The leitmotif of this paper, the article stated, was to obey the commandment not to take part in the political battles of non-Jewish parties, not out of timidity but in accordance with an ancient Jewish tradition. The Orthodox press had not rejoiced when Social Democracy was at its height, nor did it criticize it at its tragic end, since one should not speak ill of the dead. The leaders of the Austrian Social Democratic Party were mainly non-Jews, but even those accused of being Jews had very little in common with Judaism. They were renegades and hence extremely harmful to other Jews. *Unser Wort* regretted what it claimed was a relatively small number of Jews who had gone astray and appealed to them to return to the fold now that Austria was a religiously based state.[40]

Orthodox Jews had no grounds to regret the passing of the party state, *Unser Wort* asserted, since finding a place in political life had not been easy in postwar Austria. An unbridgeable chasm of an ideological nature separated the Orthodox from all free-thinking parties, whether middle-class or socialist. They needed a conservative party with interconfessional views, which unfortunately never existed. The editorial ended with the hope that the new corporate state would better serve the needs of religious Jews than the old parliamentary republic. The Orthodox could count on a state based on the premises of the recent papal encyclical, *Quadragesimo Anno*, to embrace confessional tolerance and reject racial antisemitism, it maintained.[41] While these views must be understood in the particular political context in which they were written, they reflect a basic aversion not only to the Socialists but also to the democratic process in general, which was scarcely atypical of much of Orthodox Jewry. The Orthodox were generally much more concerned about preserving their own religious lifestyle than maintaining a system of majority rule within which they constituted an ineffective minority.

While the Agudah-type Orthodox might not have publicly expressed their antipathy toward Socialism very often, they were much less reticent about openly declaring their antagonism against Zionism in any form, whether secular Jewish Nationalism or Religious Zionism in the form of Mizrachi. In December 1918, Adas Jisroel called a meeting of Orthodox groups in Vienna in order to oppose a pro-Zionist resolution recently adopted by a gathering of Galician Hasidic Jews[42] and to organize a campaign for "Yischub Erez-Jisroel," the settlement of Palestine by observant Jews. One Schiffschul spokesman emphasized the great importance of the Holy Land for Jews and Judaism. Another talked of creating a homeland for the oppressed and the persecuted. The Orthodox shared that goal with the Zionists, he said, but not their social and economic attitudes which excluded religion. The Orthodox wanted a Jewish settlement, not a settlement of Jews. They did not want to be the victims of a bloody war but spiritual conquerors instead. Wolf Pappenheim, a long-standing opponent of Zionism who before the war had been active in the Vienna branch of the ITO (Jewish Territorialist Organization),[43] delivered the main address. He claimed that the Zionists, busy with *Gegenwartsarbeit*, had neither the time nor the means to look after the poor and the needy in Palestine. The Orthodox must go their own way, he insisted, and conduct widespread activities on behalf of Palestine. Colonization must be in accordance with the spirit of the Holy Land and nothing must be done contrary to Jewish law.[44] The ultra-Orthodox vehemently opposed the idea of creating a secular Jewish state in Palestine.

By the end of 1919, the organization which grew out of this meeting had officially decided to join the world organization of Agudat Israel and adopted its name.[45] Like Orthodox leaders in postwar Slovakia and elsewhere, the Hungarian Orthodox in Vienna realized that the help of a powerful international body would be needed to fight the forces of irreligion that seemed to be gaining the upper hand on the Jewish scene and to counteract secular Zionism. In practice, this measure was tantamount to a merger between the Adas Jisroel and Agudat Israel. Not only were their names similar, but so were most of their leadership and supporters. While an Agudah women's auxiliary existed in Austria on paper only, an active youth network developed, with its largest branch located in Leopoldstadt.[46] Membership in Agudat Israel and its various affiliated groups had reached an estimated 2,300 by the end of the interwar period.[47]

In the immediate aftermath of World War I, a basic choice confronted the members of the Schiffschul community. Should they remain isolated from the Kultusgemeinde as they had done for almost fifty years, looking after their own affairs, including kosher slaughtering, or should they enter into the politics of the communal boardroom with the hope of successfully promoting Orthodox interests? While some favored complete secession, a majority reached the decision to follow the second course of action, temporarily at least.[48]

With the creation of the statutory reform commission in late 1918, the winds of change were blowing on Seitenstettengasse and the Orthodox clearly resented being left out of the decision-making process. The progressives and the nationalists must not decide the future shape of the Kultusgemeinde without consulting the third, and surely not the smallest, faction, sputtered an editorial in *Jüdische Korrespondenz*. Orthodox interests had to be taken into consideration.[49] But such protests were to no avail, since the Orthodox still lacked official representation on the communal board.

The introduction of proportional representation offered an opportunity for the first time of running an independent Orthodox list and electing several candidates who would truly represent observant Jews, without having to compromise their Orthodoxy. The Hungarian Orthodox justified their change of policy vis-à-vis the Kultusgemeinde by claiming that up until then they had been able to get along outside its framework quite well, but a dangerous new situation had arisen within the community. Radical, aggressive groups, i.e., the secular Jewish Nationalists, were striving to oust the easy-going Liberals from office. Therefore it seemed necessary for the Orthodox to adopt new tactics to protect religious interests, since their old ways were perhaps outmoded and no longer practical.[50]

In November 1919 a general meeting of the Schiffschul took place in order to formulate a policy toward the upcoming communal elections. The Orthodox decided to run their own separate list instead of joining the Liberal-sponsored slate, which called itself the "United Electoral Committee of Non-Jewish Nationalist Parties."[51] They put their reasoning into rhyme as follows: "Die Alten können wir nicht wählen, / Auch mit den Nationalen können wir nicht zählen, / Denn Kultus ist nicht Politik und nicht Partei, / Wir wählen 'Glaubenstreu,' dass uns schon Hilfe sei." (For the old [guard] we cannot vote, / Also with the Nationalists we cannot count ourselves, / For religion is not politics and parties, / We vote Orthodox, so that there should be help for us.)[52]

On the eve of the 1920 elections, the Adas Jisroel–sponsored list issued a campaign statement explaining its position and presenting its communal platform. The preamble announced: "We submit before the electorate for the first time an independent list of Torah-true Jews. Social position, secular knowledge, and character alone are not enough to enable one to lead Jewish communal life and we want to document [the fact] that the Kultusgemeinde is first and foremost a religious body which logically should only be led by men who know and follow Jewish law and Jewish teachings."[53]

The Orthodox program made several demands. First, institutions used by all communal members must meet the strictest requirements of kashrut. Second, the conduct of religious affairs must be in the "authentic" Jewish spirit and subventions to Orthodox prayer-houses should be increased. Its third and perhaps most radical demand pertained to compulsory Jewish education. Religious instruction which trains the youth in the Holy Scriptures as teachings and law should be suitably designed to educate religious Jews. If not, then a dispensation should be given to Jewish pupils in public schools whose parents wanted their children religiously educated, so that they did not have to attend "official religious instruction which to date is worthless both as to its curriculum as well as its content, and had only harmful effects due to irreligious teachers." The statement concluded with the hope and expectation that every religious Jew would vote for this list and that all those who were interested in having a Jewish community that was "really Jewish" would do the same.[54]

The list of the "United Religious Jews of Vienna" was headed by Wolf Pappenheim, the seventy-two-year-old Pressburg-born vice-president of Adas Jisroel, who later also served as president of the Viennese branch of the Agudah. While this group claimed to speak on behalf of all Orthodox Jews in Vienna, de facto it represented primarily the "Hungarian" segment.[55] This list was the only separate Orthodox slate to run in the 1920 elections. Nevertheless, the ticket only managed to draw 878 votes, 8 percent of the total cast in that election. This not particularly impressive result netted the Orthodox three out of the thirty-six seats on the communal council.[56] Pappenheim won election to a one-year term on the executive council, but was not subsequently reelected to that body during his first four years on the board. The Orthodox faction was not well represented on the various subcommittees either, although at least one of its members served on the religious affairs committee.[57] Thus, during their first term on the Kultusgemeinde, the Orthodox were not able to implement very much of their program or achieve a great deal of influence.

In the fall of 1923, the long-standing dispute between the Schiffschul contingent and the Kultusgemeinde openly flared up again and the Hungarian Orthodox threatened to secede from the community. Ostensibly, a Rosh Hashanah sermon of Chief Rabbi Chajes provided the excuse for the confrontation, since the Orthodox took exception to its content. The Schiffschul representatives on the communal board reiterated their position that their community, centered around Adas Jisroel, did not recognize the authority of the Viennese rabbinate in general and of Chief Rabbi Chajes in particular. They proceeded to issue a four-point ultimatum. First, they demanded that the Kultusgemeinde grant separate recognition to the rabbis connected with Adas Jisroel, which would enable them to perform divorces, chalitzah (exemptions from levirate marriages), and all other rabbinic functions independently. Second, they demanded that public elementary and middle school pupils associated with Adas Jisroel and affiliated Orthodox prayer-houses should be exempted from religious instruction taught by Kultusgemeinde-appointed instructors. Unless this were allowed, they felt that the Orthodox would not be able to exercise their constitutionally guaranteed freedom of religion. They could not turn over their pupils to instruction by Kultusgemeinde-sponsored teachers if the highest spiritual leader of the community presented in his sermons an areligious point of view not based on the sanctity of the Torah, they insisted. Third, they demanded that the Schiffschul community be granted equal rights with the semiautonomous Sephardic community, which was technically part of the Kultusgemeinde but enjoyed a special self-governing status and relief from payment of communal taxes. Finally, the Hungarian Orthodox deputies demanded that a part of the new Jewish cemetery be set aside for the ultra-Orthodox. In this section would be interred only the bodies of those individuals who during their lifetime had adhered strictly to religious legal requirements. The rabbinate of Adas Jisroel should have final say in the maintenance and supervision of this area. The Orthodox representatives considered their requests urgent and wanted them dealt with immediately. They regarded an accommodation to their four demands as a last chance for the Orthodox to remain within the Kultusgemeinde, thereby avoiding dissolution of the unified Jewish community. The communal council did not respond to this crisis situation with great alacrity, however.[58]

The Schiffschul ultimatum helped bring into focus the inner divisions among Viennese Orthodoxy. In response, a deputation of "Torah-true organizations of Vienna," uniting under the name Achduth Israel (unity of Israel), submitted a resolution to the presidium of the Israelitische Kultusgemeinde signed by twenty-two Orthodox prayer-houses, insisting that no concessions be made to the Agudah in reaction to its threat of secession. A spokesman for Beth Israel, the largest Polish synagogue, declared that Orthodox Jewry of Vienna opposed the "small group of men" who were attempting to "shake the foundations of the Kultusgemeinde" and threaten its unity. Likewise, a representative from Machsike Hadath, one of the oldest Orthodox prayer-houses in the Inner City, announced that the Orthodox must help to preserve the unity of the community and reject the attempts of the Hungarian separatists.[59]

Shortly thereafter, Adas Jisroel called a meeting of the boards of all Orthodox prayer-houses to organize a "Federation of Orthodox Prayer-House Associations of Vienna for Protection of the Interests and Safeguarding the Rights of Viennese Orthodoxy." Representatives of a dozen prayer-houses attended, including Machsike Hadath and two Hasidic shtiebels, as well as several Hungarian congregations known to be sympathetic to the Schiffschul. According to the report in *Jüdische Presse*, the Agudah paper, all participants supported the actions of Adas Jisroel. It was well known, one spokesman claimed, that the "entire world" regarded Adas Jisroel as the "sole effective representative of true Jewish Orthodoxy in Vienna" and that all of its institutions were the most authentically Orthodox.[60]

It is extremely doubtful, however, whether the boards of all the prayer-houses which sent representatives to this meeting actually backed the Schiffschul agenda. Two weeks later, delegates from some thirty Orthodox prayer-houses adopted a unanimous resolution to submit an open letter to the Kultusgemeinde board to protest once again the separatist demands of the Schiffschul and insist that no concessions be made to them. This sharply worded statement attacked Adas Jisroel as an "insignificant separatist group" and denied its claim to represent Viennese Orthodoxy. While the Orthodox comprised many thousands of people, it asserted, the Schiffschul with its several hundred supporters constituted a dwindling minority. The letter further maintained that granting special privileges to the Schiffschul minority ran contrary to the basic principles of Orthodoxy. The prayer-house associations whose representatives signed this statement claimed to speak in the name of the overwhelming majority of Torah-true Jews of Vienna.[61]

Most prayer-houses which had received subventions from the Kultusgemeinde in the past, or expected to do so in the future, preferred to remain within the communal framework. By contrast, a few Hungarian congregations affiliated with the Schiffschul, which did not normally accept communal subsidies except for certain educational purposes, felt they had little to lose in continuing to back Adas Jisroel and its demands for increased autonomy. Therefore, only a relatively small, albeit significant, minority among the Orthodox, predominantly made up of Jews of Hungarian origin, were actually willing to go along with a threat to secede if the ultimatum to the Kultusgemeinde board failed.

It was not until late June 1924, almost nine months after the furor had begun, that Chief Rabbi Chajes and the executive committee of the Kultusgemeinde responded formally to the Schiffschul demands. Chajes protested that a High Holyday sermon could hardly be considered as an official pronouncement of the communal rabbinate. He differentiated between his role as chairman of the rabbinical collegium and as a rabbi lecturing from the pulpit, speaking for himself. That he was a progressive in his ideas and his scholarly activity was well known before his appointment, he pointed out, but there was no contradiction between his personal freedom of expression and his desire to protect the interests of conservative Jews.[62]

The Orthodox request that was easiest to meet, Chajes felt, was that the institutions of the Kultusgemeinde be accessible to all Jews. He had supported this notion ever since his arrival five years earlier and had attempted to introduce strictly kosher kitchens in public Jewish facilities wherever possible. Chajes himself was dissatisfied with the quality of religious instruction in the public schools, but a collective exemption of the children of Orthodox parents from such classes was not a practical solution, in his opinion. According to the Chief Rabbi, the demand for a separate cemetery section for the Orthodox was not justified and any comparison of the Schiffschul situation with that of the Turkish Israelite (or Sephardic) community was simply inappropriate. With respect to a completely independent rabbinate, the demand of Adas Jisroel might perhaps have been legitimate if the communal rabbinate were in principle Liberal or if tradition and Jewish law were not being followed, but such was not the case, Chajes asserted, since the rabbinate was extremely strict in questions of divorce and other such issues. The Schiffschul community had been granted their own shechitah (kosher slaughtering) in the past, but reasons no longer existed for such a distinction, he maintained. In fact, since the communal rabbinate adopted a strict orientation with regard to all ritual affairs, there was no need whatsoever for an independent Orthodox rabbinate. Chajes had appealed to Adas Jisroel and related Orthodox groups in the past and invited their rabbis to join the local board of rabbis, but they had repeatedly rejected his offer. The Chief Rabbi was very willing to expand the already large Viennese communal rabbinate if this would better meet the needs of the Orthodox.[63]

Following the general guidelines suggested by Chajes, the Kultus-gemeinde executive committee, which lacked Orthodox representation at that time, adopted a series of resolutions in an attempt to address the issues raised in the Orthodox ultimatum. They acquiesced that all institutions supported by the Israelitische Kultusgemeinde Wien should conduct themselves in such a manner that all elements of the Jewish population would be able to use them. The requests of parents that children be exempted from religious instruction in the public schools would be dealt with, as before, on an individual rather than a collective basis, but such cases would be treated sympathetically. The executive committee was willing to approve either the expansion of the so-called Schomer Shabbos section already existing in the cemetery or the creation of another such corner, where no mausoleums or decorations would be allowed and German inscriptions would be discouraged. Admittance to this area would be made by request of the deceased or their relatives and final decisions would rest with the Kultusgemeinde. The executive also approved the suggestion to increase the membership of the rabbinical collegium, with Orthodox Jews naming their recommendations for the new positions. However, they rejected out of hand the demand for autonomy similar to that of the Sephardic community.[64] Thus, the Kultusgemeinde granted further concessions to the Orthodox with respect to kashrut in Jewish public institutions and a separate section of the cemetery, but the Orthodox had not really improved their situation appreciably, especially when viewed from the perspective of the Schiffschul faction. After all, the determination of the standards of kashrut and admission to the Schomer Shabbos sector of the cemetery remained in the hands of the communal rabbinate, which Adas Jisroel refused to join.

When their secessionist threats failed to achieve their desired goals, the Hungarian Orthodox leadership decided to change their tactics for the 1924 communal elections. Instead of fighting the Liberals as before, they would join them—and the Jewish Nationalists—in a coalition in order at least to preserve the status quo, if not actually improve their position within the Kultusgemeinde. While the Schiffschul representatives on the communal board had not succeeded in implementing their essential demands, they claimed to have brought about a greater understanding of Orthodox needs than had previously existed. The Agudah faction agreed to join an electoral partnership with its erstwhile opponents, but not to give up any of its principles.[65]

For an Agudah-oriented group to work together with Liberals to attain common goals was not an entirely unprecedented phenomenon. Gershon Bacon, in his study of Agudat Israel in Poland, alludes to an alliance between the Hasidim and the assimilationist communal leadership in Warsaw in the early twentieth century. The major political battles which the Agudah fought within the Jewish community in Austria, as in Poland, proved in many respects identical with the agenda of the Liberals. Both groups fought against the introduction of a *Volksgemeinde* and tried to prevent their adversaries, the Zionists and the Socialists, from altering the basically religious nature and functions of the Kultusgemeinde. Both the Agudists and the Liberals shared the belief that secular Jews should not be in charge of religious institutions and insisted that religious tradition formed the basis of the existence of the Jewish community and the Jewish people. That the Schiffschul faction in Vienna should align itself with the Liberals once autonomy efforts failed was therefore not particularly startling.[66] That it should agree to enter a coalition which included secular Jewish Nationalists seems much more amazing.

The Agudists quickly came to regret their decision to join this electoral alliance, especially once two rival Galician Orthodox groups submitted their own lists of candidates. The Agudists considered this unanticipated turn of events very regrettable from an Orthodox standpoint since it split the observant community internally. The Agudah press urged all Orthodox to go to the polls and vote for the joint list which included the trusted defenders of Orthodoxy.[67] But the Orthodox clearly played only a very minor role in this alliance. Wolf

Pappenheim, their top candidate, placed only tenth on the list after six Liberals and three Zionists.[68] The Schiffschul Orthodox campaigned on behalf of the coalition, but not with any great conviction or enthusiasm. Their spokesmen did not even officially endorse the common platform upon which the "United Jewish Parties" slate was running.[69]

The results of this election scarcely pleased the Agudists, even though the number of Orthodox representatives on the communal council had actually doubled from three to six. How many Orthodox voters cast their ballots for the coalition list remains in doubt, but one can assume that most of the "Hungarians" did so, if they bothered to vote at all. The Agudists, with three mandates, proved to be the only group within the electoral alliance which did not lose any of the seats they had previously held. The two Galician Orthodox lists combined received 1,394 votes or 9 percent of the total. (See Table 6.) This amounted to over 50 percent more votes than the Agudist United Religious slate had polled in the last election, but the overall explicitly Orthodox share of the vote had not increased significantly. Undoubtedly it was the "Poles," especially the recently enfranchised Galician newcomers, who voted for the Mizrachist Religious bloc and Beth Israel's Achduth Israel, however, rather than the "Hungarians." The former slate obtained two seats on the communal council and the latter, one.[70] The *Jüdische Presse* saw this growth in Orthodox representation not as an Orthodox victory but as a failure, a lack of self-confidence, and an inability on the part of the Orthodox to organize effectively. In Agudist eyes, six Orthodox deputies would not serve to strengthen their cause but to weaken it due to internal fragmentation and insufficient support for the true Orthodox leadership.[71]

While still dreaming of secession, the Hungarian Orthodox had in fact become part of the Liberal Establishment within the Kultusgemeinde. On December 29, 1924, the constituent meeting of the new communal board took place, chaired by Wolf Pappenheim, its oldest member. As a token of gratitude for his willingness to enter the coalition, Pappenheim won election to the eight-person executive committee by an almost unanimous vote. He was to serve on that body continuously for the next eight years. One Orthodox representative briefly chaired the religious affairs committee, whereas the other two served as regular members of this committee and of other committees as well. Thus, during their second term on the communal board the Schiffschul representatives participated more actively in committee work. They made their wishes heard and sometimes even gained minor victories for the Orthodox.[72]

During this period special commissions for religious and ritual affairs and for kashrut came into being, both made up of communal rabbis and Orthodox nominees. The hospital and the old age home instituted rabbinically approved dietary supervision, and a strictly controlled tagging system was introduced for kosher meat. Nevertheless, Adas Jisroel continued to maintain its own "hashgachah" or oversight of ritual slaughtering, which provided a significant portion of the kosher meat in Vienna. In 1927, the Kultusgemeinde took over control and maintenance, as well as renovation, of the mikvah or ritual bath, which in recent years had been run largely under the auspices of an Agudah-dominated committee.[73] The Orthodox had thus made some progress within the larger community. Given the general improvement in relations between the Agudists and the Liberals, it came as little surprise when the two anti-Zionist groups decided to renew their alliance on the eve of the 1928 elections.[74]

A similar modus vivendi did not develop between the Agudists and the Jewish Nationalists. Even though the joint platform upon which the three coalition partners had run in 1924 pledged that they would work together for the rebuilding of Palestine, the Agudists showed absolutely no indication of complying on that score. In 1925, the Kultusgemeinde board authorized a 20,000 schillings contribution to Keren Hayessod, the Palestine Foundation Fund, in honor of the opening of the Hebrew University.[75] The main objection to this allocation came from Wolf Pappenheim, who protested vociferously against donating communal tax monies for Jewish Nationalist purposes, especially for a university in the Holy Land which would teach antireligious views.[76] The following year, when a 50,000 schillings Palestine subvention was proposed, including 7,500 schillings for the Keren Hayishuv fund of Agudat Israel as well as 25,000 schillings for Keren Hayessod, Pappenheim again spoke out in opposition to such a measure and the *Jüdische Presse* also inveighed against it. The Agudah spokesman insisted that the rebuilding of Palestine was not among the statutory duties of the Israelitische Kultusgemeinde Wien and, while the Orthodox paper expressed pride in the success of the Orthodox working on behalf of the Land of Israel, it distinguished between individual support and communal support. The Jewish community had always supported Palestine, it claimed, but never by using communal tax money.[77]

Each year thereafter in his budget speech Pappenheim attacked Zionism in general and the Keren Hayessod in particular and then voted against the entire Palestine subsidy because Zionists fostered irreligiosity in the Holy Land, believing in free love and not providing their children with a proper religious education.[78] Despite Pappenheim's opposition, Keren Hayessod and Keren Hayishuv continued to receive communal subventions, as did other Palestine funds, including by the mid-thirties Keren Hamizrachi, which was allocated twice as much as its Agudah counterpart.[79] Meanwhile, at all times the Agudists attempted to discredit not only the secular Jewish

Nationalists but also the Mizrachists, whom they denounced as illegitimate, both religiously and in terms of their support for Zionism.

The Galician Orthodox

In Vienna, Orthodox Jews of Galician origin lacked the cohesion of the Hungarian-dominated Schiffschul community. Much more numerous than the Hungarians, the Galicians were fragmented into at least eighty prayer-houses, some of the older ones calling themselves Polish, many of the newer ones explicitly Hasidic, and the rest merely undifferentiated Orthodox, often structured as benevolent societies of Jews from a specific town or district. Some Galicians identified themselves as Religious Zionists, others were non-Zionists, while a few affiliated with the anti-Zionist Agudah. The largest of the Polish synagogues, Beth Israel, attempted to assume a centralizing leadership role similar to that of Adas Jisroel but its efforts never proved very effective or long-lasting. Beth Israel claimed to represent the interests of all Galicians and generally ran its own candidates in communal elections under the rubric of Achduth Israel or the "Apolitical Electoral Alliance."[80]

Unlike the Hungarian Jews in Vienna, who were virtually all Mitnagdim, or opponents of Hasidism, who had migrated in the nineteenth century from the western regions of the former Hungarian lands, many Polish Jews, especially war refugees from eastern Galicia, came from Hasidic backgrounds.[81] The Hasidim remained a group apart in the Austrian capital, setting up at least a dozen prayer-houses, including several dynastic courts in Alsergrund and Leopoldstadt. They rarely became actively involved in local communal politics, although several of their rabbinic leaders supported the Agudah. Some of their more established prayer-houses received communal subventions and at least three of them signed the 1923 antiseparatist petition, but the Hasidim never expressed a desire to compete for seats on the Kultusgemeinde board, even after they had obtained Austrian citizenship and had become eligible for election.[82]

In addition to the more acculturated "Poles" affiliated with the modern Orthodox Beth Israel and the isolationist Hasidim who had arrived more recently, a third identifiable faction among the Galician Orthodox organized itself around Mizrachi, the religious wing of the World Zionist Organization. A branch of the international Mizrachi association as well as a Mizrachi youth chapter had already constituted itself in Vienna on the eve of World War I,[83] but Religious Zionism never seemed to take a very firm hold in Austria. Religious Zionists played an active part in founding the "Jischub Erez Jisroel" group immediately after the war, but this effort to activate Orthodox

Jews on behalf of Zionist efforts in Palestine fizzled out after being taken over by the Agudah.[84] In 1922, the Agudas Hacharedim, a federation claiming to represent a majority of Orthodox Jews in Vienna, held a meeting to protest against the policies of the Agudah in Palestine. Prominent Mizrachi leaders dominated the gathering and urged the other Galician Orthodox to join the Austrian Mizrachi Federation and work together to rebuild Palestine.[85] Soon after, Mizrachi began publishing its own weekly, *Jüdische Wochenschrift*, which appeared for several years. It also decided to put forth its own slate of candidates for the first time in the 1924 Kultusgemeinde elections. These apparent signs of vitality did not translate themselves into any real strength of effort, either on behalf of Palestine or within the Viennese Jewish community.

Mizrachi remained the weakest element within the framework of Austrian Zionism. As in Poland, it lacked strong leadership and effective organization, often being outmaneuvered by the secular Jewish Nationalists on its left flank or the Agudah on its right.[86] Membership in Austrian Mizrachi never greatly exceeded 1,000 even at its height, and judging by its voting record for World Zionist Congresses, its rosters in Vienna were undoubtedly much more modest during most of the interwar years.[87] (See Table 7.) While Mizrachi had token representation on nearly every Zionist body, including the various Keren Hayessod commissions, there is no evidence of any great stirring of political activity among Austrian Religious Zionists, except periodically around election time.

None of the Galician Orthodox factions fielded a separate list of candidates for the first postwar communal election but a group calling itself the "United Viennese Temple Associations," centered around Beth Israel, published a program for the Kultusgemeinde in 1919. This document's recommendations were not limited to Orthodox interests but could also be endorsed by most Liberals. It defined the tasks of the Kultusgemeinde primarily in religious terms in accordance with the Austrian law of 1890 and emphasized the need for larger subventions for temple and prayer-house associations, but it also made a series of suggestions regarding vocational, as well as religious, education and social welfare. On the one hand, this program stressed that the Kultusgemeinde should not constitute a "political" body, since this would exclude a significant portion of the Jews living in Vienna from participating in communal affairs. "As a cultural community," it insisted, "it cannot be the object of national, social, or political struggle." On the other hand, it seemingly endorsed the Zionist Basle formula by stating that it favored "the acquisition of Palestine as a homeland secured by public law for those Jews who cannot or do not wish to remain in their own homelands." It then added, "Out of respect for tradition, allocations for cultural purposes in Palestine should be budgeted annually by the Kultusgemeinde and contributions for these purposes should also be accepted in the communal synagogues."[88]

This desire to keep "politics," especially Jewish Nationalist politics, out of the communal council became a hallmark of the non-Zionists and of the Beth Israel faction of the Galician Orthodox as well. Nevertheless, this document's solid support for the Zionist cause in Palestine later also characterized the "independent" Orthodox group associated with Beth Israel, which generally agreed with Palestine-centered Zionism but not *Landespolitik.*

The list of candidates running on the official Zionist list in 1920 included several Mizrachi activists, as well as at least three individuals associated with Beth Israel.[89] On the eve of this election, one of the Hasidic prayer-houses called a meeting of "tradition-true" Jews to counter what it referred to as the "misconception" generated by Agudist campaign charges that the Zionists "somehow intended to harm the religious basis of Judaism either in Vienna or anywhere else." One Mizrachist asserted that "a large number of tradition-true Jews are today in the Nationalist camp." Robert Stricker, well known for his secularist views, presented the Zionist religious agenda. The communal board should not decide religious matters; instead such concerns should rest in the hands of authoritative officials, namely the rabbis together with representatives of tradition-true Jews, whether or not they belonged to the board. All communal institutions must be set up in such a manner that the most Orthodox Jews could use them without question. The Jewish Nationalists above all stood for the absolute necessity of unity among the Jewish people. No distinctions should be made between Orthodox and progressives, Easterners and Westerners, he emphasized. The Agudists who were now rallying to protect Orthodox Jewry from the Zionist threat had in the past built barriers between Eastern and Western Jews, instead of working at tearing them down, Stricker claimed. The Zionists were thus casting themselves in the role of true defenders of the interests of Galician-born Orthodox Jews.[90]

Two Mizrachists won election to the communal council in 1920. Neither played a particularly active role on that body, but both served on the special subcommittee which instituted reforms in the supervision of kosher meat.[91] On most issues they voted together with their fellow members of the Zionist Club. However, when electoral reform came before the council on the eve of the 1924 elections, the Religious Zionists, dissenting from party discipline, objected to granting women the right to vote, let alone the right to run for communal office. On this matter the Mizrachists, like the Agudists and most Liberals, remained consistent throughout the interwar period. The Mizrachists, like the other Zionists, heartily approved the restoration of voting rights to male non citizens, however. No longer would "foreigners," i.e., Easterners recently arrived from Galicia, be discriminated against in communal voting, except for their continued ineligibility to run for office.[92] Ironically, one Mizrachist, after serving four years on the board as a Zionist, was prevented from assuming his seat upon reelection on a Mizrachi slate in 1924, since it was discovered after the fact that he had not yet obtained his official Austrian citizenship papers.[93]

The tables had turned for the Orthodox within the Kultusgemeinde in 1924. In 1920 Beth Israel and the Mizrachists had joined forces with the Zionists, while the Schiffschul community had campaigned separately to protect Orthodoxy from the dire threat posed by the progressives and the Jewish Nationalists. In 1924 Adas Jisroel entered the Liberal-Zionist coalition, whereas Achduth Israel, an "independent" Orthodox group centered around Beth Israel, and the Religious Bloc (or Mizrachi) mounted the ramparts in defense of Orthodox interests. Both groups claimed to represent Viennese Orthodoxy in general and the assorted Galician prayer-houses in particular. Indeed, they appealed to almost identical constituencies, but negotiations to unify the two slates failed.

The Mizrachists, claiming to have the backing of thirty-six prayer-houses, campaigned more actively than Achduth Israel and articulated their program more fully. They condemned the Agudah for joining what they called the "unnatural coalition," which they basically saw as a marriage of convenience and a sell-out of religious Jews. They noted how humorous it appeared to see Wolf Pappenheim sharing the same platform as Robert Stricker, ignoring the fact that they themselves had campaigned together with Stricker four years earlier. They also criticized the General Zionists for joining such an incongruous partnership. How would it have been, they asked, if the Religious Zionists had allied themselves with the assimilationists and the Agudists without, or against the wishes of, the non-Mizrachi Zionists? Surely the other Zionists would have considered this a betrayal of Zionist principles, even if the Mizrachists could claim to be acting out of religious motivation. The Mizrachists tried to appeal for the support of both the Zionists and the Orthodox on the grounds that they were the only "strictly kosher" candidates on both scores.[94]

The electoral platform of the Religious Bloc clearly delineated their position as Orthodox Jews, as Zionists, and as Easterners. The only possible basis for maintaining a Jewish community, it asserted, was according to Torah and tradition. Therefore the Kultusgemeinde must support all Jewish religious institutions with communal funds and provide for the religious needs of everyone, even the very poor, free of charge if necessary. Careful supervision of kashrut was necessary, with kosher meat being provided in the communal hospital and its old age home, while ritual baths should be available at accessible prices, especially for the poor. Intensive Jewish education, both religious and national, should supplement the obligatory general religious instruction in the public schools. As Zionists, the Mizrachists demanded that the Kultusgemeinde support the rebuilding of Palestine through financial contributions, since they viewed Eretz Israel as the Jewish homeland and a spiritual center for the diaspora. They emphasized the unity of the Jewish community and the necessity for a unified community which would protect the constitutionally guaranteed rights of Jews and represent all its members regardless of their origin, citizenship, and religious orientation. As Easterners with lower economic status, they were concerned about democratization of the community and all its institutions and an expanded welfare system, as well as a satisfactory standard of living for communal employees. Finally, they supported universal suffrage within the Kultusgemeinde, so that any Jewish male living in Vienna at least one year could enjoy both active and passive voting rights. As Religious Zionists hailing primarily from Galicia, they felt very strongly that every Jew, whether rich or poor, whether native or foreign-born, when coming into contact with the Kultusgemeinde must be able to relate to his brethren on equal terms. The organized Jewish community should no longer tolerate second-class citizenship, except for women, whom they did not mention.[95]

After a heated campaign and despite a rather low voter turnout, the Religious Bloc managed to attract 943 votes (6%), while Achduth Israel received an additional 451 (3%), for a total of 1,394 for the two lists combined. This netted the Galician Orthodox three seats on the communal council, the exact equivalent of what their Hungarian counterparts had obtained through their coalition agreement. (See Table 6.) Their main spokesman was Viktor Bauminger, the vice-president of the Austrian Mizrachi Federation, who had been born in Warsaw in 1889 and thus was thirty-five years of age when first elected to communal office.[96] During his initial term, Bauminger acted as alternate chairman of the religious affairs committee and also served on a wide variety of other committees. He was obviously an eager young volunteer who did not mind attending innumerable meetings. When reelected in 1928, Bauminger was to chair the religious affairs committee, with Wolf Pappenheim as his alternate.[97] This situation must have appeared rather incongruous, given the forty-year disparity in their ages, not to mention their radically different personalities and orientations. Pappenheim was an irascible anti-Zionist, whereas Bauminger sometimes insisted on addressing the Kultusgemeinde board in Hebrew, even though few could understand him and his remarks officially remained off the record.

In his maiden speech before the Kultusgemeinde board in 1924, Bauminger delivered a programmatic statement as to the tasks and duties of this body, which also incorporated the Mizrachi philosophy. First, he declared, Judaism comprises both a religion and a nation; the two are inseparable. Second, the community must assure its own future through the proper education of its youth. Third, the basic principle on which it rests is unity. The communal board cannot tolerate any separatism within its midst. It must take all measures to insure the confidence of all Jews, even the strictest conservatives, but it must always remain sovereign. Lastly, he issued a plea for equality. "Our Torah," he said, "recognizes no maps" or geographical boundaries. "There are neither Polish nor Hungarian Jews; there are only Jews, and all Jews, even Viennese Jews, must identify completely with our unified religious community." The Mizrachi credo, he stated, was "One God, one People, one Land, one language, and one Kultusgemeinde!"[98]

Bauminger's critiques of the Kultusgemeinde during his tenure on the board often assumed a Cassandra-like quality. He once described the communal budget as technically a financial achievement but spiritually bankrupt. He spoke of an annually increasing deficit in Jewish souls in a growing secessionist army. But he expressed little regret at those leaving Judaism, since by and large they were no great loss anyway, in his opinion. He demanded an intensive education of Jewish youth with an emphasis on Hebrew and protested against the barring of Hebrew as an official language by the communal council. Jews did not go to temple, he claimed, because they no longer understood the Hebrew service and hence found it uninteresting and boring. It was impossible, he charged, to inspire the illiterate. While services might be worthy and devout, they were not comprehensible to the average congregant. The communal synagogues should be largely self-supporting, he maintained, but due to lack of interest they required exorbitant subventions. The least frequented synagogues, he pointed out, received the highest subsidies, while the smaller prayer-houses, which were more likely to be filled daily, were allocated minimal funding, if any. Greater support should be given to those Jews who still cared about being Jewish.[99]

In 1928, while the Agudists once again joined forces with the Liberals, the Mizrachists and the independent Orthodox, now calling themselves "Apoliticals," ran on two separate lists, both claiming to be composed of men "for whom nothing Jewish is alien." Support for the two Galician Orthodox slates combined increased only slightly in absolute numbers and actually declined in relative terms. Altogether they received 1,547 votes or 8 percent of the ballots cast, almost evenly split between them. (See Table 6.) Over half of these votes came from Leopoldstadt, where most Galician Orthodox Jews lived.[100] These results proved a disappointment for the Mizrachists since they lost one of their two seats on the communal council. Viktor Bauminger

returned as the single representative of Mizrachi on the Kultusgemeinde board and was joined by Leo Landau.

Born in Przemysl, Galicia, in 1891, Landau came to Vienna in 1909
to study law. Affiliated as a Zionist since his youth, he joined the board
of the Beth Israel in the early twenties, at a time when there was
considerable hostility against Zionists. As Landau relates in his un-
published memoirs, Beth Israel had been created in the 1890s because
Poles were not allowed to hold office in the Hungarian Schiffschul
nearby. Thirty years later, according to Landau, several prominent
Zionists were excluded not only from the board of Beth Israel but even
from membership. Landau, who was not very active in Zionist affairs,
managed to persevere and eventually attained the synagogue's
presidency after a considerable shakeup on the board. Landau not only
helped to legitimize Zionism in the modern Orthodox Polish congrega-
tion, but he also claimed responsibility for the various efforts to
centralize Galician Orthodoxy around Beth Israel. He served as president of the Federation of Temple Associations and also headed the
Association of Conservative Prayer-Houses. During his ten years on
the Kultusgemeinde board, he generally voted together with the
Zionists. He served on various subcommittees and by the end of the
interwar period headed the important social welfare committee, becoming actively involved in refugee work.[101]

The declared purpose of the "Apolitical Electoral Alliance," which
Landau represented and which was backed by Beth Israel and the
Association of Conservative Prayer-Houses called Hitachdut Jereim,
was to "keep politics out of the Kultusgemeinde." Its platform, which
remained constant for several elections, focused on equality for all
Jews in Vienna and unity within the Jewish community. It stressed
religious education and the strengthening of Talmud Torah schools,
which should be free for all children, and laid great emphasis on
expansion of social welfare facilities as well. It also pledged its support
for all efforts toward the rebuilding of Palestine.[102] Although very little
differentiated the "Apolitical" program from that of the Mizrachi, the
two Galician Orthodox groups continued to compete against one
another, as well as against the Hungarian Orthodox, in communal
elections.

In the 1932 campaign, all three Orthodox factions submitted their
own slates. For the first time since 1920, the Agudists decided to put
forth their own candidates and not join the Liberal coalition which now
included the Socialists. Since the Schiffschul leadership was again
considering secession, this list received only halfhearted backing and
obtained a mere 435 votes, less than 2 percent of the total ballots cast.
In 1920 the Hungarian Orthodox had won three seats, with 8 percent
of the electorate behind them; this time they won none. Clearly the
ultra-Orthodox community was de facto, if not de jure, opting out of

the Kultusgemeinde and no longer cared whether it had its own spokesmen within that body.[103] Meanwhile the "Apolitical" list received 1,041 votes, while the Mizrachi slate got 837; combined, the two Galician Orthodox tickets obtained 7 percent of the overall vote. Both lists had been coupled with the official Zionist list before the election and each managed to hold on to its single mandate on the board.[104] Thereafter, only two, rather than five or six, Orthodox deputies served on the Kultusgemeinde. (See Table 6.)

Regardless of the Orthodox representation on the communal board, the Israelitische Kultusgemeinde Wien by and large maintained the religious status quo throughout the interwar period, whether under a Liberal or a Jewish Nationalist regime. The communal rabbinate, both in its personnel and its practices, remained essentially the same fairly conservative body it had been before the war. No new Liberal congregations formed and the existing temples retained their late nineteenth century ritual patterns or in some instances became even more traditional under the influence of Chief Rabbi Chajes. New Orthodox prayer-houses sprang up and many of them began to receive communal subsidies. Despite the economic constraints of the thirties, more of these Orthodox congregations obtained communal funding under the Zionists than had been the case during the Liberal-controlled administrations of the previous decade. The Kultusgemeinde continued to run the single mikvah or ritual bath in the Austrian capital and introduced reforms in kashrut supervision for public Jewish institutions, including the hospital and the home for the aged. While not all the demands of the Orthodox constituents were met, the Viennese Kultusgemeinde, like other Liberal-dominated European Jewish communities, went quite far in responding to most of their grievances in an attempt to keep the community united.

In post-emancipation Jewish communities, Orthodox minorities faced several fundamental choices: one, seceding from the general community completely, as in Germany or Hungary; two, trying to ignore it and concentrate exclusively on purely Orthodox institutions; or else three, working together with the majority. In interwar Vienna the various Orthodox factions, the Agudists, the Hasidim, the Mizrachists and so-called "Apoliticals," experimented with all of these alternatives. In general, secessionist strategies failed to ameliorate the position of the Orthodox segment of the population significantly, whereas conciliatory tactics toward the dominant non-Orthodox parties, whether Liberals or Jewish Nationalists, tended to yield more positive results for the Orthodox, at the expense of those with more progressive religious views. In the end, as we shall demonstrate in the next chapter, *Austritt* efforts modeled on the German secessionist communities proved neither necessary nor successful. Mutual accommodation seemed to serve the Orthodox cause much more effectively, even if the compromises which resulted were never entirely to the satisfaction of the ultra-Orthodox element.

The 1932 elections marked an important watershed in the history of the Kultusgemeinde, however. Even though the new Jewish Nationalist administration continued to support religious activities, Jewish education, and social welfare much along the same lines as the Liberal administration had done in the past, tensions within the organized Jewish community escalated. Hostilities increased not only between Liberals or Social Democrats and Jewish Nationalists but also between the Schiffschul community and the Galician Orthodox, the Agudists and the Mizrachists. As the general Jewish political situation in Austria deteriorated in the thirties, so too did harmony within the Kultusgemeinde. The battle lines had been clearly drawn between the Zionists and the non-Zionists.

6

CONTINUITY AND DISUNITY

In January 1933 Desider Friedmann, a Zionist, assumed the presidency of the Israelitische Kultusgemeinde Wien, replacing Alois Pick, the Liberal who had served in that office for twelve years. Friedmann hoped that his administration would strengthen, democratize, and unify the extremely diverse Viennese Jewish community. While out of power, the Jewish Nationalists had generally cooperated with the Liberals. Once the tables had turned, however, the Liberals and the Hungarian Orthodox experienced great difficulty getting along with the Jewish Nationalists who wanted to transform the religious community into a more broadly defined "people's community." The Liberals once attempted to convince the Austrian government to dissolve the Kultusgemeinde board, whereas the Agudists tried to secede from the community altogether. The Jewish Nationalists thus faced serious internal dissension which made it difficult for them to institute radical reforms.

At the same time, they encountered even greater external obstacles. The depression created severe financial problems for the Jewish community, compelling it to curtail its existing programs and divert its funds to social welfare purposes, while reducing the likelihood of ambitious new endeavors. In January 1933 Hitler came to power in Germany; two months later Dollfuss dissolved the Austrian parliament and subsequently banned all political parties other than the Fatherland Front. The mid-thirties scarcely proved an opportune time to democratize the Kultusgemeinde and significantly expand its sphere of activities.

During the twenties the Israelitische Kultusgemeinde Wien had faced serious crises as well. The economic hardships of the early postwar years, intensified by the inflationary spiral, demanded drastic cutbacks and emergency measures. Communal employees, protesting against starvation wages, had to be pacified and paid. The Liberal leadership of the Kultusgemeinde managed to cope with the situation by working together with the Zionists and the Orthodox in a relatively harmonious fashion. Certainly, rumblings of discontent could be heard among the Orthodox, while the Jewish Nationalists and Socialists frequently expressed their dissatisfaction with the status quo, but by and large, through coalitions and compromises, the Kultusgemeinde had functioned as a unit without interference from outside authorities. Could this body continue to operate as smoothly under the new Jewish Nationalist administration in the thirties, given the depression, more widespread antisemitism, and increasing outside pressures due to the development of a one-party Christian state? Or would internal conflicts combined with the hostile economic and political circumstances prevent the Zionists from achieving their communal goals?

The Jewish Nationalists who took over control of the Kultusgemeinde were already seasoned communal leaders with considerable years of experience behind them. More than half had previously served on the communal board, one for as many as twenty years and five others for eight to fourteen years each. For the most part, these men were in their late forties or early fifties, at the prime of their careers.

Desider Friedmann, the Jewish Nationalist chosen as president of the Viennese Kultusgemeinde, was fifty-two years of age, having been born in 1880 in Boskowitz (Boskovice), Moravia. After receiving a solid Jewish education and attending gymnasium in Brno, he came to the University of Vienna to study law. During his student days he became involved in the Zionist movement, and by the twenties he had joined the front ranks of Austrian Zionist leadership. On several occasions he served as president of the Zionist National Committee for Austria, as a delegate at Zionist Congresses and as a member of the Congress Court of the World Zionist Organization. He was also elected to the Council of the expanded Jewish Agency at its founding session in 1930. Friedmann entered the Kultusgemeinde boardroom in 1920, served as vice-president until 1924 and thereafter as a member of the executive committee. He became deeply involved with the financial affairs of the community, acting as alternate chairman of the finance committee, and was also actively engaged in personnel matters. A member of B'nai B'rith Lodge "Wien," he was well respected as a lawyer and served for many years as a member of the disciplinary council of the Viennese Chamber of Lawyers.[1] Friedmann was a very able administrator but not a charismatic leader. Although generally well liked by his colleagues, his opponents accused him of being heavily partisan and favoring Zionist over non-Zionist candidates for communal appointments. Although sympathetic to traditional Jewish religious concerns, Friedmann directed most of his efforts toward furthering the cause of Zionism, with a strong leaning toward *Landespolitik*.

In his inaugural address Friedmann outlined his objectives as president. Acknowledging the very difficult economic situation caused by the depression, with demands growing and communal income shrinking, he stressed the need for a balanced budget and strict economy measures. Nevertheless, he spoke of expanding and reforming existing social welfare institutions, especially the winter relief campaign. He wanted to strengthen the position of the Jewish middle classes suffering from unemployment by creating vocational counseling services and an employment bureau. He expressed concern for Jewish youth and wished to intensify efforts at Jewish educational reform.[2]

Friedmann believed that the unity of the Jewish community was axiomatic and that no group within Jewry should encounter discrimination. He promised to retain all synagogues and ritual institutions as before, including those of the ultra-Orthodox. He wanted to defend the civil and political rights of all Jews and transform the community into the true center of Viennese Jewish life. In order to improve the legal position of Austrian Jewry, he strongly supported the creation of a federation of Jewish communities which would represent the interests of all Jews. This step was of particular importance in order to secure a much-needed state subsidy for which the Jewish community was eligible according to the constitution. He intended to amend the communal statutes and introduce universal, equal, and direct suffrage, eliminating all restrictions, including tax requirements. Allowing all members of the Jewish community to vote would increase interest and strengthen participation within its ranks. Lastly, he considered it the duty of the community as a whole to help in the rebuilding of Palestine, especially by encouraging pioneers and supporting their preparation for a new life. Friedmann pleaded with his fellow board members to set aside all party differences and work together toward a common goal, the well-being of their community and of their fellow Jewish citizens.[3]

Central to the aspirations of the Jewish Nationalists, and formerly of the Socialists as well, was the democratization of the Kultusgemeinde. At the first plenary meeting following the elections, the new board debated two motions presented by the General and Labor Zionists: the first, to introduce universal suffrage for all members of the Jewish community in Vienna, regardless of sex and tax status, and the second, to extend eligibility to hold office to women. The Mizrachi representative, normally allied with his fellow Zionists, spoke strongly against granting such rights to women, arguing on halachic or Jewish legal grounds. The Liberals, together with their new Socialist partners, also opposed the measure, claiming that by law the Kultusgemeinde had to concern itself with the religious needs of all Jews and they did not wish to offend the religious sensibilities of the Orthodox. Electing women to communal office contradicted the millennial old basis of the Jewish faith, they maintained.

Agudat Israel, no longer represented on the Kultusgemeinde board, appealed to all religious Jews to join their protest against granting electoral rights to women. They questioned the applicability of democratic principles in the religious sphere and expressed their deepest regrets that a religious body should consider contravening religious law. Jewish women played a very active role in welfare work in Vienna; they did not miss political participation, since they were not predisposed to it anyway, the Agudah leadership insisted. It was much more important for women to be involved in the education of Jewish children instead. Once again the Schiffschul faction threatened to secede completely from the broader community if their views on this matter were not respected.[4]

The motion to create an electoral reform commission to consider universal suffrage won by a 22 to 14 margin, with the Socialists voting together with the Zionists, whereas the vote regarding exploring equality for women resulted in a tie when the Socialists opted to vote with their Liberal allies on this issue. The two Orthodox deputies on the board, both members of the Zionist camp, sided with the Liberals on both motions.[5]

The electoral commission eventually recommended the introduction of universal suffrage and the right of women to run for office, but these recommendations never actually saw implementation, since the increasingly authoritarian Austrian state had to approve any changes in communal electoral statutes. The Orthodox, with the backing of the Liberals, had de facto won a victory against the Jewish Nationalists and against women, who had lobbied unsuccessfully on their own behalf. Prospects for true democratization of the Jewish community had disappeared.

Even with a Zionist majority, the Kultusgemeinde retained the same basic religious orientation and practices as before. In 1934, an Association for Progressive Religious Judaism notified the executive committee that it planned to begin holding regular biweekly prayer meetings in the private homes of its members, with lectures on biblical topics and musical accompaniment. They wanted to hire one of the religious teachers employed by the Kultusgemeinde as their lecturer. After some debate, with only one dissenting vote the communal executive committee decided that since this group engaged in religious practices which could not be approved by the board, any participation of a communal employee in this endeavor would be contrary to the interests of the Kultusgemeinde. They did approve the next item on their agenda, however, which was installing a loudspeaker system in the Leopoldstadt temple. The communal leadership might tolerate certain minor changes contrary to Jewish custom, but they would not permit any major innovation which more traditional elements might find objectionable.[6] As a result of religious disparities as well as practical realities, continuity and conservatism generally won out over change and reform.

Financial Constraints and Shifting Priorities

The Israelitische Kultusgemeinde Wien faced serious financial difficulties throughout the interwar period, first due to the postwar inflationary spiral and then as a result of the Great Depression. The core of this dilemma lay in the lack of adequate sources of communal revenue. The community derived about 30 percent of its income in the mid- to late twenties, and as much as 35 percent in the thirties, from its religious and health departments, which exacted fees for synagogue seats and medical and other services. Education brought in very little money, because the community provided religious instruction without charge. An additional 30 percent in the twenties, but somewhat less in the thirties, came from burial receipts, since the Kultusgemeinde imposed graduated fees for interment in the communal cemetery based on ability to pay. For the remaining 35 to 38 percent of its revenues the community depended on taxation of its members. (See Table 11.)

In 1912, the Kultusgemeinde had been able to collect 1,604,211 crowns from almost 25,000 taxpaying households. By 1924, the number of taxpayers had more than doubled to nearly 53,000 but they collectively paid only 1,259,585 schillings (with the Austrian schilling stabilized at approximately two-thirds the value of the prewar gold crown). In 1928, the number of taxpayers had climbed to over 58,000, contributing 2,286,280 schillings all told. Thus, even at the height of the postwar recovery, communal tax revenues had not quite reached their prewar level in terms of actual monetary value. Although more people were contributing to the community, the vast majority continued to pay the very nominal minimum rate.

During the early twenties, despite difficult financial circumstances, the Kultusgemeinde's Liberal leadership felt reluctant to apply for a state subsidy based on the Treaty of St. Germain, because, like other patriotic Austrians, they considered the treaty to have been shamefully imposed upon their country after the war and they wanted Jews to be treated as equal citizens with no special status.[7] Nevertheless, the Jewish Nationalists eventually prevailed upon the Liberals to claim the funds for which the community was eligible as a recognized religious minority according to both the treaty and the Austrian constitution. In 1928, the Kultusgemeinde board unanimously approved a motion to request a permanent subsidy from the federal government in order to help it fulfill its statutory obligations.[8]

In its application the communal council asserted that owing to the economic circumstances of the postwar era, it was no longer able to carry out all its assigned religious, educational, and welfare tasks. Inflation had destroyed the income from its prewar endowments, while revenues from taxation and fees were not sufficient to cover all needs, and government restrictions prevented further increases. The Kultusgemeinde argued that the 1928 state budget had allocated over 16,000,000S to the Catholic Church and more than half a million to the Protestants but only 800S to the Jewish community as a subvention for the Israelite Theological Seminary, along with salaries for certain religious instructors. Since fewer Protestants than Jews lived in Austria, this constituted unequal treatment and was contrary to the constitutional guarantee of equality for all citizens, regardless of religion. The petition also cited examples of state aid given to Jewish communities in other countries, including Czechoslovakia, Germany, Hungary, and Rumania.[9] That the Liberals actually agreed to approach the government for funding, albeit on religious grounds, represented a major step forward for the Jewish Nationalists' advocacy of group rights for Jews. Unfortunately, the authorities, while not denying the validity of the claim, never granted any subsidy, despite repeated appeals in subsequent years. Although ostensibly the government based its refusal on the grounds of insufficient funds, no doubt anti-Jewish sentiments played a significant role in the discriminatory behavior of Austrian Christian Social officialdom.[10] The Social Democratic Viennese bureaucracy, which excluded all religious bodies from municipal funding, refused outright to grant any subventions for Jewish institutions on the assumption that they were sectarian in nature.

One major obstacle preventing the Jewish Nationalists from accomplishing their aims once they had attained power thus lay in the lack of available funds. When they took over, they inherited a deficit of almost 200,000S and it was all they could do to keep the communal debt from doubling. Given the financial realities of the day, a balanced budget remained out of the question. The Kultusgemeinde was forced to rely strictly on revenues from communal fees and taxation. But the number of people capable of paying for dues and services was steadily declining due to the deteriorating economic situation. By 1932 the number of households contributing to the Kultusgemeinde coffers had fallen to less than 52,000 and three years later it had dwindled to under 48,000, while the tax revenues increased only slightly, reaching 2,410,363S by 1935. Less than 10 percent of the communal taxpayers paid over 100S each and they carried 60 percent of the tax burden.[11]

As the economic situation deteriorated further and the number of taxpayers continued to decrease, the need to collect additional tax revenues acquired even greater urgency. In 1936, the Jewish Nationalists introduced a motion for a compulsory 20 percent increase in communal taxation in order to help eliminate the deficit and offset winter relief, but the Liberal deputies, who had objected to raising taxes in the past, adopted obstructionist tactics to prevent its approval. The Liberals also opposed a proposal to raise the tax maximum to 9,000S from the 6,000S ceiling established ten years earlier. Although this measure would have affected only six individuals in the highest tax bracket, it would have brought in 18,000S more revenue. As a result of Liberal objections and also the unwillingness of the state authorities to approve higher compulsory Jewish communal taxation, the tax increase became voluntary and the deficit remained.[12]

Voluntary tax raises proved insufficient to cover the costs of existing programs, let alone introducing expensive new projects.[13] The community received support once again from the Joint Distribution Committee, which allowed it to establish and maintain a credit bureau for small businesses and a fund for interest-free loans, as well as provide aid for German refugees.[14] Such help, although certainly welcome, did not provide a solution to the community's ongoing budgetary woes.

Due to persistent economic difficulties, funding priorities shifted, even under Liberal management in the twenties. While the religious and educational spheres experienced a relative decrease in funding after World War I, the social welfare branch witnessed a dramatic increase in its share of communal allocations. These same trends largely continued after the Jewish Nationalists assumed office in the early thirties.

Whereas in 1912 roughly 31 percent of the Kultusgemeinde budget had gone for social welfare purposes, in 1920, out of necessity, this department was allotted almost 45 percent of total expenditures. In 1924, which marked the beginning of the recovery from the rampant inflation, health and welfare needs were assigned about 35 percent, a ratio which remained relatively constant until the end of the decade, but by 1932, the social welfare allocation had climbed once again to 42 percent and three years later it reached 44 percent. (See Table 12.)

The largest portion of this money was channeled into communally supported health-care facilities, especially the Jewish hospital and the old age home. The remainder of the welfare allocation was divided between communal social service agencies on the one hand and subsidies to various Jewish charitable organizations on the other. After several attempts at centralizing and coordinating Jewish philanthropic activities, the Kultusgemeinde reduced its subventions to private institutions and associations from about 29 percent of its social welfare allotments in 1920 to 6 percent in 1928 and then 4 percent in the thirties. At the same time, it increased its support of direct communal relief programs, which doubled from a low of 8 percent in 1924 to 17 percent in 1928, and redoubled to 37 percent in 1932. By 1935, 46 percent of the welfare budget was spent on public relief. (See Table 13.)

In 1932, 11,000 cases appeared on the communal welfare rolls, representing approximately 40,000 individuals or almost one-quarter of Viennese Jewry. By 1936, the number of families on relief had risen dramatically to 23,000, conservatively estimated at 60,000 persons, totaling more than one-third of the Jewish population. By then, as many as one out of three Jews faced unemployment. The Kultusgemeinde continued to try to provide emergency aid to all the needy who applied to its Central Welfare Bureau, created in 1930. The annual winter campaign, based primarily on voluntary donations, distributed food, clothing, and fuel to several thousand families and provided free meals at soup kitchens as well. Numerous private Jewish charitable organizations provided similar services on a smaller scale. The demand, however, far exceeded the facilities and the funds available. By 1935, the Kultusgemeinde had to cover, either fully or partially, the burial expenses of an estimated 65 percent of Jewish corpses in Vienna.[15]

Along with numerous special agencies to assist children and youth, the community set up self-help and retraining programs for the unemployed. Loan societies and vocational rehabilitation courses came into existence and in 1935 the Kultusgemeinde established an employment agency. In its first year, the placement bureau handled 4,116 job applicants, of whom the majority were adults and almost half were women. Of these, 2,293 received job offers and 1,089 others remained registered.[16]

While communal welfare services undoubtedly helped to take the edge off the misery of many Jews, such activities could not provide a solution to the urgent problems of the day. Some people managed to find new jobs and get back on their feet, but many more discovered themselves out of work. Although these people had nowhere else to turn, the community and its affiliated charitable organizations could not possibly meet their needs. Emigration did not become a realistic alternative for most individuals until after the *Anschluss*, since the few countries that would admit Jews were already flooded by German refugees, some of whom passed through Vienna on their way to other destinations.[17] It is difficult to blame the Viennese Kultusgemeinde for its inability to cope with the dire economic situation. The crisis resulting from the depression combined with antisemitic discrimination was simply more than the means at its disposal could handle.

The Jewish Nationalists could take the credit for whatever limited advances occurred in the welfare sphere and blame lack of funds rather than lack of effort for failure to achieve greater successes. They were largely responsible for the reorganization and centralization of welfare activities which began under their Liberal predecessors in the late twenties as a result of constant Zionist and Socialist pressure. After 1932 the Jewish Nationalists merely continued and intensified the same trends in social welfare policy as before, although the new administration focused its efforts more on vocational retraining and economic self-help than did the old.[18] The most pressing problem facing the Kultusgemeinde, however, remained the lack of sufficient funds with which to implement its programs and effectively deal with increasing Jewish poverty and unemployment.

While funding for social welfare activities increased in the postwar period, funding for educational purposes decreased both in relative and in absolute terms. Although both Liberals and Jewish Nationalists emphasized education as the main weapon in combating assimilation and strengthening the Jewish community, allocations in this sphere declined significantly. Between 1912 and 1920, the Kultusgemeinde reduced the proportion of its budget assigned to education by half, from 12 to 6 percent, but by 1932 Jewish education's appropriation had risen to 9 percent where it remained thereafter. (See Table 12.) This allocation primarily covered the costs of Jewish religious instruction within the public school system, but it also went toward such programs as youth religious services and confirmation classes for girls, as well as supporting communal and associational, or private, Bible and Hebrew schools.

The number of Jewish children receiving compulsory rudimentary religious instruction in public elementary schools fluctuated considerably during the interwar years. It declined from a high of 27,635 in 1917–18 to 10,689 in 1925–26 as a result of the expulsion of Galician refugees and the low birth rate during the war, then rose to 13,194 in 1930–31 but fell again to 9,065 by 1935–36, reflecting the plummeting Jewish birth rate. Despite this volatile situation, the number of children receiving supplementary Jewish education grew slowly but steadily. In 1923–24, the ten communally supported Bible and Hebrew schools in Vienna had only 1,300 pupils; four years later, forty-five schools receiving Kultusgemeinde subsidies reported a total of 2,252 pupils. By 1935–36, at the end of the Jewish Nationalists' first term in office, 2,824 pupils attended thirty-two communal schools and 1,642 more pupils enrolled in twenty-three subsidized associational schools, for a total of 4,466 children, 3,581 of elementary school age and 885 at the secondary level.[19]

In education, as in the social welfare arena, the Jewish Nationalists intensified rather than altered the policies instituted under the Liberals. For the most part they expanded existing programs, rather than creating new alternatives of their own. They increased the number of communal Bible and Hebrew schools, doubling the number of pupils receiving free supplementary Jewish education. They continued the practice of their predecessors of providing subsidies to private schools sponsored by various organizations, three-quarters of which called themselves Talmud Torah or Bible schools, while the rest described themselves as Hebrew schools. The educational content in these schools undoubtedly varied considerably from an emphasis on Hebrew language in some to liturgy, Bible, and Talmud in others, but most combined both religious and Hebrew elements to some degree. Under Jewish Nationalist control, the Kultusgemeinde also gave subventions to district Zionist associations which offered courses in modern Hebrew. In addition, it continued granting annual allocations to numerous youth groups, including those affiliated with the Union and the Agudah, as well as the entire spectrum of Zionist factions. While the Zionists clearly preferred supporting secular, Hebrew language institutions and their own youth affiliates, they did not discriminate against other political or religious orientations when distributing the limited funds available.[20]

The Liberals had been trying to foster weekly Sabbath youth services at communal as well as associational synagogues. In 1924–25, annual attendance was reported at 6,662; four years later, it reached 44,069; and by 1931–32, this total had doubled to 88,698. Under Jewish Nationalist auspices, attendance at youth services, which had become mandatory for certain pupils, climbed to a remarkable 156,453 in 1935–36, which amounted to an average of 4,229 children per week attending Liberal synagogues during the thirty-seven Sabbaths of the school year. The Viennese Jewish community, whether headed by Liberals or Jewish Nationalists, retained a strong commitment to traditional Jewish education and values, at least at a basic level.[21]

Children attended communal schools without charge. The Kultusgemeinde also supplied confirmation classes for girls and free Bar Mitzvah training for needy boys. The community presented a Mannheimer prayer book to every girl who was confirmed and to every boy who had a Bar Mitzvah in a communal synagogue, and each poor boy also received a *tallit* (prayer shawl) and *tefillin* (phylacteries). The Jewish Nationalists continued largely unchanged the educational policies which the Liberals had introduced in the nineteenth century.[22]

In addition to supporting religious instruction in public schools and supplementary Jewish education, the Kultusgemeinde provided funding for several full-time Jewish institutions of learning. In 1919, the Jewish Modern Secondary School, later known as the *Chajes Realgymnasium*, came into existence, which taught general and Jewish studies at the high school level, including modern Hebrew literature, Jewish history, and the geography of Palestine, as well as Bible and Talmud. Located in Leopoldstadt, with most of its students the children of Galician parents who could not afford to pay full tuition, it functioned as a predominantly Jewish Nationalist institution. The school received an annual subsidy from the Kultusgemeinde, as well as grants from various American sources, including the Joint Distribution Committee.[23] The community also accepted supplementary American aid to help it support the Israelite Theological Seminary, an institution for the training of rabbis established in 1893, which hovered on the brink of financial collapse throughout the interwar years.

Although the Jewish Nationalists had for some time favored the establishment of separate Jewish day schools on an elementary level and had incorporated this demand into their 1928 communal program, they themselves did not initiate such a venture until pressure was exerted from the outside. Indeed, the only community-sponsored elementary school which existed in Vienna prior to the mid-thirties was the Agudah-affiliated Talmud Torah school with 370 pupils, situated in Leopoldstadt.[24] Despite the existence of antisemitism in the public school system and the lack of very high quality supplementary Jewish education, there does not appear to have been a great demand for a non-Orthodox Jewish day school in the Austrian capital, and the Jewish Nationalists did not push the issue until the state threatened to create separate classes for Jewish children within the public schools in 1934.

After a bitter controversy within the communal leadership, which we shall discuss in greater detail in the next chapter, the Kultusgemeinde opened a new Jewish elementary school in September 1935. The communal *Volksschule* took over the building formerly occupied by the *Chajes Realgymnasium*, which with 470 students, including girls, had recently moved to a new location. The Liberals argued that the elementary school should be resituated either elsewhere in Leopoldstadt or in Brigittenau, since it would compete with the nearby Orthodox Talmud Torah school. The Jewish Nationalists denied that the new school would adversely affect the existing one, since the two had very different orientations and were likely to attract different pupils. The communal elementary school, unlike the high school, did not provide a very intensive secular Jewish education. It adhered to the public school curriculum but included an extra hour of Jewish religious instruction plus several hours of Hebrew language per week. In its first year, it enrolled one class of 29 pupils and the next year it had two classes with a total of 107 children; on the eve of the *Anschluss* no more than 200 attended.[25] Because of its very late start, this school remained small and had relatively little impact on the Jewish educational scene as a whole.

By the late thirties, three Jewish day schools existed in Vienna, the communal *Volksschule*, the Orthodox Talmud Torah, and the *Chajes Realgymnasium*, as well as the faltering Israelite Theological Seminary and a small girls' trade school. There was talk of creating additional schools, especially at the intermediate level, which would emphasize vocational training and the study of Hebrew and other foreign languages.[26] The Jewish Nationalists strengthened Jewish education in Vienna somewhat, but for the most part their educational programs continued to follow much the same practices as before. Lacking time and money, and perhaps impetus as well, they failed to create a strong secularist alternative to the relatively weak traditional Jewish educational network in Vienna.

Even though the Liberals consistently maintained that the primary task of the Kultusgemeinde was to fulfill the religious needs of its members, the proportion of the total budget appropriated for religious affairs declined by one-third after World War I, from 22 percent in 1912 to 14 percent in 1920. By 1932 ritual activities had risen slightly to 17 percent of communal expenditures, but by 1935, under the Jewish Nationalist administration, this category fell back to 15 percent. (See Table 12.)

This allocation largely maintained the communal and associational synagogues, but also funded the rabbinate, kosher meat supervision, the ritual bath, and temporary prayer services for the High Holydays. In addition, the religious affairs budget provided subsidies for Orthodox prayer-house associations. In 1924, fifty-six Orthodox *minyanim* had received only 4 percent of communal funding for religious purposes from the Liberal administration, whereas by 1935 the Jewish Nationalists were distributing 17 percent of the religious appropriation to a total of eighty-nine *minyanim.*[27] The Zionists, far from diminishing the traditional religious activities of the Kultusgemeinde, actually increased the level of communal contributions to Orthodox prayer-houses. Despite the fact that relatively little had changed when the Jewish Nationalists assumed control, some of the ultra-Orthodox expressed increasing dissatisfaction with their situation within the Viennese Jewish community and once more threatened to secede.

Orthodox Secession Attempts

The Hungarian Orthodox presented the greatest obstacle to unifying the Jewish community of the Austrian capital and creating a national federation of Jewish communities during the thirties. After the Jewish Nationalist victory in the 1932 communal elections, the Schiffschul faction again began contemplating complete secession from the Kultusgemeinde, since they, as Agudah supporters, refused to recognize secular Zionists as the legitimate leaders of the Jewish community. Like the Liberals, the Hungarian Orthodox feared that the Jewish Nationalist demand for a *Volksgemeinde* based on the recognition of Jews as a national rather than a religious minority would threaten the religious essence of Judaism. Now that an authoritarian Christian state had replaced the democratic Austrian republic, the Hungarian Orthodox hoped that by basing their demands for separate status on religious grounds they would be allowed to form their own independent community and no longer have to pay Kultusgemeinde taxes.

In April 1934, the Christian Social *Reichspost* reported that a general meeting of the Agudat Israel youth group in Leopoldstadt had introduced a motion challenging the legitimacy of the Kultusgemeinde, claiming that the communal board consisted almost entirely of men who led irreligious lives. The Agudah supporters recommended that such individuals be forced to resign and persons be appointed or elected in their stead who, by their tradition-true lifestyle, were suited to represent the community. If this advice was not heeded, the leadership of religious Jewry in Vienna should meet with Chancellor Dollfuss, inform him of the unacceptable state of affairs in the Kultusgemeinde, and convince him to introduce a law that only those persons who live in accordance with the Shulchan Aruch should be eligible to serve on the Kultusgemeinde, since only Orthodox Jews were capable of conducting the community in a true religious fashion.[28]

The Zionist press reacted strongly against this proposal that the Kultusgemeinde be governed by tradition, rather than majority rule. *Neue Welt* recognized that the Agudah group was trying to take advantage of the new Christian religious course of the Austrian government but accused them of allying themselves with Christian Socials and condemned them for conducting an internal Jewish dispute on non-Jewish turf. By contrast, the Orthodox *Unser Wort* justified the actions of its youth group, accusing the Zionists of turning the Kultusgemeinde into a party instrument instead of protecting communal interests. It demanded a separate community which would fulfill its religious obligations. The Orthodox had floated their trial balloon and the battle lines were being drawn.[29]

The Union, while opposing the idea of secession, expressed sympathy with the Agudah. Ernst Feldsberg, a Union spokesman affiliated with an Orthodox prayer-house, empathized with the embitterment of religious Jewry at the failure of secular Jewish Nationalists to understand their demands. He felt that more credit should be given the Agudah for their role in building Eretz Israel and supported their stand on Palestine. Clearly the Agudists would not have embarked on plans to abandon the community formally had the Liberals remained in power.[30] Their demands had not changed appreciably over the years and neither had the conduct of Kultusgemeinde affairs. The situation seemingly resembled an Agudah-Union vendetta against their Zionist rivals.

Meanwhile, a group of Galician Orthodox rabbis and prayer-house leaders called a mass meeting of Orthodox Jews in May 1934 to protest, as they had done a decade earlier, against the efforts by the Agudah separatists to destroy the unified Jewish community and to deny their claim to be sole representatives of Torah-true Judaism in Vienna. Rabbi Salomon Friedmann, president of Mizrachi, criticized the Agudah for appealing to non-Jewish authorities against their fellow Jews and pleaded for communal unity. Other speakers also declared their support for the Kultusgemeinde as presently constituted and condemned Josef Ticho, a prominent Liberal leader, for publishing an article asserting that the powers of the Kultusgemeinde should be limited to purely confessional matters. This meeting, obviously orchestrated by the Zionists, concluded with a unanimous resolution giving a vote of confidence to the Kultusgemeinde board, recognizing its "work in the renewal and deepening of Jewish life and building of religious institutions" and thanking it for its compassion for all religious orientations.[31] The informal alliance which had been formed in the twenties between the Jewish Nationalists and the Galician conservatives remained in place in the thirties even after the Zionists attained control over the Jewish community.

The Schiffschul faction began marshaling its arguments against the Zionist-dominated Kultusgemeinde. Complaints against communal subvention policies assumed a prominent place within their lengthy litany of grievances. The Orthodox press accused the Jewish Nationalists of misusing communal funds for partisan purposes. While providing niggardly sums to Orthodox prayer-houses and educational institutions, the Zionists allegedly increased allocations for secular, nationalist endeavors, such as the *Chajes Realgymnasium* and sports associations. The Orthodox also charged the Zionists with numerous infractions against Jewish law, including support for women's suffrage and the introduction of a loudspeaker system in the Leopoldstadt temple. Their greatest offense, however, lay in trying to turn a religious body into a national *Volksgemeinde*.[32]

The Kultusgemeinde had an exclusive obligation to look after the religious needs of the community, the Orthodox dissidents claimed. The religious indifference of the Liberals had forced the Orthodox to set up their own institutions for kosher slaughtering, ritual baths, and religious education. The Orthodox themselves had to intervene with school and state authorities to enable Jewish students to observe Sabbath in school and to protect the religious needs of Jewish employees and workers. The Jewish Nationalists had an even worse record than the Liberals, according to *Unser Wort*, and did not really represent the Jewish masses. They did not even observe kashrut and the Sabbath, let alone other Jewish customs. Such secular Jews should not have the power to determine the religious affairs of the community. Instead, the Hungarian Orthodox spokesmen demanded statutory revisions whereby only religiously observant men would be eligible for election to the communal board and the rabbinate would have the deciding word on all religious matters, rather than merely serving in an advisory capacity. Religious Jews must see to it that Jewish law hold sway in the statutes and practices of the Kultus-gemeinde. If the Kultusgemeinde proved unwilling or unable to implement this "just demand," then the Orthodox must have the opportunity to establish an independent religious community.[33]

In November 1934, the Schiffschul officially announced its desire to secede from the Kultusgemeinde. A statement to this effect appeared in the Catholic Clerical *Reichspost* several days before a formal petition reached the governmental authorities. The signatories to this document included the president and vice-presidents of Adas Jisroel, but the synagogue board had approved the decision to separate by only a bare majority. No general meeting of the Schiffschul community had taken place, apparently because the leadership feared lack of support within its own ranks. This endeavor thus had limited backing, even within the Hungarian Orthodox camp itself.[34] As in German Orthodox communities, such as Frankfurt-am-Main, most Orthodox balked against a complete split with the non-Orthodox *Gemeinde*, preferring to maintain a guise of *k'lal yisrael* or Jewish unity. [35]

A committee of Galician Orthodox rabbis and lay leaders, including members of the Agudah and various Hasidic dynasties, as well as representatives of most of the Orthodox prayer-houses in Vienna, organized to combat secession. Claiming to speak on behalf of 95 percent of Viennese Orthodox Jews, they strongly condemned the Schiffschul's actions and expressed their support for a unified community under the existing leadership.[36] Even the Union, which had expressed sympathy with at least some of the Schiffschul's demands, opposed the idea of formally dividing the community.[37] The Adas Jisroel board thus found virtually no allies for its separatist goals.

Desider Friedmann, as president of the Kultusgemeinde, forcefully and bitterly denounced the secession attempt. He maintained that Adas Jisroel represented only a small and dwindling part of Viennese Orthodoxy and that the vast majority of Orthodox Jewry stood behind the Kultusgemeinde. The claims upon which the Schiffschul had based its need to separate were patently false, according to Friedmann, since the Kultusgemeinde in Vienna was one of the few large communities which rejected Reform. Especially in recent years, the community had become recognizably more conservative and even the ultra-Orthodox considered the ritual orientation of the Kultusgemeinde exemplary, he insisted. The Schiffschul community, as part of the Kultusgemeinde, had its own recognized communal rabbi and also enjoyed the right to its own *shechitah* or kosher slaughtering, along with far-ranging autonomy and power. According to the law of 1890, secession was illegal. Friedmann stressed the importance of Jewish communal unity, especially in these difficult times.[38]

The Schiffschul community would have derived few material advantages from leaving the larger community. Fewer than half of its 600 members could afford to pay communal taxes. Their combined contribution to Kultusgemeinde coffers amounted to 17,000S out of a total communal budget of 6,758,806S. Among the rest, many were indigent and dependent on communal welfare. Although the Schiffschul itself did not accept direct subventions, indirectly the Kultusgemeinde claimed to provide as much as 100,000S of the 250,000S budget of the Orthodox subcommunity. The Schiffschul complained that its members could not afford the burden of double taxation, yet in practice it apparently received considerably more from the parent body than its supporters contributed. Clearly, this faction, like other Hungarian or German Orthodox secessionist groups, decided to withdraw for a combination of religious and political reasons, rather than out of economic considerations.[39]

The Austrian authorities turned down the Schiffschul petition to form an autonomous community. They concluded that only a small minority among Viennese Orthodox Jews backed this venture. The fact that only the board of Adas Jisroel, rather than a general meeting of its membership, had approved secession rendered this decision statutorily invalid. Furthermore, the move to secede lacked the support of other Orthodox associations and merely involved fewer than 500 members of the Hungarian rite. Allowing secession of this small faction would set a very dangerous precedent. If other Orthodox groups followed suit, chaos would result.[40]

The official response noted that when the Austrian law mandating a single community encompassing all Viennese Jews had been issued in 1890, the Orthodox problem already existed. The unified Jewish community did not prevent freedom of activity for all religious elements, whereas secession threatened the financial stability of the Kultusgemeinde, which already barely managed to balance its budget. Given that Austrian religious communities had the obligation of maintaining official registries, the creation of a smaller Orthodox community alongside the main Kultusgemeinde would complicate the task unnecessarily, since no sharp differences distinguished old and new believers.[41]

The governmental assessment pointed out that the motives behind the demand for secession were not purely religious ones. The victory of the Jewish Nationalists had become a thorn in the side of Adas Jisroel, which proved unable to accept the electoral defeat of their Liberal allies. The state recognized that a power struggle for control of the Kultusgemeinde was taking place and that the creation of a small second community did not constitute an end in itself but was merely a means to the end of weakening, or even destroying, the larger Kultusgemeinde. The Ministry of Education and Religion therefore decided that intervention in this internal dispute within the Jewish community was not appropriate.[42]

The Schiffschul had not succeeded in legally dividing the Viennese community, but it did not accept this verdict with equanimity. The leaders of Adas Jisroel continued to hope that the government authorities would change their minds and allow an independent Orthodox community to function de jure as well as de facto. For the Schiffschul faction had indeed ceased to participate in Kultusgemeinde affairs, except in the role of critic. In the 1936 communal elections, the secretary of Adas Jisroel had to resign his position on the synagogue board in order to run on the Union list as a representative of Orthodox interests. The Schiffschul had unofficially opted out and by doing so had undermined the attempts of the Zionists to unify and strengthen the Jewish community.[43]

Before and during World War I, Alfred Stern, the Liberal president of the Kultusgemeinde, had attempted to set up a federation of Jewish communities to defend the interests of all the Jews in the Austrian Empire. His efforts proved ephemeral, however, since the more conservative Galician communities refused to join and the body which he managed to create out of most of the remaining communities never actually functioned.[44] During the interwar years, thirty-two small provincial communities existed in the Austrian Republic with a combined population of less than 20,000 Jews. Just as the Hungarian Orthodox jeopardized the unity of the Viennese Kultusgemeinde, so too did Hungarian Orthodox provincial communities prevent the Jewish Nationalists from achieving their goal of unifying all Jewish communities into an officially recognized Austrian communal federation.

In the mid-twenties, several of the outlying communities revived the idea of a communal federation, this time with Zionist support, but the Liberal leadership in Vienna now refused to participate in the formation of a national organization, claiming that such a body would infringe upon the authority of the Viennese Kultusgemeinde and that the demands of the smaller communities would become a financial drain for the Jews of the capital.[45]

The Hungarian Orthodox also objected to such a federation, fearing that it would undermine Orthodox authority in provincial communities, especially in the Burgenland, which had formerly belonged to Hungary. The seven Burgenland Orthodox communities declined to join a provincial association formed in the twenties and also the national organization which the Jewish Nationalists in Vienna tried to establish in the thirties.[46] Thus, although the Liberals were no longer in a position to thwart the creation of a communal federation once the Jewish Nationalists had taken over control in the thirties, their former allies, the Hungarian Orthodox, were able to do so.

The governmental authorities used the fact that not all communities wanted to belong to a federation as a pretext for denying recognition to any such umbrella organization. In 1935, after several years of negotiations, a voluntary association of almost all Austrian communities, including Vienna but excluding the Burgenland Orthodox, came into being in order to represent the interests of Austrian Jewry as a whole, but since it had no official status, it lacked any real clout.[47] Although the Schiffschul contingent in Vienna failed to reach their goal of communal autonomy, the Hungarian Orthodox in the Burgenland succeeded in preventing the establishment of an effective federation of Austrian Jewish communities. Together they obstructed the Jewish Nationalists from achieving their goal of communal unity.

Filling the Vacancies

Like the Agudists, the Liberals had considerable difficulty accommodating themselves to the mere idea of a Zionist-dominated Israelitische Kultusgemeinde Wien. The underlying hostilities between the Liberals and the Jewish Nationalists came to the fore especially during disputes over the filling of vacancies on the communal council after the expulsion of Socialist deputies in 1934 and then selecting a communal librarian and an executive director for the Kultusgemeinde after the death of the Liberal incumbents.

At first it seemed as if the reins of office had shifted with relatively little friction. In 1933, the Jewish Nationalist majority on the newly elected board consisted of fifteen General Zionists, four Labor Zionists, one Mizrachist, and one "apolitical" independent Orthodox. The nonnationalist minority faction included eleven Liberals and four Socialists. Once again, Jakob Ornstein, president of the Union, and Josef Löwenherz, a leading General Zionist, resumed their positions as vice-presidents, and the Union coalition received four out of the eight places on the executive committee, three for Liberals and one for their Socialist allies, while the remaining four seats went to the Jewish Nationalists, three to General Zionists, and one to a Labor Zionist. The Liberals had to renounce several important committee chairmanships, including finance and education, and also their majority on the various committees.[48] Even though they were well represented within the new administration, the Liberal/Socialist alliance considered themselves the opposition and hence not responsible for the actions of the board. Nevertheless, the non-Zionists agreed to work together with the Zionists, temporarily at least, for the general good of the community.[49]

This equilibrium based on parity between the Zionists and non-Zionists within the executive committee did not last more than one year, however. The Austrian Civil War of February 1934 precipitated the tipping of the delicate balance within the Kultusgemeinde. After the Social Democrats had suffered a total rout, both militarily and politically, at the hands of their Christian Social adversaries, the victorious Dollfuss government immediately issued a decree banning all activity of the Austrian Social Democratic Party, dissolving all its affiliated organizations and forbidding the creation of any new Socialist bodies. The aftermath of this action almost led to a civil war within the Jewish community.

Initially the Kultusgemeinde board saw no need to take any measures against the Socialists within its midst, since neither the non-Zionists allied with the Liberals nor the Labor Zionists had been officially designated as representatives of the Social Democratic Party. Soon, however, the government promulgated a revised order whereby mandates to any general elective body faced dissolution if they came to office on the program of the Social Democratic Party or with its help. This new version clearly left no doubt that it included more than simply the Austrian Social Democratic Party itself. The Jewish Workers' Alliance had for many years openly advocated that Jews should affiliate politically with the Social Democrats, while it was public knowledge that Poale Zion–Hitachdut members were also all adherents of the Party and participated actively in its campaigns. In addition, the Labor Zionist group belonged to the Second International, the world Socialist parent organization. Since the deputies of both factions belonged to the party and had been elected under its influence, in early March, the president of the Jewish community, Desider Friedmann, after consulting with the Ministries of Interior and Education, issued an administrative decree expelling all who had been elected as Socialists from the community council, its district committees and its welfare offices.[50] Thus all official Socialists were formally purged from the Kultusgemeinde and its subsidiaries.

After annulling the eight mandates held by Labor Zionist and Jewish Workers' Alliance deputies, Friedmann attempted to clarify the impact of this action. The exclusion of the Socialist deputies from the communal board would not limit the scope of activity of the Israelitische Kultusgemeinde, he stated. The exemplary social aid work of the Jewish community and its welfare institutions, the expansion of which was in large measure due to Zionist efforts, would continue uncurtailed. The Jewish community had never let itself be guided by any class viewpoint, Friedmann claimed, and had always emphasized the fact that its welfare and relief work benefited all needy, regardless of class or estate. The community would maintain these unshakable principles in the future, as in the past.[51]

Despite reassurances that communal business would continue as usual, the Kultusgemeinde was considerably shaken up by these events. Not only were the Jewish Socialist groups themselves outlawed, with some of their leaders temporarily arrested and eventually seeking exile, but even their non-Socialist sympathizers experienced a sense of vulnerability. The Jewish Nationalists publicly accused the Union of Austrian Jews of seeking the favor of the Dollfuss regime in order to make the government forget the Union's connections with the Social Democrats. Even the longtime vocal opponent of the Social Democrats, Leopold Plaschkes, and his Association of Radical Zionists became the subject of a complaint to the Ministry of Interior which claimed that he and his party were tainted by Social Democratic affinities, since they were willing to accept former members of the banned Poale Zion into their ranks.[52]

Since so many Viennese Jews had openly identified themselves as supporters of the Social Democratic Party, the atmosphere within the Jewish community must have resembled a witch-hunt. Certainly any hopes for introducing universal suffrage into the Kultusgemeinde had to be shelved indefinitely, because one did not dare initiate new democratic practices within a Christian authoritarian quasi-dictatorship which had outlawed parliamentary government and officially banned all party as well as Socialist activities. The communal council indeed continued to function, but the cloud hanging over it was growing ever darker.

As a result of the loss of the eight Socialist deputies, instead of its normal contingent of thirty-six members, the Kultusgemeinde board found itself reduced to twenty-eight, including eleven Liberals and seventeen Zionists. The Union Club demanded to be allowed to fill the four vacancies left by their Socialist coalition partners with Liberals, since they had been elected on the same list. The Jewish Nationalists refused to permit this, preferring instead to allow the seats to remain vacant, undoubtedly because the Labor Zionists had run on their own separate list and it was unclear who could legitimately fill their places. Tensions between the two bourgeois groups significantly increased rather than diminished in the absence of their respective Socialist allies. Indeed, the issue of who should occupy the seats vacated by the Socialists became the pretext for a major confrontation between the Liberals and the Zionists.[53]

The Liberals had become increasingly unhappy with their minority status within the Kultusgemeinde and decided to adopt a more militant stance vis-à-vis the Jewish Nationalist regime. Jakob Ornstein gave up his communal vice-presidency in May 1934 and subsequently the Union presidency as well, and was replaced by Josef Ticho in the former position and Hermann Oppenheim in the latter. According to Jewish Nationalist sources, Ornstein resigned involuntarily under pressure from members of the Union leadership who considered him neither willing nor robust enough to conduct a successful fight against the Zionist majority. Ornstein had once briefly served as a non-Zionist delegate to the Jewish Agency, but Ticho and Oppenheim can best be classified as ardent anti-Zionists.[54]

Ironically enough, Josef Ticho had grown up together with his future rival, Desider Friedmann, in the small Moravian community of Boskowitz (Boskovice). The two men on opposite sides of the political fence shared very similar backgrounds. Born in 1877, Ticho, like Friedmann, was raised in a traditional Jewish household and remained attached to the teachings of his childhood throughout his life. He also studied at a gymnasium in Brno and later graduated with a law degree from the University of Vienna. While the Austrian capital provided the meeting ground for both Liberals and Zionists, Moravia seems to have provided the breeding ground for leaders of both camps.[55]

In the first postwar communal election in 1920, Ticho won a Kultusgemeinde seat and began serving as a member of the executive committee, an office which he held until his elevation to vice-president in 1934. Like other Liberal leaders (and Friedmann), he joined B'nai B'rith Lodge "Wien" in 1920 and he also become active in the Israelitische Allianz. A Union board member in the twenties and its vice-president in the thirties, he occupied the position of chairman of the Club of Union Deputies, or Liberal whip, within the communal council. A religious conservative, he chaired the Kultusgemeinde's education committee and maintained close ties with the Agudah.[56]

Upon assuming the position of communal vice-president in 1934, Ticho reiterated his personal credo, which essentially corresponded to the basic position of the Union. Judaism was a religion, and without religion, there could be no Jewry. The Kultusgemeinde should limit its activities to the religious sphere; if it exceeded those bounds, he claimed, it was on foreign territory. Even Jews who adhered to the strictest observances must feel comfortable within the Kultusgemeinde, Ticho insisted. Jews must be patriotic citizens of the state in which they live, differing from their Christian fellow citizens only by religion. They must have equal rights and equal obligations in helping to rebuild their country. For Ticho, any form of Jewish Nationalism was anathema.[57]

With Ticho leaving to join the presidium and the Socialists vacating two seats, three empty slots existed on the executive committee. The Jewish Nationalists initially proposed to fill two of these vacancies with their own supporters and one with a Liberal, thereby providing themselves with a five to three advantage. After prolonged negotiations, the Zionists announced their willingness to accept a four to three ratio in their own favor, but the Union was not satisfied with a proportional rather than a parity solution. The Jewish Nationalists then proceeded to fill all three vacancies with their own loyalists, leaving the Liberals with only two seats out of eight. As a result, the Union Club decided to resign from all its seats on the executive and on standing committees as well, limiting its involvement to plenary participation only, with Ticho continuing as vice-president.[58] Now that Ticho had replaced Ornstein as the Union's primary spokesman within the Kultusgemeinde, the Liberals adopted a policy that they would only play ball with the Jewish Nationalists according to their own rules of the game; if the Zionists would not "play fair," the Liberals would refuse to play at all. Temporarily, Jewish Nationalists assumed all executive and committee assignments, but after the summer recess had ended, they capitulated to the Union's demands and agreed to return to the status quo ante of parity on the executive committee.[59] This skirmish proved merely a precursor of more serious battles yet to come.

The tempests over the exclusion of the Socialists and the Schiffschul secession attempt had not yet died down before a new controversy threatened to undermine the strength of the Kultusgemeinde even further. A dispute over communal hiring practices generated increased animosity between the Liberals and the Jewish Nationalists and aroused conflict within the Zionist camp as well. Once again the Zionists' opponents appealed to outside forces in an effort to overthrow Jewish Nationalist predominance within the Kultusgemeinde.

In the spring of 1935, following the death of the Liberal director of the communal library, Moses Rath, a Zionist who was a Kultusgemeinde board member and Ticho's successor as chairman of the education committee, was appointed librarian. Six months later, the long-standing executive director of the Kultusgemeinde died and six candidates applied for the publicly advertised position as his replacement. The Jewish Nationalist leadership decided that the person best qualified for this job was none other than Josef Löwenherz, the prominent Viennese Zionist who had been serving as communal vice-president since being elected to the Kultusgemeinde in 1924. The Liberals, who had previously objected to the hiring of Rath, immediately raised a loud hue and cry against the Löwenherz appointment, accusing the Jewish Nationalists of nepotism and corruption.[60] The Schiffschul faction, no longer represented on the communal council, vehemently joined the protest against these nominations on similar grounds.[61] Some board members within the Zionist camp also publicly expressed reservations concerning the propriety of these hiring practices.[62] Clearly the Jewish Nationalists had not geared their personnel choices toward improving their popularity among rival factions within the Kultusgemeinde.

Despite threats by the Union to retaliate, in January 1936 Löwenherz relinquished his vice-presidency and, with fifteen out of twenty-eight votes in his favor, provisionally became the top administrator of the Jewish communal bureaucracy.[63] Thereupon the Union instructed its eleven deputies to resign from the board and submitted a formal complaint to the Viennese municipal authorities asking them to annul this appointment and dissolve the Kultus-gemeinde board, which now had only seventeen members instead of its statutory complement of thirty-six. The Liberals hoped thereby to force an early communal election.[64]

The lengthy petition which the Union leadership presented to the Mayor of Vienna articulated the major grievances which the Liberals had accumulated against their adversaries over the years. The Union charged the Jewish Nationalists with conducting Zionist party politics instead of looking after the religious needs of Viennese Jewry and with politicizing the administration by systematically packing the communal bureaucracy, formerly heavily Liberal, at least at the highest levels, with their own party adherents, regardless of their qualifications. Moses Rath, they claimed, might perhaps be a very good religious instructor for elementary schools, but he was scarcely suitable for the job of director of the communal library, especially since he had been elected to the honorary position of member of the communal board on a Jewish Nationalist ticket.[65] Zionist sources asserted that Rath was indeed eminently qualified to head the library, since he was an ordained rabbi with a degree in philosophy and a leading Hebraist who had taught at the Hebrew Teachers Institute and for many years been active in the publishing and book trade.[66]

The Union complaint did not challenge Löwenherz's professional qualifications to be executive director, but wanted to deny him the job on the basis of his age, origins, and partisanship. A lawyer by profession, Josef Löwenherz was then fifty-two years old, which was relatively young for a Kultusgemeinde board member, especially by Liberal standards, and remarkably young for someone who had already served as communal vice-president for twelve years. The Union maintained, however, that fifty-two was too advanced an age for a new communal employee, since his salary would be more than the Kultusgemeinde could afford, given its difficult financial situation, and since he would soon become eligible for a high pension, which the community could also ill afford. Even more damning from the Union's point of view was the fact that Josef Löwenherz, like Moses Rath, had been born in Galicia and did not receive his Austrian citizenship until after World War I. The petition claimed that Löwenherz had arrived in Vienna in 1919 and been naturalized two years later, and that for this reason alone the Zionists had not chosen him as communal president in 1932, instead of Desider Friedmann. His recent advent from the East made Löwenherz unacceptable as a member of the Viennese Jewish elite and unlike Zionist leaders born in Moravia he never joined B'nai B'rith. According to the Union, someone who had been an Austrian citizen for a mere fifteen years was not an appropriate choice as the official representative of the Jewish community before the authorities, whether in an elected or an appointed capacity. Furthermore, they declared, the executive director of the Kultusgemeinde must be completely above partisan politics. Löwenherz, a former vice-president of the Zionist National Committee, had been actively involved in Viennese Zionist affairs ever since his arrival in the capital and had been an elected Jewish Nationalist officer within the Kultusgemeinde since 1924. Therefore he should not, in their opinion, be considered eligible for paid employment of any kind within the Jewish community, let alone its most powerful administrative post.[67]

The Union recommended that Emil Engel, who held an interim appointment as executive director, continue in that position permanently. Engel, who had been born in Vienna, was three years older than Löwenherz and had retired from communal employ after twenty-five years of service but had been rehired on a temporary basis after the death of the incumbent administrator. Interestingly enough, Engel also had served as an elected Kultusgemeinde board member within the Liberal camp from 1924 to 1930 and had acted as alternate chairman of the social welfare committee until he resigned to take over the position of chief welfare administrator for the Jewish community.[68] It would thus almost appear to be a case of the pot calling the kettle black!

The Union denounced the Jewish Nationalists for dishonest practices and avowed that the appointment of Löwenherz was invalid. They claimed that the Zionist leaders had deliberately hired Löwenherz in order to force the Liberal deputies to resign and to facilitate a Jewish Nationalist takeover of the communal electoral apparatus. Desider Friedmann and Robert Stricker had made a deal whereby Stricker would become Löwenherz's successor as vice-president in return for the support of the Striickeer facttion on the board for this appointment. The Liberals insisted that Stricker, an overtly secular Jew, was not a fit person to hold office in a community which by law and statute was restricted to looking after the religious needs of its members. Stricker, incidentally, had already served briefly as a communal vice-president in 1920 and at that time had received the electoral support of the Liberal majority.

The Union challenged the right of the Jewish Nationalist leadership to refuse to seat the four deputies whom the Union had presented as replacements for their Socialist colleagues who had lost their mandates in 1934. With those four extra votes, the Union figured that it might have been able to prevent the Löwenherz appointment. As it was, the Union asserted that the seventeen Jewish Nationalists who remained on the board after the resignation of the eleven Unionists did not constitute a majority of the statutory thirty-six-member body or even a quorum, hence they did not have the proper authority to appoint a new executive director or indeed to conduct any communal business whatsoever. In sum, the Union considered the appointment of Löwenherz to be invalid, unnecessary, and detrimental to the community, both religiously and economically, and demanded that the state intervene and appoint a temporary commissar to be in charge of the community until new elections could be held.[69]

The Union complaint went on to blame "foreign Jews" for the shifts in the composition of the Viennese communal board in recent years. Before the war, suffrage in communal elections had not depended on citizenship because, they claimed somewhat inaccurately, very few members of the Viennese Jewish community were not Austrian citizens and the Kultusgemeinde did not "engage in politics." In 1920 when a citizenship requirement was in force, the Union had won a majority of seats; after the requirement was rescinded, they pointed out, the non-nationalists obtained only half the seats in 1928 and became a minority in 1932. It seemed obvious to the Union, therefore, that the Jewish Nationalists owed their victory largely to the votes of "foreign Jews," i.e. Galicians. The Liberals claimed for themselves a monopoly over Austrian patriotism and they concluded their lengthy memorandum to the authorities with an impassioned plea: "The Union of Austrian Jews is the organization of all Viennese Jews who take their stand on behalf of this positive-religious and patriotic Austrian soil. We stand firmly on the soil of this country, whose fate we have shared for centuries in suffering and in joy and for which at any time we would gladly make sacrifices. Austria is our fatherland and our homeland. We reject any form of nationalist separatist politics; as Austrian Jews we want no special status within the state and we especially object [to the fact] that the Kultusgemeinde, which is intended for the satisfaction of the religious needs of its members, be misused for nationalist political purposes."[70]

These efforts on the part of the Union leadership to proclaim their loyalty to the fatherland and validate their objections against the Jewish Nationalists by implying their disloyalty to Austria failed miserably, since the authorities at all levels rejected their complaint in its entirety.[71] By the mid-thirties, the Austrian government clearly recognized the Zionists, rather than the Liberals, as the legitimate leaders of the Viennese Jewish community. The Kultusgemeinde was not dissolved but instead continued to function with only seventeen Jewish Nationalists participating, while the eleven Unionists maintained their boycott of the boardroom. The Liberals had to wait until regular communal elections in November 1936 to attempt to exonerate their position with the Jewish electorate.

Tensions between the Liberals and the Orthodox on the one side and the Jewish Nationalists on the other were escalating at the same time that the Kultusgemeinde was experiencing growing external pressures created by the changing conditions in Austrian society, mounting antisemitism, and the depression. Various Jewish organizations attempted to bridge the gap between the opposing factions so that the community might present a united front to the outside world. In late 1933, even before the vacancy crises, Adolf Böhm, a B'nai B'rith leader who was also a prominent Zionist activist, wrote a long article in the B'nai B'rith paper describing the difficulties inherent in defending the rights of a beleaguered Jewry which was so internally divided. He suggested creating a committee composed of all Zionist factions to negotiate with the non-Zionist groups in an effort to unite all of Austrian Jewry. However, Wilhelm Knöpfmacher, the president of the Austrian Grand Lodge, vetoed this proposal to unite Jewry under B'nai B'rith auspices, since his organization officially stood above politics.[72]

In 1936, the Alliance of Jewish War Veterans, which had been created four years earlier to defend Jewish honor and combat antisemitism, decided that as the largest nonpartisan Jewish organization in Austria it had the obligation to try to bring an end to what it viewed as an actual civil war within the Jewish community. The Veterans' Alliance had objected to the Schiffschul secession controversy primarily because it had resulted in the public airing of dirty laundry. It felt that such disputes should be kept within the confines of the community and be conducted in a dignified manner so as not to provide additional ammunition for the antisemitic press.[73] The Alliance of Jewish War Veterans, which like B'nai B'rith comprised both Zionists and non-Zionists, made intensive behind-the-scenes efforts to try to find a formula which might lead to a compromise solution to the "Löwenherz case," which continued to drag on. It also took upon itself the initiative to form a supra-party Jewish defense front to deal with antisemitism and take a stand on all public affairs affecting the interests of Jews. At all costs, the Alliance wanted to avoid holding new communal elections, since a campaign would only serve to poison the atmosphere further. It sought to bring about a single unified list in order to spare Austrian Jewry a tragic spectacle in what it regarded as the twelfth hour.[74] All such peacemaking efforts proved in vain, however, when individual Zionists threatened to withdraw from the Alliance of Jewish War Veterans if it continued to engage in political activities, and none of the parties involved demonstrated a willingness to cooperate.[75]

The 1936 Elections

Given the ugly mood of the day, the 1936 election campaign degenerated into a series of unusually sharp and heated exchanges between the Liberals and the Zionists. While the Jewish Nationalists denounced the Unionists as "Naumann-Juden," comparing them with the small group of ultra-assimilated Jews in Germany who wanted to support Hitler,[76] the Liberals equated Robert Stricker with the German Nazi publicist Julius Streicher and Desider Friedmann with the Austrian Nazi leader Walter Riehl, and they classified the Zionist press with the *Völkische Beobachter* and other Nazi papers. The Unionists claimed that the very existence of Austrian Jewry was at stake in this election. If the Jewish Nationalists won, thousands of antisemites would rejoice at their victory and the rescinding of Jewish rights would begin immediately with the institution of official quotas which would generate defamation in the social sphere, loss of class status in the cultural sphere, and loss of power in the economic sphere. Zionist separatist politics would lead to Jews being *in* Austria but not *for* Austria; they would be for Palestine instead and no longer 100 percent Austrian citizens. In sum, the Union insinuated that a renewed success for the Jewish Nationalists would bring about doomsday for Austrian Jewry.[77] In return, the Zionists accused the Liberals of attacking Jewish honor and dignity in an unheard-of fashion and harming the interests of Austrian Jewry by their vindictiveness.[78]

The Liberals, for the first time in many years running on their own, presented the Jewish voters with a nine-point platform that reiterated much of their old program but also introduced several new planks in keeping with the needs of the day. As in the past they insisted upon strictly limiting the sphere of activity of the Kultusgemeinde to fulfilling the religious needs of its members. They promised ideological and material help for the upbuilding of Palestine for the benefit of coreligionists who could not remain in their own homelands but supported Jewish settlement elsewhere as well, while rejecting all Jewish Nationalist politics as harmful. They upheld the idea of the bonds of destiny which are shared by all Jews and pledged to support their "Eastern coreligionists" (i.e., the Galicians), a gesture which was supposedly continuing the old traditions of the Union. They agreed to give full consideration to the religious needs of various rites and pay special attention to the demands of the Orthodox, promising extensive subventions to temple associations and prayer-houses.[79] This conciliatory statement of goals portrayed the Liberals as non-Zionists, rather than anti-Zionists, and demonstrated their eagerness for the Orthodox, and particularly the Galician, vote.

In addition the 1936 Union agenda advocated educational reform, with an emphasis on vocational training of Jewish youth for crafts, industry, and agriculture, and a thoroughgoing reorganization and modernization of the social welfare institutions of the Jewish community, as well as simplification of the taxation system.[80] Such recommendations seem to resemble the policies of the Jewish Nationalist and Socialist opposition rather than the old Liberal program. They also appear to exceed the bounds of the purely religious definition which the Liberals had adopted for the Kultusgemeinde.

The Union's platform concluded with the demand that communal statutes be revised to prevent party maneuvering in personnel matters and subventions and the misuse of public funds for party purposes. In addition, board members must be excluded from paid communal positions during the duration of their incumbency and for a number of years thereafter and public competition must be made obligatory for all Kultusgemeinde jobs and supply contracts. Here we have a rather blatant condemnation of Jewish Nationalist practices and the Löwenherz case in particular.[81]

The Jewish Nationalists countered with a six-point platform of their own. They continued to demand that the Kultusgemeinde be expanded into a *Jüdische Volksgemeinde* so that in addition to looking after the religious needs of Vienna's Jewish inhabitants, it would fulfill cultural, economic, and social needs as well. The preamble stated that "the inseparable relationship with Jewry around the world obligated the community to take an active part in the reestablishment and strengthening of the Jewish people, as well as the rebuilding of the national homeland in the Land of Israel." The Jewish Nationalists officially supported the following principles: (1) the unification of all Austrian Jewish communities into a legally recognized communal federation; (2) the equality of all communal members; (3) protection of the civil rights of Jews collectively as guaranteed by the constitution; (4) strengthening of communal bodies and institutions for ritual, cultural, educational, and social welfare purposes through expansion and timely reform of existing institutions as well as the creation of necessary new ones; (5) promoting the economic and social well-being of the Jewish population; and (6) participation of the Kultusgemeinde in all matters affecting Jewry as a whole. The elaboration of this basic Jewish Nationalist program did not include any significant changes from the platform upon which the Zionists had come to power four years earlier. Owing to economic and political circumstances, the Jewish Nationalists had not yet succeeded in implementing their blueprint for an ideal *Volksgemeinde*, but they appealed to the electorate to give them more time.[82]

As a result of a significant reduction in the number of communal taxpayers due to the depression, 11 percent fewer Jews were eligible to vote in the 1936 elections than four years earlier. Nevertheless, given the serious political situation and vigorous campaigning, voter turnout increased by 18 percent. Out of 44,480 eligible voters, 31,760 cast their ballots, which amounted to a record voter participation of over 70 percent.[83] (See Table 5.) The Liberals had always claimed that those eligible voters who did not bother to come to the polls were most likely to be non-Zionist sympathizers. Perhaps this generalization held true for the minority who did not vote in this election as well, but out of the more than 5,500 new voters who appeared on the scene in 1936, only about one quarter chose to support the Union list. The Liberals received 11,593 votes, 12 percent more than in 1932, but their share of the total vote fell from 39 to 36.5 percent. (See Table 6.) Even in their former stronghold, the affluent Inner City, they attracted only 48 percent of the votes.[84]

The fact that the Union lost this election badly not only in those districts, like Leopoldstadt and Brigittenau, which were heavily settled by Galician-born Jews, but also in those areas, like the villa districts and the other suburbs, inhabited largely by "Western" or "native" Jews belied the assertion by the Liberals that Jewish Nationalist victories were due primarily to the vote of "foreigners."[85] The Zionists went to the trouble of verifying with the police the citizenship of all those who had voted in 1936 and discovered that 83 percent were Austrians and, among those who were actually foreigners, fewer than half were Polish citizens. Less than 45 percent of the votes cast by Austrian citizens had gone to the Union list.[86] By 1936, the vast majority of Jews remaining in Vienna were already citizens, but whatever their status most voters in communal elections clearly preferred Jewish Nationalists over Liberals. This election marked a major defeat for the Liberal camp, since it proved conclusively that by the mid-thirties only a minority of Viennese Jews continued to endorse the old regime.

For the Jewish Nationalists, this election resulted in an unequivocal victory. On its eve, the Zionists had managed to form a unified electoral list, including almost the entire spectrum from Center to Right: General Zionists, Radicals, Jewish State Party, Revisionists, and Mizrachi, as well as the independent Orthodox candidate, Leo Landau.[87] This united Zionist list received 16,438 votes, or 52 percent of all ballots cast. Two peripheral dissident Zionist lists got 957 votes for an additional 3 percent. Thus the Zionists, excluding the left wing, had 55 percent of the vote, having gained a majority in all districts, except for one small outlying suburban community. The Labor Zionists fielded their own list, which was somewhat surprising in light of the fact that all Social Democratic groups had been outlawed in Austria two years previously, and acquired 2,772 votes for a further 9 percent. The Zionist camp thus controlled a clear majority of the seats on the Kultusgemeinde board, occupying a total of twenty-three out of the thirty-six places on the communal council.[88] (See Table 6.) With almost two-thirds of the vote and proportional representation on the board, the Jewish Nationalists should have felt themselves securely in power. The communal electorate had given them a resounding vote of confidence, believing that they could provide stronger leadership than their Liberal rivals in such troubled times.

Unfortunately, the Löwenherz controversy continued to cast its shadow over Kultusgemeinde affairs. The Liberals, although definitely in the minority, had actually gained two seats in this election, since for the first time since 1920 the Union had not entered into a coalition with any other group and hence did not have to share the thirteen mandates allotted to the non-Zionist list.[89] They demanded one vice-presidency and proportional representation on the executive committee and the various standing committees, as had become customary. The Jewish Nationalists, however, bore a grudge against the Union leaders for having submitted their complaint to the municipal authorities and, while they were willing to accede to the Liberals' request for appropriate representation, they tried to prevent any person whose name had appeared on that petition from assuming the post of vice-president. Hermann Oppenheim, as president of the Union, maintained that the Liberals had the right to choose their own candidate for this position and insisted that Josef Ticho, who was one of the seven signatories, resume his vice-presidency. Thereupon, a majority of the Jewish Nationalists proceeded to elect two of their own as vice-presidents, an action reminiscent of Liberal behavior eight years earlier. Interestingly enough, all three of the Unionists elected to the executive committee at that same constituent meeting had affixed their signatures to the complaint.[90]

After nearly two months of fruitless negotiations and obstructionist tactics on the part of the Union, the Jewish Nationalists finally agreed to meet nearly all of the Liberals' conditions. Once again, Ticho assumed his vice-presidency, although Oppenheim relinquished his seat on the executive committee and moderate Unionists who had not signed the infamous petition filled the remaining vacancies. In addition to three seats on the executive committee, the Liberals received four seats on each of the major committees and three committee chairmanships. While participating in the administration of communal affairs, they nevertheless played a strictly oppositional role.[91]

Despite what looked like a comfortable majority, the Jewish Nationalist Club could not always enforce party discipline due to lingering hostilities within its own ranks. When Josef Löwenherz had been appointed acting executive director of the Kultusgemeinde in early 1936, not only Liberals but some Zionists as well had raised objections on grounds of partisanship. While Stricker and his faction had been won over with the promise of a vice-presidency for their leader, the Radicals and the Religious Zionists remained dissatisfied.[92] When the Löwenherz appointment came up for approval on a permanent basis the following year, eight Zionists outside the General Zionist mainstream were reluctant to support the motion. If any six of these board members voted against the measure, the Jewish Nationalists would no longer have the necessary majority to appoint Löwenherz as their new top administrator. After considerable bargaining within Zionist circles, extending as far as London and Jerusalem, the Radicals and the Labor Zionists agreed to abstain from voting so that the Löwenherz appointment could pass with a sixteen to thirteen vote, with six abstentions and two Jewish Nationalist absentees.[93] This was scarcely a sign of cohesion but instead represented serious dissension among the Zionists.

Given that Löwenherz had been a Zionist spokesman since the early twenties and his fellow Jewish Nationalists certainly could not have lacked confidence in his excellent administrative abilities, one can only conclude that this dispute was based on factional partisanship rather than higher principles of communal welfare. The Löwenherz affair did not create the internal conflicts among the various factions within the Kultusgemeinde, but it certainly brought them into the open and consumed a great deal of time and energy which might have been more constructively utilized elsewhere. In retrospect, one cannot help but think of Nero fiddling while Rome burned.

From January 1933 until the *Anschluss* in March of 1938, the Jewish Nationalists proved unable to introduce many radical changes into the Israelitische Kultusgemeinde Wien. Due to the authoritarian regime in Austria, they did not dare to institute universal suffrage. Therefore only taxpayers could vote in communal elections and women remained ineligible to run for office, much to the delight of both the Orthodox and the Liberals. The community continued to conduct its religious affairs exactly as it had done in the past, with slightly larger subsidies allocated to the various Orthodox prayer-houses. Jewish education also followed the pattern set by the Liberals, although communal schools expanded their efforts and the number of children receiving supplementary Jewish education and attending youth services increased substantially. Despite the strenuous objections of the Liberals, the Jewish Nationalists managed to establish a non-Orthodox communal elementary day school, which never had the chance to attract very many students. The greatest achievements of the new administration lay in the social welfare sphere which considerably extended its relief efforts and services for the unemployed. But here too lack of sufficient funds hampered the Jewish Nationalists' ability to transform an essentially religious Kultusgemeinde into a *Volksgemeinde* in any really meaningful sense of that term.

The multiple problems confronting the Viennese Kultusgemeinde during the interwar era were by no means unique to the Austrian capital, but typified the dilemmas facing many other twentieth century Jewish communities. Desider Friedmann and his vice-president, and later executive director, Josef Löwenherz, served as very competent administrators of the communal bureaucracy and ably handled the financial crises of the day. Unfortunately, they did not succeed as well in reaching a modus vivendi with the opposition within the Kultusgemeinde. As strongly partisan Zionists, they alienated their non-

Zionist opponents, both the Agudists and the Liberals, to such a degree that on several occasions the Kultusgemeinde board almost ceased to function. Although the Schiffschul community's threat to secede and the Liberals' attempt to dissolve the communal council both met with failure when the governmental authorities refused to condone these actions, nevertheless such incidents proved extremely divisive and sapped the organized Jewish community of much needed strength to combat outside threats to its existence.

Such escalating inner conflicts might have been almost inevitable given the great diversity and major transitions which characterized the Viennese Jewish community during the interwar period. It was extremely difficult for the Westernized Liberals who had controlled the Kultusgemeinde administration for over half a century to concede their power to the Jewish Nationalists, whom they considered dangerous Eastern upstarts. Similarly, the Hungarian Agudist Schiffschul community, which had dominated Viennese Orthodoxy since the late nineteenth century, undoubtedly felt threatened at being outnumbered by the Galician Orthodox and outvoted by the Zionists. A different breed of Jewish leaders, primarily Moravian in origin, like Desider Friedmann, but including some more recently arrived Galicians, like Josef Löwenherz, had taken over the reins of the community. Although the innovations they succeeded in introducing were rather modest, this new guard represented the winds of change; hence the older Establishment did not welcome their advent and tried to prevent them from achieving their goals using all possible means.

Bickering over religious practices and personnel matters was not a new phenomenon in Kultusgemeinde politics. The squabbles of the thirties over who should hold certain offices bring to mind similar disputes in the twenties. Both the Liberals and the Jewish Nationalists often adopted each other's tactics from the previous decade, when they occupied opposite positions of power. But whereas the Zionists eventually agreed to cooperate with the Liberal administration in the twenties, the Jewish Nationalist regime of the thirties evidently made accommodation more difficult, and the Liberals, as well as the Agudists, resorted to appealing to governmental bodies to intervene in Jewish communal affairs. This threatened communal autonomy and set a very dangerous precedent, especially considering the increasingly authoritarian nature of the Austrian government.

By the mid thirties, neither the Orthodox nor the Socialists functioned any longer as significant factors within the Kultusgemeinde board. In both cases, the Zionists and the non-Zionists within their ranks tended to cancel each other out. After the Socialists had lost their mandates in 1934, the non-Zionist Social Democrats officially disappeared from the communal scene, while the Labor Zionists continued to participate but maintained a low profile. Meanwhile, the

Agudists had voluntarily opted out of the Kultusgemeinde framework, while the Galician Orthodox joined forces with the Jewish Nationalists on nearly all issues. The main standard bearers of the Zionists and the non-Zionists, the Jewish Nationalists and the Liberals, thus had the battlefield within the communal boardroom virtually to themselves again. They refused to call a permanent truce, although intermittently they observed a cease-fire.

Meanwhile, other battles even more critical to Jewish survival in the long run were taking place in Vienna outside the framework of the Kultusgemeinde. Antisemitism steadily intensified and exacerbated Jewish economic difficulties. By 1934, Austria had become a one-party authoritarian state. How did the Viennese Jewish community respond to the spread of antisemitism in Austrian society, the development of a Christian corporate state, and the rise of Nazism? To what extent did Liberal and Jewish Nationalist policies really differ when it came to combating anti-Jewish external pressures? Was an internally divided Kultusgemeinde equipped to cope with such serious outside threats? The next chapter will explore these questions.

CONFRONTING
ANTISEMITISM

Antisemitism was neither a new nor a unique phenomenon in interwar Vienna. As elsewhere in Europe, modern antisemitism had developed in the Austro-Hungarian Monarchy during the last two decades of the nineteenth century and had become personified in the popular Christian Social mayor of Vienna, Karl Lueger, and the rabble-rousing Pan-German demagogue, Georg von Schönerer, both of whom Adolf Hitler acknowledged as his teachers. Antisemitic attitudes and slogans had become socially acceptable and even fashionable in the Austrian capital. But whereas before the war antisemitism generally manifested itself in verbal form, thereafter these same words were more likely to lead to concrete actions against Jews, which the state never officially sanctioned but tacitly condoned.

While rapid acculturation proceeded apace among Viennese Jewry, antisemitism prevented complete assimilation into Viennese society. In the interwar Austrian republic antisemitism took on several configurations, which Edmund Schechter vividly describes in his memoirs. Violent antisemitism revealed itself in clashes at the university, in scuffles at sports events with Jewish competitors, in fistfights in beer or wine establishments, and in curses and racial slurs. More subtle forms of antisemitism also existed. Few Jews were accepted into government service; there were virtually no Jewish judges or public prosecutors and relatively few unbaptized tenured professors at the universities. This "silent antisemitism" showed itself also in the restricted nature of many social and sports clubs and professional associations, and above all in the increased separatism of personal relations and friendships.[1] Even though Jewish education and Jewish Nationalism did not always succeed in instilling a positive sense of Jewish identity, antisemites in the Austrian capital constantly reminded Jews of their Jewishness.

Interwar Vienna witnessed frequent outbreaks of violence against Jews, especially at the universities. Even before the war, Vienna's institutions of higher learning had become hotbeds of radical German Nationalism, and, given the general impoverishment and dismal employment prospects of the postwar era, this trend among both students and faculty intensified considerably after the war. Demands for Jewish quotas and the exclusion of foreigners became rallying calls for regular attacks on Jewish students, which often resulted in the temporary closing of various educational institutions.[2] In the early twenties, mass demonstrations by antisemitic groups sometimes led to physical attacks on Jews in the streets. By the late twenties, such outbursts had become less frequent but Jews were experiencing systematic exclusion from many tourist resorts, and Jewish businessmen and professionals were increasingly subject to boycotts and other forms of economic discrimination.

With the spread of Nazism coupled with the depression and rampant unemployment, the early thirties brought renewed anti-Jewish riots. After 1933, in its attempts to suppress the Nazis, the one-party Christian corporate state muted the physical violence against Austrian Jews, but in its desire to counteract German Nationalism and maintain popularity with the masses the authoritarian government, dominated by Christian Social and Heimwehr leaders who had never been sympathetic toward Jews, intensified economic and social discrimination against them. As the decade progressed, the situation steadily deteriorated.

Kultusgemeinde Defense Activities

How did the Viennese Jewish community respond to these external pressures which threatened its security and survival? Could the various political factions work together to combat their common foe, antisemitism? As a rule the Orthodox and the Socialists did not become actively involved in defense endeavors, but left the field to the Liberals and the Jewish Nationalists. The Union of Austrian Jews saw itself as the major Jewish defense organization and continued to lobby for civil equality and to engage in legal actions, trying to protect individual Jews from various forms of discrimination, whereas the Jewish Nationalists held protests, ran electoral candidates, and made innumerable speeches in defense of Jewish interests.

In most instances Jewish efforts to protect themselves relied on the effectiveness of words, although in the immediate postwar years the Jewish Nationalists did attempt to organize self-defense units, and in the early thirties the Alliance of Jewish War Veterans followed suit, while Jewish Nationalist student fraternities frequently tried to ward off the attacks of their German Nationalist counterparts. Nevertheless, in times of crisis, both the Liberals and the Jewish Nationalists, despite their differences in outlook, generally turned to the central communal body, the Israelitische Kultusgemeinde Wien, to intervene with state authorities on behalf of persecuted Austrian Jews. The primary form of Jewish defense in interwar Austria, as in Germany or Poland, thus remained the time-honored method of *shtadlanut* or lobbying with government officials behind the scenes, and sometimes publicly as well, in order to protect the interests of the Jewish minority.[3] In the field of defense, the traditional strategies of the Union usually prevailed over more radical Zionist alternatives.

Although combating antisemitism did not constitute one of its statutorily defined tasks, in the absence of any other officially recognized Austrian Jewish representative body the Viennese Kultusgemeinde in the twentieth century reluctantly assumed the responsibility of registering protests with high government representatives against antisemitic manifestations. In July 1918, the communal council joined together with some three hundred other wartime Austrian Jewish communities in unanimously adopting a resolution condemning the dangerous escalation in antisemitism. In introducing the resolution, Kultusgemeinde president Alfred Stern alluded to the alarming agitation of antisemitic parties in the press, in public meetings, in city council, and in the national parliament. The situation had grown intolerable, he maintained, and the specter of pogroms was haunting the Austrian capital. The resolution denounced the systematic incitement against Jews by antisemitic groups and vowed that Jews would organize themselves to protect their very existence against the threatened dangers. Although not wishing to stoop to reply to antisemitic accusations, the joint statement emphasized the patriotism of Austrian Jewry during the war and the sacrifices Jews had made on behalf of the fatherland.[4] Despite such protests, the authorities did nothing to stem the growing tide of antisemitism and fears of pogroms continued unabated, due to the unrestrained rhetoric which flowed during antisemitic demonstrations.[5] In 1919, the Liberal-controlled Kultusgemeinde granted a subsidy to a defense troop of demobilized soldiers organized by the Jewish Nationalists to protect heavily Jewish neighborhoods in times of emergency.[6]

In March 1923, the Kultusgemeinde together with the Jewish Nationalist deputies on the municipal council called a mass meeting attended by several thousand Jews to protest against Nazi Jew-baiting activities and lack of government protection. With a Nazi counter-demonstration taking place outside, police efforts to maintain order resulted in several injuries.[7] Later that month, in an unusual act of unanimity, a special committee representing all Jewish parties and major organizations in Vienna, including the Kultusgemeinde, the Union of Austrian Jews, Agudat Israel, and the Zionist National Committee for Austria, as well as B'nai B'rith and the Israelitische Allianz, issued another joint statement on the need for a unified defense against antisemitism, stating that the antisemitic movement in Austria had recently adopted such excessive forms that the Jewish citizenry saw itself endangered in its constitutionally guaranteed equality and could no longer remain silent. Inflammatory placards, publications, and meetings disparaged the honor of the Jewish population, incited hatred and violence against Jewish citizens, and discredited the teachings of their religion through fabrication and misrepresentation. The efforts to curtail the freedom of Jewish instructors to teach and of Jewish students to study had encountered little opposition from the competent authorities.

As citizens of Austria who professed loyalty to their republic, the Jewish spokesmen demanded that the government effectively confront this treacherous movement which provoked hatred against the Jewish population and damaged the authority of the state internally and the reputation of the republic abroad. The resolution concluded with the assertion that Austrian Jewry firmly resolved to oppose with decisive resistance any encroachment upon their civic equality and diminution of their civil and political rights, and that all Jews considered themselves united in this effort, regardless of ideology and party orientation.[8]

This joint appeal for government support against antisemitism, reflecting a coalition spirit within the Viennese Jewish community which did not last long, was in large measure due to the serious problems which continued to plague Jewish students at Viennese institutions of higher learning. As John Haag has described the situation, "To be a democrat, pacifist or Socialist (let alone a Jew) at the University of Vienna in the years 1919–33 meant accepting a *vogelfrei* [outlaw] status; neither professors, nor other students, nor the Rector himself would lift a finger to protect such individuals from the periodic attacks by the *völkisch* [nationalist] rowdies of the *Deutsche Studentenschaft* [German student federation]."[9] Riots against Jewish students, and sometimes against Socialists as well, occurred on campus on a regular basis, generally on Saturdays, but tended to be more intense at the beginning of each semester. Sometimes Jewish students, especially members of Jewish Nationalist fraternities, fought back, but they were usually overwhelmingly outnumbered by the German Nationalists.[10] Antisemitic student groups made frequent attempts to bar Jews from attending classes. An incident at one university often had ripple effects leading to violent outbreaks at other universities. As a result, the temporary closing of educational institutions, including the University of Vienna, the Institute for World Trade, the Polytechnical Institute, and the Institute for Agriculture, became a common practice in order to quell antisemitic disturbances in the twenties and early thirties.[11] In 1932, violent attacks against Jews and Socialists at the university resulted in injury to at least fifteen Jewish students, including three American citizens; this led to a minor international crisis.[12] Despite repeated petitions from various Jewish student organizations, the Kultusgemeinde and other Jewish representatives, in the name of academic freedom, the state authorities refused to intervene before 1933.[13]

Throughout the interwar years, the German Student Federation, which was made up of German Nationalist, German Liberal, and Catholic student societies, stridently demanded the introduction of a numerus clausus or quota on Jewish students and faculty, as in neighboring Hungary, and the exclusion of foreigners, especially Polish Jews, from Austrian universities. Although the number of foreign students declined considerably due to higher fees and other restrictions, the antisemitic German student body did not fully achieve its goal of restricting the admission of Jews to Austrian universities, except for the Polytechnical Institute and the Institute for Agriculture which put into effect de facto quotas by the mid-twenties.[14] In 1930, the Rector of the University of Vienna attempted to implement a policy which would have discriminated against Jews by categorizing students according to their national origins, but the Austrian Constitutional Court declared these new regulations illegal the following year.[15] In late 1931, the Christian Social Minister of Education, Emmerich Czermak, submitted to the Austrian parliament a similar piece of draft legislation on student rights based on racial principles, but this too never went into effect.[16] Therefore, despite the extremely hostile atmosphere in academia, without an official numerus clausus, the overall numbers of Austrian Jewish citizens attending Viennese universities did not decline significantly until the mid-thirties.[17]

Undoubtedly the steady stream of protests against a numerus clausus emanating from the Kultusgemeinde, as well as the Union of Austrian Jews and various Zionist and student groups, helped to ward off the introduction of an official quota system at most Viennese institutions of higher learning. But while the Liberals and the Jewish Nationalists both opposed the principle of mandatory quotas based on religion or race, they differed as to the rationale behind their objections and hence rarely managed to present a united front. The Liberals feared that the Jewish Nationalists' demand for national minority status for Jews would provide additional ammunition for the antisemitic student arsenal, as well as for antisemitic politicians; they were convinced that the recognition of Jews as a separate nationality would inevitably lead to official quotas. Hence, they repeatedly urged their opponents to abandon this aspect of their program.[18] By contrast, the Zionists believed that Jewish minority rights would improve their situation; in the words of Bruce Pauley, they "hoped that withdrawal from Austrian politics and society (dissimilation), along with the building of a separate Jewish culture, would win the respect of gentiles and would lessen outbursts of antisemitism." The Jewish Nationalists were willing to appeal to the League of Nations to enforce the minority rights provisions of the Treaty of St. Germain; the Liberals were utterly appalled by this idea.[19]

Whereas the Liberals rejected outright the proposed new student regulations and the subsequent Czermak draft legislation because these formulations classified Jews as a nationality or a race rather than a religious denomination,[20] the Jewish Nationalists opposed them because they threatened the equality of Jewish students as a group and reduced them to second-class citizenship without allowing them to determine their own nationality freely. The Czermak bill, which was racial in nature, would have counted baptized and *konfessionslos* former Jews as Jews, a concept which the Jewish Nationalists could not accept because they believed in national self-determination for all individuals.[21] This ongoing dispute between the Zionists and the non-Zionists delayed the adoption of a joint Kultusgemeinde resolution against these student regulations in 1931 and resulted in a watered-down compromise statement condemning attacks against Jewish students and entreating the authorities to protect Jewish rights.[22] Ultimately the Christian Social government leaders decided to reject quotas at the universities not because they had succumbed to decisive pressure from within the Jewish community but because, as members of a Clerical party based on Christian religious doctrines, they were unwilling to accept racial classifications officially.

Even under the pre–1933 parliamentary regime, Kultusgemeinde appeals to the administration to help combat antisemitism rarely brought positive results. Christian Social officialdom on the national level evinced even less interest in defending Jews, either publicly or privately, than the Social Democratic municipal authorities. Shielding Jews against antisemitism might help improve the Clerical party's image abroad, but it would definitely not increase its popularity with the Austrian electorate. Relations between the organized Jewish community and the central government remained proper, but not cordial. Along with public demonstrations and joint resolutions which followed renewed outbreaks of violence against Jews, members of the Kultusgemeinde presidium met privately with various ministers and with the Austrian chancellor to present their grievances; they received polite reassurances that Jewish rights would be protected, but no concrete actions ensued from these discussions.[23]

In practice, the Kultusgemeinde and the Union of Austrian Jews shared the burden of defending Austrian Jewry against antisemitism before 1933. For the most part, communal leaders representing both Zionists and non-Zionists interceded with the authorities when Viennese Jews encountered physical or economic harm or after particularly vicious antisemitic propaganda campaigns.[24] The Union generally assumed responsibility for protesting against exclusion of Jews from Alpine tourist clubs and summer resorts, as well as other forms of social discrimination.[25] It also insisted upon representing Jewish interests with respect to libel reform legislation, since its leaders felt that the community itself should not be implicated in any demand which might impinge upon freedom of the press.[26] Although the Jewish Nationalists often belittled the tactics of the Liberals in defending Jewish interests, they came up with few practical alternatives of their own. Once the Zionists assumed control over the Kultusgemeinde in 1933, little changed with respect to the role of communal leaders as *shtadlanim* or intercessors with the authorities.

In the Austrian Corporate State

The year 1933 marked a major turning point for Austria and Austrian Jewry. Fearing a Nazi takeover following Hitler's assumption of power in Germany, Engelbert Dollfuss, Austria's Christian Social Chancellor, suspended parliament, restricted assemblies, and increased censorship. In February 1934, after a brief but bitter Civil War, he outlawed the Austrian Social Democratic Party and all affiliates. In place of a democratic republic, he instituted an authoritarian, corporate Christian state, based on Catholic social philosophy and the medieval concept of estates rather than classes. Only a single political organization, known as the Fatherland Front, functioned legally. After the assassination of Dollfuss in July 1934, Kurt von Schuschnigg became Chancellor and continued the same policies until the German *Anschluss* in March 1938.

The top Austrian government and Fatherland Front leaders did not overtly espouse racial antisemitism, although many of their henchmen were avid antisemites. Dollfuss and Schuschnigg repeatedly affirmed their commitment to the 1934 constitution, which, like its 1919 predecessor, guaranteed the equality of all citizens before the law regardless of birth, estate, or class and promised complete equality to all legally recognized religions. Nevertheless, despite frequent reassuring statements aimed at Jewish and foreign audiences, leadership pronouncements regarding Jews for local consumption sounded much more ambiguous. Whille C Chriistian Social and d Heimweehr spokesmen voiced objections to violent forms of antisemitism, they de facto encouraged antisemitic behavior, especially in economic and social spheres, in the hope of retaining the support of the Austrian populace, who they feared might otherwise be attracted to their National Socialist adversaries.[27]

The authoritarian regime had transformed Austria into a German Christian state. Since the Jews were clearly not Christian and only Christians were considered true Germans, their status in this new entity was bound to become problematic. Christian Social politicians, along with members of the Catholic clergy, disagreed among themselves as to the proper position of Jews in this society. As in the twenties, the Christian Socials generally condemned racial antisemitism as un-Christian, but condoned "cultural" antisemitism aimed at ridding the state of "harmful Jewish influences."

Within the church hierarchy, the Jews considered the Archbishop of Vienna, Theodor Innitzer, to be the Catholic spokesman most friendly to their interests. In the twenties, as Rector of the University of Vienna and Minister of Social Welfare, he had attempted to combat outbreaks of student antisemitism, and as a supporter of Zionism, he had belonged to the short-lived Pro-Palestine Committee. However, his stance on Jews was definitely exceptional and in 1938 he too was to welcome Hitler to Austria.[28] The Bishop of Linz, Johannes Maria Gföllner, provides a more typical example of Austrian clerical attitudes. In January 1933, Gföllner issued a pastoral letter accusing the Jews of "base materialism," "mammonism," and other "destructive social characteristics." He blamed "prevailing Jewish influence" for all the existing "spiritual trash" and the "inundation of moral slime" in the world. While claiming to oppose racial antisemitism and persecution of Judaism, the Bishop of Linz called for the disenfranchisement of Austrian Jewry through special legislation.[29]

This strongly worded attack on Jewish values and rights from an official Catholic source provoked vehement objections from the Jewish community. The Alliance of Jewish War Veterans immediately called a protest rally, attended by representatives of the Kultusgemeinde, the Union, and various other Jewish organizations. Addressing a packed hall, leaders of the Veterans' Alliance urged Jews to defend their honor against attack, while a Union spokesman pleaded for Jewish solidarity, comparing the situation of Austrian Jewry with that of their coreligionists in Germany, where Hitler had just assumed the office of Chancellor of the Reich. The gathering adopted a resolution objecting to the blatant antisemitism of the Linz pastoral letter and vehemently opposing the proposed revocation of emancipation. While criticizing the Church, albeit politely, the joint statement appealed once again to the government to protect the equality of Jewish citizens. In addition, the Union published a letter of protest in the local Sunday newspapers, and the Kultusgemeinde board unanimously passed a lengthy proclamation which appeared in the Jewish press, countering the criticisms contained in Gföllner's message. Once again, Viennese Jewry responded to an antisemitic incident with remarkable unanimity, but as usual their remonstrances produced little or no effect.[30]

The Austrian corporate state never proclaimed antisemitism as official government policy, yet the phenomenon clearly permeated the entire system, with at least tacit support from its highest officials. The press, especially the various Christian and Nationalist publications, constantly spewed forth antisemitic venom and antisemitic placards and pamphlets abounded. Antisemitic organizations operated openly, while the Pan Germans and the National Socialists functioned semi-clandestinely. Nevertheless, physical outbreaks of violence against Jews, while occurring sporadically, manifested themselves less frequently after the authoritarian regime formally banned the Austrian Nazi Party and clamped down upon such activities.[31]

The most serious threat to Austrian Jewish existence in the mid-thirties lay in the economic sphere. Jews continued to fear the introduction of a formal numerus clausus, not only at the universities but also in various occupations, which would exacerbate the already mounting economic discrimination against them. Prominent Christian Social political figures advocated instituting various quota systems. Emmerich Czermak, the former Minister of Education, supported official minority status for Jews, including a separate electoral curia and separate schools, as well as proportional numeric quotas in those occupations in which Jews were "overrepresented."[32] Christian Social Workers' Movement leader Leopold Kunschak demanded that Jews, even baptized Jews, be treated as a foreign minority by limiting their numbers at universities and in certain occupations and excluding them formally from teaching and public service.[33] Deputy Mayor Kresse, accusing Jews of profiteering in Socialist Vienna, advocated an economic boycott and the banning of Jews from trade union membership.[34] The Jewish press of all shades vociferously objected to these recommendations, many of which Austrian Jews had heard before. The Liberals had always opposed minority status of any kind, whereas the Jewish Nationalists only favored minority rights which would not infringe on the civil equality of Jewish citizens.[35] While few of these antisemitic proposals formally became law before the *Anschluss*, many were actually implemented much earlier.

Discrimination against Jews in the workplace had begun long before the imposition of the Christian corporate state. The Austrian capital experienced an unusually high level of unemployment throughout the interwar period and the depression served to intensify Vienna's economic plight. Amid the generally antisemitic political climate, limited job opportunities fostered growing resentment against Jewish competition in virtually all fields. Ever since World War I, Jews had been systematically excluded from both national and municipal public service positions, including the judiciary and the teaching profession. Christian applicants filled all vacancies, even those which resulted from the retirement of the few Jews who had previously held government jobs. Austrian industry rarely employed Jewish workers, and even in such branches of the economy as banking and insurance, where Jews had formerly been prominent, they were gradually being replaced by non-Jews. In December 1932, Nazi newspapers and leaflets, as well as placards posted on churches, announced a formal boycott against Jewish businesses during the Christmas season. Despite complaints from individuals and the Kultusgemeinde, Austrian officials did little or nothing to curb these practices.[36]

Employment prospects, especially for younger Jews, became even bleaker as an outcome of the authoritarian Dollfuss regime and the 1934 Civil War. The outbreak of violence between the government forces and the Socialist Schutzbund resulted in relatively little physical harm to Jews. Several Jews received injuries during the fighting, but none were killed. Perhaps a third of the Socialist leaders arrested after these events were Jews, at least by origin, and many of the more prominent Jewish Social Democrats went underground or into exile to avoid persecution. Those Jews employed within the Socialist party and educational apparatus lost their jobs once these bodies were outlawed. Other Jewish Socialists faced dismissal on political grounds as well.[37]

Jewish physicians were particularly hard hit by these anti-Socialist measures. While the Social Democrats had control over Vienna's city hall, a high percentage of Jewish doctors had worked for the Socialist sick fund and practiced medicine in municipal hospitals. By August 1933, rumors began circulating that henceforth public hospitals were no longer hiring Jewish physicians unless they could provide baptismal certificates, that Jews would not receive promotions, and that they might even be fired.[38] In the aftermath of the Civil War, these fears increasingly became reality. The Association of Jewish Physicians in Vienna reported that no Jews had been appointed to public positions since 1933, and that in the summer of 1934, of the fifty-eight individuals dismissed, fifty-six were Jews. The physicians' organization predicted that there would soon be virtually no more Jewish interns or residents left at municipal hospitals and that this policy would result in many vacancies due to a lack of sufficient Aryan replacements. Ostensibly Jewish doctors lost their jobs because they were Socialists, but given the fact that almost no non-Jewish Socialist doctors found themselves unemployed, it became abundantly clear that most of the Jewish doctors affected were unable to practice medicine merely because they were Jews.[39]

All avenues of protest, whether by the Kultusgemeinde, the Union, the Zionists, or the physicians themselves, led nowhere. The Association of Jewish Physicians of Austria attempted a variety of methods of alleviating the crisis facing its membership. Once joining the Fatherland Front became a requirement for obtaining a position in a public hospital, the organization affiliated en masse in February 1934.[40] But despite all its efforts, speeches, petitions, and negotiations on behalf of younger colleagues, it was unable to report any success. It had become almost impossible for young Jewish medical school graduates to complete their accreditation requirements. The one practical option available was to expand the training facilities at the communally supported Rothschild Hospital. This provided only a very partial solution to the much larger problem, however. While some Jewish doctors continued to practice in their field, others joined the expanding ranks of the unemployed.[41]

Physicians were certainly not the only Jewish group adversely affected by discrimination in the thirties. Jewish lawyers, who had always been excluded from public service, found earning their livelihoods in the private sector increasingly precarious. The Federation of German Aryan Lawyers demanded the introduction of a numerus clausus in the legal profession. Although the Union of Austrian Bar Associations rejected this proposal, it removed its Jewish president and other Jewish board members from its own ranks.[42] Jews were also being eased out of the cultural sphere, including the theater and the press.[43] Jewish businessmen and tradesmen suffered from boycott efforts and the denial of licenses and municipal contracts, while in 1934 the Fatherland Front-sponsored trade union adopted an Aryan paragraph which officially excluded Jews. In November 1937, the Deputy Mayor of Vienna spearheaded a movement for Christians to buy only from Christians, claiming that Jews only patronized other Jews. Such measures caused incalculable misery for members of the Jewish community.[44]

Employment prospects for Jews looked extremely bleak. Non-Jewish employers rarely hired Jews, whereas Jewish employers often preferred Christian employees over fellow Jews in the hope of ridding their firms of a Jewish image. By 1937, due to the economic effects of the depression combined with antisemitism, roughly one-third of the Jewish work force in Vienna found itself without jobs and as many as 60,000 individuals were receiving some form of relief from the Kultusgemeinde, which took care of the Jewish needy as best it could.[45]

Defense Efforts in the Thirties

How could Viennese Jewry effectively combat antisemitism in authoritarian Austria? They depended upon the state to protect them and their civil rights, yet the leadership, both on the national and municipal levels, condoned anti-Jewish discrimination, especially in the economic realm. Complaining to the authorities and receiving reassuring replies thus did little good. Various Jewish groups, including the war veterans, the Liberals, and the Zionists, as well as the Kultusgemeinde itself, attempted to deal with antisemitic manifestations piecemeal but they failed to combine their efforts. The frustrations they encountered in trying to deal with this intractable problem only intensified the internal divisions among Jews, further polarizing the Zionists and the Liberals. The magnitude of Austrian antisemitism far exceeded the ability of the Jewish community to cope with it, whether as a united force or as factions squabbling among themselves.

The Alliance of Jewish War Veterans formed in July 1932 for the express purpose of taking appropriate measures, including self-defense, to defend Jewish honor and protect the right of Jews to earn their living in Austria. During the High Holydays that fall, a veterans' militia, together with a Zionist defense group and members of the celebrated Hakoah soccer team, warded off a Nazi attack on several synagogues and prayer-houses in Leopoldstadt and sustained some serious injuries before the police arrived.[46] This marked the first and last attempt by the Veterans' Alliance to employ physical force against antisemites.

With the new authoritarian government taking over in 1933 and ostensibly reducing the threat of violence against Jews, the Alliance changed its tactics to protest rallies, commemorations for the Jewish war dead, and proclamations of Jewish loyalty to the state.[47] This organization, which emphasized the military virtues of discipline, obedience, and physical fitness, claimed 8,000 members by 1934.[48] The Alliance, a nonpartisan group, devoted a great deal of its energy, unsuccessfully, to trying to mediate between the Liberals and the Zionists and forge a united Jewish defense front.[49] An article entitled "The Obligation for Harmony and Unity," appearing in the Veterans' Alliance paper *Jüdische Front* in late February 1938, expressed its basic philosophy that "honor is as important as bread" and that Jews needed self-esteem more than anything else. Jews should set aside all divisive tendencies and "march in the same step."[50] The Alliance's formula for alleviating antisemitism in Vienna remained unclear, however.

The Union of Austrian Jews continued to view itself as the premier defense organization and true guardian of the interests of Austrian Jewry. Its methods of coping with antisemitism in the thirties did not differ significantly from those of the twenties or the prewar period. Despite increasingly difficult circumstances, it proudly adhered to its old principles of defending Jewish rights by legal means. Its leaders met with government officials and submitted petitions protesting antisemitic statements and actions. It exposed examples of illegal exclusion of Jews from jobs and vacation resorts, submitting documented complaints for individual cases. The Union tried to stem the distribution of antisemitic propaganda, and published pamphlets and articles countering various slanderous accusations. In addition, it supported the activities of the few exceptional non-Jews, such as Richard Coudenhave-Kalergi and Irene Harand, who were also involved in combating antisemitism through education.[51]

While such efforts were by no means unimportant and produced occasional minor successes, they had virtually no effect in improving the overall situation. The Union dealt with antisemitism as if it were a rational phenomenon and as if antisemites were reasonable human beings subject to persuasion by logical arguments, which unfortunately was not the case. Its leadership counted on the state to protect Jewish rights, repeatedly expressing confidence in the good will of the authorities and frequently being taken in by empty promises.

In the twenties, Jewish Nationalists involved in *Landespolitik* had concerned themselves primarily with participating in elections and trying to achieve minority status for Jews as a group, but by the early thirties Viennese Zionist leaders had largely abandoned these goals and were becoming increasingly preoccupied with the question of defense and basic Jewish survival in Austria. In June 1932, a group of prominent General Zionists, including Desider Friedmann and Josef Löwenherz, called a mass meeting and issued an appeal to "all upright Jews" to join together and form a General Jewish Association which would engage in active Jewish politics and energetic defense against antisemitic attacks. In their plea for support, they described the daily escalation of Jewish need. While the misery of the Jewish masses had increased enormously, militant Nazi antisemitism threatened Jewish honor, life, civil rights, and their very economic existence. Austrian Jewry must take their fate in their own hands, the Jewish Nationalists insisted, and band together to fight for their civil rights and equal status before Austrian law.[52]

This General Jewish Association soon joined forces with Robert Stricker's Jewish People's Party, which redefined its role as representing "conscious Jewry" to the outside world and fighting for equal rights of Jewish citizens and their security.[53] Once political parties were banned in Austria, the Jewish People's Party renamed itself the Jewish People's Alliance and attempted to function as a defense organization, with much the same concerns as the Union of Austrian Jews. Despite frequent appeals for membership, it never attracted a significant following and remained largely ineffectual. This group became increasingly associated with Stricker after the General Zionist leadership decided that the Kultusgemeinde, as the officially recognized Jewish community, constituted the only body capable of defending Jewish interests effectively.[54]

While the Jewish Nationalists frequently disdained the Union and its methods, they were unable to devise practical defense tactics of their own. Three rival Jewish bodies, the Veterans' Alliance, the Union, and the very weak People's Alliance, thus engaged in similar but separate defense endeavors in Vienna. All of them preached the need for Jewish solidarity, but they refused to heed their own advice and join together to attain their common goals. In practice, responsibility for Jewish defense in Vienna had largely shifted out of the hands of the separate defense organizations and into the domain of the Kultus-gemeinde and the Jewish Nationalist communal leadership.[55]

By 1933 Jewish Nationalists had become the official representatives of Austrian Jewry in the public arena. After the Dollfuss regime dissolved all elected legislatures, it replaced them with appointed councils. Desider Friedmann, president of the Kultusgemeinde, received an appointment to the Council of State, while Jakob Ehrlich, the former municipal councilor, was named to the Citizens' Council. The Jewish position on the Cultural Council went to Professor Salomon Frankfurter, the former director of the University of Vienna Library and also former chairman of the library committee of the Kultus-gemeinde, but no Jew was to serve on the Economic Council. The three appointees were very prominent members of the Jewish community, belonging to B'nai B'rith Lodge "Wien," and all were Jewish Nationalists.[56] Friedmann and Ehrlich, both strong proponents of *Landespolitik*, had long served as Zionist leaders within the Kultus-gemeinde.

Evidently the Austrian authorities perceived the Jewish Nationalist leadership as less tainted than the Union leaders by ties with the now outlawed Social Democratic Party. Perhaps the Christian Social administration decided to appoint Zionists rather than Liberals because they preferred the ultimate Zionist goal of a separate Jewish state to assimilation. They hoped to eliminate Jews from Austrian society, and Palestine might provide the appropriate solution. As one commentator has pointed out, "In no case were appointments made on the basis of prior participation in Austria's political parties or on the ground that the appointees had declared their foremost allegiance to Austria; the declaration of loyalty to Judaism [sic] as a national minority was held to be the decisive criterion."[57] Whatever motivated these appointments, it is clear that by the mid-thirties the government viewed the Jewish Nationalists as the proper spokesmen for Austrian Jewry.

It seems ironic that the Jews had greater formal representation on the appointed bodies of the thirties than on their elected counterparts a decade earlier. All these councils, however, served primarily as window-dressing and rubber stamps and had very little actual power. Desider Friedmann maintained a low profile on the Council of State, but Jakob Ehrlich made an annual speech during the budget debate condemning discrimination against Jews. These addresses, delivered by the lone Jew on the city council, echoed many familiar themes but were accompanied by a heightened sense of urgency.

In his first such speech in 1934, Ehrlich insisted that no one wanted to deny the German-Christian character of the Austrian state and promised that the Jewish minority would be loyal to the new constitutional system, as long as it was based on true Christianity and not on racial concepts. Protection of minorities, he asserted, was anchored in the constitution, which guaranteed civil equality and respect for cultural life. Minorities should receive state subsidies for educational and welfare purposes. Thus, Jewish schools should be eligible for public funding and the Jewish hospital, which also served non-Jews, should receive external financial support as well. Jews should not be excluded from public medical positions, as had become the case.[58] In 1935 and again the following year, Ehrlich focused his speech more exclusively on the personnel policies of the municipal administration. He complained about the exclusion of Jews from municipal service due to religious affiliation, claiming that this practice was both unconstitutional and harmful. In addition, he pointed out that municipal contracts were only granted to members of the new trade unions, which excluded Jews.[59] In what was to be his final address in December 1937, Ehrlich denounced the boycott of Jewish businesses, condoned by Deputy Mayor Kresse, and the damaging effects of racial restrictions on Austrian tourism.[60] As before, his complaints were recorded but exerted no effect on policy.

While the Zionist press applauded these efforts, the Liberal paper, *Die Wahrheit*, denied that Ehrlich had the right to speak on behalf of Viennese Jewry, even though he was the most senior member of the Kultusgemeinde, having served on that body since 1912 in virtually every capacity except as president. The Union's press organ severely criticized Ehrlich's arguments, which in fact did not differ greatly from those of the Union itself.[61] Personal political animosities had once again won out over the desire for a united front in the face of outside threats. In January 1938 all Union members absented themselves from a special session of the communal board which met to honor Ehrlich for his courageous stand on behalf of Jewish interests before the municipal council. He received a unanimous vote of confidence from the Zionists present, however.[62]

Since the federation of Austrian Jewish communities had failed to receive formal recognition, the Israelitische Kultusgemeinde Wien remained the only official representative of Austrian Jewry before the authorities. The Kultusgemeinde board continued to register protests against antisemitic occurrences all over the country and intervened behind the scenes on frequent occasions. Its president, Desider Friedmann, and other members of the presidium regularly had audiences with Chancellors Dollfuss and then Schuschnigg to discuss the status of Jews in Austria. They then reported back to the executive committee and the gist of these conversations often appeared in the minutes of the communal board and in the Jewish press as well.[63] As before, the Kultusgemeinde followed the tradition of *shtadlanut* and maintained a polite and correct relationship with the top figures of the Austrian state. Perhaps this policy helped to prevent the Jewish situation from further deteriorating before the *Anschluss*, but it could not claim very many successes in alleviating the effects of antisemitism.

The Jewish Nationalist leadership recognized even more clearly than their Liberal opponents the growing dangers of both official and unofficial antisemitism in Austria and they spoke out strongly against it. They were aware of the situation of Jews in Nazi Germany and openly admitted that they too might be faced with a similar plight. They did all that they could to try to ensure the continued existence of an independent Austrian state, since the available alternative seemed far worse than the dismal realities they already faced. They certainly understood the problems that beset Austrian Jewry, but they lacked effective means to cope with antisemitism even before 1938, let alone thereafter.

Austrian Jews and the Fatherland Front

By and large the organized Viennese Jewish community outwardly supported the authoritarian German-Christian government during the mid-thirties. Some leftist critics argue that the Jews would have been better off if they had continued to back the forces for Social Democracy even after they were outlawed following the disastrous 1934 Civil War,[64] but one must keep in mind that the most likely alternative to the corporate state in Austria after 1933 was not Socialism but National Socialism. In reality Jews had little choice of allies. The enemy of their enemy Hitler had to be their friend.

In an age of censorship and quasi-dictatorship, Viennese Jewish newspapers cannot be considered an accurate barometer of the real opinion of the average Jew concerning the Austrian government. Indubitably the press did not even present the true views of the leadership. The vast majority of Viennese Jews had voted Social Democratic before 1933 and, while many might have preferred a viable Liberal or Jewish Nationalist party, very few, except for some wealthy industrialists and perhaps some of the Orthodox, had ever backed the Christian Social Party, which was widely known to be antisemitic. Jewish political preferences did not change overnight, but the dissolution of parliamentary government and the subsequent outlawing of the Social Democratic Party had radically altered the picture. Jews of nearly all political shades immediately began dissociating themselves from the Socialists and declaring their loyalty to the new Austrian state and the Fatherland Front. One might term such behavior opportunistic, but to a greater extent, like previous Jewish support for the Social Democrats, it was merely pragmatic. In the Austria of Dollfuss and Schuschnigg, one either came out in favor of the Fatherland Front or else kept silent.

Those committed Jewish Socialists who did not leave the country obviously had to choose the latter course of action. After the Civil War, the most prominent went underground, while the rest tried to become inconspicuous so as not to lose their jobs. While some Socialists, especially Labor Zionists, continued their involvement in Jewish communal politics, Jewish Socialists as a group ceased to be a significant factor in Jewish affairs. Like many other Jews, they staunchly opposed the regime in private but dared not openly speak out against it.

At the other end of the spectrum, the Orthodox press associated with Agudat Israel welcomed the authoritarian government with the greatest degree of enthusiasm. As the most vocal element within Viennese Orthodoxy but also the faction least enamored by democratic ideals, the Agudah spokesmen did not necessarily typify all Orthodox Jews. Nevertheless, an editorial in *Unser Welt* in February 1934 claimed not to regret the passing of the multiparty state and the Social Democratic Party, and asserted that a Christian state might better serve the needs of religious Jews.[65] The Schiffschul held a special service in honor of the new Austrian constitution of 1934 and both Adas Jisroel and Agudat Israel wrote letters to Dollfuss thanking him for guaranteeing the equality of all religious groups.[66] The Agudists had hoped that the government of the new German-Christian state would sympathize with their aspirations to secede from a Kultusgemeinde dominated by secular Jewish Nationalists. Although disappointed by the rejection of the Orthodox bid to leave the community, the Agudah press continued to express confidence in the Schuschnigg administration.[67]

The Fatherland Front admitted Jews into its ranks but did not allow them to rise within the party hierarchy. While the Orthodox did not enroll as a group in this Christian association, the Liberals urged their fellow Jews to become members of the patriotic national organization. Already in May 1933 the Union of Austrian Jews formally affiliated itself with this body and encouraged all of its membership to join as individuals. The Union had never previously backed the Christian Socials, let alone their Heimwehr partners, but had eventually openly allied themselves with the Social Democrats instead. They were able to read the anti-Socialist writing on the wall quite early, however, and jumped on the Dollfuss bandwagon even before the Civil War, although they still had serious reservations about the strong antisemitic tendencies among the governing Clerical party. For most Liberals, joining the Front meant supporting the future existence of Austria, rather than a commitment to the principles of the Christian corporate state.[68]

The Union had always vaunted its Austrian patriotism and it continued to do so even more vehemently in the thirties. In its *Festschrift* published in 1936, past president Jakob Ornstein asserted that Jews had been natives of Austria for more than a millennium and that the burning love of Austrian Jewry for this ancient homeland also extended to the new Austria, even when acts of its administration were not based on principles of equality.[69] Liberal leaders lost no opportunity to declare their loyalty to the state as Jews. During the Civil War the editor of *Die Wahrheit* quickly tried to dissociate the Jews from the Social Democrats and vouch for their fidelity.[70] Another Union spokesman acknowledged the debt which Jews owed to democracy and expressed regret at its decline and abuses, but felt that Jews should welcome the new authoritarian constitution as loyal citizens. "Austria is our state and our homeland," he maintained, and its Jews would remain true to their religion and their fatherland, as long as they enjoyed equality before the law.[71] Despite growing disillusionment with the realities of the day, the Liberals publicly backed the Schuschnigg regime until its end.[72]

Like the Union, the Alliance of Jewish War Veterans constantly emphasized Jewish patriotism to Austria, both in war and in peace. During the February 1934 Civil War, the veterans' organization, which had also already joined the Fatherland Front as a group, declared its willingness to fight against the Social Democratic Schutzbund if called upon to do so. Based on the service record of its members during World War I, the Alliance claimed that its loyalty to the state could not be questioned and demanded the protection of Jewish civil equality as a right that was due, not a favor.[73] The Veterans' Alliance wanted to work within the Fatherland Front to bolster Austria and at the same time tried to unify Austrian Jewry to fight against antisemitism. They saw themselves as the "shield of Austrian Jewry: true to Austria, true to Judaism and true to the Alliance of Jewish War Veterans."[74]

Stricker's Jewish People's Party issued a program on the eve of the Civil War affirming its recognition of the new Austrian state and its preparedness to cooperate in its development, while at the same time rejecting the ideology of class struggle. It wanted to keep Austrian Jewry away from involvement in "foreign," i.e., non-Jewish, parties and their struggles. Any entanglements with either the Social Democrats or the Christian Socials could only bring harm to Jewry and be of no use to the parties themselves. The People's Party opposed participation by Jews in any form of *Kulturkampf*, but instead supported order and social justice. Its platform combined Austrian patriotism and anti-socialism with advocacy for civil equality and Zionism.[75] The People's Party, unlike the Union, strongly discouraged Jews from entering the Fatherland Front.

The Jewish Nationalists could not recommend that Jews join the Front, either as individuals or as a group, because this body was clearly based on German-Christian principles. They did not consider Jewish entry into the Fatherland Front as beneficial either for the Jews or for the patriotic organization. Since Jews were neither Germans nor

Christians, they should remain outside its framework and relate to the political body of German Austrians as one nation to another nation.[76] Viennese Zionists undoubtedly joined the Front as individuals for pragmatic reasons or as members of other affiliated organizations, such as the Alliance of Jewish War Veterans or the Association of Jewish Physicians, but unlike the Union of Austrian Jews the Jewish Nationalists never signed up collectively. They expressed willingness to support the authoritarian state, however, and backed all efforts to bolster Austrian independence.

Separate but Not Equal

As an officially German Catholic entity, the Austrian corporate state was extremely unlikely to acquiesce to Jewish demands for complete civil equality for Jews, even on paper. The Union of Austrian Jews rejected out of hand "separate but equal" status as a possible alternative. For these Liberals, any form of segregation meant ghettoization and was therefore completely unacceptable. They consistently maintained that they were patriotic Austrians with equal duties and hence deserving of equal rights in their state.[77] Unlike the Liberals, the Jewish Nationalists could accept a separate status for Jews as a national or religious minority, as long as they were treated as equals rather than second-class citizens.

In September 1934, the Ministry of Education issued a directive that parallel classes be set up dividing Catholic from non-Catholic students in overcrowded middle and normal schools. The authorities attempted to justify this action by claiming that it was not based on antisemitism or racism but on purely technical grounds and that it would spare non-Catholics, i.e., Jews, Protestants, and declared agnostics, from recently instituted compulsory attendance in Catholic religion classes. In actuality, the small Protestant minority in Vienna, who generally did not live among Jews, remained unaffected by this edict, but some Jews and pupils "without religion" were indeed segregated from their Christian classmates.[78]

The decree caused a great deal of consternation among the Kultusgemeinde leadership, who viewed this unilateral action as deliberately discriminatory against Jews. They immediately protested and unanimously approved a resolution stating that the creation of parallel classes based on religion was contrary to an agreement which had been made between the authorities and representatives of the Jewish community earlier that year. The Jewish population, the resolution went on to say, considered this act unsettling and disturbing, since forced segregation was likely to arouse feelings of inferiority among Jewish pupils. The board appealed unsuccessfully to the Ministry of Education to rescind the order.[79]

Even though all the members of the Kultusgemeinde board agreed that compulsory separation of Jewish pupils into parallel classes with the same curriculum and the same teachers as before would be harmful, no consensus existed as to whether or not state-supported Jewish schools with more Jewish content and Jewish teachers might be a desirable alternative. The Liberals protested vociferously against the idea of a secular Jewish day school. Ostensibly their objections were based on the claim that such a school was unnecessary and would compete with the existing Orthodox Talmud Torah, but in reality they were opposing any form of Jewish education which was not primarily religious in content. While they were willing to tolerate supplementary Hebrew language training under Zionist auspices and even the *Chajes Realgymnasium* they refused to support a modern elementary day school. Jewish children, they felt, should receive their primary education not in "ghetto schools" but in public schools, where they would learn to get along with their Christian neighbors and become good Austrian citizens, differing from the majority only in their religion.[80]

The Orthodox, including the Agudists who were no longer repre-sented on the communal board, disagreed somewhat with the Liberals on this issue. Since they favored the creation of Jewish religious schools, they did not oppose mandating separate classes for Jewish pupils, as long as the instruction in such classes was in accordance with Orthodox religious views. The Agudist press, however, protested against expanding secular Jewish education in Vienna.[81]

The Jewish Nationalists regarded separate schooling for Jewish pupils in a more positive light than the Liberals. They did not object to the principle of special state-supported schools or youth groups for Jewish children, but such arrangements had to meet certain criteria of equality and be voluntary rather than obligatory. If the state wanted to give Catholics the opportunity to educate their children as German-Christians, it had the obligation to provide Jews with the same opportunity to educate their children as Jews. Unlike the Liberals, the Zionists felt that, instead of eradicating antisemitism, the public schools often fostered it and caused humiliation for Jewish pupils. Jewish parents should have the option of sending their children to Jewish schools at state expense. Thus, while the Liberals advocated continued integration, the Jewish Nationalists favored separate but equal educational opportunities for Jews.[82]

The Jewish Nationalists, however, joined the Liberals in strenuously objecting to the mandatory imposition of parallel classes for non-Catholics, but these protests largely failed. By the end of 1937, eleven segregated middle school classes had come into existence, with an almost exclusively Jewish student body. While Jewish symbols were allowed in these classrooms, neither the curriculum nor the teachers had changed and the textbooks remained inappropriate for Jewish education. Although the Zionists set up their own communal elementary school as a result of this dispute, they had not achieved their goal of establishing separate but equal Jewish schools with public funding.[83]

Unlike the Liberals, the Jewish Nationalists could accept the creation of a special Jewish section within the Austrian Young People's Organization, the junior branch of the Fatherland Front, which was strictly organized on Christian-German principles and excluded Jews from regular membership. Once again, they would agree to "separate but equal" minority status, as long as this did not relegate them to de facto second-class citizenship.[84] Trying to maintain their balance on this rather delicate tightrope was no easy feat for the Zionists.

When the Jewish Nationalist president of the Kultusgemeinde, Desider Friedmann, came out in favor of the creation of a Jewish Youth Federation within the Austrian Young People's Organization, Hermann Oppenheim, president of the Union, charged him with not being the true representative of Austrian Jews or Austrian Jewish youth, on the grounds that foreigners had elected him and his responsibilities only extended to religious, not political, matters. The proper spokesman for Austrian Jewish youth was the Union of Austrian Jews, claimed its president. The Jewish Nationalists had no right to set up a separate Jewish subsidiary, since Austrian Jewish youth should belong to the Young People's Organization itself.

Oppenheim publicly questioned the Austrian loyalty of Jewish Nationalists, especially focusing on the Revisionist youth group Betar, whom he referred to as fascists. He claimed that instead of wearing a medieval yellow badge, the Zionists wore a blue-white badge, whereas the Union recognized only the red-white banner and only one national anthem, that of Austria. The central board of the Union reaffirmed Oppenheim's stand in a unanimous resolution published several weeks later.[85] By February 1938 yellow badges were no longer a purely medieval symbol but represented a new reality of life in Nazi Germany.

Despite Liberal denials, Desider Friedmann, as president of the Kultusgemeinde, member of the Council of State, and spokesman for the Jewish Nationalist majority, had indeed become the officially recognized representative of Austrian Jewry. He, like the leaders of the Union and the Alliance of Jewish War Veterans, dutifully went through the formalities of demonstrating Jewish loyalty to the state. On behalf of the Jewish community, he formally expressed his thanks for the new constitution guaranteeing civil equality, eulogized Dollfuss after his assassination and met with Schuschnigg to clarify the Jewish position and reiterate Jewish support. While he clearly recognized the negative aspects of the Jewish situation in Austria and expressed serious reservations about government policy in private, in his public utterances and articles he generally lauded the regime.[86] Did he, or any other Viennese Jewish leader, really have much choice?

The Union repeatedly attacked Jewish Nationalists, particularly Robert Stricker but also Desider Friedmann and Jakob Ehrlich, as unpatriotic, foreign, and fascist, sometimes comparing them to Nazis. Such charges were not only unfounded but also extremely dangerous and likely to backfire and tarnish the positive image of Jews which the Liberals were trying to create. This internal Jewish feuding, conducted openly in the press, could only have further undermined the already weak position of the Kultusgemeinde and Friedmann as its leading spokesman. Surely the Union leaders should have realized that, despite ideological differences, they and the Jewish Nationalists had a common goal, a secure position for Austrian Jewry, and a common enemy, the Austrian antisemites but especially the National Socialists.

A recent leftist critic of Zionism, Lenni Brenner, has adopted an opposite view to that of the Union in the thirties and taken the stand that the Jewish Nationalists were, if anything, too patriotic during that period. He accuses them of acting as local and international apologists for the Christian Socials, condemning Nahum Sokolow, a prominent leader within the World Zionist Organization, for eulogizing Dollfuss as a friend of Zionism and Nahum Goldmann of the World Jewish Congress for his quiet diplomacy with Mussolini on behalf of Austrian Jewry.[87] He condemns Stricker for denying reports that Jews were being persecuted during the 1934 Civil War and for supposedly welcoming segregated Jewish classes. Brenner also denounces Friedmann for serving on the Council of State and supporting the Schuschnigg government, including the March 1938 plebiscite. According to Brenner, "Austrian Jewry had only one hope: a resolute alliance, locally and international with the Social Democrats. . . . However, instead of looking to the socialists, in Austria and abroad, for succor, the local Zionists looked to the regime, which was ultimately to surrender to Hitler without firing a shot."[88]

A less biased observer would probably conclude, however, that the Jewish Nationalists would clearly have preferred working with Social Democrats rather than dealing with an antisemitic right-wing government if that had been a realistic option after 1933. Most Jewish Nationalists in Vienna had voted Social Democratic during the democratic republic and the Austrian Zionist leadership had given at least their tacit support to the Austrian Social Democratic Party in the early thirties instead of continuing to back their own candidates against the antisemitic Christian Socials and Nationalists. The Jewish Nationalists never developed an alliance with the Christian Socials, either before or after the Civil War. They did not support the authoritarian regime out of choice but out of necessity. Such a misreading of history, accusing Zionist leaders of actively abetting fascism, deserves even less credence when it comes from subsequent analysts than from contemporaries.

Jewish survival in Austria depended on the existence of an independent Austrian state. Like the Union of Austrian Jews, the Alliance of Jewish War Veterans, and the Orthodox Agudat Israel, the Jewish Nationalists publicly gave their support to Dollfuss and then to Schuschnigg, and eventually his plebiscite, not because they approved of the Christian corporate state but because they realized that the only other likely alternative was National Socialism. Discrimination formally based on religious grounds, while scarcely desirable, was certainly preferable to discrimination officially based on racial principles. Austrian antisemitism one could live with, if necessary. Its German Nazi counterpart would not let you live. While the Austrian Jewish leadership could not possibly have foreseen all the dire consequences of a German *Anschluss*, they understood the situation well enough to do everything in their very limited power to attempt to prevent its occurrence. As one historian has pointed out, "Viennese Jews, like those in Hungary at this time, found themselves in the absurd position of looking to moderate antisemites for protection against radical ones."[89]

With growing apprehension, Austrian Jewry closely followed the negotiations between Austria and the German Reich, culminating in February 1938.[90] On the 24th of that month, Chancellor Schuschnigg met separately with Desider Friedmann, president of the Israelitische Kultusgemeinde, and with his adversary, Hermann Oppenheim, president of the Union of Austrian Jews. In his discussion with Friedmann, Schuschnigg reaffirmed his government's absolute commitment to maintaining the 1934 constitution, which guaranteed the rights of all Austrian citizens as well as the protection of minorities. At the same time, he agreed to the creation of the Jewish Youth Federation of Austria, providing equal rights for Jewish youth and an organizational link with the Austrian Young People's Organization. He also assured Oppenheim that the constitution would remain unchanged and that citizenship rights gained during or after the war would not be altered. Oppenheim thanked Schuschnigg in the name of Austrian Jewry and pledged the patriotic support and unquestioning loyalty to the fatherland of all Jewish citizens of Austria.[91]

In early March, Jews of all political shades rallied around Schuschnigg, collecting money and actively campaigning on behalf of the plebiscite in favor of continued Austrian independence. Every Jewish paper, from the Orthodox *Jüdische Presse* and the Liberal *Die Wahrheit* to the Zionist *Die Stimme* and *Neue Welt*, strongly urged Jews to come out and vote "yes."[92] While some might blame Austrian Jewry for unwisely putting all their eggs in a single basket, by that time no other receptacles were available. For once all Viennese Jews were in agreement. Their only hope for avoiding a far worse fate was that a victory in this plebiscite would guarantee Austria's future.

EPILOGUE

After the *Anschluss*

In March 1938 Hitler marched triumphantly into Vienna amid cheers from much of the Austrian populace, but for the Viennese Jewish community, Germany's annexation of Austria spelled catastrophe. Almost overnight Austrian Jewry lost virtually everything they had ever had. Nazi antisemitism, with its sadistic public humiliations and rapacious private plundering, made all previous anti-Jewish manifestations in Vienna look like child's play. Within six months Vienna's Jews experienced even greater horrors and more punitive legislation than German Jewry had witnessed over six years, but the worst was yet to come. Viennese Jews clearly had only one choice: to leave or to die. The Nazi occupation brought Jewish life to an end in Vienna; within less than four years, the former Austrian capital was to become, in effect, *judenrein*.[1]

The *Anschluss* brought about cataclysmic upheaval for the Israelitische Kultusgemeinde Wien and its leadership, as well as the Jewish population as a whole. Soon after their arrival in Vienna, the Nazis ransacked the Kultusgemeinde offices on Seitenstettengasse, confiscated the list of contributors to the Schuschnigg plebiscite, and arrested most members of the communal board. Many of the top Jewish leaders, including Desider Friedmann, Robert Stricker, Jakob Ehrlich, and Hermann Oppenheim, were sent on the first transports to Dachau in April. Although some of these deportees eventually returned to Vienna, at least temporarily, others, including Ehrlich, did not. The Gestapo demanded payment of a sum equal to the amount the Jewish community had raised on behalf of Schuschnigg's referendum before the Kultusgemeinde could resume functioning even on a limited basis. This marked only the beginning of Nazi extortion from the Jewish community.[2]

For all intents and purposes, the Israelitische Kultusgemeinde Wien, which had previously avoided large-scale governmental intervention, turned into a Gestapo agency with an autocratic executive officer. To head its apparatus the Nazis selected Josef Löwenherz, the controversial, Galician-born Jewish Nationalist chief communal administrator, who, unlike most prominent Jewish leaders, had never belonged to

B'nai B'rith. Instead of an elected communal board made up of a wide range of factions, Löwenherz, with Nazi approval, appointed an eight-man advisory council, almost exclusively Zionist, with a single Agudat Israel representative but no Liberals or Socialists. Löwenherz, a decent man and a competent manager, acted as an efficient bureaucrat rather than an eager collaborator for the Nazis. He remained in Vienna and directed its "non-Aryan" community until the end of the war.[3] The Nazis had confirmed Jewish Nationalist dominance within the Viennese Jewish community, but the new structure they imposed and the disappearance of the opposition within the Kultusgemeinde signaled a complete reversal in the democratization process and the termination of the long-standing tradition of Jewish communal autonomy.

The Kultusgemeinde constituted one of the very few Jewish organizations allowed to operate in post-*Anschluss* Vienna. It continued to provide services for an increasingly destitute Jewish population deprived of its wealth and livelihood. With assistance from the Joint Distribution Committee, it ran soup kitchens which fed many thousands of undernourished men, women, and children daily. It expanded its elementary and secondary school network to accommodate Jewish children excluded by law from public schools. It also developed extensive retraining and foreign language programs for both youth and adults in the hope of facilitating emigration abroad.[4] Alongside its ongoing activities which provided assistance for Jews as long as they remained in Vienna, the most crucial task of the Kultusgemeinde became helping Jews leave Austria.

From the outset it had been made abundantly clear that Jews had no future in Nazi Vienna, and immediately after the *Anschluss* they began seeking escape hatches, either legally or illegally. Some Jews who could see no another way out of their grim situation committed suicide.[5] Despite the incredible bureaucracy and the fact that no country in the world wanted to accept more refugees from Nazism, many Jews managed to emigrate on their own in the first few weeks and months after the Nazi takeover. The Gestapo set up a temporary Zionist umbrella organization with the primary function of arranging for the emigration of Jews to Palestine. Agudat Israel helped to locate new homes for some fellow Orthodox Jews, but for the most part emigration to destinations other than Palestine had become the responsibility of the Kultusgemeinde.[6]

Although the international Evian Conference, which Löwenherz attended as an observer in August 1938, failed to open up any new havens willing to accommodate large numbers of Jewish refugees, soon thereafter Adolf Eichmann implemented his Jewish agent's suggestion of establishing a centralized agency to expedite the processing of Jewish applicants who wanted to leave Austria. According to this system, a Jew would enter the mansion which had formerly belonged to the Rothschild family with papers ascertaining his or her identity, wealth, and property and exit with only a few pennies left but permission to cross the border legally and immediately. According to this Robin Hood scheme, the rich subsidized the poor to allow them to leave the country and attempt to reach a more secure shelter from the Nazi storm. Whether rich or poor while in Vienna, most Austrian Jews, unlike their German counterparts who emigrated earlier, left the country of their birth or adoption with nothing. By December 1939, more than 100,000 of the approximately 175,000 Viennese Jews had emigrated; within the next two years, another 25,000 followed in their footsteps.[7]

With some help from fellow Jews and much determination, a majority of Viennese Jews managed to find sanctuary in many different parts of the globe; some, however, had not gotten far enough away to escape Hitler's clutches. More than 55,000 remained in Europe; of these, the majority had gained entry into England. The United States accepted the next largest group, numbering some 28,000. About 11,000 former Viennese made new homes for themselves in Latin America, while over 18,000 reached at least a temporary haven in Shanghai, which was one of the few places in the world which did not require a visa once you got there. Due to strict British restrictions, few official certificates for entry into Palestine were available for Viennese Jews, but approximately 9,000 émigrés, including a few prominent Zionist leaders such as Leopold Plaschkes, managed to find asylum in Palestine before 1941; many of them arrived illegally on small unseaworthy boats.[8] When World War II broke out in September 1939, only about 66,000 persons classified as Jews by religion, most of them women and many of them elderly, remained in Vienna.[9]

Those Jews who did not leave Vienna voluntarily faced subsequent forcible deportation "to the East," with transports beginning as early as October 1939 and continuing intermittently for the next three years. In September and October 1942, with fewer than 20,000 Jews left in the city, most of the remaining communal employees and former leaders, including Desider Friedmann and Robert Stricker, were sent to Theresienstadt. Nearly all of them perished there or else in Auschwitz, except for a few like Rabbi Benjamin Murmelstein, a former communal rabbi and Löwenherz's assistant, who became the last administrator of the so-called model ghetto. In November 1942, the Nazis officially dissolved the Israelitische Kultusgemeinde Wien and created instead a Council of Elders, still headed by Josef Löwenherz, whose purpose was to look after the few thousand "privileged" Jews, mainly baptized or *konfessionslos* individuals married to Aryans, who still were allowed to live in Vienna. For all practical purposes, Jewish existence in former Austria had been wiped out.[10]

An estimated 65,500 Austrian Jews, including approximately

15,000 who had emigrated to other countries in continental Europe, lost their lives during the Holocaust.[11] This figure represents more than one-third of prewar Austrian Jewry. Among the survivors, fewer than 10,000 reestablished residence in the Austrian capital after the war, although many thousands more Jews from all over Europe passed through Vienna on their way to other destinations. Josef Löwenherz, by then a broken man, eventually emigrated to the United States with his wife, Sophie, who had also been a Zionist activist before the war. Other survivors preferred to leave Europe as well; some chose to make *aliyah* to Israel. After 1945, one was much more likely to encounter Viennese Jews in Jerusalem, New York, or London than in their native city where Jews now constituted an insignificant percentage of the population.[12]

The second Austrian Republic proved no more hospitable to its Jewish inhabitants than the first, and antisemitism continued to pervade Viennese society. Little had changed. Austrians, unlike Germans, never acknowledged responsibility for their involvement with Nazism, and the Austrian government only very reluctantly agreed to pay reparations to individual Jewish survivors. When Bruno Kreisky, a Jew by birth but a Social Democrat by conviction, served as Austrian Chancellor in the seventies and eighties, he bent over backwards to accommodate antisemites and, following the example of his Jewish Socialist predecessors before the war, actively disassociated himself from Israel. It came as no surprise that the Austrian electorate chose Kurt Waldheim as their country's president in the mid-eighties despite his Nazi war record and that Jewish protests in Vienna and elsewhere led to renewed public manifestations of antisemitism.[13]

The Viennese Jewish community, which never exceeded 12,000 in the postwar era and by the mid-eighties had declined to about 6,500, generally maintains an extremely low profile.[14] The Israelitische Kultusgemeinde Wien, which reconstituted itself after the war, continues to provide religious, educational, and welfare services for a Jewish population roughly 5 percent of its former size. From 1945 to 1947 it operated under Communist control.[15] Its first postwar elections took place in 1948; in 1952 and the following four quadrennial elections, the Socialist faction, the Alliance of Jewish Workers, won a majority of seats on the communal board and their representative served as its president.[16] Thus the mantle of authority in the organized Viennese Jewish community had shifted from the Liberals to the Jewish Nationalists in 1932, but after 1949 had switched to the Social Democrats who had formerly been allied with the Liberals. Now that a Jewish State was in existence, most of the surviving Jewish Nationalists had emigrated to Israel or elsewhere and given up their dreams of achieving national recognition for Jews in the diaspora. The former non-Zionists were once again firmly in control of the Kultusgemeinde, which they clearly regarded as a religious community struggling for bare survival.

A thread of continuity between pre- and post-Holocaust Jewish communal leadership can be discovered in Ernst Feldsberg, who as a young Liberal representative and former treasurer of the Union of Austrian Jews had been elected to the Kultusgemeinde board in 1932 and had served on its executive committee from 1936 to the *Anschluss.* Born in Moravia in 1894, Feldsberg belonged to an Orthodox prayer-house before the war but had long been a Social Democratic sympathizer. After returning from Theresienstadt in 1945, he immediately resumed his communal activities, serving as vice-president of the Kultusgemeinde until 1963 and then as its president until his death in 1970. Feldsberg, who epitomized the non-Zionist camp both before and after the war, devoted much of his life to the well-being of the Viennese Jewish community.[17] His lengthy career in communal office demonstrates the paradox that Social Democrats, normally secular by definition, can remain actively involved in Jewish religious life.

Although the debate still continues among diaspora Jewry as to whether Jews constitute a religious group or a nationality, the fate of Jews everywhere has become inextricably linked with the existence of the State of Israel. Supporters of the Palestine Liberation Organization spearheaded attacks in the seventies and eighties against Jews and Jewish property in Vienna, including the main synagogue still located on Seitenstettengasse in the Inner City. Although Austrian authorities provide some protection for Jewish institutions and have allowed many Jewish émigrés, especially from the Soviet Union, to pass through Vienna en route to Israel or other destinations, the Austrian government generally expresses greater sympathy for Arab interests than for Israel.[18] While many former Viennese Jews reside in Israel, some Israeli citizens also live in Vienna. The Viennese Jewish community, however, no longer plays a significant role in Jewish political life, whether as active supporters of Israel, passive fellow-travelers, or vocal anti-Zionists.

The post–World War II Viennese community is only a shadow of its former self. It appears more internally united than its pre-*Anschluss* predecessor, but it largely remains impotent. Not a major community in either size or stature, it can no longer provide a battleground for various factions to argue over the nature and destiny of diaspora Jewry. Like the capital of the neutral Austrian Republic in which it is situated, the Viennese Jewish community has lost most of its former importance as the world passes it by.

Viennese Jewry, like Vienna itself, lives on in people's memories as it was in the past, more than fifty years ago, rather than as it is today. Some Viennese Jews, wherever they may be living, can still nostalgically recall the "good old days" before the war when they felt at home in Vienna and its vibrant cultural life. Today few Jews still hold on to the illusion that they could ever be fully accepted as Viennese. No matter how assimilated a Viennese Jew may seem, he or she still remains a Jew, rather than a Viennese, in the eyes of other Austrians.[19]

Before the Holocaust, Vienna had harbored one of the largest and most vibrant Jewish communities in Europe. Jews had constituted a very important and conspicuous element in Viennese society. With their strong support for the Austrian Social Democratic Party, they had helped to create and maintain "Red Vienna," that Socialist oasis surrounded by a conservative hinterland. Even the Christian Social authoritarian regime after 1934 could not afford to ignore Jewish interests entirely. Not until the Nazis decided to eradicate the Jewish presence in Vienna completely did Jews cease to make valuable contributions to Viennese life and culture. When Vienna rid itself of its Jewish population, it also lost much of its greatness and its dynamism.

The Viennese Jewish community certainly faced many serious economic, political, and demographic problems before World War II. Its leadership, split between Zionists and non-Zionists, could never agree as to how best to resolve these dilemmas and assure the continued survival of Viennese Jewry. In the end, the virulence and thoroughness of Nazi antisemitism precluded any possible solutions. But the factionalism which so permeated Jewish politics in interwar Vienna can be seen in retrospect not only as a sign of weakness but also a sign of inner vitality. Liberals and Jewish Nationalists, Agudists and Mizrachists, Social Democrats and Labor Zionists all were deeply concerned with reshaping the Israelitische Kultusgemeinde Wien according to their own definitions of the ideal Jewish community. Despite internal schisms, the Kultusgemeinde managed to cope with its predicaments, whether under Liberal or Jewish Nationalist leadership, and functioned reasonably effectively without outside intervention before the *Anschluss.*

Jewish politics in interwar Vienna strongly resembles Jewish politics in other major Jewish communities in the twentieth century. Whenever the problems are the greatest and the Jewish community is least able to devise viable solutions, the Jewish leadership seems unable to forge a united front and factionalism runs rampant. In an independent Jewish community, in times of stress, political parties more often splinter than cooperate. This phenomenon might constitute a dangerous syndrome, but it embodies a deeply rooted commitment to Jewish survival, especially when the means to achieve that goal are by no means obvious.

Abbreviations

AJYB	*American Jewish Yearbook*
AU	Austria
AVA	Allgemeines Verwaltungsarchiv, Vienna
AW	Austria/Vienna
BKA-I	Bundeskanzleramt-Inneres
CAHJP	Central Archives for the History of the Jewish People, Jerusalem
CZA	Central Zionist Archives, Jerusalem
d-öst.	deutsch-österreichisch
DBOW	*Dr. Blochs Oesterreichische Wochenschrift*
DJA	*Der jüdische Arbeiter*
DJW	*Der jüdische Weg*
DS	*Die Stimme*
DW	*Die Wahrheit*
EJ	*Encyclopaedia Judaica*
GR	Gemeinderat, Vienna
HWK	Hauptwahlkomitee
IKGW	Israelitische Kultusgemeinde Wien
JA	Jewish Agency
JDC	Joint Distribution Committee, New York
JF	*Jüdische Front*
JJO	*Jüdisches Jahrbuch für Oesterreich*, 1932/33 (5693)
JK	*Jüdische Korrespondenz*
JNR	Jüdischer Nationalrat
JP	*Jüdische Presse*
JW	*Jüdische Wochenschrift*
JZ	*Jüdische Zeitung*
KG	Kultusgemeinde
KH	Keren Hayessod
KKL	Keren Kayemet L'israel
KV	Kultusvorstand
LBI	Leo Baeck Institute, New York
LBIYB	*Leo Baeck Institute Yearbook*

NFP	*Neue Freie Presse*
NW	*Neue Welt*
Oest./öst.	Oesterreich/österreichisch
OIU	Oesterreichisch-Israelitische Union
Stenog.	Stenographische
UW	*Unser Wort*
WIKG	Wiener Israelitische Kultusgemeinde
WJF	*Wiener Jüdisches Familienblatt*
WM	*Wiener Morgenzeitung*
ZLK (fO)	Zionistisches Landeskomitee (für Oesterreich)
ZLO	Zionistische Landesorganisation
ZLVfO	Zionistischer Landesverband für Oesterreich

Tables

TABLE 1.

Viennese Population By Religious Affiliation, 1910–1934

Religion	1910		1923		1934	
	No.	%	No.	%	No.	%
Catholic	1,767,223	87.0	1,520,732	81.5	1,478,139	78.9
Jewish	175,318	8.6	201,513	10.8	176,034	9.4
Protestant	75,854	3.7	88,508	4.7	110,421	5.9
None	4,766	0.2	33,087	1.8	75,906	4.0
Other	8,337	0.5	21,940	1.2	33,630	1.8
Total	2,031,498	100%	1,865,780	100%	1,874,130	100%

SOURCE: Bundesamt für Statistik, *Die Ergebnisse der österreichischen Volkszählung vom 22. März 1934*, Vols. I and II.

TABLE 2.

Jewish Residential Distribution in Vienna (1923)

District	Name	Socioeconomic Composition	No. of Jews	% of Residents	% of Jews
I	Inner City	UC/UMC	10,462	24.3	5.2
II	Leopoldstadt	MC/LMC	59,722	38.5	29.7
III	Landstrasse	MC/inner	14,204	9.8	7.1
IV	Wieden	UC/UMC/inner	5,570	9.7	2.8
V	Margareten	MC/WC/inner	4,471	5.0	2.2
VI	Mariahilf	MC/inner	8,941	16.4	4.4
VII	Neubau	MC/inner	9,838	15.6	4.9
VIII	Josefstadt	MC/inner	6,932	13.8	3.4
IX	Alsergrund	MC/LMC/inner	23,746	25.1	11.8
X	Favoriten	WC Czech/outer	4,011	2.8	2.0
XI	Simmering	MC/suburban	400	0.9	0.2
XII	Meidling	WC/outer	2,405	2.5	1.2
XIII	Hietzing	WC/MC/villas	5,977	4.6	3.0
XIV	Rudolfsheim	WC/LMC/outer	3,706	4.7	1.8
XV	Fünfhaus	WC/LMC/outer	2,904	5.5	1.4
XVI	Ottakring	WC/outer	4,881	3.1	2.4
XVII	Hernals	WC/villas	3,829	4.3	1.9
XVIII	Währing	UC/MC/villas	4,601	5.4	2.3
XIX	Döbling	UC/MC/villas	5,665	10.2	2.8
XX	Brigittenau	WC/LMC	17,572	18.0	8.7
XXI	Floridsdorf	WC/rural	1,676	2.0	0.8
Total	Vienna		201,513	10.8	100.0

SOURCE: Bundesamt für Statistik, *Statistisches Handbuch für die Republik Oesterreich*, VI, 1925.
CODE: UC = upper class; UMC = upper middle class; MC = middle class; LMC = lower middle class; WC = working class; inner = inner district along Ringstrasse; outer = outer suburb

TABLE 3.

Candidates for Communal Office
by Place of Birth (1928)

Birthplace	Liberals		Zionists		Socialists		Orthodox		All
	No.	%	No.	%	No.	%	No.	%	
WESTERN JEWS									
Austria									
Vienna	11		4		10		1		26
Provinces	0		1		0		0		1
Subtotal	11	28.2	5	13.9	10	31.2	1	3.7	27
Hungarian Lands									
Hungary	4		0		2		3		9
Burgenland	3		1		0		1		5
Slovakia	3		1		1		3		8
Subtotal	10	25.6	2	5.6	3	9.4	7	25.9	22
Czech Lands									
Bohemia	4		1		2		0		7
Moravia	10		6		5		0		21
Silesia	0		1		0		0		1
Subtotal	14	35.9	8	22.2	7	21.9	0	0	29
Total	35	89.7	15	41.7	20	62.5	8	29.6	78
EASTERN JEWS									
Habsburg Empire									
Galicia	4		16		10		11		41
Bukovina	0		1		0		1		2
Subtotal	4	10.3	17	47.2	10	31.2	12	44.5	43
Elsewhere									
Russian Empire	0		2		1		5		8
Rumania	0		2		1		2		5
Subtotal	0	0	4	11.1	2	6.3	7	25.9	13
Total	4	10.3	21	58.3	12	37.5	19	70.4	56
GRAND TOTAL	39	100	36	100	32	100	27	100	134

SOURCE: CAHJP, AW, 60/3, Wahlen 1928.

TABLE 4.

Kultusgemeinde Board Members, 1920–38

A. Non-Zionists

	Liberals	Social Democrats	Agudists	All Non-Zionists	All
	N=44	N=10	N=6	N=60	N=109
Terms of Office					
One	56.9%	80.0%	33.3%	58.4%	53.2%
Two	13.6	20.0	50.0	18.3	22.9
Three	15.9		16.7	13.3	13.8
Four or more	13.6			10.0	10.1
	100.0	100.0	100.0	100.0	100.0
Occupations					
Businessmen	31.8	30.0	50.0	33.3	34.8
Professionals	27.3	10.0		21.7	30.3
White Collar	34.1	40.0		31.7	23.9
Other	6.8	20.0	50.0	13.3	11.0
	100.0	100.0	100.0	100.0	100.0
Academic Degree					
Yes	43.2	10.0		33.3	41.3
No	56.8	90.0	100.0	66.7	58.7
	100.0	100.0	100.0	100.0	100.0
Residence					
Inner City (I)	18.2			13.3	22.0
Leopoldstadt (II)	20.5	40.0	100.0	31.7	30.3
Alsergrund (IX)	18.2	20.0		16.7	12.8
Other	43.1	40.0		38.3	34.9
	100.0	100.0	100.0	100.0	100.0
	N=24	N=6	N=3	N=33	N=57
Age First Elected					
30s	12.5			9.1	21.1
40s	33.3	50.0	33.3	36.4	36.8
50s	29.2	33.3	33.3	30.3	19.3
60s or older	25.0	16.7	33.3	24.2	22.8
	100.0	100.0	99.9	100.0	100.0
Place of Birth					
Vienna	21.7	66.6		28.1	25.0
Czech lands	34.8			25.0	25.0
Hungarian lands	34.8		100.0	34.4	19.6
Galicia	8.7	16.7		9.4	25.0
Other		16.7		3.1	5.4
	100.0	100.0	100.0	100.0	100.0

B. Zionists

	General Zionists	Labor Zionists	Mizrachi/ Ind.Orth.	All Zionists	All
	N=36	N=8	N=5	N=49	N=109
Terms in Office					
One	44.4%	62.5%	40.0%	46.9%	53.2%
Two	27.8	25.0	40.0	28.6	22.9
Three	13.9	12.5	20.0	14.3	13.8
Four or more	13.9			10.2	10.1
	100.0	100.0	100.0	100.0	100.0
Occupation					
Businessmen	30.6	37.5	80.0	36.7	34.8
Professionals	47.2	25.0	20.0	40.8	30.3
White Collar	13.9	25.0		14.3	23.9
Other	8.3	12.5		8.2	11.0
	100.0	100.0	100.0	100.0	100.0
Academic Degree					
Yes	55.6	37.5	40.0	51.0	41.3
No	44.4	62.5	60.0	49.0	58.7
	100.0	100.0	100.0	100.0	100.0
Residence					
Inner City (I)	38.8		40.0	32.6	22.0
Leopoldstadt (II)	27.9	25.0	40.0	28.6	30.3
Alsergrund (IX)	8.3	12.5		8.2	12.8
Other	25.0	62.5	20.0	30.6	34.9
	100.0	100.0	100.0	100.0	100.0
	N=19	N=3	N=2	N=24	N=57
Age First Elected					
30s	21.1	100.0	100.0	37.5	21.1
40s	47.3			37.5	36.8
50s	5.3			4.2	19.3
60s or older	26.3			20.8	22.8
	100.0	100.0	100.0	100.0	100.0
Place of Birth					
Vienna	15.8	66.7		20.8	25.0
Czech lands	31.6			25.0	25.0
Hungarian lands					19.6
Galicia	42.1	33.3	100.0	45.8	25.0
Other	10.5			8.4	5.4
	100.0	100.0	100.0	100.0	100.0

TABLE 5.

Kultusgemeinde Taxpayers and Voters

Year	No. of Taxpayers	Eligible Voters		Actual Voters	
		No.	% of Taxpayers	No.	% of Eligible Voters
1910	25,276	12,289	48.6	4,446	36.2
1912	24,684	18,632	75.5	1,960	10.5
1920	34,210	19,303	56.4	10,553	54.7
1924	52,986	35,628	67.2	14,865	41.7
1928	58,690	37,557	64.0	19,348	51.5
1932	51,813	49,929	96.4	26,178	52.4
1936	47,782	44,480	93.1	31,760	71.4

SOURCES: *Bericht der IKGW, 1912–24*, p.8 and Tables XIII and XIV; *Bericht der IKGW, 1925–28*, p.3 and Tables XVII and XVIII; *Bericht der IKGW, 1929–32*, p.3 and Tables XIX and XX; IKGW, *Bericht des Präsidiums, 1933–36*, pp.9 and 96; CAHJP, AW, 72/23, Protokoll, November 8, 1936.

TABLE 6.

Kultusgemeinde Election Results

A. VOTES

Slate	1920	1924	1928	1932	1936
Non-Nationalist/ Union	5,912	+	9,068 *	10,194*	11,593
United Jewish		11,205*			
Zionist/ General Zionist	3,714 *	+	5,834	8,934	16,438*
Zionist/Democrat/ Adolf Stand				1,331	957
Socialist/ Social Democrat		2,266	2,899	+	
Socialist/ Labor Zionist				2,859	2,772
Other Socialist	49			547	
Orthodox/ Adas Jisroel	878	+	+	435	
Mizrachi	+	943	789	837	+
Beth Israel/ Apolitical	+	451	758	1,041	+
Total	10,553	14,865	19,348	26,178	31,760

B. MANDATES

Slate	1920	1924	1928	1932	1936
Non-Nationalist/	20		18*	15*	13
Union		(15)+	(15)+	(11)+	
United Jewish		28*			
Zionist/	13*		11	14	19*
General Zionist	(11)+	(10)+			(17)+
Other Zionist				1	1
Socialist/SD		5	5	(4)+	
Labor Zionist				4	3
Orthodox	3	(3)+	(3)+	0	
Mizrachi	(2)+	2	1	1	(1)+
Apolitical	(0)+	1	1	1	(1)+
Total	36	36	36	36	36

SOURCES: *Bericht der IKGW, 1912–24*, p.8; *Bericht der IKGW, 1925–28*, p.3; *Bericht der IKGW, 1929–32*, p.3; IKGW, *Bericht des Präsidiums, 1933–46*, p.9; CAHJP, AW, 72/23, Protokoll, November 8, 1936.
* = Coalition Total; +/( )+ = Coalition Partner

TABLE 7.

World Zionist Congress Election Results for Vienna/Austria
(Number of delegates in parentheses)

Slate	1927	1929	1931	1933	1935	1937
Pro-Jewish Agency/	551	862	1,376	2,462	3,581	5,717S*
General Zionist B	(1)	(1)	(1)	(2)	(3)	(4)
Radical/	663 S	1,602 S	340	659	1,063	1,168
General Zionist A	(1)	(2)			(1)	(1)
Revisionist/	264	192	1,955 S	1,319 S	2,149 S	S*
Jewish State			(2)	(1)	(1)	
Hitachdut-Poale Zion/	189	663	852	1,457	2,646	2,758
Labor Zionist			(1)	(1)	(2)	(2)
Mizrachi/	114	172	269	404	747	681
Religious Zionist						
Other (Jabotinsky/				765	302	
Adolf Stand)						
Total	1,781	3,491	4,792	7,066	10,488	10,324
% of Shekel Payers	34%	NA	43%	65%	67%	60%

SOURCES: *WM*, IX, 3037 (August 13, 1927), p.3; *DW*, XLV, 27 (July 4, 1929), pp.1–2; *NW*,
    V, 195 (July 12, 1931), p.1; *NW*, VII, 305 (July 14, 1933), p.2; *NW*, IX, 477 (July
    5, 1935), p.1; *NW*, XI, 668 (July 2, 1937), p.1.
S = Robert Stricker's Slate; S* = Coalition with Stricker's Slate

TABLE 8.

Occupations and Education of Jewish Nationalist and Liberal Supporters (1928)

Occupations	Zionist Electoral Committee		Union Electoral Committee	
Businessmen	293	49.9%	276	53.5%
Professionals	141	24.0	62	12.0
White Collar Employees	84	14.3	72	14.0
Manufacturers	31	5.3	45	8.7
Artisans	27	4.6	45	8.7
Other	11	1.9	16	3.1
Total	587	100.0	516	100.0

University Degrees	Zionist Electoral Committee		Union Electoral Committee	
Yes	143	24.4	66	12.8
No	444	75.6	450	87.2
Total	587	100.0	516	100.0

SOURCE: CAHJP, AW, 60/4, "Das Zionistische Wahlkomitee," *Mitteilungen des ZLKfO*, I, 1 (October 25, 1928) and "Das grosse Wahlkomitee der 'Union'" (1928).

TABLE 9.

Candidates for Communal Elections
by Occupation, Residence and Age
1920–1936

	Liberals	Zionists	Socialists	Orthodox	Total
	N=92	N=149	N=170	N=113	N=524
Occupations					
Businessmen	37.0%	43.6%	51.7%	73.5%	51.5%
Professionals	22.8	24.8	13.5	10.6	17.8
White Collar	23.9	18.8	16.5	0.9	15.1
Other	16.3	12.8	18.3	15.0	15.6
Total	100.0	100.0	100.0	100.0	100.0
Residence					
Inner City (I)	14.1	20.1	3.5	8.0	11.1
Leopoldstadt (II)	17.4	26.8	44.7	60.2	38.2
Alsergrund (IX)	16.3	9.4	10.6	7.1	10.5
Other	52.2	43.7	41.2	24.7	40.2
Total	100.0	100.0	100.0	100.0	100.0
	N=39	N=36	N=32	N=27	N=134
*Age**					
30s	2.6	8.3	25.0	7.4	10.4
40s	17.9	50.0	43.7	22.2	33.6
50s	43.6	13.9	18.8	33.3	27.6
60s	20.5	22.2	9.4	33.3	20.9
70s	15.4	5.6	3.1	3.8	7.5
Total	100.0	100.0	100.0	100.0	100.0

* in 1928

SOURCES: CAHJP, AW, 57/12, Amtlicher Stimmzettel, June 27, 1920; 60/3, ibid., November 9, 1924; 60/4, ibid., December 2, 1928 and Wahlen 1928; 61/2, Amtlicher Stimmzettel, December 4, 1932; 62/2, ibid., November 8, 1936.

TABLE 10.

Communal Revenues and Expenditures

Year	Revenues	Expenditures	Surplus/(Deficit)
1912	3,496,862K	3,307,006K	189,856K
1920	28,496,104K	31,495,610K	(2,999,506K)
1924	3,591,710S	3,695,316S	(103,606S)
1928	5,977,558S	6,047,221S	(69,663S)
1932	6,138,272S	6,179,752S	(41,480S)
1935	6,743,903S	6,758,806S	(14,903S)

SOURCES: *Bericht der IKGW, 1912–24*, Table VII; *Bericht der IKGW, 1925–28*, Table XI; *Bericht der IKGW, 1929–32*, Table XVIII; IKGW, *Bericht des Präsidiums, 1933–36*, p.108.
K = Austrian Crowns; S = Austrian Schillings

TABLE 11.

Communal Revenue Sources

Source	1912	1920	1924	1928	1932	1935
Taxation	45.9%	16.9%	35.1%	38.2%	37.5%	35.7%
Cemetery	28.7	39.4	29.3	28.0	23.6	20.8
Social Welfare	12.4	30.6	14.5	18.2	25.7	27.8
Religious Affairs	7.1	10.9	11.9	10.6	10.0	7.3
Education	3.1	1.1	2.9	0.4	1.2	1.5
Other	2.8	1.1	6.3	4.6	2.0	6.9
Total	100.0	100.0	100.0	100.0	100.0	100.0

SOURCES: *Bericht der IKGW, 1912–24*; *Bericht der IKGW, 1925–28*; *Bericht der IKGW, 1929–32*; IKGW, *Bericht des Präsidiums, 1933–36*.

TABLE 12.

Communal Allocations

Branch	1912	1920	1924	1928	1932	1935
Social Welfare	30.9%	44.5%	35.2%	33.9%	41.9%	44.0%
Religious Affairs	21.6	14.4	13.8	16.0	17.1	15.0
Education	11.9	6.1	7.7	6.7	9.2	9.1
Administration	19.1	14.6	20.5	24.4	16.7	15.4
Other	16.5	20.4	22.8	19.0	15.1	16.5
Total	100.0	100.0	100.0	100.0	100.0	100.0

SOURCES: Ibid.

TABLE 13.

Social Welfare Allocations

Agency	1912	1920	1924	1928	1932	1935
Communal Hospital	24.0%	20.8%	37.5%	45.8%	34.9%	29.5%
Home for the Aged	21.3	29.9	26.4	20.9	19.1	17.2
Other Institutions	5.8	0.3	5.8	10.3	4.4	3.3
Direct/Youth Relief	30.0	20.3	8.1	16.7	37.3	45.8
Philanthropic Societies	18.9	28.7	22.2	6.3	4.3	4.2
Total	100.0	100.0	100.0	100.0	100.0	100.0

SOURCES: Ibid.

Notes

1. Introduction: Jews, Politics, and Vienna

1. For a detailed analysis of Jewish migration to Vienna before World War I, see Marsha Rozenblit, *The Jews of Vienna, 1867–1914: Assimilation and Identity* (Albany: State University of New York Press, 1983), pp.13–45. See also Ivar Oxaal and Walter R. Weitzmann, "The Jews of Pre-1914 Vienna: An Exploration of Basic Sociological Dimensions," *LBIYB*, XXX (1985), pp.397–403, and Arieh Tartakower, "Jewish Migration Movements in Austria in Recent Generations" in Josef Fraenkel, ed., *The Jews of Austria* (London: Valentine-Mitchell, 1967), pp.286–289.

2. Cf. Jack Wertheimer, *Unwelcome Strangers: East European Jews in Imperial Germany* (New York: Oxford University Press, 1987); Salomon Adler-Rudel, *Ostjuden in Deutschland 1880–1940* (Tübingen, 1959); Trude Maurer, *Ostjuden in Deutschland, 1918–33* (Hamburg, 1986); Steven E. Aschheim, *Brothers and Strangers* (Madison: University of Wisconsin Press, 1982).

3. For comparative data on Germany, see Ernest Hamburger and Peter Pulzer, "Jews as Voters in the Weimar Republic," *LBIYB*, XXX (1985), pp.3–66, and Donald L. Niewyk, *The Jews in Weimar Germany* (Baton Rouge: Lousiana State University Press, 1980). For East Central Europe, see Ezra Mendelsohn, *The Jews of East Central Europe between the World Wars* (Bloomington: Indiana University Press, 1983) and *The Jews of Czechoslovakia: Historical Studies and Surveys*, 2 vols. (Philadelphia: Jewish Publication Society, 1971).

4. See William O. McCagg, *A History of Habsburg Jews, 1670–1918* (Bloomington: Indiana University Press, 1989), pp.83–101.

5. See Gary B. Cohen, *The Politics of Ethnic Survival: Germans in Prague, 1861–1914* (Princeton: Princeton University Press, 1981).

6. Carl E. Schorske, "Politics in a New Key: An Austrian Triptych," *Journal of Modern History*, XXXIX, 4 (December 1967), pp.343–381. See also Adam Wandruszka, "Oesterreichs politische Struktur" in Heinrich Benedikt, ed., *Geschichte der Republik Oesterreich* (Munich: Oldenbourg, 1954), pp.289–486.

7. For information on antisemitism in prewar Vienna, see John W. Boyer, *Political Radicalism in Late Imperial Vienna* (Chicago: University of Chicago Press, 1981); Andrew G. Whiteside, *The Socialism of Fools* (Berkeley: University of California Press, 1975); William A. Jenks, *Vienna and the Young Hitler* (New York: Octagon, 1976); and P.G.J. Pulzer, *The Rise of Political Anti-Semitism in Germany and Austria* (New York: John Wiley & Sons, 1964).

8. For an anecdotal account of Viennese Jewry focusing on antisemitism, see George E. Berkley, *Vienna and Its Jews* (Cambridge: Abt Books, 1988).

9. Klaus Berchtold, ed., *Oesterreichische Parteiprogramme, 1868–1966* (Munich: Oldenbourg, 1967), p.357.

10. Ibid., pp.374–376.

11. Klemens von Klemperer, *Ignaz Seipel: Christian Statesman in a Time of Crisis* (Princeton: Princeton University Press, 1972), pp.255–258, 404–405n213; *WM*, I, 306 (November 27, 1919), p.2; *WM*, IX, 2830 (January 14, 1927), p.1; *DW*, XLIII, 4 (January 21, 1927), pp.1–2; *DW*, XLVIII, 32 (August 5, 1932), pp.1–2.

12. CZA, KH4/280I, Memorandum to Zionist Executive, London, February

17, 1928, and letter from Chancellor Seipel to Nahum Sokolow, Vienna, February 18, 1928; *NW*, II, 23 (February 24, 1928).

13. Berchtold, ed., *Oesterreichische Parteiprogramme*, pp.478–482.

14. F.L. Carsten, *Fascist Movements in Austria: From Schönerer to Hitler* (London and Beverly Hills: Sage, 1977), pp.97–101; Bruce F. Pauley, "Political Antisemitism in Interwar Vienna" in Ivar Oxaal, Michael Pollak, and Gerhard Botz, eds., *Jews, Antisemitism and Culture in Vienna* (London and New York: Routledge & Kegan Paul, 1987), pp.163–164.

15. For information on the Austrian Communist Party, see Herbert Steiner, *Die Kommunistische Partei Oesterreichs von 1918–1933: Biographische Bemerkungen* (Vienna: Europa Verlag, 1968).

16. See Jack Jacobs, "Austrian Social Democracy and the Jewish Question in the First Republic" in Anson Rabinbach, ed., *The Austrian Socialist Experiment: Social Democracy and Austro-Marxism, 1918–34* (Boulder: Westview Press, 1985), pp.157–168, and Leopold Spira, *Feindbild "Jud"* (Vienna: Löcker Verlag, 1981).

17. Hamburger and Pulzer, "Jews as Voters in the Weimar Republic," pp.4–5, 26–31. Cf. also Jacob Toury, *Die politische Orientierung der Juden in Deutschland von Jena bis Weimar* (Tübingen, 1966), and Mordechai Breuer, *Jüdische Orthodoxie im Deutschen Reich* (Frankfurt: Jüdischer Verlag, 1986), pp.295–301.

18. *WM*, IV, 1338 (November 1, 1922), pp.2–3.

19. In the 1923 census only 2,434 individuals in Vienna reported Yiddish as their mother tongue. Of these 614 were Austrian citizens and 1,820 foreign citizens, including 1,275 Polish nationals. According to the 1934 census, there were only 510 native speakers of Yiddish left in Vienna. (Source: Bundesamt für Statistik, *Statistisches Handbuch für die Republic Oesterreich*, 1925; *Statistisches Jahrbuch der Stadt Wien*, 1929 and 1935.) These official figures are undoubtedly much too low, but most Galician Jews evidently deemed it prudent to claim German rather than Yiddish for census and naturalization purposes at least.

20. *DW*, XXXVII, 20 (October 12, 1922), pp.9–10; *WM*, IV, 1338 (November 1, 1922), pp.2–3; *WM*, V, 1519 (May 6, 1923), p.2; Union d-öst. Juden, *Festschrift zur Feier des 50-jährigen Bestandes der Union österreichischer Juden* (Vienna, 1937), pp.90–94.

21. For details on Jewish occupational structure in Vienna before World War I, see Rozenblit, *The Jews of Vienna*, pp.47–70, and Oxaal and Weitzmann, "The Jews of Pre-1914 Vienna," pp.424–427.

22. IKGW, *Bericht des Präsidiums über die Tätigkeit in den Jahren 1933–36* (Vienna, 1936), p.94; JDC, Austria, 439, General, 1934–38, The Jews in Austria (March 1938) and (Dr. W.B.), Data on the Jews of Austria (April, 1938).

23. Rozenblit, *Jews of Vienna*, p.195 and passim.

24. Cf. Steven M. Lowenstein, "Jewish Residential Concentration in Post-Emancipation Germany," *LBIYB*, XXVIII (1983), pp.471–495.

25. Rozenblit, *The Jews of Vienna*, pp.96–98; Ivar Oxaal, "The Jews of Young Hitler's Vienna: Historical and Sociological Aspects" in Ivar Oxaal, et al., eds., *Jews, Antisemitism and Culture in Vienna*, p.29.

26. See Rozenblit, *The Jews of Vienna*, pp.76–97.

27. *WM*, VIII, 2789 (December 2, 1926), pp.4–5; ibid., 2812 (December 25, 1926), pp.3–4; Leo Goldhammer, *Die Juden Wiens: Eine statistische Studie* (Vienna: R. Löwit Verlag, 1927), pp.59–64.

28. See Ivan T. Berend and György Ranki, *Economic Development in East-Central Europe in the 19th and 20th Centuries* (New York: Columbia University Press, 1974), pp.174–175; K.W. Rothschild, *Austria's Economic*

Development between the Two Wars (London: Frederick Muller, 1947), pp.14–19; Eduard März, *Austrian Banking and Financial Policy* (New York: St. Martin's Press, 1984), pp.281–299.

29. März, *Austrian Banking and Financial Policy*, Table A6: Postwar inflation, November 1918–December 1922.

30. See Berend and Ranki, *Economic Development in East-Central Europe*, p.180; Rothschild, *Austria's Economic Development*, pp.19–31; März, *Austrian Banking and Financial Policy*, pp.402–420.

31. CZA, Z4/2116, Letter from JNR, Vienna to Zionist Office, London, December 15, 1918 (in English).

32. Tartakower, "Jewish Migratory Movements," p.290. See also Pauley, "Political Antisemitism in Interwar Vienna," p.153.

33. *JK*, V, 35/36 (September 23, 1919), pp.3–4; *WM*, I, 232 (September 11, 1919), p.3; *WM*, IV, 1204 (July 28, 1922), p.3.

34. JDC, Austria, 111, General 1919–20, Mr. Gillis's Report to JDC (1919).

35. Josef Roth, *Juden auf der Wanderschaft* (Berlin, 1930), pp.53–64.

36. März, *Austrian Banking and Financial Policy*, pp.284–285, 416.

37. JDC, Austria, 117, Cultural-Religious, Letter from H.P. Chajes to Cyrus Adler, February 3, 1921.

38. Martin Kitchen, The Coming of Austrian Fascism (London: Croom Helm, 1980), pp.83–88; Rothschild, Austria's Economic Development, pp.31–42; Berend and Ranki, Economic Development in East-Central Europe, pp.213–214.

39. Felix Butschek, *Die österreichische Wirtschaft im 20. Jahrhundert* (Stuttgart: Gustav Fischer, 1985), p.35.

40. *WM*, VIII, 2476 (January 14, 1926), pp.4–5; ibid., 2789 (December 2, 1926), pp.4–5; *DJA*, IV, 10 (September 14, 1927), pp.1–2; *DS*, I, 18 (March 5, 1928), p.9; ibid., 22 (May 31, 1928), p.1.

41. März, *Austrian Banking and Financial Policy*, pp.297–302.

42. Peter Marcuse, "The Housing Policy of Social Democracy: Determinants and Consequences" in Anson Rabinbach, ed., *The Austrian Socialist Experiment*, pp.201–218; Anson Rabinbach, *The Crisis of Austrian Socialism: From Red Vienna to Civil War, 1927–34* (Chicago: University of Chicago Press, 1983), pp.27–28; Goldhammer, *Die Juden Wiens*, pp.61–62.

43. Berend and Ranki, *Economic Development in East-Central Europe*, pp.252–255; Butschek, *Die öst. Wirtschaft im 20. Jahrhundert*, pp.35–61; Kitchen, *The Coming of Austrian Fascism*, pp.91–94; Rothschild, *Austria's Economic Development*, pp.47–76.

44. *NW*, VI, 229 (January 29, 1932), p.1; DS, XI, 677 (September 24, 1937), p.2.

45. *DS*, V, 230 (June 2, 1932), pp.1–2; *NW*, VII, 308 (August 8, 1933), pp.3–4; *DS*, VI, 294 (August 10, 1933), p.5; *NW*, VIII, 411 (November 6, 1934), p.2; *DS*, VIII, 434 (March 15, 1935), p.1.

46. *DS*, V, 259 (December 22, 1932), pp.4–5; CAHJP, AW, 71/20, Protokoll der öffentlichen Plenarsitzung, February 6, 1933; *DS*, VII, 323 (January 26, 1934), p.3; *NW*, VIII, 411 (November 6, 1934), pp.1–2; *AJYB*, XXXIII (1931–32), p.80; *AJYB*, XXXIV (1932–33), pp.63–64; *AJYB*, XXXVII (1935–36), pp.188–190, 410–411; JDC, Austria, 439, General, 1934–36, Memo from Abraham Flexner to Felix Warburg, October 22, 1934; JDC, Poland, 788, General, 1933–35, Neville Laski, Report on Journey to Austria, Poland and Danzig, August 15–31, 1934; *DS*, XI, 742 (March 9, 1938), p.1; Charles Gulick, *From Habsburg to Hitler* (Berkeley: University of California Press, 1948), II, pp.1478–1479. See also Sylvia Maderegger, *Die Juden im österreichischen Ständestaat* (Vienna: Geyer, 1973), pp.224–245.

47. *NW*, IX, 510 (November 5, 1935), pp.1–2.

48. *DS*, VI, 266 (February 9, 1933), p.3; *WJF*, II, 5 (March-April 1934), pp.1–5; *NW*, IX, 473 (June 21, 1935), p.2; *DS*, XI, 684 (October 18, 1937), p.3.

49. *DS*, VIII, 398 (November 6, 1934), p.1; IKGW, *Bericht des Präsidiums, 1933–36* (Vienna, 1936), p.63; JDC, Austria, 439, General, 1934–38, Data on the Jews in Austria (1938), p.5; Yehuda Bauer, *My Brother's Keeper: A History of the American Jewish Joint Distribution Committee, 1929–39* (Philadelphia: Jewish Publication Society, 1974), p.224.

50. Rozenblit, *The Jews of Vienna*, pp.132–140. See also Oxaal and Weitzmann, "The Jews of Pre-1914 Vienna," pp.414–417. Cf. Peter Honigmann, *Die Austritte aus der Jüdischen Gemeinde Berlin 1873–1941* (Frankfurt: Peter Lang, 1988).

51. Arnold Ascher, *Die Juden im statistischen Jahrbuche der Stadt Wien für das Jahr 1911* (Vienna: Oesterreichische Wochenschrift, 1913), pp.9–11; IKGW, *Bericht der IKGW über die Tätigkeit in der Periode 1912–1924* (Vienna, 1924), Table XVI; IKGW, *Bericht des Präsidiums, 1933–36*, p.109, Table I. See also *Statistisches Handbuch für die Republic Oesterreich*, III (1923); *Statistisches Handbuch für den Bundesstaat Oesterreich*, XV (1935), p.36; Goldhammer, *Die Juden Wiens*, pp.30–34.

52. Arthur Ruppin, *Die Soziologie der Juden* (Berlin, 1930), I, pp.305–308; Arthur Ruppin, *The Jews in the Modern World* (London: Macmillan & Co., 1934), pp.330–332; *Statistisches Handbuch für die Republik Oesterreich*, XI (1920).

53. *Statistisches Jahrbuch der Stadt Wien*, 1938.

54. IKGW, *Bericht der IKGW über die Tätigkeit in der Periode 1925–28* (Vienna, 1928), Table XIX; IKGW, *Bericht der IKGW über die Tätigkeit in der Periode 1929–32* (Vienna, 1932), Table XXI; IKGW, *Bericht des Präsidiums, 1933–36* (Vienna, 1936), Table I; Goldhammer, *Die Juden Wiens*, p.26; Leo Goldhammer, "Von den Juden Oesterreichs," *JJO*, pp.11–12.

55. For greater detail on Jewish communal organization in Vienna before World War I, see Walter R. Weitzmann, "The Politics of the Viennese Jewish Community, 1890–1914" in Ivar Oxaal, et al., *Jews, Antisemitism and Culture in Vienna*, pp.121–151. For further information on the interwar period, especially communal elections, consult Avraham Palmon, "The Jewish Community of Vienna between the Two World Wars, 1918–1938" (Ph.D. diss., Hebrew University, Jerusalem, 1985) (in Hebrew).

56. Bundesamt für Statistik, *Ergebnisse der öst. Volkszählung vom 22 März 1934*, vols. I and II.

57. JDC, Austria, 117, Cultural-Religious, Letter from H.P. Chajes to Cyrus Adler, February 3, 1921; 174, Relief Supplies, Präsidium der IKGW, Bericht über die Tätigkeit und die Leistungen der WIKG (1922); *Mitteilungen der IKGW*, 1 (September 1930), p.4.

58. *Bericht der IKGW, 1912–24*, Table XIII; *Bericht der IKGW, 1929–32*, Table XIX; IKGW, *Bericht des Präsidiums, 1933–36*, p.94.

59. Samuel Krauss, *Die Geschichte der israelitischen Armenanstalt in Wien* (Vienna, 1922), pp.58–63; Weitzmann, "The Politics of the Viennese Jewish Community," p.132.

60. *JZ*, VIII (November 27, 1914), p.4; *JZ*, X, 15/16 (April 14, 1916), pp.7–8; JDC, Austria, 111, General, 1919–20, A.M., The Present State of Nutrition in the Jewish Population of Vienna (February 1919) and Mr. Gillis's Report to JDC (1919); CAHJP, AW, 2317, Zehn Jahre Arbeit des Vereines "Soziale Hilfsgemeinschaft Anitta Müller," 1914–24; *Bericht der IKGW, 1912–24*, p.29.

61. JDC, Austria, 111, General, 1919–20, Mr. Gillis's Report to JDC (1919); *JK*, V, 39 (October 24, 1919), p.2; 117, Cultural-Religious, Letter from Leon

Wechsler, JDC, Vienna to Albert Lucas, JDC, NY, May 18, 1920 and October 17, 1920; *WM*, III, 765 (March 13, 1921), pp.13–14; JDC, Austria, 112, General, April 1920–21, Boris D. Bogen, Activities of the JDC in Austria (1921); Bauer, *My Brother's Keeper*, p.14.

62. IKGW, *Bericht des Präsidiums, 1933–36*, pp.63–66. See also *Bericht der IKGW, 1929–32*, pp.41–43; *DS*, V, 241 (August 8, 1932), p.3; *DS*, VI, 308 (November 9, 1933), p.6; *DS*, VII, 398 (June 11, 1934); *NW*, X, 526 (January 3, 1936), p.2.

2. The Liberals

1. Cohen, *Politics of Ethnic Survival*, p.60.

2. For background on Jews and Liberals before World War I, see P.G.J. Pulzer, "The Austrian Liberals and the Jewish Question, 1867–1914," *Journal of Central European Affairs*, XXIII, No. 2 (July 1963), pp.131–142; Robert Kann, "German-Speaking Jewry during Austria-Hungary's Constitutional Era, 1867–1918," *Jewish Social Studies*, X, No. 3 (1948), pp.240–242; Walter B. Simon, "The Jewish Vote in Austria," *LBIYB*, XVI (1971), pp.103–112; Diethild Harrington-Müller, *Der Fortschrittsklub im Abgeordnetenhaus des österreichischen Reichsrats 1873–1910* (Vienna: Hermann Böhlau, 1972), pp.58–66; and Eva Holleis, *Die Sozialpolitische Partei* (Munich: Oldenbourg Verlag, 1978), passim.

3. See Marsha L. Rozenblit, "The Struggle over Religious Reform in Nineteenth-Century Vienna," *AJS Review*, XIV, 2 (1989), pp.179–221, and Michael A. Meyer, *Response to Modernity: A History of the Reform Movement in Judaism* (New York: Oxford University Press, 1988), pp.192–193.

4. Union, *Festschrift*; *DW*, L, 15 (April 6, 1934), p.3.

5. Werner Cahnman, "Adolf Fischhof and His Jewish Followers," *LBIYB*, IV (1959), p.127; Robert S. Wistrich, *Socialism and the Jews* (East Brunswick: Associated University Presses, 1982), pp.208–209.

6. For comparative data on the Centralverein, especially before World War I, consult Ismar Schorsch, *Jewish Reactions to German Anti-Semitism* (New York: Columbia University Press, 1972), pp.103–148; Jehuda Reinharz, *Fatherland or Promised Land* (Ann Arbor: University of Michigan Press, 1975), pp.37–89; Marjorie Lamberti, *Jewish Activism in Imperial Germany* (New Haven: Yale University Press, 1978); Arnold Paucker, "Zur Problematik einer jüdischer Abwehrstrategie in der deutschen Gesellschaft" in Werner E. Mosse, ed., *Juden im Wilhelminischen Deutschland 1890–1914* (Tübingen: J.C.B. Mohr, 1976), pp.479–548.

7. On the Israelitische Allianz, see N.M. Gelber, "Die Wiener Israelitische Allianz," *Bulletin des LBI*, No. 11 (1960), pp.198–203; *AJYB*, II (1900–1901), p.507; *JJO*, pp.54–55.

8. On Josef Bloch and the early years of the Union, see Jacob Toury, "Troubled Beginnings: The Emergence of the OIU" in *LBIYB*, XXX (1985), pp.457–475 and "Years of Strife: The Contest of the OIU for the Leadership of Austrian Jewry," *LBIYB*, XXXIII (1988), pp.179–199. See also Joseph S. Bloch, *My Reminiscences* (Vienna: R. Löwit, 1923; Arno reprint, 1974); Rozenblit, *The Jews of Vienna*, pp.155–157; Cahnman, "Adolf Fischhof and His Jewish Followers," pp.126–128; Wistrich, *Socialism and the Jews*, pp.208–211; Kann, "German-Speaking Jewry during Austria-Hungary's Constitutional Era," pp.250–255; Max Grunwald, *Vienna* (Philadelphia: Jewish Publication Society, 1936), pp.430–447.

9. CAHJP, AW, 2862, Statut des Vereines "OIU" in Wien (1886), p.2, articles 1 and 2.

10. Union, *Festschrift*, pp.113–115; DW, XXXVIII, 20 (October 12, 1922), p.8; *DW*, XXXIX, 11 (May 30, 1923), p.11; *DW*, XLI, 32/33 (August 17, 1925), pp.1–4; *DW*, XLVIII, 1 (January 1, 1932), pp.1–2.

11. Sigmund Mayer, *Ein jüdischer Kaufmann, 1831 bis 1911* (Leipzig: Duncker und Humblot, 1911), pp.313–316; Rozenblit, *The Jews of Vienna*, pp.157–159; Union, *Festschrift*, pp.78–90; DBOW, XXIX, 19 (May 10, 1912), p.309; DBOW, XXX, 17 (April 25, 1913), p.300; *DBOW*, XXXI, 22 (May 29, 1914), pp.376–378.

12. Union, *Festschrift*, pp.9–13, 105–107; DBOW, XXXIII, 19 (March 31, 1916), pp.314–319.

13. Union, *Festschrift*, pp.14–25, 73–77, 95–96; DW, XXXIX, 11 (May 30, 1923), pp.9–12; *DW*, XLIII, 22 (May 27, 1927), pp.8–10; CAHJP, AW, 72/29, Protokoll der Vertretersitzung, November 25, 1929; 75/11, Stellungnahme zum Pressgesetz (1929).

14. AVA, BKA-I, 15/4, 310.081–31, Statuten der "Union d-öst. Juden" (1920) and Statuten der "Union öst. Juden" (1937).

15. Union, *Festschrift*, pp.90–94; DW, XXXVIII, 20 (October 12, 1922), pp.9–10; WM, IV, 1338 (November 1, 1922), pp.2–3; *DW*, XXXIX, 11 (May 30, 1923), pp.9–14; *DW*, XL, 11 (March 14, 1924), p.8.

16. Union, *Festschrift*, pp.95–98; DW, XLVI, 22 (May 30, 1930), pp.5–6; ibid., 38/39 (September 22, 1930), pp.5–6; *DW*, XLVII, 26 (June 26, 1931), p.1; ibid., 49 (December 4, 1931), pp.2–3.

17. CAHJP, AW, 71/20, Protokoll der Plenarsitzung, September 13, 1934; *DW*, L, 40 (October 5, 1934), p.1; *DW*, LI, 14 (April 5, 1935), pp.5–6; ibid., 28 (July 12, 1935), pp.1–2.

18. Union, *Festschrift*, pp.99–102; DW, XLIII, 28 (July 8, 1927), pp.9–10; *DW*, XLV, 24 (June 15, 1929), pp.10–12; ibid., 26 (June 28, 1929), pp.8–9.

19. AVA, BKA-I, 15/4, 310.081–31, Statuten der "Union öst. Juden" (1937); Union, *Festschrift*, pp.19, 102–104; *DW*, LI, 11 (March 15, 1935), p.1.

20. For comparative information on the defense activities of the Central-verein, see Schorsch, *Jewish Reactions to German Antisemitism*, pp.117–148, and Reinharz, *Fatherland or Promised Land*, pp.37–89. For an indictment of the defense strategy of the Centralverein, and by analogy the Union as well, see David Joshua Engel, "Organized Jewish Responses to German Antisemitism during the First World War" (Ph.D. diss., UCLA, 1979), especially pp.8–12.

21. Union, *Festschrift*, p.112; JJO, pp.56–57.

22. DBOW, XXIX, 19 (May 10, 1912), p.310; DBOW, XXX, 17 (April 25, 1913), p.300; DBOW, XXXI, 22 (May 29, 1914), p.377.

23. DBOW, XXXIII, 19 (March 31, 1916), p.315.

24. DW, XXXIX, 11 (May 30, 1923), p.11.

25. This figure may be somewhat low, since it originates from an official Kultusgemeinde list compiled by Zionists. CAHJP, AW, 299, Ueberblick über das jüdische Organisationswesen im Lande Oesterreich (1938).

26. AVA, BKA-I, 15/4, 310.081–31, Statuten der "Union d-öst. Juden" (1920), article 4, and Statuten der "Union öst. Juden" (1937), article 4.

27. CAHJP, AW, 60/3, Wahlen 1928, Wahlvorschlag der Wählergruppe "Jüdische Union."

28. Holleis, *Die Sozialpolitische Partei*, p.74; CAHJP, AW, 2862, Statut des Vereines "OIU" in Wien (1886), article 4; DBOW, XXX, 17 (April 25, 1913), p.301; AVA, BKA-I, 15/4, 310.081–31, Statuten der "Union d-öst. Juden" (1920).

29. DW, XXXIX, 11 (May 30, 1923), p.11.

30. DW, XLVII, 21 (May 22, 1931), p.3; JJO, p.57; Union, *Festschrift*, p.113.

31. CAHJP, AW, 60/4, Das grosse Wahlkomitee der "Union" (1928).

32. *DW*, L, 18 (April 27, 1934), p.1; Union, *Festschrift*, pp.109–110.

33. *DW*, XLV, 24 (June 14, 1929), p.12; Union, *Festschrift*, pp.109–110; CAHJP, AW, 2828/38, XLVI Jahresbericht der Israelitischen Allianz zu Wien, 1925; 2828/39, XLVII, Bericht der Israelitischen Allianz zu Wien für die Jahre 1925–28; *JJO*, pp.55–56; Wilhelm Knöpfmacher, *Entstehungsgeschichte und Chronik der Vereinigung "Wien" B'nai B'rith in Wien 1895–1935* (Vienna, 1935); B'nai B'rith in Wien, Eintracht, *Festschrift anlässlich des 25-jährigen Bestandes des Israelitischen Humanitätsvereines "Eintracht"* (Vienna, 1928).

34. *DW*, XLV, 23 (June 7, 1929), p.9.

35. *DW*, XLVII, 21 (May 22, 1931), p.3; *JJO*, p.57; Union, *Festschrift*, p.113; CAHJP, AW, 289, Verzeichnis der jüdischen Vereine (1938).

36. Harrington-Müller, *Der Fortschrittsklub im Abgeordnetenhaus*, pp.62–66; Pulzer, "The Austrian Liberals and the Jewish Question," pp.136–142; Gordon Marshall Patterson, "The Misunderstood Clown: Egon Friedell and His Vienna" (Ph.D. diss., UCLA, 1969), pp.38–41.

37. Boyer, *Political Radicalism in Late Imperial Vienna*, p.454n225.

38. Sigmund Mayer, *Ein jüdischer Kaufmann*, pp.288–289.

39. Ibid., pp.299–301.

40. Ibid., pp.307–312.

41. See Lamberti, *Jewish Activism in Imperial Germany*.

42. Holleis, *Die Sozialpolitische Partei*, pp.30–31, 35, 39–42; Cahnman, "Adolf Fischhof and His Jewish Followers," p.125.

43. Holleis, *Die Sozialpolitische Partei*, pp.22, 86–87, and passim; *WM*, VI, 2018 (September 27, 1924), pp.1–2; *NFP*, 21568 (September 27, 1924, AM), p.2; *DW*, XL, 41 (October 10, 1924), p.5; Arthur Freud, "Um Gemeinde und Organisation," *Bulletin des LBI*, 10 (1960), pp.88–89.

44. Rozenblit, *The Jews of Vienna*, pp.181–184; Mayer, *Ein jüdischer Kaufmann*, pp.351–354.

45. Holleis, *Die Sozialpolitische Partei*, pp.86–89; Pulzer, "Austrian Liberals and the Jewish Question," p.140; *JZ*, VII, 22 (May 30, 1913), p.1.

46. Harrington-Müller, *Der Fortschrittsklub im Abgeordnetenhaus*, pp.64–66; Pulzer, "Austrian Liberals and the Jewish Question," pp.138–142; Patterson, "The Misunderstood Clown," pp.40–41.

47. Union, *Festschrift*, pp.25–26.

48. *DW*, XXVIII, 9 (March 1, 1912), pp.3–4; ibid., 10 (March 8, 1912), p.3; ibid., 15 (April 19, 1912), p.4; ibid., 17 (May 3, 1912), p.3.

49. *DBOW*, XXIX, 19 (May 10, 1912), p.310.

50. IKGW, *Bericht der IKGW, 1912–24*, p.3.

51. *DBOW*, XXXV, 13 (March 29, 1918), pp.194–196; *DBOW*, XXXVI, 28 (July 18, 1919), pp.444–445; *WM*, II, 596 (September 20, 1920), p.1; GR, B29–10, Stenog. Berichte 1923, pp.1901–1912; *DS*, V, 237 (July 21, 1932), p.7; *DJW*, I, 13 (August 2, 1932), p.3.

52. Wandruszka, "Oesterreichs politische Struktur," pp.293–300; Simon, "The Jewish Vote in Austria," pp.111–113.

53. Simon, "The Jewish Vote in Austria," pp.113–115; Walter Simon, "The Jewish Vote in Vienna," *Jewish Social Studies*, XXIII, 1 (January 1961), pp.38–39; Franz Patzer, *Der Wiener Gemeinderat, 1918–38* (Vienna: Jugend und Volk, 1961), pp.105–106, 140.

54. *NFP*, 19572 (February 17, 1919, PM), p.2; *NFP*, 20167 (October 18, 1920), p.2; *NFP*, 21235 (October 22, 1923), p.3; Wandruszka, "Oesterreichs politische Struktur," pp.297–298.

55. *NFP*, 19572 (February 17, 1919, PM), p.2; *WM*, I, 106 (May 5, 1919), p.1.

56. *NFP*, 19646 (May 5, 1919, PM), pp.2–3; *DBOW*, XXXVI, 18 (May 9,

1919), pp.282–283; *NFP*, 21235 (October 22, 1923), p.5; Patzer, *Der Wiener Gemeinderat*, pp.106–107, 140–142; *DJW*, I, 13 (August 2, 1932), p.3.

57. *DBOW*, XXXVI, 1 (January 3, 1919), pp.8–9.

58. *DW*, XXXIX, 1 (January 1, 1923), p.8.

59. Ibid., 10 (May 15, 1923), pp.11–12; ibid., 16 (August 10, 1923), pp.10–11; *WM*, V, 1656 (September 24, 1923), p.2; *DW*, XXXIX, 20 (October 5, 1923), pp.11–12; CAHJP, AU, 210, Wahlen in den Nationalrat und in den Gemeinderat (1923), Die "Bürgerlich-demokratische Arbeitspartei" und die Juden; Union, *Festschrift*, p.27.

60. *Statistik der Nationalratswahlen des Jahres 1920; NFP*, 20167 (October 18, 1920, PM), p.2; *NFP*, 21235 (October 22, 1923), pp.3, 5; Simon, "The Jewish Vote in Austria," pp.113–116; *WM*, V, 1685 (October 23, 1923), p.3; Patzer, *Der Wiener Gemeinderat*, pp.106–109.

61. *DW*, XXXIX, 22 (November 2, 1923), p.11; *Jüdische Volksstimme*, 29 (October 31, 1923), p.1.

62. *DW*, XLIII, 14 (April 1, 1927), pp.1–2; ibid., 16 (April 15, 1927), p.9; ibid., 17 (April 22, 1927), pp.1–8.

63. *DW*, XLVI, 42 (October 17, 1930), pp.1–2; ibid., 44 (October 31, 1930), p.1; *JP*, XVI, 45 (November 14, 1930), p.1; Simon, "The Jewish Vote in Austria," p.113; Patzer, *Der Wiener Gemeinderat*, pp.106, 140.

64. *DW*, XLVIII, 16 (April 15, 1932), pp.2–3; Simon, "The Jewish Vote in Austria," p.113.

65. *DW*, XLVI, 46 (November 14, 1930), p.1; Simon, "The Jewish Vote in Vienna," pp.45–47; Simon, "The Jewish Vote in Austria," pp.120–121; Walter B. Simon, "The Political Parties of Austria" (Ph.D. diss., Columbia University, 1957), pp.27–28. See also Herbert Solow, "Unrest in Austria," *Menorah Journal*, February 1930, pp.141–147.

66. Simon, "The Jewish Vote in Vienna," p.47; Patzer, *Der Wiener Gemeinderat*, pp.105, 141, 176–177.

67. Patterson, "The Misunderstood Clown," pp.48–49.

68. IKGW, *Bericht der IKGW, 1912–24*, pp.1–3.

69. CAHJP, AW, 744/9, Dr. Alfred Stern, Gedenkrede von Vizepräsident Dr. Ornstein, August 29, 1931.

70. *DBOW*, XXXIII, 34 (August 25, 1916), pp.557–558; *DBOW*, XXXV, 45 (November 15, 1918), pp.724–725; *JZ*, XII, 49 (December 6, 1918), p.4; Moritz Rosenfeld, ed., *H.P. Chajes, Reden und Vorträge* (Vienna, 1933), pp.205–206.

71. *Die Neuzeit*, XLI, 34 (August 23, 1901), p.241; *NFP*, 19495 (December 2, 1918, PM), p.4; CAHJP, AW, 744/9, Dr. Alfred Stern, Gedenkrede. . . Ornstein, 1931.

72. *WM*, VIII, 2535 (March 14, 1926), pp.10–11; *DBOW*, XXXV, 45 (November 15, 1918), pp.725–726; CAHJP, AW, 744/8, Dr. Alfred Stern (1918).

73. *DBOW*, XXX, 16 (April 18, 1913), pp.284–286; *DBOW*, XXXV, 45 (November 15, 1918), pp.724–725; CAHJP, AW, 744/8 and /9, Dr. Alfred Stern (1918 and 1931).

74. CAHJP, AW, 744/9, Dr. Alfred Stern (1931); *JZ*, XII, 39 (September 27, 1918), p.3; ibid., 49 (December 6, 1918), p.4.

75. *JZ*, VII, 4 (January 24, 1913), p.2; *DBOW*, XXX, 16 (April 4, 1913), pp.284–286; *JZ*, VII, 17 (April 25, 1913), p.1; *JZ*, VIII, 11 (March 13, 1914), pp.3–4; CAHJP, AW, 71/16, Beilage zum Protokolle der Plenarsitzung vom 5 November 1918.

76. CAHJP, AW, 79, Demission des Präsidenten Stern (1918); 71/16, Protokoll der Plenarsitzung vom 5 November 1918 and Beilage; 102, Vorlage des Tätigkeitsberichtes, 1912–24, pp.10–13; *DBOW*, XXXV, 44 (November 8, 1918), pp.712–713; *JZ*, XII, 49 (December 6, 1918), p.4.

77. *Bericht der IKGW, 1912–24,* pp.1–3; *Bericht der IKGW, 1925–28,* pp.3–4; *Bericht der IKGW, 1929–32,* pp.4–5; IKGW, *Bericht des Präsidiums, 1933–36,* pp.10–11.

78. Cf. Rozenblit, *The Jews of Vienna,* pp.47–70.

79. *Bericht der IKGW, 1912–14; Bericht der IKGW, 1925–28; Bericht der IKGW, 1929–32;* IKGW, *Bericht des Präsidiums, 1933–36; DW,* XLV, 24 (June 14, 1929), p.13; Union, *Festschrift,* p.4.

80. *DS,* II, 96 (October 17, 1929), p.3; "Pick, Alois," *Biographisches Lexikon Hervorragender Aerzte, Neuzeit,* II, p.1212; "Pick, Alois," *EJ,* XIII, p.499.

81. *DBOW,* XXXV (December 5, 1918), p.780.

82. *JK,* IV, 36 (December 5, 1918), p.2.

83. Knöpfmacher, *Entstehungsgeschichte,* p.75.

84. Kurt Lewin, "The Problem of Minority Leadership" in Alvin W. Gouldner, ed., *Studies in Leadership: Leadership and Democratic Action* (New York, 1950), pp.192–194.

85. *DS,* II, 96 (October 17, 1929), p.3; *JJO,* p.16; *DW,* XLIX, 2 (January 13, 1933), p.2; *EJ,* XIII, p.499.

86. CAHJP, AW, 26/9, Statut der IKGW (with 1914 and 1919 amendments), Anhang 1, Wahlordnung, pp.1–2; Letter from IKG to Magistrat der Stadt Wien, June 6, 1919 and reply, April 21, 1920; 74/6, Protokoll der Plenarsitzung, March 23, 1919; *DBOW,* XXXVI, 21 (May 30, 1919), pp.332–333.

87. IKGW, *Bericht, 1912–24,* Table XIV.

88. Ibid., pp.4–5; CAHJP, AW, 71/17 and 74/7, Protokoll der Plenarsitzung des KVS vom 30 September 1920; 71/17 and 74/8, Protokoll der Plenarsitzung des KVS vom 13 Januar 1921; 71/17, Protokoll der Plenarsitzung vom 6 März 1922.

89. CAHJP, AW, 71/18, Protokoll der öffentlichen Plenarsitzung vom 14 April 1924 and Wahlordnung (1924), pp.1–2; 74/10, Protokoll der öffentlichen Plenarsitzung vom 14 April 1924; *WM,* VI, 1857 (April 16, 1924), p.3; *Jüdische Volksstimme,* 20 (June 20, 1924), p.2.

90. *Bericht der IKGW, 1924–28,* Tables XVII and XVIII; *Bericht der IKGW, 1929–32,* Table XX.

91. *DW,* XL, 39/40 (September 26, 1924), p.23; *WM,* VI, 2034 (October 16, 1924), p.4; *DW,* XL, 43 (October 24, 1924), p.8.

92. CAHJP, AW, 72/10 and 59/5, Protokoll der Vertretersitzung vom 10 November 1924; *DW,* XL, 46/47 (November 18, 1924), pp.1–3.

93. CAHJP, AW, 71/18 and 74/10, Protokoll der Plenarsitzung vom 29 Dezember 1924.

94. *DW,* XLIV, 39 (September 28, 1928), p.12 (also CAHJP, AW, 60/4).

95. Ibid.

96. Ibid.

97. Ibid.

98. CAHJP, AW, 60/12, KG Election Results (1928); *DS,* I, 50 (December 13, 1928), pp.5–7; *DW,* XLIV, 50 (December 12, 1928), p.7; *Bericht der IKGW, 1929–32,* Table XX.

99. *Bericht der IKGW, 1929–32,* pp.3–4.

100. CAHJP, AW, 74/14, Protokoll der Plenarsitzung vom 3 Januar 1929; *DS,* II, 54 (January 10, 1929), pp.6–7; *NW,* III, 69 (January 11, 1929), p.4; *DW,* XLV, 2 (January 11, 1929), p.1.

101. *DS,* II, 56 (January 24, 1929), pp.8–9; ibid., 57 (January 31, 1929), pp.6–8; ibid., 58 (February 7, 1929), p.7; *DW,* XLV, 6 (February 8, 1929), pp.1–7; ibid., 7 (February 15, 1929), pp.1–5; CAHJP, AW, 74/14, Protokoll der Plenarsitzung vom 31 Januar 1929; *Bericht der IKGW, 1929–32,* pp.4–7.

102. *DS*, V, 250 (October 20, 1932), pp.1–2; *DW*, XLVIII, 43 (October 21, 1932), p.2; *DJW*, II, 1 (October 11, 1932), p.1; *DW*, XLVIII, 46 (November 11, 1932), pp.3–4; *Der Kultuswähler*, I, 1 (November 14, 1932), pp.5–6.

103. CAHJP, AW, 61/2, Jüdische Wähler und Wählerinnen (1932) and Nichtnationale Liste (1932); *DW*, XLVIII, 46 (November 11, 1932), pp.2–3; ibid., 47 (November 18, 1932), p.1.

104. *DS*, V, 246 (November 22, 1932), pp.1,6; *DW*, XLVIII, 39 (September 23, 1932), p.2.

105. *Bericht der IKGW, 1929–32*, Tables XIX and XX; *DJW*, II, 3 (November 8, 1932), p.2.

106. CAHJP, AW, 72/21, Protokoll betreffend die Ermittlung der Ergebnisse der Abstimmung (1932); *DS*, V, 257 (December 8, 1932), p.1; *DW*, XLVIII, 50 (December 12, 1932), pp.1–2; IKGW, *Bericht des Präsidiums, 1933–36*, pp.8–9.

3. The Jewish Nationalists

1. Cf. Ezra Mendelsohn, *The Jews of East Central Europe between the Wars* and *Zionism in Poland, The Formative Years, 1915–1926* (New Haven: Yale University Press, 1981); A.M.K. Rabinowicz, "The Jewish Party" in *The Jews of Czechoslovakia*, vol. II, pp.253–346; and Harriet Pass Freidenreich, *The Jews of Yugoslavia: A Quest for Community* (Philadelphia: Jewish Publication Society, 1979), pp.139–189. For Germany, see Jehuda Reinharz, *Dokumente zur Geschichte des deutschen Zionismus 1882–1933* (Tübingen: J.C.B. Mohr, 1981).

2. For information on Jewish national autonomism in pre–World War I Austria, see Oscar Janowsky, *The Jews and Minority Rights* (New York: Columbia University Press, 1933); Kurt Stillschweig, "Nationalism and Autonomy among Eastern European Jewry," *Historia Judaica*, VI, No.1 (April, 1944), pp.35–40; Rozenblit, *The Jews of Vienna*, pp.170–178; S.A. Birnbaum, "Nathan Birnbaum and National Autonomy" in Josef Fraenkel, ed., *The Jews of Austria* (London, 1967), pp.131–146.

3. See Mendelsohn, *The Jews of East Central Europe*, pp.46–51, and Freidenreich, *The Jews of Yugoslavia*, pp.146–153.

4. For further information on Kadimah, see Harriet Z. Pass (Freidenreich), "Kadimah: Jewish Nationalism in Vienna before Herzl," *The Dean's Papers, 1969, Columbia Essays in International Affairs*, V, pp.119–136; Julius H. Schoeps, "Modern Heirs of the Maccabees: The Beginning of the Vienna Kadimah, 1882–1897," *LBIYB*, XXVII (1982), pp.155–170; Ludwig Rosenhek, ed., *Festschrift zur Feier des 100. Semesters der akademischen Verbindung Kadimah* (Mödling, 1933); Edmund Schechter, *Viennese Vignettes* (New York: Vantage Press, 1983), pp.43–53; Rozenblit, *The Jews of Vienna*, pp.161–164.

5. See David Vital, *Zionism: The Formative Years* (New York: Oxford University Press, 1982), pp.470–475.

6. Adolf Böhm, *Die zionistische Bewegung* (Berlin: Jüdischer Verlag, 1937), I, pp.342–347; Stillschweig, "Nationalism and Autonomy among Eastern European Jewry," pp.37–40; Robert S. Wistrich, "The Clash of Ideologies in Jewish Vienna (1880–1918): The Strange Odyssey of Nathan Birnbaum," *LBIYB*, XXXIII (1988), pp.201–230.

7. *JZ*, XII, 12 (March 22, 1918), p.1.

8. Hermann Kadisch, *Die Juden und die österreichische Verfassungsrevision* (Vienna: Verlag Berkelhammer, 1918).

9. See Mendelsohn, *The Jews of East Central Europe*; Rabinowicz, "The Jewish Party," pp.254–267; and Hillel Kieval, *The Making of Czech Jewry* (New York: Oxford, 1988), p.189.

10. CAHJP, AW, 79, Declaration of the JNR im d-öst. Staate to all Jews, November 6, 1918; *JZ*, XII, 45 (November 8, 1918), pp.1–3.

11. CAHJP, AW, 79, Kundgebung des WIKG, November 5, 1918; *JZ*, XII, 45 (November 8, 1918), p.2.

12. *JK*, IV, 36 (December 5, 1918), p.2; *DBOW*, XXXV, 48 (December 6, 1918), p.780.

13. *JZ*, XII, 45 (November 8, 1918), p.4.

14. CAHJP, AW, 72/17, Protokoll der Vertretersitzung vom 8 Februar 1919; *JZ*, XIII, 20 (May 16, 1919), p.1; Aryeh (Leo) Sahawi-Goldhammer, *Dr. Leopold Plaschkes* (Tel Aviv: Orgun Olej Merkaz Europea, 1943), p.40.

15. *JZ*, XIII, 3 (January 17, 1919), p.3; *JK*, IV, 36 (December 5, 1918), p.2; Union, *Festschrift*, p.49.

16. CAHJP, AU, 157, D-öst. Staatsamt des Inneren, Letters from Robert Stricker to Chancellor Karl Renner, z.z.36228/19 (September 27, 1919 and October 19, 1919)(copies); *JZ*, XIII, 32 (August 8, 1919), pp.1–2; *WM*, I, 232 (September 11, 1919), p.3.

17. *DBOW*, XXXV, 46 (November 22, 1918), pp.737–738; *WM*, II, 662 (November 28, 1920), p.2.

18. Union, *Festschrift*, pp.50–54; *JZ*, XIV, 3 (January 16, 1920), pp.1–2.

19. *NFP*, 19501 (December 8, 1918, AM), p.5; CZA, Z4/2116, Telegram sent by Zionist Office, London, December 15, 1918.

20. *JZ*, XIII, 20 (May 16, 1919), p.1; *WM*, II, 509 (June 23, 1920), p.3.

21. CZA, Z4/2116, Letter from JNR für D-öst. to Zionist Organization, London, July 25, 1919; *WM*, II, 509 (June 23, 1920), p.3.

22. *WM*, I, 82 (April 4, 1919), p.4; *WM*, II, 509 (June 23, 1920), pp.3–4; Supplement, List of Educational Institutions, Austria, *Jewish Social Studies*, VIII, 3 (July 1946), pp.9–14.

23. *JZ*, XII, 43 (October 25, 1918), p.2.; *JZ*, XIII, 20 (May 16, 1919), p.1.

24. *WM*, I, 111 (May 10, 1919), p.1; *JZ*, XIII, 14 (April 4, 1919), pp.2–3; ibid., 19 (May 9, 1919), p.1.

25. *WM*, I, 1 (January 19, 1919), p.1; CZA, Z4/1089, Letter from *WM* to Zionist Actions Committee, London, September 24, 1919; Z4/2672, Letter from Colonel Kisch to Felix Rosenblüth, September 14, 1926 and reply, September 29, 1926; *NW*, I, 1 (September 23, 1927), p.1; *DS*, I, 1 (January 5, 1928), p.1; *DS*, IX, 500 (November 19, 1935), p.1; *DJW*, 1932–1938.

26. Internal Zionist politics in Poland and especially in Czechoslovakia bore some uncanny resemblances to the Austrian situation. See Mendelsohn, *Zionism in Poland* and Oskar K. Rabinowicz, "Czechoslovak Zionism: Analecta to a History" in *The Jews of Czechoslovakia*, vol. II, pp.19–136.

27. Rosenfeld, *Chajes' Leben und Werk*, pp.77–98; Böhm, *Die zionistische Bewegung*, II, 511–513.

28. CZA, Z4/2422, Letter from ZLK to Zionist Executive, London, February 3, 1926 and CZA, Z4/2672, Oesterreich (questionnaire, n.d., 1926).

29. CAHJP, AW, 57/12, Amtlicher Stimmzettel, June 27, 1920; 60/3, ibid., November 9, 1924; 60/4, ibid., December 2, 1928; 61/2, ibid., December 4, 1932; 62/2, ibid., November 8, 1936.

30. CAHJP, AW, 60/3, Wahlen 1928, "Wahlvorschlag der Wählergruppe 'Zionistische Liste'" and "Wahlvorschlag der Wählergruppe 'Jüdische Union.'"

31. CAHJP, AW, 60/4, "Das Zionistische Wahlkomitee" *Mitteilungen des ZLKfO*, I, 1 (October 25, 1928) and "Das grosse Wahlkomitee der 'Union'" (1928); *DS*, V, 252 (November 4, 1932), pp.2–3.

32. See Gideon Kaminka, *Ins Land, das Ich dir zeigen werde* (Zurich: Judaica Verlag, 1977), pp.44–45, 84–85, 104; and CZA, KKL/Box 331, Report of KKL Zentralbureau für Oest. to KKL, Jerusalem, October 17, 1927.

33. CAHJP, AW, 60/3, Wahlen 1928, "Wahlvorschlag der Wählergruppe 'Zionistische Liste'"; IKGW, *Bericht, 1912–1924*, pp.1–3; *Bericht, 1925–1928*, pp.3–4; *Bericht, 1929–1932*, pp.4–5; *Bericht des Präsidiums, 1933–36*, pp.10–11.

34. *WM*, I, 1 (January 19, 1919), p.3; ibid., 93 (April 22, 1919), p.3; *JZ*, XIII, 17 (April 25, 1919), p.2; *WM*, II, 601 (September 26, 1920), p.1; CZA, Z4/231/6, Delegiertenwahlen zum XVIII Zionistenkongress (1933) and Z4/234/4, Abschrift des Protokolls der Sitzung der HWK vom 11 Juli 1935; S5/1717, Letter from ZLVfO to Zionist Executive, Zurich, July 6, 1937.

35. *WM*, VI, 1854 (April 13, 1924), p.4; *WM*, IX, 2877 (March 2, 1927), pp.3–4; *DS*, I, 1 (January 5, 1928), p.2; *DS*, VI, 263 (January 19, 1933), p.7; *DW*, XLIX, 3 (January 20, 1933), pp.1–2.

36. *WM*, V, 1505 (April 22, 1923), p.2; ibid., 1519 (May 6, 1923), p.2; ibid., 1522 (May 9, 1923), p.1; ibid., 1528 (May 15, 1923), p.2.

37. Böhm, *Die zionistische Bewegung*, I, pp.343–344.

38. Rozenblit, *The Jews of Vienna*, p.178.

39. *WM*, I, 30 (February 17, 1919), p.1; *WM*, II, 631 (October 26, 1920), p.2; *WM*, V, 1666 (October 4, 1923), p.3; ibid., 1685 (October 23, 1923), p.2; *WM*, IX, 2909 (April 3, 1927), p.1; ibid., 2930 (April 25, 1927), p.1; *NW*, IV, 165 (November 14, 1930), p.1.

40. Arthur Freud, "Gestalten um Herzl in Wien," *Zeitschrift für die Geschichte der Juden*, IX, No.3/4 (1972), p.145; "Isidor Schalit," *EJ*, XIV, pp.940–941.

41. Rozenblit, *The Jews of Vienna*, p.176.

42. CZA, Z4/215/2, Memo from ZLK to Zionist Executive, August 11, 1925; Z4/2422, Die Freie Zionistische Vereinigung (n.d., 1925); DW, XLI, 39 (October 2, 1925), pp.3–4.

43. Siegfried Graubart, "Robert Stricker and the Wiener *Kultusgemeinde*," in Josef Fraenkel, ed., *Robert Stricker* (London, 1950), p.36.

44. Fraenkel, ed., *Robert Stricker*, pp.12–13, 77–79.

45. Louis Lipsky, *Memoirs in Profile* (Philadelphia: Jewish Publication Society, 1975), p.168.

46. Fraenkel, ed., *Robert Stricker*, pp.15, 26, 79–80.

47. CAHJP, AU, 122, "Rede des Kandidaten für die Leopoldstadt: Robert Stricker," *JZ Extraausgabe*, No. 3 (1911).

48. Statistische Zentralkommission, *Die Wahlen für die Konstituierende Nationalversammlung*, I (1919) and II (1920); *Statistik der Nationalratswahlen des Jahres 1920*, X and XI; *NFP*, 19572 (February 17, 1919, PM), p.2; *NFP*, 20167 (October 18, 1920, PM), p.2.

49. Ibid.; *Statistisches Handbuch für die Republik Oesterreich*, VI (1925).

50. CAHJP, AU, 121, An die jüdische Wählerschaft Oesterreichs! (1920); *WM*, II, 582 (September 4, 1920), p.4; ibid., 601 (September 26, 1920); ibid., 606 (October 1, 1920), p.3.

51. *WM*, II, 606 (October 1, 1920), p.3; ibid., 621 (October 16, 1920), p.4.

52. *Statistik der Nationalratswahlen des Jahres 1920*, X and XI.

53. *JZ*, XIII, 8 (February 21, 1919), p.1.

54. Robert Stricker, *Wege der jüdischen Politik* (Vienna: Löwit, 1929), pp.116–118.

55. Ibid., pp.122–124.

56. Ibid., pp.155–156.

57. Ibid., pp.150–151.

58. Ibid., pp.119–120.

59. Ibid., pp.125–127.

60. *WM*, I, 272 (October 22, 1919), p.2; *JZ*, XIII, 41 (October 24, 1919), p.1; *JK*, V, 40 (October 31, 1919), pp.2–3.

61. Stricker, *Wege der jüdischen Politik*, p.149.

62. *NFP*, 19646 (May 5, 1919 PM), p.3.

63. Sahawi-Goldhammer, *Dr. Leopold Plaschkes*, pp.9–22, 66–67; *DJW*, III, 13 (March 13, 1934), p.1.

64. Sahawi-Goldhammer, *Dr. Leopold Plaschkes*, pp.27–29, 46–50, 65–69; GR, B29–28, Stenog. Berichte, December 19, 1924, p.3868.

65. *WM*, VII, 2251 (May 27, 1925), p.3; *NW*, II, 35 (May 18, 1928), p.5; Sahawi-Goldhammer, *Dr. Leopold Plaschkes*, pp.54–61.

66. *NW*, VIII, 366 (May 18, 1934), p.2; *WJF*, II, 8 (June 1934), p.5; CZA, K4/B, Box 10, Letter from S. Altmann to KH, Jerusalem, November 10, 1937.

67. *DBOW*, XXX, 17 (April 25, 1913), p.302; *DBOW*, XXXIII, 19 (March 31, 1916), p.319; *DBOW*, XXXVI, 1 (January 3, 1919), pp.9–10; Union, *Festschrift*, p.109.

68. *NFP*, 19646 (May 5, 1919, PM), p.1.

69. GR, B6–89, Sitzungsprotokolle des Gemeinderates 1919, June 27, 1919; B29–3, Stenog. Berichte, October 9, 1920, pp.460–462; and December 10, 1920, pp.718–719; B29–5, ibid., June 24 1921, pp.766–770, June 28, 1921, pp.929–930 and December 19, 1921, pp.1400–1404; B29–7, ibid., December 20, 1922, pp.992–994; B29–10, ibid., March 9, 1923, pp.871–917. Plaschkes's and Ehrlich's speeches were also reported in *WM*, II, 675 (December 11, 1920), pp.1–2; III, 866 (June 25, 1921), pp.2–3; IV, 1388 (December 21, 1922), pp.2–3; IV, 1391 (December 24, 1922), p.2; and V, 1463 (March 10, 1923), pp.1–2.

70. Felix Czeike, *Liberale, Christlichsoziale und Sozialdemokratische Kommunalpolitik, 1861–1934* (Munich: Oldenbourg, 1962), pp.25–26; GR, B29–14, Stenog. Berichte, July 24, 1923, pp.2371–2377; *WM*, V, 1598 (July 25, 1923), p.7.

71. *WM*, V, 1657 (September 25, 1923), p.1; *DW*, XXXIX, 20 (October 5, 1923), p.12; CAHJP, AU, 210, Wahlen in den Nationalrat und Gemeinderat, October 21, 1923, "Jüdische Wähler und Wählerinnen!" and "Die bürglich-demokratische Arbeitspartei und die Juden!"; *WM*, V, 1662 (September 30, 1923), p.1 and *DW*, XXXIX, 23 (October 5, 1923), p.10.

72. *WM*, V, 1679 (October 17, 1923), pp.2–3; 1681 (October 19, 1923), pp.2–3; 1682 (October 20, 1923), pp.2–3.

73. *NFP*, 21235 (October 22, 1923), pp.5–6; *WM*, IV, 1684 (October 22, 1923), pp.1–2; *Statistik der Nationalratswahlen des Jahres 1920*, X and XI; Walter B. Simon, "The Jewish Vote in Austria," pp.113–117.

74. GR, B29–28, Stenog. Berichte, December 19, 1924, pp.3859–3868; B29–38, December 16, 1925, pp.2817–2829; B29–49, December 15, 1926, pp.2917–2928.

75. CZA, Z4/2422, Communique on founding of Freie Zionistische Vereinigung (n.d., 1925) and letter from Freie Zionistische Vereinigung to Zionist Organization, London, January 12, 1926.

76. CZA, Z4/2094II, Protokoll des Parteitages, November 11, 1923.

77. CZA, Z4/3563I, Speech by Desider Friedmann to Delegiertentag, 1926; *DW*, XLII, 46 (November 11, 1926), pp.1–2.

78. CZA, KH4/277I, Protokoll der Sitzung des Zionistischen Parteirates, February 2, 1927; *WM*, IX, 2874 (February 27, 1927), p.2; ibid., 2892 (March 17, 1927), p.1.

79. CAHJP, AU, 211, Wahlen in den Nationalrat und in den Gemeinderat (1927).

80. CZA, KH4/277I, Letter from KH (Gelber) to KH, Jerusalem, March 17, 1927; *WM*, IX, 2930 (April 25, 1927), p.1; ibid., 2932 (April 27, 1927), p.2.

81. *DS*, III, 147 (October 16, 1930), pp.1–2; ibid., 148 (October 23, 1930), p.7; *NW*, IV, 161 (October 17, 1930), p.8.

82. *NW*, IV, 161 (October 17, 1930), pp.1–2; 163 (October 31, 1930), p.1.

83. *NW*, IV, 165 (November 14, 1930), p.1; *DS*, III, 152 (November 20, 1930), p.2.

84. *NW*, VI, 239 (April 5, 1932), pp.2–3; *DS*, V, 224 (April 21, 1932), p.2.

85. *DS*, III, 131 (June 19, 1930), pp.4–5.

86. *DS*, IV, 163 (February 12, 1931), pp.3–4; *NW*, V, 178 (February 13, 1931), pp.4–5; *DW*, XLVII, 7 (February 13, 1931), pp.1–2.

87. AVA, BKA-I, 15/Wien/1699, 215.380–30, Verein "Jüdischer Volksverein" (politischer Verein) in Wien, Bildung, November 21, 1930.

88. *NW*, VI, 239 (April 15, 1932), pp.2–3.

89. *JZ*, VI, 41 (October 18, 1912), pp.1–2; *DS*, I, 39 (September 27, 1928), p.1; Rozenblit, *The Jews of Vienna*, pp.187–188; *Bericht der IKGW, 1912–1924*, Table XIV.

90. *JZ*, XIV, 20 (June 25, 1920), p.2.

91. CAHJP, AW, 71/16, Protokoll der Plenarsitzung, November 5, 1918 and 71/17, Beilage zum Protokoll der Plenarsitzung, February 27, 1919; *JZ*, XII, 45 (November 8, 1918), p.2; *JZ*, XIII, 1 (January 3, 1919), pp.1–2.

92. CAHJP, AW, 74/6, Protokoll der Plenarsitzung, March 13, 1919 and March 26, 1919; 71/17, Beilage zum Protokolle, February 27, 1919; *DBOW*, XXXVI, 10 (March 7, 1919), pp.151–154; ibid., 12 (March 21, 1919), pp.184–186; ibid., 14 (April 4, 1919), pp.216–218; ibid., 21 (May 21, 1919), pp.332–333; CAHJP, AW, 26/9, Memo from IKG to Magistrat der Stadt Wien, June 6, 1919; *Bericht der IKGW, 1912–24*, pp.5–6.

93. Ibid.

94. *JZ*, VI, 40 (October 11, 1912), pp.1–2; *JZ*, XIV, 20 (June 25, 1920), p.2.

95. *JZ*, XIV, 17 (May 14, 1920), p.2.

96. *WM*, II, 492 (June 6, 1920), p.3; 512 (June 26, 1920), p.1.

97. *Bericht der IKGW, 1912–24*, p.4; *JZ*, VI, 41 (October 18, 1912), pp.1–2; *WM*, II, 514 (June 28, 1920), p.1; *JZ*, XIV, 21 (July 9, 1920), p.1.

98. CAHJP, AW, 57/12, IKGW, Kundmachung Z.1808/130 ex 1920 (October 1920) and letter from Jakob Engel to Benjamin Rappaport, September 23, 1920; 71/17 and 74/7, Protokoll der Plenarsitzung, September 30, 1920 and Beilage zum Protokolle; *WM*, II, 608 (October 3, 1920), pp.3–4.

99. CAHJP, AW, 71/17 and 74/8, Protokoll der Plenarsitzung, January 13, 1921.

100. *WM*, III, 830 (May 20, 1921), p.4; *Jüdische Rundschau*, November 8, 1921; CAHJP, AW, 71/17, Protokoll der Plenarsitzung, March 6, 1922.

101. *WM*, III, 852 (June 11, 1921), p.3; *WM*, IV, 1366 (November 29, 1922), pp.2–4; *Bericht der IKGW, 1912–24*, p.12.

102. *Bericht der IKGW, 1912–24*, pp.7–14.

103. CAHJP, AW, 71/18 and 74/10, Protokoll der öffentlichen Plenarsitzung, April 4, 1924; *WM*, VI, 1857 (April 16, 1924), p.3.

104. *WM*, VI, 2034 (October 16, 1924), p.4; 2046 (October 28, 1924), p.1.

105. CAHJP, AW, 59/3 and 60/3, Kultuswahlen 1924; *WM*, VI, 2948 (October 30, 1924), p.4.

106. CAHJP, AW, 59/5 and 72/10, Protokoll der Vertretersitzung, November 10, 1924; *Bericht der IKGW, 1925–28*, pp.3–6; *WM*, VI, 2058 (November 10, 1924), p.1; ibid., 2059 (November 11, 1924); p.1; *DW*, XL, 46/47 (November 18, 1924), pp.1–3; CAHJP, AW, 74/10, Protokoll der Plenarsitzung, December 11, 1924 and December 29, 1924.

107. *WM*, VII, 2181 (March 17, 1925), p.1; *Bericht der IKGW, 1925–28*, p.12; CAHJP, AW, 383, Palästina Zuwendungen, 1925–36.

108. *DW*, XLII, 11/12 (March 15, 1926), pp.27–29; *JP*, XII, 20/21 (May 18, 1926), p.153.

109. *WM*, VIII, 2467 (January 5, 1926), p.1.

110. *WM*, VIII, 2541 (March 20, 1926), p.2; CZA, Z4/2422, Letter from N.M. Gelber, Vienna to KH, London, March 23, 1926; CAHJP, AW, 71/19, Protokoll der öffentlichen Plenarsitzung, May 6, 1926; *WM*, VIII, 2587 (May 7, 1926), p.4.

111. CAHJP, AW, 71/19 and 74/12, Protokoll der öffentlichen Plenarsitzung, January 5, 1927; *WM*, IX, 2877 (March 2, 1927), pp.3–4; CAHJP, AW, 75/9, Protokoll der Vertretersitzung, November 28, 1927; *DS*, I, 1 (January 5, 1928), pp.2, 9; CAHJP, AW, 74/13, Protokoll der Plenarsitzung des KV, January 16, 1928.

112. *WM*, VIII, 2468 (January 6, 1926), p.5; 2507 (February 14, 1926), p.6; 2517 (February 24, 1926), p.6; *DS*, I, 1 (January 5, 1928), p.2; 6 (February 9, 1928), p.9.

113. *DS*, I, 29 (July 19, 1928), p.1; *NW*, II, 53 (September 21, 1928), p.2; CAHJP, AW, 60/4, *Mitteilungen des ZLKfO*, I, 1 (October 25, 1928) and 61/2, ibid., 5 (November 7, 1928).

114. CAHJP, 60/4, *Mitteilungen des ZLKfO*, I, 8 (November 28, 1928) and "Juden, lasset Euch nicht irreführen!" (1928).

115. *Bericht der IKGW, 1929–32*, p.3; *DS*, I, 49 (December 6, 1928), pp.1–2; ibid., 50 (December 13, 1928); *DW*, XLIV, 50 (December 14, 1928), p.7.

116. CAHJP, AW, 74/14, Protokoll der Plenarsitzung, January 3, 1929 and January 31, 1929; *DW*, XLV, 6 (February 8, 1929), pp.1–7; ibid., 7 (February 15, 1929), pp.1–5; *DJA*, VI, 2 (February 15, 1929), p.1; *Bericht der IKGW, 1929–32*, pp.4–6.

117. CAHJP, AW, 61/2, "Achtung vor Irrtum! Zionistische Liste" (1932); *DS*, V, 252 (November 4, 1932), pp.1–3; ibid., 255 (November 24, 1932), p.7; *NW*, VI, 271 (November 25, 1932), p.1.

118. *DJW*, II, 2 (October 25, 1932), p.1; ibid., 3 (November 8, 1932), p.1; CAHJP, AW, 61/2, "36 Männer und keine Frau!" (1932).

119. CAHJP, AW, 61/2, Amtlicher Stimmzettel (1932).

120. CAHJP, AW, 72/21, Protokoll betreffend die Ermittlung der Ergebnisse der Abstimmung vom 4 Dezember 1932; CZA, Z4/3563III, Letter from ZLKfO to Zionist Executive, London, December 5, 1932; *DS*, V, 257 (December 8, 1932), p.1.

121. In his memoirs, Gideon Kaminka, a Zionist who was not sympathetic to *Landespolitik*, attributes the Jewish Nationalist victory to a reaction against antisemitism. See Kaminka, *Ins Land, das Ich dir zeigen werde*, p.104. Walter Simon sees the shift as "a reaction to the frustrating situation that confronted the Jewish voters at the polls when voting for their country's legislative bodies." Walter Simon, "The Political Parties of Austria" (Ph.D. diss., Columbia University, 1957), p.280.

4. The Socialists

1. See Steiner, *Die Kommunistische Partei Oesterreichs*.

2. For comparative information on Jews and the German Left, see Hans-Helmuth Knütter, *Die Juden und die deutsche Linke in der Weimarer Republik 1918–1933* (Düsseldorf: Droste Verlag, 1971).

3. For comparative information on Labor Zionists elsewhere in East

Central Europe, see Mendelsohn, *Zionism in Poland* and Oskar K. Rabinowicz, "Czechoslovak Zionism: Analecta to a History."

4. Wistrich, *Socialism and the Jews*, pp.311–312; Mendelsohn, *The Jews of East Central Europe*, p.50.

5. Cf. Bernard Johnpoll, *The Politics of Futility* (Ithaca: Cornell University Press, 1967), and Ezra Mendelsohn, *The Jews of East Central Europe between the Wars*, pp.77–78 for Poland; Paula Hyman, *From Dreyfus to Vichy*, pp.101–114, 206–216 for Paris; and for New York, Irving Howe, *World of Our Fathers* (New York: Harcourt, Brace, Jovanovich, 1976).

6. Patzer, *Der Wiener Gemeinderat*, pp.62, 107, 142, 177; Czeike, *Liberale, Christlichsoziale und Sozialdemokratische Kommunalpolitik*, pp.25–26; John Bunzl, "Arbeitsbewegung und Antisemitismus in Oesterreich vor und nach dem Ersten Weltkrieg," *Zeitgeschichte*, V (1975), p.167.

7. George Clare, *Last Waltz in Vienna: The Destruction of a Family, 1842–1949* (New York: Holt, Rinehart, Winston, 1982), p.105.

8. Hamburger and Pulzer, "Jews as Voters in the Weimar Republic," p.55.

9. Rabinbach, *The Crisis of Austrian Socialism*, pp.27–28.

10. Simon, "The Jewish Vote in Vienna," p.43.

11. Simon, "The Jewish Vote in Austria," pp.117–119.

12. *WM*, I, 102 (May 1, 1919), p.1; *NW*, IV, 161 (October 17, 1930), pp.1–2; Simon, "The Jewish Vote in Austria," pp.108–110; Edmund Silberner, "Austrian Social Democracy and the Jewish Problem," *Historia Judaica*, XIII, No. 2 (October 1951), pp.120–123, 127–128; Wistrich, *Socialism and the Jews*, pp.209, 225–261.

13. See Spira, *Feindbild "Jud'*," passim.

14. GR, B29–19, Stenog. Berichte, January-February 1924, pp.96–97.

15. Spira, *Feindbild "Jud'*," pp.65–67; Avraham Barkai, "The Austrian Social Democrats and the Jews, II," *Wiener Library Bulletin*, XXIV, No.2 (1970), pp.20–21.

16. *WM*, I, 89 (April 17, 1919), p.4; *JK*, V, 15 (April 24, 1919), p.3; CZA, Z4/2116, Memorandum from Jüdische Pressbüro to Zionist Central Bureau, Berlin, July 3, 1919; Spira, *Feindbild "Jud'"*, pp.71–80.

17. *WM*, III, 959 (September 27, 1921), pp.1–3; *WM*, IV, 1338 (November 1, 1922), pp.2–3; *WM*, V, 1519 (May 6, 1923), p.2; GR, B29–28, Stenog. Berichte, December 19–20, 1924, pp.3862–3863.

18. Spira, *Feindbild "Jud'*," pp.80–86.

19. Simon, "The Jewish Vote in Austria," p.108.

20. *DS*, I, 1 (January 5, 1928), p.10.

21. This has been amply demonstrated for the pre–World War I period in Rozenblit, *The Jews of Vienna*, pp.132–141, and undoubtedly held true for the interwar years as well. Roughly 13,650 Viennese Jews abandoned Judaism between 1920 and 1935, an overwhelming majority of whom became *konfessionslos*. (*Statistisches Handbuch für den Bundesstaat Oesterreich*, XV, 1935, p.36 and XVII, 1937.)

22. *DW*, XXIX, 20 (October 5, 1923), pp.11–12.

23. *DW*, XLVIII, 16 (April 15, 1932), pp.2–3.

24. *JZ*, XII, 45 (November 8, 1918), p.4; *JZ*, XIII, 19 (May 9, 1919), p.1; ibid., 42 (October 24, 1919), p.1; *WM*, VIII, 2796 (December 9, 1926), pp.2–3.

25. GR, B29–3, Stenog. Berichte, June-December 1920, Speech by Plaschkes, p.462.

26. *NFP*, 20167 (October 18, 1920, PM), p.4.

27. *WM*, III, 993 (November 3, 1921), pp.3–4 (also *Jüdische Rundschau*, November 8, 1921); Wistrich, *Socialism and the Jews*, p.334.

28. *WM*, V, 1662 (September 30, 1923), pp.3–4.

29. *WM,* V, 1668 (October 6, 1923), p.2.

30. *NFP,* 21235 (October 22, 1923), p.6. See also GR, B29–19, Stenog. Berichte, January-February 1924, pp.94–106.

31. GR, B29–28, Stenog. Berichte, December 19–20, 1924, p.3868; GR, B29–38, Stenog. Berichte, December 16–17, 1925, p.2892; GR, B29–49, Stenog. Berichte, November-December 1926, p.2929.

32. GR, B29–38, Stenog. Berichte, December 16–17, 1925, pp.2823–2826.

33. CZA, KH4/2771, Protokoll der Sitzung des Zionistischen Parteirats, February 13, 1927; *DS,* I, 8 (February 21, 1928), pp.1–6 (also CZA, KH4/2801); *DW,* XLIV, 8 (February 24, 1928), pp.1–2.

34. CZA, Z4/2422, Letter from Freie Zionistische Vereinigung to Zionist Organization, London, January 12, 1926.

35. *DJW,* I, 4 (April 12, 1932), pp.1–2; *NW,* VI, 239 (April 15, 1932), pp.2–3; *DW,* XLVIII, 16 (April 15, 1932), pp.2–3; *DS,* V, 224 (April 21, 1932), pp.1–2; *DJA,* IX, 9 (April 28, 1932), p.1.

36. *DJA,* IX, 6 (March 18, 1932), p.1; ibid., 8 (April 15, 1932), p.1.

37. Patzer, *Der Wiener Gemeinderat,* p.180.

38. Rabinbach, *The Crisis of Austrian Socialism,* pp.26–27; Julius Braunthal, *In Search of the Millennium* (London: Victor Gollancz, 1945), pp.254–255, 286–288.

39. Joseph Buttinger, *In the Twilight of Socialism* (New York: F.A. Praeger, 1953), p.80.

40. Norbert Leser, ed., *Werk und Widerhall: Grosse Gestalten des österreichischen Sozialismus* (Vienna: Wiener Volksbuchhandlung, 1964).

41. Wistrich, *Socialism and the Jews,* pp.332–333; Rabinbach, *The Crisis of Austrian Socialism,* pp.27–28.

42. Buttinger, *In the Twilight of Socialism,* p.81.

43. Spira, *Feindbild "Jud',"* pp.35–36, 55, 64–65; Silberner, "Austrian Social Democracy and the Jewish Problem," p.125; Wistrich, *Socialism and the Jews,* pp.332–333.

44. See Leser, *Werk und Widerhall.*

45. Braunthal, *In Search of the Millennium,* pp.304–305.

46. Clare, *Last Waltz in Vienna,* p.105.

47. Braunthal, *In Search of the Millennium,* p.288.

48. *DS,* III, 151 (November 13, 1930), pp.5–6.

49. See Wistrich, *Socialism and the Jews,* pp.335–343; Silberner, "Austrian Social Democracy and the Jewish Problem," pp.124–125, 133–140; Avraham Barkai, "The Austrian Social Democrats and the Jews," *Wiener Library Bulletin,* XXIV, No.2 (1970), pp.17–18.

50. Braunthal, *In Search of the Millennium,* p.305; Wistrich, *Socialism and the Jews,* p.334.

51. *WM,* V, 1666 (October 4, 1923), p.3; *DJA,* IV, 5 (April 30, 1927), pp.2–3.

52. *DJA,* IV, 4 (April 20, 1927), pp.2–3.

53. *DJA,* IX, 6 (March 18, 1932) and 8 (April 15, 1932), pp.1–2.

54. *DJA,* X, 30 (July 28, 1933), pp.1–2.

55. Franz Goldner, *Austrian Emigration 1938–45* (New York: Frederick Ungar, 1979), pp.5–7.

56. *NW,* VII, 320 (October 27, 1933), p.1; *DJW,* III, 4 (November 14, 1933), p.1; ibid., 11 (February 28, 1934), p.1; *DW,* L, 11 (March 3, 1934), pp.1–2.

57. Berchtold, ed., *Oesterreichische Parteiprogramme,* pp.258–259.

58. *Bericht der IKGW, 1925–28,* pp.24–27; GR, B29–5, Stenog. Berichte, June-December 1921, p.728; GR, B29–28, Stenog. Berichte, December 19–20, 1924, p.3866; *WM,* VIII, 2796 (December 9, 1926), pp.2–3; GR, B29–49, Stenog. Berichte, November-December 1926, pp.2925–2927.

59. *WM*, III, 1000 (November 10, 1921), pp.1–3; ibid., 1001 (November 11, 1921), p.1; GR, B29–5, Stenog. Berichte, June-December 1921, p.1403; *Bericht der IKGW, 1912–24*, pp.24–25.

60. *WM*, VIII, 2517 (February 24, 1926), p.6; GR, B29–49, Stenog. Berichte, November-December 1926, p.2925.

61. *WM*, VIII, 2517 (February 24, 1926), p.6; *WM*, IX, 2831 (January 15, 1927), pp.2–3.

62. *DW*, XLIV, 13 (March 30, 1928), pp.8–9; ibid., 26 (June 29, 1928), pp.1–3; ibid., 42 (October 19, 1928), pp.15–16; ibid., 43 (October 26, 1928), pp.1–4; *DS*, I, 28 (July 12, 1928), p.8.

63. *WM*, VI, 2043 (October 25, 1924), p.3; *DW*, XLIV, 12 (March 23, 1928), pp.1–2; *DS*, I, 46 (November 15, 1928), pp.1–2; *Mitteilungen des ZLKfO*, I, 8 (November 28, 1928), p.3.

64. CAHJP, AW, 71/18, Deklaration der Mandatare der Vereinigung für soziale Tätigkeit in der KG, December 1924; *DW*, XLVIII, 43 (October 21, 1932), p.1; Union, *Festschrift*, p.64.

65. CAHJP, AW, 59/3, Programm der Wahlvereinigung für soziale Tätigkeit in der IKG (1924).

66. CAHJP, AW, 57/12, Amtlicher Stimmzettel, June 27, 1920; 60/2, ibid., November 9, 1924; 60/4, ibid., December 2, 1928; 61/2, ibid., December 4, 1932; 62/2, ibid., November 8, 1936.

67. Ibid.

68. Saul Raphael Landau, *Sturm und Drang im Zionismus* (Vienna: Neue National Zeitung, 1937), pp.165–166.

69. *Unsere Tribune*, I, 8 (September 11, 1924), p.1.

70. CAHJP, AW, 59/3, An die Wähler der jüdischen KG! and Programm der Wahlvereinigung für soziale Tätigkeit in der IKG (1924); 71/18, Deklaration der Mandatare der Vereinigung für soziale Tätigkeit in der KG (December 1924).

71. Ibid.

72. Ibid.

73. Ibid.

74. Ibid.

75. Ibid.

76. *DW*, XL, 46/47 (November 18, 1924), pp.1–3.

77. *Bericht der IKGW, 1925–28*, p.3.

78. Ibid., pp.3–4; CAHJP, AW, 71/18 and 74/10, Protokoll der Plenarsitzung vom 29 Dezember 1924.

79. *WM*, VII, 2182 (March 18, 1925), p.3; ibid., 2183 (March 19, 1925), p.4; *DW*, XLI, 12 (March 27, 1925), pp.10–11; *Unsere Tribune*, II, 6 (April 29, 1925), p.3.

80. CAHJP, AW, 74/12, Protokoll über die vertrauliche Plenarsitzung, December 9, 1926; 71/19, Beilage zum Protokoll, December 22, 1926.

81. CAHJP, AW, 71/19 and 74/12, Protokoll der öffentlichen Plenarsitzung vom 23 Dezember 1926 and Protokoll der vertraulichen Plenarsitzung vom 5 Januar 1927; *DJA*, IV, 1 (January 12, 1927), pp.1–3.

82. CAHJP, AW, 71/20, Protokoll der Plenarsitzung vom 28 Juni 1928.

83. *DW*, XLIV, 12 (March 3, 1928), pp.1–2; *DS*, I, 47 (November 22, 1928), pp.7–8.

84. *DJA*, IV, 13 (December 9, 1927), pp.1–3. See also *DW*, XLIV, 6 (February 10, 1928), pp.3–5.

85. *Jüdische Volkszeitung; DW*, XLIV, 12 (March 23, 1928), pp.1–2; *DS*, I, 31 (August 2, 1928), p.7; ibid., 35 (August 30, 1928), p.8.

86. *DW*, XLIV, 34 (August 24, 1928), pp.1–4.

87. Ibid., 36 (September 7, 1928), pp.1–4.

88. Ibid., 12 (March 23, 1928), pp.1–2; ibid., 43 (October 26, 1928), pp.1–4.

89. *DJA*, V, 15 (October 25, 1928), p.1; *Jüdische Volkszeitung*, I, 17 (November 30, 1928), pp.2–3.

90. CAHJP, AW, 74/14, Protokoll der Plenarsitzung vom 3 Januar 1929; *DS*, II, 54 (January 10, 1929), pp.6–7; *NW*, III, 69 (January 11, 1929), p.4; *DW*, XLV, 2 (January 11, 1929), p.1.

91. CAHJP, AW, 74/14, Protokoll der Plenarsitzung vom 31 Januar 1929; *DS*, II, 58 (February 7, 1929), p.7; *DW*, XLV, 6 (February 8, 1929), pp.1–7; ibid., 7 (February 15, 1929), pp.1–5; *DJA*, VI, 2 (February 15, 1929), p.1.

92. *DW*, XLV, 16 (April 19, 1929), pp.5–7; *NW*, III, 83 (April 19, 1929), p.6; *DJA*, VI, 5 (May 31, 1929), p.1.

93. *DW*, XLV, 21 (May 24, 1929), pp.4–5.

94. AVA, BKA-I, 15/4, 102.194–32, Vereinigung der Werktätigen Juden Oesterreichs (1930).

95. *DS*, III, 117 (March 30, 1930), pp.2–3.

96. *DJA*, VIII, 6 (April 13, 1931), pp.2–3; *DS*, V, 215 (February 18, 1932), pp.5–6; *DJA*, IX, 5 (March 4, 1932), pp.1–2.

97. AVA, BKA-I, 15/4, 102.194–32, Statuten der "Vereinigung der Werktätigen Juden Oesterreichs" (1931).

98. *DW*, XLVIII, 43 (October 21, 1932), p.2; ibid., 48 (November 25, 1932), p.1.

99. CAHJP, AW, 61/2 (Sozialistische Liste,) Jüdische Wähler und Wählerinnen! (1932); *DW*, XLVIII, 48 (November 25, 1932), p.1.

100. *DJA*, IX, 23 (December 16, 1932), p.1.

101. CAHJP, AW, 72/21, Protokoll betreffend die Ermittlung der Ergebnisse der Abstimmung (December 4, 1932); IKGW, *Bericht des Präsidiums, 1933–36*, p.9; *DS*, V, 257 (December 8, 1932), p.1.

102. CAHJP, AW, 71/20, IKGW, Präsidium usw. (1933); *DS*, VI, 262 (January 12, 1933), pp.1–2; *DW*, XLIX, 2 (January 13, 1933), pp.1–2; ibid., 3 (January 20, 1933), p.3.

103. IKGW, *Bericht des Präsidiums, 1933–36*, p.9.

104. CAHJP, AW, 71/20, Protokoll der öffentlichen Plenarsitzung, January 22, 1934; *DJW*, III, 10 (February 6, 1934), p.2.

105. CAHJP, AW, 71/20, Desider Friedmann, Bericht betreffend das Erlöschen der Mandate der der "Vereinigung werktätiger Juden" und der Gruppe "Poale Zion-Hitachduth-Verband sozialistischer Juden" angehörigen Mandatare der KG, March 8, 1934; IKGW, *Bericht des Präsidiums, 1933–36*, p.11.

106. AVA, BKA-I, 15/4, 124.719–34, Verein "Zionistisch-sozialistische Arbeiterorganisation Poale Zion-Hitachduth" mit dem Sitz in Wien behördliche Auflösung (1934); CZA, Z4/3563III, Letter from Grünbaum (Paris) to Zionist Executive, London, February 25, 1934; CZA, S5/2179, ibid., November 25, 1935.

107. CAHJP, AW, 62/2, Amtlicher Stimmzettel, November 8, 1936; 72/23, Protokoll betreffend die Ermittlung des Ergebnisses der Abstimmung bei der am 8 November 1936 stattgehalten Wahl.

108. Meir Henisch, "Galician Jews in Vienna" in Josef Fraenkel, ed., *The Jews of Austria* (London: Valentine-Mitchell, 2nd ed., 1970), pp.368–373; Rozenblit, *The Jews of Vienna*, pp.96–97.

5. The Orthodox

1. Hamburger and Pulzer, "Jews as Voters in the Weimar Republic," pp.4–5, 26–31, 55–66. For comparative information on German Orthodoxy before World War I, see Breuer, *Jüdische Orthodoxie im Deutschen Reich,* especially pp.295–301.

2. See Gershon C. Bacon, "The Politics of Tradition: Agudat Israel in Polish Politics, 1916–1939" in *Studies in Contemporary Jewry,* II (1986), pp.144–163.

3. JDC, 112, Austria, General, April 1920–21, Leon Wechsler and Saul Sokal, Third Report of Vienna Branch of JDC for January-February 1920, March 15, 1920.

4. *B'nai B'rith Mitteilungen für Oesterreich,* XXX, No. 5 (May 1930), pp.216–217; *Bericht der IKGW, 1929–32,* p.25; *JJO,* p.31.

5. Gertrude Hirschler, "The History of Agudath Israel in Slovakia (1918–39)" in *The Jews of Czechoslovakia,* II, pp.156–157.

6. See Rozenblit, "The Struggle over Religious Reform in Nineteenth-Century Vienna."

7. For comparative information on Germany, see Jack Wertheimer, *Unwelcome Strangers,* pp.123–142, and "The Duisberg Affair: A Test Case in the Struggle for 'Conquest of the Communities,'" *AJS Review,* VI, 1981, pp.185–206.

8. *Bericht der IKGW, 1912–1924,* p.4; *Bericht der IKGW, 1925–28,* p.3; *Bericht der IKGW, 1929–32,* p.3; IKGW, *Bericht des Präsidiums, 1933–36,* p.9.

9. Gershon Bacon, "Agudath Israel in Poland, 1916–39" (Ph.D. diss., Columbia University, 1979), esp. pp.86, 117; Bacon, "The Politics of Tradition," pp.150–151.

10. AVA, BKA-I, 15/2, 353.587-35, Statuten des Vereines Agudas Jisroel Wien (June 26, 1929).

11. Gideon Aran, "From Religious Zionism to Zionist Religion," *Studies in Contemporary Jewry,* II (1986), p.123, and Aryei Fishman, "The Religious Kibbutz Movement," ibid., p.101.

12. For further detail on Reform efforts in Vienna before World War I, see Marsha Rozenblit, "Jewish Identity and the Modern Rabbi: The Cases of Isak Noa Mannheimer, Adolf Jellinek, and Moritz Güdemann in Nineteenth Century Vienna," *LBIYB,* XXXV (1990), and "The Struggle over Religious Reform in Nineteenth Century Vienna." See also Meyer, *Response to Modernity,* which includes extensive comparative data.

13. The following analysis, unless otherwise indicated, is based on a compilation of information on Viennese synagogues and prayer-houses taken from the following sources: *Bericht der IKGW, 1912–24,* pp.16–19; *Bericht der IKGW, 1924–28,* pp.18–22; *Bericht der IKGW, 1929–32,* pp.20–25; IKGW, *Bericht des Präsidiums, 1932–36,* pp.32–36; *JJO,* pp.23–41; CAHJP, AW, 289, Verzeichnis der jüdischen Vereine, (A) Tempel und Bethausvereine (1938); Gold, *Die Geschichte der Juden in Wien,* pp.117–128.

14. The seventh communal synagogue, with ca. 1,000 members, belonged to the Association of Turkish Israelites, the Viennese Sephardic community. While Orthodox, it does not concern us here because, although affiliated with the Kultusgemeinde and the recipient of communal subventions, it operated as a completely separate entity. For information on the Sephardim in Vienna, see N.M. Gelber, "The Sephardic Community in Vienna," *Jewish Social Studies,* X, No. 4 (1948), pp.359–396; Rudolf Till, "Geschichte der Spaniolischen Juden in Wien," *Jahrbuch des Vereins für Geschichte der Stadt Wien,*

V-VI, 1946/47, pp.108–123; M. Papo, "The Sephardi Community of Vienna" in Josef Fraenkel, *The Jews of Austria*, pp.327–346.

15. *B'nai B'rith Mitteilungen für Oesterreich*, XXX, 5 (May 1930), pp.215–216.

16. IKGW, *Bericht des Präsidiums, 1933–36*, pp.32–35.

17. *JP*, XV, 12 (March 22, 1929), pp.1–2; *JJO*, pp.32–41.

18. CAHJP, AW, 60/3, Wahlen 1928.

19. CAHJP, AW, 731/3, Letter from Güdemann to Kultusvorstand, March 10, 1914; *DBOW*, XXXI, 15 (April 10, 1914), pp.245–246.

20. CAHJP, AW, 725/5, Plenum, April 24, 1918, and Sitzung des Vertreterkollegiums, April 24, 1918.

21. Rosenfeld, *H.P. Chajes*, pp.10–42.

22. *JK*, IV, 15 (May 2, 1918), pp.1–2; Rosenfeld, *H.P. Chajes*, pp.45–46.

23. Rosenfeld, *H.P. Chajes*, pp.52, 118–119; Kopel Blum, "Aufklärung und Reform bei den Wiener Juden" (Ph.D. diss., University of Vienna, 1935), p.164; CAHJP, AW, 72/19, Protokoll, Vertreterkollegium, June 25, 1924, "Forderungen der Orthodoxie"; Gideon Kaminka, *Ins Land, das Ich dir zeigen werde*, p.47.

24. Rosenfeld, *H.P. Chajes*, p.116.

25. Ibid., pp.62–66; Kaminka, *Ins Land . . .*, pp.47–48; Schechter, *Viennese Vignettes*, p.105.

26. CAHJP, AW, 725/2, Vorstand der IKGW, Instruktion ad Z.2064 ex 1918.

27. *JZ*, XII, 41 (October 11, 1918), p.2; *DBOW*, XXXV, 40 (October 11, 1918), p.650; Rosenfeld, *H.P. Chajes*, pp.83–85; Hugo Gold, *Zwi Perez Chajes: Dokumente aus seinem Leben und Wirken* (Tel Aviv: Olamanu, 1971), pp.30–31.

28. CAHJP, 725/4, Letters to President of IKGW, October 17, 1918 and November 2, 1918; letter from Präsidium der IKGW (signed Rappaport) to H.P. Chajes, February 2, 1919; and Beschluss des Vertreterkollegiums, February 11, 1919; *JZ*, XI, 43 (October 25, 1918), p.4; Gold, *Chajes: Dokumente*, pp.32–39.

29. CAHJP, AW, 72/19, "Forderungen der Orthodoxie," Protokoll, Vertreterkollegium, June 25, 1924; Gold, *Chajes: Dokumente*, p.48.

30. *Jüdische Korrespondenz, Wochenblatt für jüdische Interessen* (Vienna, 1915–1919); *Jüdische Presse, Organ für die Interessen des orthodoxen Judentums* (Vienna/Bratislava, 1920–38); *JP*, XXI, 1 (January 4, 1935), pp.1–2. *Unser Wort*, another Agudist paper, also briefly appeared in Vienna during 1933–34.

31. *JK*, IV, 5 (February 14, 1918), pp.2–3.

32. *JK*, IV, 6 (February 21, 1918), pp.3–4.

33. *JK*, IV, 13 (April 18, 1918), pp.1–3.

34. *JK*, V, 4 (January 23, 1919), p.1; see also ibid., 1 (January 2, 1919), p.1; 2 (January 16, 1919), p.1; and 16 (May 1, 1919), p.1.

35. *JK*, V, 17 (May 8, 1919), pp.1–2.

36. *DW*, XXXIX, 22 (November 2, 1923), p.11.

37. *JK*, V, 1 (January 2, 1919), p.1.

38. *JK*, V, 3 (January 16, 1919), p.1; Bacon, "Agudat Israel in Polish Politics," p.154.

39. *JP*, XVI, 45 (November 14, 1930), p.1.

40. *UW*, II, 8 (February 23, 1934), p.1.

41. Ibid.

42. *JZ*, XII, 46 (November 15, 1918), pp.3–4.

43. Marsha Leah Rozenblit, "Assimilation and Identity: The Urbanization of the Jews of Vienna, 1880–1914" (Ph.D. diss., Columbia University, 1980), p.383.

44. *JK*, V, 1 (January 2, 1919), pp.1–3.

45. *JK*, V, 46/47 (December 19, 1919), pp.1–2.

46. *JJO*, p.53.

47. CAHJP, AW, 299, Ueberblick über das jüdische Organisationswesen im Landes Oesterreich (1938).

48. *JK*, V, 28 (August 1, 1919), pp.1–2; ibid., 39 (October 24, 1919), pp.1–2.

49. *JK*, IV, 36 (December 5, 1918), p.2; *JK*, V, 3 (January 16, 1919), p.1.

50. *JK*, V, 27 (July 25, 1919), pp.1–2.

51. *JK*, V, 43 (November 21, 1919), pp.1–2.

52. CAHJP, AW, 57/3, Vereinigte glaubenstreue Judenschaft Wiens (1920).

53. CAHJP, AW, 57/3, An die Judenschaft Wiens! (1920)

54. Ibid.

55. CAHJP, AW, 57/12, Amtlicher Stimmzettel, June 27, 1920; *JJO*, pp.38–39, 52–53.

56. *Bericht der IKGW, 1912–24*, pp.3–4.

57. CAHJP, AW, 57/12, IKGW, Kundmachung, Z.1808/130, October 1924; 74/8, Protokoll der Plenarsitzung des KV vom 13 Januar 1921; 71/17, Protokoll der Plenarsitzung vom 6 März 1922; 71/18 and 74/10, Protokoll der Plenarsitzung vom 22 Mai 1924.

58. *JP*, IX, 40 (October 5, 1923), pp.311–312; *DW*, XXIX, 20 (October 5, 1923), p.14; *AJYB*, XXVI (1924–25), pp.86–87.

59. *WM*, V, 1689 (October 27, 1923), p.4.

60. *JP*, IX, 45 (November 9, 1923), p.353.

61. *WM*, V, 1717 (November 25, 1923), p.7.

62. CAHJP, AW, 72/19, "Forderungen der Orthodoxie," Protokoll des Vertreterkollegiums, June 25, 1924.

63. Ibid.

64. Ibid.

65. *JP*, X, 41/42 (October 10, 1924), pp.277–278.

66. Bacon, "Agudath Israel in Poland," pp.267, 292.

67. *JP*, X, 41/42 (October 10, 1924), pp.277–278; 43 (October 24, 1924), p.285; and 45 (November 7, 1924), p.298.

68. CAHJP, AW, 60/3, Amtlicher Stimmzettel, November 9, 1924; *Bericht der IKGW, 1925–28*, pp.3–4.

69. *WM*, VI, 2034 (October 16, 1924), p.4.

70. *Bericht der IKGW, 1925–28*, pp.3–4.

71. *JP*, X, 46 (November 14, 1924), p.303.

72. CAHJP, AW, 60/16, IKGW, Mitglieder der Kommissionen pro 1928.

73. *Bericht der IKGW, 1925–28*, p.23.

74. *JP*, XI, 13 (March 27, 1925), pp.81–82; *DW*, XLI, 12 (March 27, 1925), pp.10–11; *JP*, XII, 11 (March 12, 1926), pp.81–82; *DW*, XLIV, 37/38 (September 14, 1928), pp.28–29; *JP*, XIV, 46a (November 30, 1928), p.1.

75. *DW*, XL, 43 (October 24, 1924), p.8; *Bericht der IKGW, 1925–28*, p.12; CAHJP, AW, 363, Palästina Zuwendungen, 1925–35.

76. *JP*, XI, 13 (March 27, 1925), p.82.

77. *JP*, XII, 20/21 (May 18, 1926), p.153; *WM*, VIII, 2708 (September 6, 1926), p.2.

78. CAHJP, AW, 71/19, Protokoll der öffentlichen Plenarsitzung vom 23 März 1926; *WM*, VIII, 2545 (March 24, 1926), p.4; ibid., 2587 (May 7, 1926), p.4; CAHJP, AW, 75/9, Protokoll der Vertretersitzung vom 30 März 1927; *DS*,

I, 20 (May 5, 1928), p.1; ibid., 47 (November 22, 1928), pp.8–9; CAHJP, AW, 74/14, Oeffentliche Plenarsitzung vom 15 April 1929; *DJW*, I, 9 (May 10, 1929), p.4.

79. CAHJP, AW, 383, Palästina, 1925–36.

80. Yad Vashem, 01/244, Leo Landau, "In Wien von 1909 bis 1939" (manuscript); *WM*, V, 1544 (June 1, 1923), p.5.

81. Rozenblit, *The Jews of Vienna*, pp.32–33.

82. J. Heschel, "The History of Hassidism in Austria" in Josef Fraenkel, ed., *The Jews of Austria*, pp.354–355; *JJO*, pp.32–41; *Bericht der IKGW, 1912–24*, pp.16–19; *Bericht der IKGW, 1915–28*, pp.18–22; *Bericht der IKGW, 1929–32*, pp.20–25; IKGW, *Bericht des Präsidiums*, pp.32–36; CAHJP, AW, 289, Verzeichnis der jüdischer Vereine, (A) Tempel und Bethausvereine (1938).

83. Rozenblit, *The Jews of Vienna*, p.168.

84. *JZ*, XII, 46 (November 15, 1918), pp.3–4; *JK*, V, 1 (January 2, 1919), pp.2–3.

85. CZA, Z4/2665I, Protokoll der Protestversammlung gegen die Aguda am 12 März 1922 . . . veranstaltet von Agudas Hacharedim.

86. For comparative information on Poland where Mizrachi was the strongest, see Mendelsohn, *Zionism in Poland*.

87. CZA, Z4/2672, Oesterreich, questionnaire (n.d., 1926).

88. CAHJP, AW, 1406, Das Aktionskomitee der vereinigten Wiener Tempelvereine, *KG-programm der vereinigten Wiener Tempelvereine* (Vienna, 1919) (also found at YIVO, 8/42739).

89. CAHJP, AW, 57/12, Amtlicher Stimmzettel, June 21, 1920.

90. *WM*, II, 492 (June 6, 1920), p.3.

91. *Bericht der IKGW, 1912–24*, pp.3–4; CAHJP, AW, 71/18, Protokoll der Plenarsitzung, December 11, 1924.

92. *Jüdische Volksstimme*, 20 (June 20, 1924), p.2 (LBI, Rudolf Seiden Collection, I, Article II); *JP*, X, 16/17 (April 18, 1924), p.113.

93. CAHJP, AW, 74/10, Protokoll der Plenarsitzung, December 11, 1924.

94. *JW*, II, 42 (October 24, 1924), pp.1–4; 43 (October 31, 1924), pp.1, 3.

95. *JW*, II, 42 (October 24, 1924), pp.2–3.

96. *Bericht des IKGW, 1925–28*, pp.3–4; *JW*, II, 45 (November 14, 1924), pp.1–2; *JW*, III, 12 (March 27, 1925), pp.2–3; CAHJP, AW, 17/18, Protokoll der Plenarsitzung, December 11, 1924.

97. *Bericht des IKGW, 1925–28*, p.5; CAHJP, AW, 60/16, IKGW, Mitglieder der Kommissionen pro 1928; *Bericht der IKGW, 1929–32*, p.5.

98. CAHJP, AW, 71/18, Protokoll der Plenarsitzung December 29, 1924; *DS*, V, 250 (October 20, 1932), p.5; *JJO*, pp.60–62.

99. *DW*, XLIV, 6 (February 10, 1928), pp.3–5; *NW*, II, 21 (February 10, 1928), pp.1–2; *DS*, I, 7 (February 16, 1928), p.9; CAHJP, AW, 74/14, Zum Protokoll vom 22 April 1929.

100. *DS*, I, 50 (December 13, 1928), p.7; *DW*, XLIV, 50 (December 14, 1928), p.7.

101. Yad Vashem, 01/144, Leo Landau, "In Wien von 1909 bis 1939."

102. CAHJP, AW, 60/4, Leo Landau, Unpolitische Wahlvereinigung (1928); AW, 61/2, ibid., 1932.

103. *DW*, XLVIII, 46 (November 11, 1932), pp.1–2; CAHJP, AW, 61.2, Amtlicher Stimmzettel (1932); IKGW, *Bericht des Präsidiums*, pp.9–10.

104. CAHJP, AW, 72/21, Protokoll betreffend die Ermittlung der Ergebnisse der Abstimmung bei der am 4 Dezember 1932 stattgehalten Wahl; IKGW, *Bericht des Präsidiums*, pp.9–10; *DS*, V, 257 (December 8, 1932), p.1; *NW*, VI, 274 (December 9, 1932), p.1.

6. Continuity and Disunity

1. *DS*, III, 152 (November 20, 1930), p.3; *DS*, VI, 262 (January 12, 1933), p.2.

2. CAHJP, AW, 61/6 and 71/20, Antrittsrede des neugewählten Präsidenten der IKG—Dr. Desider Friedmann, January 9, 1933.

3. Ibid.

4. *DW*, XLIX, 5 (February 3, 1933), p.5; *JP*, XXI, 1 (January 4, 1935), p.2.

5. *DS*, VI, 263 (January 19, 1933), p.7; *DW*, XLIX, 3 (January 20, 1933), pp.1–2; *NW*, VII, 280 (January 20, 1933), p.3; *DJW*, II, 10 (January 24, 1933), pp.1–2.

6. CAHJP, AW, 72/22, Protokoll der Vertretersitzung vom 29 Januar 1934.

7. *DW*, XLIV, 13 (March 30, 1928), p.9; *DS*, I, 13 (March 20, 1928), p.11.

8. *DS*, I, 20 (May 17, 1928), pp.1–2; *DW*, XLIV, 20 (May 18, 1928), pp.1–4; ibid., 23 (June 8, 1928), pp.1–2.

9. CAHJP, AW, 161/1, Letter from IKGW (signed by Löwenherz and Ornstein) to Bundesregierung, No. 5539 ex 1928 (July 15, 1928).

10. CAHJP, AW, 161/1, Correspondence between IKGW and various state ministries, 1928–33.

11. *Bericht der IKGW, 1929–32*, p.64 and Tables I-VII, XVIII and XIX; IKGW, *Bericht des Präsidiums*, pp.38, 55, 93–96, 108.

12. *DS*, IX, 607 (December 31, 1936), pp.3–4; *DJW*, VI, 7 (January 5, 1937), pp.3–4; *DS*, X, 635 (April 13, 1937), p.3.

13. IKGW, *Bericht des Präsidiums, 1933–36*, pp.7–8, 93–96; *DW*, XLVIII, 7 (February 12, 1932), pp.2–3; *DS*, VI, 273 (March 30, 1933), p.4; ibid., 301 (September 20, 1933), p.2; CAHJP, AW, 72/22, Protokoll der gemeinsamen Sitzung des Vertreterkollegiums und der Finanz-Kommission vom 10 Januar 1934; *DS*, VII, 322 (January 23, 1934), p.2; ibid., 411 (December 21, 1934), p.5; *DS*, IX, 526 (February 25, 1936), pp.2–3; *DS*, X, 631 (March 26, 1937), pp.3–4; *DS*, XI, 737 (February 2, 1938), pp.3–4.

14. JDC, 439, Austria, General, 1934–38, B. Kahn, Situation of Jews in Austria, February 28, 1934; Joseph G. Hyman, Memorandum of Discussion at Meeting with Dr. Josef Loewenherz, August 27, 1934; and B. Kahn, Report on Poland, March 3, 1936.

15. IKGW, *Bericht des Präsidiums, 1933–36*, pp.63–71; *DS*, VIII, 398 (November 6, 1934), p.2; *NW*, IX, 473 (June 21, 1935), p.2; Bauer, *My Brother's Keeper*, p.224.

16. Ibid.

17. CAHJP, AW, 2010, Protokoll der Wanderfürsorge-Konferenz in Wien, November 26, 1933; 71/10, Beilage, Interterritoriale jüdische Wanderfürsorge-Konferenz in Wien, December 21, 1933; 75/18, Protokoll der Besprechung in Angelegenheit der Deutschlandhilfe, January 14, 1936; 2013, Report to HICEM, Paris, December 1, 1936; Yad Vashem, 30/23, IKGW, Protokoll der interterritorialen Wanderfürsorge-Konferenz in Wien am 15 November 1937; IKGW, *Bericht des Präsidiums, 1933–36*, pp.67–68, 72–74. See also Michael R. Marrus, *The Unwanted: European Refugees in the Twentieth Century* (New York: Oxford University Press, 1985).

18. *Bericht der IKGW, 1912–24*, Tables III, VII and VIII and pp.31–34; *Bericht der IKGW, 1925–28*, Tables III, VIII and XI; *Bericht der IKGW, 1929–32*, pp.37–55 and Tables III, VIII and XVIII; IKGW, *Bericht des Präsidiums, 1933–36*, pp.3–7, 55–93, 108.

19. *Bericht der IKGW, 1912–24*, pp.21–24 and Tables II, VII and XV; *Bericht der IKGW, 1925–28*, pp.24–27 and Tables II and XI; *Bericht der IKGW, 1929–32*, pp.26–28 and Tables II and XVIII; IKGW, *Bericht des Präsidiums, 1933–36*, pp.2, 37–42, 53–55, 108.
20. Ibid.
21. Ibid.
22. Ibid.
23. A. Fürst, "Die jüdischen Mittelschulen in den Ländern der ehemaligen österreichisch-ungarischen Monarchie," *Monatschrift für Geschichte und Wissenschaft des Judentums*, vol. 75 (1931), p.218; *DS*, VIII, 434 (March 15, 1935), p.5.
24. *DS*, VI, 315 (December 29, 1933), p.2.
25. CAHJP, AW, 71/20, Protokoll der Plenarsitzung vom 27 Mai 1935; *DW*, LI, 28 (July 12, 1935), pp.1–2; *DS*, VIII, 487 (September 27, 1935), p.3; *DW*, LII, 15/16 (April 6, 1936), pp.5–6; IKGW, *Bericht des Präsidiums, 1933–36*, pp.49–51.
26. CAHJP, AW, 1571, Bericht über der Schulunterricht der jüdischen Jugend in Wien vom 21 Juni 1938.
27. *Bericht der IKGW, 1912–24*, pp.16–17 and Tables I and VII; *Bericht der IKGW, 1925–28*, pp.18–24 and Tables I and XI; *Bericht der IKGW, 1929–32*, pp.20–23 and Tables I and XVIII; IKGW, *Bericht des Präsidiums, 1933–36*, pp.1, 31–37, 108.
28. *NW*, VIII, 356 (April 13, 1934), p.1; *UW*, II, 14 (April 20, 1934), pp.1–2.
29. Ibid.; *NW*, VIII, 360 (April 27, 1934), p.4.
30. Ibid., p.4; *JP*, XXI, 18 (May 10, 1935), p.1.
31. *NW*, VIII, 364 (May 11, 1934), p.2.
32. *UW*, II, 5 (February 2, 1934), p.1; 17 (May 5, 1934), pp.1–2; ibid., 20 (June 15, 1934), p.1; *JP*, XXI, 5 (February 1, 1935), p.1.
33. *UW*, II, 16 (May 5, 1934), pp.2–3; 17 (May 11, 1934), pp.1–2; and 18 (May 18, 1934), p.4.
34. *DW*, L, 47 (November 23, 1934), p.2; *DS*, VII, 409 (December 14, 1934), p.2.
35. Cf. Robert Liberles, *Religious Conflict in Social Context* (Westport: Greenwood Press, 1985), and Breuer, *Jüdische Orthodoxie im Deutschen Reich*.
36. *DS*, VIII, 407 (January 11, 1935), p.3.
37. *DW*, L, 47 (November 23, 1934), p.2; *JP*, XXI, 18 (May 10, 1935), p.1.
38. *DS*, VII, 409 (December 14, 1934), p.2.
39. *JK*, XII, 2/3 (February 14, 1935), pp.1–2; *JP*, XXI, 16 (April 17, 1935), p.6; ibid., 23 (June 14, 1935), p.1; *DS*, IX, 514 (January 14, 1936), p.7.
40. AVA, BKA-I, 15/2, 334.113–35, Israelitischer Bethausverein "Adas Jisroel" in Wien, Gesuch um Anerkennung als selbständige Religionsgesellschaft (1935).
41. Ibid.
42. Ibid.
43. *JP*, XXI, 45 (November 22, 1935), p.1; *JP*, XXII, 3 (January 17, 1936), p.1; ibid., 36 (November 23, 1936), p.1.
44. *DW*, XXVIII, 19 (May 17, 1912), p.6; CAHJP, AW, 2819, Letter from K.k. niederöst. Statthalterei to Praesidium of IKGW, March 23, 1914; 71/16, Resolution des Vorstandes der WIKG, July 25, 1916; 72/15, Protokoll der Vertretersitzung, July 25, 1916; *B'nai B'rith Oesterreich Zweimonats-bericht*, XIX, 5 (1916), pp.169–181; *JZ*, XII, 19 (May 10, 1918), pp.1–2.
45. CAHJP, AW, 75/8, Protokoll der Vertretersitzung, December 8, 1926;

74/12, Protokoll über die vertrauliche Plenarsitzung, December 9, 1926; *DW*, XLII, 52 (December 17, 1926), pp.2–4.

46. *WM*, VIII, 2800 (December 13, 1926), p.3; AVA, BKA-I, 15/2, 122.219–27, Verein "Verband der Israelitischen Kultusgemeinden Oesterreichs"—Bildung, May 24, 1927; *WM*, IX, 3005 (July 10, 1927), p.3; CAHJP, AW, 2819, Memorandum, April 26, 1928; *JP*, XXI, 24 (June 21, 1935), pp.1–2.

47. CAHJP, AW, 2819, Correspondence between IKGW and IKG Graz (1934) and Protokoll über die Sitzung der Konferenz der Delegierten der IKG Oest., June 10, 1935; *DS*, VIII, 458 (June 18, 1935), p.5; CAHJP, AW, 2819, Protokoll über die Tagung der "Arbeitsgemeinschaft der IKG des Bundesrepublik Oest." angeschlossenen Gemeinden, April 26, 1936.

48. CAHJP, AW, 71/20, Protokoll der Plenarsitzung des KV, January 9, 1933 and IKGW, Präsidium, 1933; *DS*, VI, 262 (January 12, 1933), p.1; *DW*, XLIX, 2 (January 13, 1933), pp.1–2; *NW*, VII, 279 (January 13, 1933), pp.3–4; IKGW, *Bericht des Präsidiums, 1933–36*, pp.10–11.

49. *DW*, XLIX, 2 (January 13, 1933), p.2; and 3 (January 20, 1933), p.3.

50. CAHJP, AW, 71/20, Desider Friedmann, Bericht betreffend das Erlöschen der Mandate der der "Vereinigung werktätiger Juden" und der Gruppe "Poale Zion-Hitachduth-Verband sozialistischer Juden" angehörigen Mandatare der KG, March 8, 1934; IKGW, *Bericht des Präsidiums, 1933–36*, p.11.

51. *DS*, VII, 333 (March 6, 1934), p.1; *JF*, III, 4 (March 10, 1934), p.5.

52. *AJYB*, XXXVI (1934–35), pp.146–148; CZA, Z4/3563III, Letter from Oskar Grünbaum (written in Paris) to Zionist Executive, London, February 25, 1934; also March 12, 1934; AVA-BKA-I, 15/4, 124.719–34, Verein "Zionistisch-sozialistische Arbeiterorganisation Poale Zion-Hitachduth" mit dem Sitz in Wien behördliche Auflösung (1934); and 161.147–31, Verband radikaler Zionisten in Wien, Verdacht getainter marxistischer Betätigung (1934).

53. *DW*, L, 25 (June 15, 1934), p.1; ibid., 26 (June 22, 1934), pp.1–2; CAHJP, AW, 71/20, Protokoll der öffentlichen Plenarsitzung, June 20, 1934.

54. *NW*, VIII, 362 (May 4, 1934), p.3; *DW*, L, 19 (May 4, 1934), pp.3–6; ibid., 20 (May 11, 1934), p.3–4; *DW*, LI, 11 (March 15, 1935), pp.1–2.

55. *DW*, L, 19 (May 4, 1934), p.5.

56. *DW*, XLIX, 5 (February 3, 1933), p.5; *DW*, L, 19 (May 4, 1934), p.5.

57. *DW*, L, 20 (May 11, 1934), p.2; *NW*, VIII, 364 (May 11, 1934), p.2.

58. *DW*, L, 25 (June 15, 1934), p.1; ibid., 26 (June 22, 1934), pp.1–2; CAHJP, AW, 71/20, Protokoll der öffentlichen Plenarsitzung, June 20, 1934.

59. CAHJP, AW, 71/20, Protokoll der Plenarsitzung, October 9, 1934; *DW*, LI, 11 (March 15, 1935), pp.2–3.

60. *DW*, LI, 44 (November 1, 1935), p.3; 45 (November 8, 1935), pp.3–4; and 46 (November 15, 1935), p.4.

61. *JP*, XXI, 43 (November 8, 1935), pp.1–2; 46 (November 29, 1935), p.2; and 49 (December 20, 1935), p.3.

62. *DJW*, IV, 17 (April 30, 1935), p.2; *DJW*, V, 5 (December 11, 1935), pp.3–4; ibid., 9 (February 12, 1936), pp.1–2; *DW*, LII, 43 (October 16, 1936), pp.6–8.

63. *DW*, LI, 50 (December 13, 1935), p.1; ibid., 51 (December 20, 1935), p.5; *NW*, X, 526 (January 3, 1936), p.2; *DW*, LII, 2 (January 10, 1936), p.3.

64. *DW*, LII, 6 (February 7, 1936), pp.1–4; AVA, BKA-I, 15/4, 310.081–31, Petition from the Union öst. Juden to Magistrat der Stadt Wien, February 5, 1936.

65. Ibid.

66. *DS*, X, 591 (October 29, 1936), p.5.

67. AVA, BKA-I, 15/4, 310.081–31, Petition, February 5, 1936.

68. CAHJP, AW, 60/3, Wahlvorschlag der Wählergruppe "Jüdische Union" (1928); *Bericht der IKGW, 1925–28*, pp.3–5; *Bericht der IKGW, 1929–32*, pp.4–6; *DS*, X, 591 (October 29, 1936), p.5.

69. AVA, BKA-I, 15/4, 310.081–31, Petition, February 5, 1936.

70. Ibid.

71. *DS*, IX, 560 (July 2, 1936), pp.1–2; *NW*, X, 573 (July 3, 1936), p.2; ibid., 606 (November 6, 1936), p.1; IKGW, *Bericht des Präsidiums, 1933–36*, pp.26–31.

72. *B'nai B'rith Mitteilungen für Oesterreich*, XXXIII, 9 (November 1933), pp.321–324; ibid., XXXIV, 1 (January 1934), pp.1–3.

73. *JF*, IV, 6 (March 15, 1935), p.1.

74. *JF*, V, 2 (January 15, 1936), p.1; 3 (February 1, 1936), p.1; 7 (April 1, 1936), pp.3–6; 20 (October 15, 1936), p.1; and 21 (November 1, 1936), p.1.

75. *DJW*, V, 8 (January 29, 1936), p.3; *NW*, X, 566 (June 5, 1936), p.6; ibid., 568 (June 12, 1936), p.4; ibid., 575 (July 10, 1936), p.4; *JF*, V, 22 (November 15, 1936), p.1; *JF*, VI, 1–2 (January 12, 1937), pp.1–2.

76. *DS*, IX, 521 (February 7, 1936), pp.2–3; ibid., 580 (September 11, 1936), p.3; *DS*, X, 585 (October 7, 1936), pp.1–3; ibid., 589 (October 23, 1936), p.1. For information on the Naumann group in Germany, see Niewyk, *The Jews of Weimar Germany*, pp.165–177.

77. *DW*, LII, 42 (October 8, 1936), pp.1–2; ibid., 43 (October 16, 1936), p.8; *NW*, X, 603 (October 27, 1936), pp.1–2; *DW*, LII, 46 (November 3, 1936), p.3.

78. *DS*, X, 591 (October 29, 1936), p.2; ibid., 595 (November 10, 1936), p.1.

79. *DW*, LII, 44 (October 23, 1936), p.1.

80. Ibid.

81. Ibid.

82. *DS*, X, 591 (October 29, 1936), p.1.

83. *DS*, X, 595 (November 10, 1936), p.1; *NW*, X, 607 (November 10, 1936), p.1.

84. Ibid.; *DS*, X, 596 (November 13, 1936), p.2; and 597 (November 17, 1936), p.4.

85. Ibid.; "Konfessionsgliederung der Bevölkerung Oesterreichs," *Die Ergebnisse der österreichischen Volkszählung*, II (1934).

86. *NW*, XII, 725 (February 8, 1938), p.1.

87. *DJW*, VI, 2 (October 8, 1936), p.1; *DS*, X, 587 (October 16, 1936), p.5; ibid., 588 (October 20, 1936), p.1; *DJW*, VI, 3 (October 23, 1936), p.3; *DW*, LII, 43 (October 16, 1936), pp.6–8.

88. CAHJP, AW, 62/3, Kultuswahlen 1936, Ergebnis; 72/23, Protokoll betreffend die Ermittlung des Ergebnisses (1936); *NW*, X, 607 (November 10, 1936), p.1; *DS*, X, 595 (November 10, 1936), p.1; ibid., 597 (November 17, 1936), p.4; CZA, S5/2228, Letter from ZLVfO (Grünbaum) to Zionist Executive, London, February 26, 1937.

89. CAHJP, AW, 72/23, Protokoll betreffend die Ermittlung des Ergebnisses (1936).

90. *DW*, LII, 55 (December 18, 1936), pp.2–3; *NW*, X, 617 (December 18, 1936), p.2; *DS*, X, 605 (December 18, 1936), pp.1–2; *DJW*, VI, 6 (December 18, 1936), p.2.

91. *DW*, LII, 57 (December 31, 1936), pp.1–3; *DS*, X, 607 (December 31, 1936), pp.3–4; *DJW*, VI, 7 (January 5, 1937), pp.3–4; ibid., 8 (January 22, 1937), p.3; ibid., 9 (February 5, 1937), pp.1–2; *DW*, LIII, 5 (February 5, 1937), pp.1–2; *DS*, X, 635 (April 13, 1937), p.3.

92. *DJW*, V, 5 (December 11, 1935), pp.3–4; ibid., 9 (February 12, 1936), pp.1–2; *DJW*, VI, 9 (February 10, 1937), p.3; DS, X, 622 (February 23, 1937), p.2.

93. CZA, S5/2228, Correspondence between ZLVfO (usually Oscar Grünbaum, sometimes Plaschkes) and Zionist Executive, London and Jerusalem (Jizchak Grünbaum and S. Brodetsky)(1937); *DW*, LIII, 12 (March 26, 1937), pp.4–5; ibid., 13 (April 2, 1937), pp.1–2.

7. Confronting Antisemitism

1. Schechter, *Viennese Vignettes*, p.28.

2. John Haag, "Blood on the Ringstrasse: Vienna's Students 1918–33," *Wiener Library Bulletin*, XXIX, 39–40 (1976), pp.29–34; John Haag, The Political Consequences of Academic Unemployment in Austria, 1918–1933 (paper delivered at Social Science History Association, Columbus, Ohio, November 4, 1978); Erika Weinzierl, "Hochschulleben und Hochschulpolitik zwischen den Kriegen" in Norbert Leser, ed., *Das geistige Leben Wiens in der Zwischenkriegszeit* (Vienna, 1981), pp.72–85.

3. For comparative data on Germany, see Jehuda Reinharz, "The Zionist Response to Antisemitism in Germany," *LBIYB*, XXX (1985), pp.105–140, and Niewyk, *The Jews in Weimar Germany*; for Poland, see Bacon, "The Politics of Tradition," Ezra Mendelsohn, "The Politics of Agudas Yisroel in Inter-War Poland," *Soviet Jewish Affairs*, II (1972), pp.47–60, and Mendelsohn, *Zionism in Poland*.

4. CAHJP, AW, 325, Letter from Alfred Stern to Vorstand, Z.2789 ex 1918, July 18, 1918 and letter from President, IKGW to Regierungsrat Ignaz Wilhelm, Z.2789 ex 1918, July 26, 1918; *JK*, IV, 25 (August 8, 1918), pp.3–4; *DBOW*, XXXV, 30 (August 2, 1918), pp.474–475; *JZ*, XII, 31 (August 2, 1918), p.1; ibid., 32 (August 9, 1918), p.1.

5. *NFP*, 19786 (September 25, 1919, PM), p.1; *WM*, I, 247 (September 26, 1919), p.4; ibid., 248 (September 27, 1919), p.1; ibid., 255 (October 5, 1919), p.4; *New York Times*, March 14, 1921; *NFP*, 209965 (January 22, 1923, AM), p.5; *WM*, V, 1417 (January 23, 1923), pp.2–3.

6. CAHJP, AW, 72/17, Protokoll der Vertretersitzung, February 8, 1919.

7. *WM*, V, 1457 (March 4, 1923), pp.1–2; *NFP*, 21006 (March 4, 1923, AM), p.9; *DW*, XXIX, 6 (March 15, 1923), pp.9–10.

8. *WM*, V, 1468 (March 15, 1923), p.1; *DW*, XXIX, 11 (May 30, 1923), pp.9–12.

9. Haag, "Blood on the Ringstrasse," p.31.

10. Ibid., pp.32–33; Schechter, *Viennese Vignettes*, p.57; Richard Berczeller, *Time Was* (New York: Viking, 1971), p.46.

11. *WM*, II, 457 (April 30, 1920), pp.1–2; ibid., 460 (May 4, 1920), p.4; *WM*, IV, 1366 (November 29, 1922), pp.1–2; *WM*, V, 1499 (April 16, 1923), p.1; ibid., 1688 (October 26, 1923), p.5; ibid., 1713 (November 21, 1923), pp.4–5; ibid., 1718 (November 26, 1923), p.2; *Jüdische Volksstimme*, 33 (December 10, 1923), p.2; *WM*, VII, 2244 (May 20, 1925), pp.1–2; ibid., 2252 (May 28, 1925), p.3; *NFP*, 21805 (May 28, 1925, AM), p.7; *WM*, IX, 2979 (June 14, 1927), p.1; *AJYB*, XXX (1928–29), pp.41, 193; *AJYB*, XXXI (1929–30), pp.47–48; *AJYB*, XXXII (1930–31), pp.101–102.

12. *DS*, V, 252 (November 4, 1932), p.3; ibid., 260 (December 20, 1932), p.2; *AJYB*, XXVI (1934–35), p.455.

13. *WM*, II, 671 (December 7, 1920), p.2; CZA, Z4/2094I, Vereinigung jüdischer Hörer an der Hochschule für Welthandel to Rektorat, Communique des Jüdischen Hochschulausschusses über die Vorfälle an den Wiener

Hochschulen, November 28, 1922 and Letter from ZLK to Zionist Executive, December 22, 1922; JDC, Austria, 172, Cultural-Religious, Reply to the Academic Senate of the University of Vienna to German-National Memorandum (n.d., 1922); *WM*, IV, 1367 (November 30, 1922), pp.1–2; ibid., 1370 (December 3, 1922), p.1; *WM*, V, 1471 (March 18, 1923), p.2; AW, 72/19, Protokoll der Vertretersitzung, November 21, 1923, 75/5, Protokoll der Sitzung des Vertreterkollegiums, October 11, 1923 and 81/18, Protokoll der Plenarsitzung, November 22, 1923; *WM*, V, 1719 (November 27, 1923), pp.2–3; *WM*, VII, 2244 (May 20, 1925), pp.1–2; AW, 328, Letter from Präsidium to Rudolf Ramek, Bundeskanzler, Z.446 ex 1925, May 26, 1925; *NFP*, 21797 (May 20, 1925), p.7; *NW*, II, 63 (November 30, 1928), pp.2–3; *DS*, II, 100 (November 15, 1929), p.3; *DS*, III, 153 (November 27, 1930), p.2; *DS*, VI, 282 (May 30, 1933), p.2.

14. Goldhammer, *Die Juden Wiens*, p.39; Haag, "Blood on the Ringstrasse," pp.31–32; Weinzierl, "Hochschulleben und Hochschulpolitik," pp.72–80; *JZ*, XII, 34 (August 23, 1918), p.2; JDC, Austria, 111, General, 1919–20 and 117, Cultural-Religious, Telegram from Kann to JDC, March 4, 1919; *WM*, III, 790 (April 9, 1921), p.3; *WM*, IV, 1388 (December 21, 1922), p.1; *NFP*, 20965 (January 22, 1923), p.5; *DW*, XXIX, 8 (April 13, 1923), p.9; ibid., 21 (October 17, 1923), pp.13–14; *WM*, VI, 2016 (September 25, 1924), p.4; *WM*, VII, 2182 (March 18, 1925), p.2.

15. *DW*, XLVI, 22 (May 30, 1930), pp.5–6; AW, 74/16, Protokoll der Plenarsitzung des KV, June 24, 1931 and Letter to Dr. Rudolf Maresch, Rektor, Z.6419 ex 1931, October 1, 1931; *DS*, IV, 180 (June 25, 1931), pp.1–2; *DW*, XLVII, 26 (June 26, 1931), p.1. See also Brigitte Fenz, "Zur Ideologie der 'Volksburgerschaft': Die Studentenordnung der Universität Wien vom 8 April 1930 vor dem Verfassungsgerichthof," *Zeitgeschichte*, V, 4 (1978), pp.125–145, and Weinzierl, "Hochschulleben und Hochschulpolitik," pp.80–82.

16. *DS*, IV, 202 (November 19, 1931), p.1; *DW*, XLVII, 48 (November 27, 1931), p.1; ibid., 49 (December 4, 1931), pp.2–3; *DS*, IV, 206 (December 17, 1931), p.3; *DS*, V, 212 (January 28, 1932), p.1.

17. Ruppin, *Die Soziologie der Juden*, II, pp.166–167; *Statistisches Handbuch für die Republic Oesterreich*, XIV (1933) and XVI (1935); *Statistisches Jahrbuch der Stadt Wien*, 1938.

18. *DW*, XXVIII, 24 (December 15, 1922), pp.8–9; *DW*, XLVI, 22 (May 30, 1930), pp.5–6; *DW*, XLVII, 49 (December 4, 1931), pp.1–2.

19. Pauley, "Political Antisemitism in Interwar Vienna," p.117.

20. *DW*, XLVII, 49 (December 4, 1931), pp.2–3; 50 (December 11, 1931), p.2; and 51 (December 18, 1931), p.4.

21. *DS*, IV, 202 (November 19, 1931), p.1; 203 (November 26, 1931), pp.1–2; 204 (December 12, 1931), p.1; and 206 (December 17, 1931), p.3; *NW*, V, 222 (December 18, 1931), pp.2–3.

22. *DS*, IV, 203 (November 26, 1931), pp.1–2; CAHJP, AW, 74/16, Protokoll über die Plenarsitzung des KV, November 30, 1931; *DS*, V, 215 (February 18, 1932), pp.5–6; *DW*, XLVIII, 8 (February 19, 1932), pp.2–3; *DS*, V, 216 (February 25, 1932), p.4; *Bericht der IKGW, 1929–32*, pp.11–13.

23. CAHJP, AW, 75/7, Protokoll der Vertretersitzung, January 14, 1925; 75/9, Protokoll der Sitzung des Vertreterkollegiums, March 16, 1927; *DW*, XLIII, 19 (May 6, 1927), pp.5–7; CAHJP, 71/9, Präsidialbericht für die Plenarsitzung, September 9, 1927; *DS*, III, 150 (November 6, 1930), p.4; *DS*, V, 222 (April 7, 1932), p.1.

24. *Bericht der IKGW, 1925–28*, p.11; IKGW, *Bericht, 1929–32*, pp.10–15.

25. *DW*, XLIII, 28 (July 8, 1927), pp.9–10; *DS*, I, 23 (June 7, 1928), p.1;

DW, XLV, 24 (June 15, 1929), pp.10–12; ibid., 26 (June 28, 1929), pp.8–9; ibid., 39 (September 27, 1929), pp.1–4.

26. CAHJP, AW, 72/20 and 75/11, Protokoll über die Vertretersitzung, November 11, 1929.

27. Maderegger, *Die Juden im österreichischen Ständestaat,* pp.115–128; Bruce Pauley, *Hitler and the Forgotten Nazis* (Durham: University of North Carolina Press, 1981), pp.160–161; Pauley, "Political Antisemitism in Interwar Vienna," pp.167–169; Oskar Karbach, "The Liquidation of the Jewish Community of Vienna," *Jewish Social Studies,* II, 3 (July 1940), pp.255–259; *NW,* VIII, 352 (March 27, 1934), p.1; *DW,* L, 19 (May 4, 1934), p.1; *NW,* VIII, 386 (July 7, 1934), pp.1–2; *DW,* L, 43 (October 26, 1934), p.1; *DS,* VII, 407 (December 7, 1934), p.2; *DW,* LI, 5 (February 1, 1935), p.2; *NW,* IX, 444 (March 5, 1935), pp.1–2; *NW,* X, 532 (January 28, 1936), p.1; *JF,* VI, 4 (February 2, 1937), p.1; *DS,* XI, 686 (October 22, 1937), p.1; *JF,* VII, 4 (February 23, 1938), p.1.

28. *DW,* XLVIII, 39 (September 9, 1932), p.2; *DS,* V, 247 (September 29, 1932), p.1.

29. *DW,* XLIX, 5 (February 3, 1933), pp.3–5; CAHJP, AW, 71/20, Protokoll der öffentlichen Plenarsitzung, February 6, 1933; Maderegger, pp.130–131.

30. CAHJP, AW, 72/22, Protokoll der Vertretersitzung, January 30, 1933; 71/20, Protokoll der öffentlichen Plenarsitzung, February 6, 1933; *DW,* XLIX, 5 (February 3, 1933), pp.3–5; *DS,* VI, 266 (February 9, 1933), p.4; *DW,* XLIX, 6 (February 10, 1933), p.4; *JF,* II, 2 (February 27, 1933), pp.3–4; Union, *Festschrift,* pp.31–32.

31. See Maderegger, pp.152–214.

32. Emmerich Czermak and Oskar Karbach, *Ordnung in der Judenfrage* (Vienna: Reinhold Verlag, 1933; 2nd ed., 1934); *WJF,* I, 2 (December 1933), pp.9–11; *DS,* XI, 496 (November 5, 1935), pp.1–2; *DW,* LI, 44 (November 1, 1935), p.2; *NW,* 512 (November 12, 1935), p.2.

33. *DS,* IX, 521 (February 7, 1936), pp.1–2; *DW,* LII, 6 (February 7, 1936), pp.4–5; *DJW,* V, 12 (March 25, 1936), pp.1–2; Gold, *Geschichte der Juden in Wien,* p.49.

34. *DJW,* V, 12 (March 25, 1936), pp.1–2; *JP,* XXII, 13 (March 3, 1936), p.1; *JF,* V, 7 (April 1, 1936), pp.3–6.

35. *DS,* VI, 310 (November 23, 1933), p.5; *UW,* I, 6 (December 1, 1933), p.2; *JF,* II, 14 (December 10, 1933), p.3; *DJW,* III, 6 (December 12, 1933), p.3; *JF,* IV, 22 (November 15, 1935), p.1; *DS,* IX, 521 (February 7, 1936), pp.1–2; *DW,* LII, 6 (February 7, 1936), pp.4–5; *DJW,* V, 9 (February 12, 1936), p.2; *JP,* XXII, 13 (March 27, 1936), p.1; *JF,* V, 7 (April 1, 1936), pp.3–6; Union, *Festschrift,* pp.29–33.

36. Haag, The Political Consequences of Academic Unemployment in Austria; *DS,* I, 24 (June 14, 1928), p.6; *AJYB,* 32 (1930–31), p.103; *AJYB,* 33 (1931–32), p.80; *NW,* VI, 228 (January 29, 1932), p.1; *DS,* V, 230 (June 2, 1932), pp.1–2; ibid., 259 (December 22, 1932), pp.1, 4–5; CAHJP, AW, 71/20, Protokoll der öffentlichen Plenarsitzung, February 6, 1933; *DS,* VII, 323 (January 26, 1934), p.3.

37. *DW,* L, 7 (February 17, 1934), p.1; ibid., 8 (February 24, 1934), pp.1–2; *DJW,* III, 11 (February 28, 1934), p.1; JDC, Austria, 439, General, 1934–38, B. Kahn, The Situation of the Jews in Austria, February 28, 1934.

38. *NW,* VII, 308 (August 4, 1933), pp.3–4; *DS,* VI, 294 (August 8, 1933), p.5; *NW,* VII, 309 (August 11, 1933), p.3.

39. *DW,* L, 12 (March 23, 1934), pp.1–2; *NW,* VIII, 352 (March 27, 1934), p.1; ibid., 354 (April 5, 1934), p.2; ibid., 411 (November 11, 1934), p.2; *DJW,*

IV, 7 (December 11, 1934), p.3; *DS*, VIII, 434 (March 15, 1935), p.1; JDC, Austria, 439, General, 1934–38, Memo from Abraham Flexner to Warburg, Situation of Jews in Austria, October 22, 1934; Maderegger, pp.224–235.

40. Maderegger, pp.225–230.

41. *NW*, IX, 467 (May 28, 1935), p.1; *DS*, IX, 496 (November 5, 1935), p.2; IKGW, *Bericht des Präsidiums, 1933–36*, pp.3–4.

42. *NW*, VII, 322 (November 10, 1933), p.2; ibid., 328 (December 22, 1933), p.2; *AJYB*, 38 (1936–37), pp.273–274; Gulick, *Austria from Habsburg to Hitler*, II, pp.1478–1479; Maderegger, pp.236–240.

43. *NW*, IX, 510 (November 5, 1935), pp.1–2.

44. *DS*, VII, 323 (January 26, 1934), p.3; *DW*, L, 10 (March 9, 1934), p.1; *NW*, IX, 510 (November 15, 1935), p.1; *DS*, IX, 521 (February 7, 1936), p.3; *JF*, V, 7 (April 1, 1936), pp.3–6; *DW*, LIII, 47 (November 26, 1937), p.1; Maderegger, pp.167–169, 242–243.

45. *DW*, XLVI, 51 (December 19, 1930), pp.1–2; *AJYB*, 34 (1932–33), pp.63–64; *DS*, VI, 266 (February 9, 1933), p.3; *DW*, XLIX, 22 (June 2, 1933), pp.2–3; *DS*, VI, 297 (August 29, 1933), p.7; *DS*, VIII, 398 (November 6, 1934), p.1; *DW*, L, 45 (November 9, 1934), p.3; *NW*, IX, 473 (June 21, 1935), p.2; IKGW, *Bericht des Präsidiums, 1933–36*, pp.63–64; Bauer, *My Brother's Keeper*, pp.223–224.

46. *NW*, VI, 255 (August 3, 1932), p.2; *DS*, V, 239 (August 4, 1932), p.3; *DW*, XLVIII, 32 (August 5, 1932), pp.2–3; *DS*, V, 248 (October 6, 1932), p.1; *JF*, III, 2 (February 10, 1934), pp.1–3; Gold, *Geschichte der Juden in Wien*, p.60.

47. *JF*, III, 2 (February 10, 1934), pp.1–3; ibid., 3 (February 28, 1934), p.1; *JF*, IV, 4 (February 15, 1935), pp.1–3; *DS*, VIII, 447 (May 7, 1935), p.5; *DJW*, IV, 19 (May 14, 1935), p.3; *JF*, V, 1 (January 1, 1936), p.1; *JF*, VI, 1–2 (January 12, 1937), pp.1–2.

48. Pauley, "Political Antisemitism in Interwar Vienna," p.171.

49. *JF*, V, 2 (January 15, 1936), p.1; 3 (February 1, 1936), p.1; 7 (April 1, 1936), pp.3–6; 20 (October 15, 1936), p.1; and 21 (November 1, 1936), p.1.

50. *JF*, VII, 4 (February 23, 1938), p.1.

51. *DW*, XLVI, 38/39 (September 22, 1930), pp.5–6; *DW*, LI, 10 (March 8, 1935), p.4; Union, *Festschrift*, pp.29–39, 76–104.

52. *DS*, V, 231 (June 9, 1932), pp.1, 5.

53. *NW*, VII, 284 (February 17, 1933), p.3.

54. *DW*, L, 11 (March 16, 1934), pp.1–2; *NW*, IX, 452 (April 2, 1935), pp.1–2.

55. *NW*, VIII, 354 (April 4, 1934), pp.3–4; *DS*, VIII, 432 (March 8, 1935), pp.3–4; *DW*, LI, 11 (March 3, 1935), p.4; *DJW*, IV, 14 (March 19, 1935), p.1; *JP*, XXI, 13 (March 29, 1935), p.1.

56. *NW*, VIII, 410 (November 2, 1934), p.2; *DS*, VIII, 397 (November 2, 1934), p.1; "Salomon Frankfurter," *Grosse Jüdische National-Biographie*, II, pp.296–300; Knöpfmacher, *Entstehungsgeschichte und Chronik der Vereinigung "Wien" B'nai B'rith in Wien*, p.124; Maderegger, p.95.

57. Franz Goldner, *Austrian Emigration 1938 to 1945* (New York: Frederick Ungar, 1979), p.6.

58. *DS*, VIII, 412 (December 28, 1934), p.3; *DW*, L, 52 (December 28, 1934), p.1; *NW*, IX, 426 (January 1, 1935), p.2.

59. *NW*, IX, 523 (December 20, 1935), pp.1–2; *DS*, IX, 509 (December 20, 1936), p.1.

60. *DS*, XI, 708 (December 20, 1937), p.2; *NW*, XI, 711 (December 21, 1937), p.1; *DJW*, VII, 5 (December 24, 1937), p.3.

61. *DW*, LIII, 51 (December 24, 1937), p.2; *DJW*, VII, 5 (December 12, 1937),

p.1; *DS*, XI, 715 (January 5, 1938), pp.1–2; *NW*, XII, 716 (January 7, 1938), p.1.

62. *DS*, XI, 719 (January 14, 1938), p.3; *NW*, XII, 719 (January 18, 1938), p.2.

63. *NW*, VIII, 354 (April 5, 1934), p.2; *DW*, L, 15 (April 6, 1934), p.1; *Zionistische Rundschau*, I, 11 (May 6, 1934), p.6; *DW*, L, 43 (October 26, 1934), p.1; CAHJP, AW, 72/22, Beilage, Protokoll der Vertretersitzung vom 30 April 1935, Bericht über die Rücksprache des Präsidiums mit dem Bundeskanzler Dr. Kurt von Schuschnigg; 2819, Protokoll über die Tagung der "Arbeitsgemeinschaft der IKG des Bundesrepublik Oest." angeschlossenen Gemeinden, November 14, 1937.

64. See, for example, Lenni Brenner, *Zionism in the Age of Dictators* (London: Lawrence Hill, 1983), pp.160–165.

65. *UW*, II, 8 (February 23, 1934), p.1.

66. Ibid., 16 (May 4, 1934), pp.1–2.

67. *JP*, XXIII, 24 (July 30, 1937), pp.1–2; ibid., 34 (October 8, 1937), p.1.

68. *DW*, XLIX, 30 (July 28, 1933), pp.1–2; *DW*, L, 11 (March 16, 1934), pp.1–2; *DW*, LI, 10 (March 8, 1935), p.4; Union, *Festschrift*, p.36.

69. Union, *Festschrift*, p.36.

70. *DW*, L, 8 (February 23, 1934), pp.1–2.

71. Ibid., L, 19 (May 4, 1934), p.1.

72. *DW*, LIV, 6 (February 11, 1938), pp.1–2; ibid., 10 (March 4, 1938), p.1.

73. *JF*, III, 2 (February 10, 1934), pp.1–3; ibid., 3 (February 28, 1934), p.1; *DS*, VIII, 447 (May 7, 1935), p.5; *DJW*, IV, 19 (May 14, 1935), p.3.

74. *JF*, IV, 4 (February 15, 1935), pp.1–3; *JF*, VI, 1–2 (January 12, 1937), pp.1–2; *NW*, XII, 718 (January 14, 1938), p.4; *JF*, VII, 3 (February 3, 1938), p.1; Maderegger, pp.96–100.

75. *NW*, VII, 327 (December 12, 1933), p.3.

76. Ibid., 319 (October 20, 1933), p.2; and 320 (October 27, 1933), p.1.

77. CAHJP, AW, 71/20, Protokoll der Plenarsitzung, September 9, 1934; *DW*, L, 40 (October 5, 1934), p.1; *DW*, LI, 14 (April 5, 1935), pp.5–6; ibid., 28 (July 7, 1935), pp.1–2; *DW*, LIV, 2 (January 14, 1938), pp.1–3; ibid., 5 (February 4, 1938), pp.1–2.

78. CAHJP, AW, 71/20, Protokoll (und Beilagen) der Plenarsitzung vom 13 September 1934; *New York Times*, September 23, 1934, sec. 4, p.3; Gulick, *Austria from Habsburgs to Hitler*, II, pp.1553–1554.

79. Ibid.; *NW*, VIII, 401 (September 28, 1934), pp.1–2; *New York Times*, September 28, 1934, p.9; IKGW, *Bericht des Präsidiums, 1933–36*, pp.48–49.

80. CAHJP, AW, 71/20, Protokoll der Plenarsitzung vom 27 Mai 1935; *DW*, L, 40 (October 5, 1934), p.1; *DW*, LI, 14 (April 5, 1935), pp.5–6; ibid., 18 (May 3, 1935), p.2; ibid., 22 (May 31, 1935), pp.2–3; *DW*, LII, 15/16 (April 6, 1936), pp.5–6.

81. *JP*, XXI, 20 (May 24, 1935), p.1.

82. CAHJP, AW, 71/20, Protokoll der Plenarsitzung vom 13 September 1934; *NW*, VIII, 401 (September 28, 1934), pp.1–2; 402 (October 5, 1934), p.1; and 405 (October 16, 1934), p.1.

83. Ibid.; CAHJP, AW, 2819, Protokoll über die Tagung der "Arbeitsgemeinschaft der IKG des Bundesrepublik Oest." angeschlossenen Gemeinden, November 14, 1937.

84. *NW*, XII, 717 (January 11, 1938), p.1; ibid., 724 (February 4, 1938), p.2.

85. *DW*, LIV, 2 (January 14, 1938), pp.1–2; ibid., 5 (February 4, 1938), pp.1–2.

86. *DJW*, III (May 8, 1934), pp.1–2; CAHJP, AW, 71/20, Protokoll der Plenarsitzung, July 26, 1934; 2819, Protokoll über die Tagung der "Arbeitsgemeinschaft der IKG des Bundesrepublik Oest." angeschlossenen Gemeinden, November 14, 1937.

87. American Jewish Historical Society, American Jewish Congress, I-77, Box 3, Administrative Committee Minutes, Committee of 7 (Foreign Affairs), December 4, 1934, pp.2–3, and Nahum Goldmann, *The Autobiography of Nahum Goldmann* (transl. by Helen Sebba) (New York: Holt, Rinehart and Winston, 1969), pp.158–159, provide a different view of Goldmann's meeting with Mussolini.

88. Brenner, *Zionism in the Age of the Dictators*, pp.161–165.

89. Pauley, "Political Antisemitism in Interwar Vienna," p.168.

90. *DS*, XI, 734 (February 18, 1938), p.1; *NW*, XII, 729 (February 22, 1938), p.1; *JF*, VII, 4 (February 2, 1938), p.1; *JP*, XXIV, 8 (February 25, 1938), p.1.

91. *DS*, XI, 737 (February 25, 1938), pp.1–2; *NW*, XII, 730 (February 25, 1938), p.1; *DW*, LIV, 9 (February 25, 1938), p.1.

92. *JP*, XXIV, 9 (March 4, 1938), p.1; *DW*, LIV, 10 (March 4, 1938), pp.1–2; ibid., 11 (March 11, 1938), p.1; *DS*, XI, 743 (March 11, 1938), p.1; *NW*, XII, 734 (March 11, 1938), p.1.

Epilogue: After the *Anschluss*

1. For contemporary accounts, see CZA, S25/9813, Leo Lauterbach, The Jewish Situation in Austria, April 29, 1938; JDC, 439, C.M. Levy, Report on Trip to Vienna, December 24, 1938; CAHJP, A/W, 11, Gesetze und Verordnungen, Judenbetreffend, sowie deren Auswirkung (1938); Oswald Dutch, *Thus Died Austria* (London: Edward Arnold, 1938), pp.242–263; G.E.R. Gedye, *Fallen Bastions* (London: Victor Gollancz, 1939), pp.303–313, 340–350; *AJYB*, XL (1938–39), pp.208–214; and Oskar Karbach, "The Liquidation of the Jewish Community of Vienna," pp.255–278. See also Herbert Rosenkranz, *Verfolgung und Selbstbehauptung: Die Juden in Oesterreich 1938–1945* (Vienna: Herold Verlag, 1978); Wolfgang Neugebauer, ed., *Widerstand und Verfolgung in Wien 1934–1945: Eine Dokumentation* (Vienna: Oest. Bundesverlag, 1975), III, pp.194–202; Radomir Luza, *Austro-German Relations in the Anschluss Era* (Princeton: Princeton University Press, 1975), pp.215–227; Gerhard Botz, "The Jews of Vienna from the *Anschluss* to the Holocaust" in Oxaal, et al., *Jews, Antisemitism and Culture in Vienna*, pp.185–204; Berkley, *Vienna and Its Jews*, pp.259–287.

2. CZA, S26/1191, Report on Visit to Vienna, London, April 1, 1938 and letter from Wyndham Deedes, London, April 28, 1938; Israel Cohen, "The Doom of Austrian Jewry," *Contemporary Review*, June 1938; Dutch, *Thus Died Austria*, pp.245, 253–254; Charles J. Kapralik, "Erinnerungen eines Beamten der WIKG 1938/39," *Bulletin des LBI*, 58 (1981), pp.52–78; Jonny Moser, *Die Judenverfolgung in Oesterreich 1938–45* (Vienna: Europa Verlag, 1966), pp.5–7; Gold, *Geschichte der Juden in Wien*, p.77; Rosenkranz, *Verfolgung und Selbstbehauptung*, pp.34–36.

3. CZA, KKL5/1149, Einige vertrauliche Bemerkungen, Tel Aviv, August 1938; Gold, *Geschichte der Juden in Wien*, p.77; Rosenkranz, *Verfolgung und Selbstbehauptung*, pp.71–74; Berkley, *Vienna and Its Jews*, passim.

4. CAHJP, A/W, 300, Protokoll über die . . . Besprechung, May 5, 1938; JDC, 439, Office Memorandum on the visit to Vienna by Mr. Landesco and Mr. Schweitzer, May 1938; Report by Capt. B.M. Woolf on his Visit to Austria, July 25, 1938; Financial and Statistical Data, 1938; CAHJP, A/W, 106, Die

Tätigkeit der KGW in der Zeit vom 13 März bis 31 Dezember 1938, pp.1–28; Rosenkranz, *Verfolgung und Selbstbehauptung*, pp.137–144 and passim.

5. Dutch, *Thus Died Austria*, pp.248–251; Gedye, *Fallen Bastions*, p.305; Neugebauer, ed., *Widerstand und Verfolgung*, III, p.213.

6. CZA, KKL5/1149, Georg Landauer, Zweiter Bericht betreffend Wien, May 9, 1938; S6/1646, Tätigkeitsbericht des Palästinaamtes Wien, 1938; CAHJP, A/W, 2329, Bericht über die bisherige Tätigkeit des orthodoxen Hilfskomitees in Wien, May 20, 1938; Mark Wischnitzer, "Jewish Emigration from Germany 1933–38," *Jewish Social Studies*, II, 1 (January 1940), pp.30–31; Rosenkranz, *Verfolgung und Selbstbehauptung*, pp.73–74.

7. CAHJP, A/W, 2819, Protokoll über die Tagung der Kultusgemeinden Oesterreichs, August 7, 1938; Marrus, *The Unwanted*, pp.167–172; Nora Levin, *The Holocaust: The Destruction of European Jewry 1933–1945* (New York: Schocken, 1973), pp.98–112; Bauer, *My Brother's Keeper*, p.227; Botz, "From the Anschluss to the Holocaust," pp.193–194; Luza, *Austro-German Relations*, pp.224–225; Rosenkranz, *Verfolgung und Selbstbehauptung*, pp.104, 191.

8. Marrus, *The Unwanted*, pp.180–181; Gold, *Geschichte der Juden in Wien*, p.133; Rosenkranz, *Verfolgung und Selbstbehauptung*, pp.106, 115, 227, 270.

9. IKGW, Report of the Vienna Jewish Community, July 1-October 31, 1939; Botz, "From the Anschluss to the Holocaust," pp.199–200; Rosenkranz, *Verfolgung und Selbstbehauptung*, p.198.

10. Moser, *Judenverfolgung in O*; Rosenkranz, *Judenverfolgung und Selbstbehauptung*; Philip Friedman, "Aspects of the Jewish Communal Crisis in the Period of the Nazi Regime," in Joseph L. Blau, et al., eds., *Essays on Jewish Life and Thought* (New York: Columbia University Press, 1959), pp.212–230; Neugebauer, ed., *Widerstand und Verfolgung*, III, pp.200–201; Berkley, *Vienna and Its Jews*, pp.289–299; Raul Hilberg, *The Destruction of the European Jews* (New York: Harper and Row, 1961), p.292.

11. Moser, *Judenverfolgung in O*, p.51; Rosenkranz, *Verfolgung und Selbstbehauptung*, p.310; Neugebauer, ed., *Widerstand und Verfolgung*, III, p.202.

12. Berkley, *Vienna and Its Jews*, pp.342–344.

13. Ibid., pp.345–355.

14. Ibid., p.364.

15. Kapralnik, "Erinnerungen eines Beamten der WIKG," p.78.

16. Anton Pick, "Zur Geschichte der Wiener IKG," in Klaus Lohrmann, ed., *1000 Jahre Oesterreichisches Judentums* (Eisenstadt: Roetzer, 1982), p.127.

17. Ibid., p.128.

18. Berkley, *Vienna and Its Jews*, p.360.

19. See Peter Sichrovsky, *Strangers in Their Own Land* (Philadelphia: Jewish Publication Society, 1986).

Selected Bibliography

Archives and Archival Collections

Allgemeines Verwaltungsarchiv, Vienna
  15-Bundeskanzleramt-Inneres, 1929–37
Archiv der Stadt Wien, Vienna
  B6-Gemeinderat, Minutes, 1919–20
  B29-Gemeinderat, Minutes, 1920–26
Central Archives for the History of the Jewish People, Jerusalem
  AW-Israelitische Kultusgemeinde Wien Collection, 1912–39
  AU-Austrian Collection, 1910–34
Central Zionist Archives, Jerusalem
  Z4-Correspondence of Zionist Organization, London, 1918–36
  S5-Correspondence of Organization Department, Jerusalem, 1935–39
  S6-Correspondence of Immigration Department, Jerusalem, 1920–38
  KH4-Keren Hayessod, 1926–38
  KKL5-Keren Kayemet L'israel, 1926–39
Joint Distribution Committee, New York
  111, 112, 117, 174-Austria, 1919–22
  439-Austria-General, 1934–38
Leo Baeck Institute, New York
  Rudolf Seiden Collection
Yad Vashem, Jerusalem
  0-1/244-Leo Landau (oral history)

Primary Sources
Newspapers

B'nai B'rith Mitteilungen für Oesterreich. Vienna, 1924–34.
Dr. Blochs Oesterreichische Wochenschrift. Vienna, 1912–19.
Der Jude, Organ für das Arbeitende Palästina. Vienna, 1934–36.
Der jüdische Arbeiter. Vienna, 1920–33.
Jüdische Front, Offizielles Organ des Bundes jüdischer Frontsoldaten Oester-
    reichs. Vienna, 1932–38.
Jüdische Korrespondenz, Wochenblatt für jüdische Interessen. Vienna, 1916–
    19 and 1935.
Jüdische Presse, Organ für die Interessen des orthodoxen Judentums. Vien-
    na/Bratislava, 1921–38.
Jüdische Volkszeitung. Vienna, 1928.
Der jüdische Weg. Vienna, 1932–38.
Jüdische Wochenschrift. Vienna, 1923–25.
Jüdische Zeitung. Vienna, 1912–20.
Neue Freie Presse. Vienna, 1918–25.
Die Neue Welt. Vienna, 1927–38.
Die Stimme. Vienna, 1928–38.
Unsere Tribune, Organ der jüdischen sozial-demokratischen Arbeiterorganiza-
    tion Poale Zion. Vienna, 1924–26.
Unser Wort. Vienna, 1933–34.
Die Wahrheit. Vienna, 1912–38.
Wiener jüdisches Familienblatt. Vienna, 1933–35.
Wiener Morgenzeitung. Vienna, 1919–27.

Zionistische Rundschau. Vienna, 1938.

Statistical Publications

Ascher, Arnold. *Die Juden im statistischen Jahrbuch der Stadt Wien für das Jahr 1911.* Vienna: Oesterreichische Wochenschrift, 1913.

Bundesamt für Statistik. "Die Bewegung der Bevölkerung in den Jahren 1914–21." In *Beiträge zur Statistik der Republik Oesterreich.* VIII. Vienna: Verlag der österreichischen Staatsdruckerei, 1923.

_____. *Die Ergebnisse der österreichischen Volkszählung vom 22 März 1934.* I and II. Vienna: Verlag der österreichischen Staatsdruckerei, 1935.

_____. *Statistisches Handbuch für die Republik Oesterreich.* I–XVII. Vienna: Verlag der österreichischen Staatsdruckerei, 1920–37.

Goldhammer, Leo. *Die Juden Wiens: Eine statistische Studie.* Vienna: R. Löwit Verlag, 1927.

Magistratsabteilung für Statistik. *Statistisches Jahrbuch der Stadt Wien.* Vienna: Statistisches Amt, 1929–38.

Statistische Zentralkommission. *Die Wahlen für die Konstituierende National-versammlung.* I and II. Vienna, 1919.

Published Reports, Documents, and Brochures

Berchtold, Klaus, ed. *Oesterreichische Parteiprogramme, 1868–1966.* Munich: Oldenbourg, 1967.

B'nai B'rith, Loge Eintracht. *Festschrift anlässlich des 25-jährigen Bestandes des israelitischen Humanitätsvereines "Eintracht."* Vienna, 1928.

Israelitische Allianz zu Wien. *Bericht.* Vienna, 1908, 1911, 1925, 1929, and 1931.

Israelitische Kultusgemeinde Wien. *Bericht der Israelitischen Kultusgemeinde Wien über die Tätigkeit in der Periode 1912–24.* Vienna, 1924.

_____. *Bericht der Israelitischen Kultusgemeinde Wien über die Tätigkeit in der Periode 1925–28.* Vienna, 1928.

_____. *Bericht der Israelitischen Kultusgemeinde Wien über die Tätigkeit in der Periode 1929–32.* Vienna, 1932.

_____. *Bericht des Präsidiums über die Tätigkeit in den Jahren 1933–36.* Vienna, 1936.

_____. *Statut der Israelitischen Kultusgemeinde Wien.* Vienna, 1926.

Jüdisches Jahrbuch für Oesterreich 1932/33 (5693). Ed. by Löbel Taubes and Chajim Bloch. Vienna, 1933.

Knöpfmacher, Wilhelm. *Entstehungsgeschichte und Chronik der Vereinigung "Wien" B'nai B'rith in Wien, 1895–1935.* Vienna, 1935.

Krauss, Samuel. *Die Krise der Wiener Judenschaft.* Vienna, 1919.

Rosenfeld, Moritz. *Der jüdische Religionsunterricht.* Vienna: R. Löwit Verlag, 1920.

Stricker, Robert. *Jüdische Politik in Oesterreich.* Vienna: Wiener Morgen-zeitung, 1920.

_____. *Der Vertreter des jüdischen Volkes.* Vienna: Verlag des Zionistischen Landeskomitees, 1919.

_____. *Wege der jüdischen Politik.* Vienna: R. Löwit Verlag, 1929.

Tschiassny, Moritz. *Jüdische Kultus- und Erziehungsfragen: Eine Denkschrift.* Vienna, 1918.

Union deutsch-österreichischer Juden. *Festschrift zur Feier des 50-jährigen Bestandes der Union österreichischer Juden.* Vienna, 1937.

Vereinigte Wiener Tempelvereine. *Kultusgemeindeprogramm.* Vienna, 1919.

Weltsch, Robert. *Jüdischer Nationalrat für Deutsch-österreich 1918.* Tel Aviv, 1927.

Published Eye-Witness Accounts and Memoirs

Bloch, Joseph S. *My Reminiscences*. Vienna: R. Löwit, 1923.
Braunthal, Julius. *In Search of the Millennium*. London: Victor Gollancz, 1945.
Clare, George. *Last Waltz in Vienna: The Destruction of a Family, 1842–1949*. New York: Holt, Rinehart and Winston, 1982.
Dutch, Oswald. *Thus Died Austria*. London: Edward Arnold, 1938.
Frankel, Josef, ed. *Robert Stricker*. London, 1950.
Gedye, George Eric Rowe. *Fallen Bastions: The Central European Tragedy*. Vienna: Victor Gollancz, 1939.
Gold, Hugo, ed. *Zwi Perez Chajes, Dokumente aus seinem Leben und Wirken*. Tel Aviv: Olamenu, 1971.
Kaminka, Gideon. *Ins Land, das Ich dir zeigen werde*. Zurich: Judaica Verlag, 1977.
Kapralnik, Charles J. "Erinnerungen eines Beamten der WIKG 1938–39." *Bulletin des LBI*, 58 (1981), pp.52–78.
Mayer, Sigmund. *Ein jüdischer Kaufmann, 1831 bis 1911*. Leipzig: Verlag von Duncker und Humblot, 1911.
———. *Wiener Juden: Kommerz, Kultur, Politik*. Vienna: R. Löwit Verlag, 1918.
Rosenfeld, Moritz, ed. *H.P. Chajes: Reden und Vorträge*. Vienna, 1933.
———. *Oberrabbiner H.P. Chajes, Sein Leben und Werk*. Vienna, 1933.
Roth, Josef. *Juden auf der Wanderschaft*. Berlin, 1930.
Schechter, Edmund. *Viennese Vignettes: Personal Reflections*. New York: Vantage Press, 1983.
Zehavi-Goldhammer, Arjeh. *Dr. Leopold Plaschkes: Zwei Generationen des österreichischen Judentums*. Tel Aviv: Irgun Olej Merkas Europe, 1943.

Secondary Sources

Books

Beckermann, Ruth, ed. *Die Mazzeinsel: Juden in der Wiener Leopoldstadt, 1918–1938*. Vienna: Löcker Verlag, 1984.
Benedikt, Heinrich, ed. *Geschichte der Republik Oesterreich*. Vienna: Verlag für Geschichte und Politik, 1954.
Berkley, George. *Vienna and Its Jews*. Cambridge: Abt Books, 1988.
Fraenkel, Josef, ed. *The Jews of Austria*. London: Valentine-Mitchell, 1967; 2nd ed., 1970.
Gold, Hugo. *Die Geschichte der Juden in Wien: Ein Gedenkbuch*. Tel Aviv: Olamenu, 1966.
Harrington-Müller, Diethild. *Der Fortschrittsklub im Abgeordnetenhaus des österreichischen Reichsrats, 1873–1918*. Vienna: Hermann Böhlau Verlag, 1972.
Holleis, Eva. *Die Sozialpolitische Partei*. Munich: Oldenbourg, 1978.
Kitchen, Martin. *The Coming of Austrian Fascism*. Montreal: McGill-Queens University Press, 1980.
Lohrmann, Klaus, ed. *1000 Jahre Oesterreichisches Judentums*. Eisenstadt: Roetzer, 1982.
Maderegger, Sylvia. *Die Juden im österreichischen Ständesstaat, 1934–38*. Vienna: Geyer, 1973.
Oxaal, Ivar; Pollak, Michael; and Botz, Gerhard, eds. *Jews, Antisemitism and Culture in Vienna*. London: Routledge and Kegan Paul, 1987.
Patzer, Franz. *Der Wiener Gemeinderat, 1918–39*. Vienna: Verlag für Jugend und Volk, 1961.

Rosenkranz, Herbert. *Verfolgung und Selbstbehauptung: Die Juden in Oesterreich, 1938–1945.* Vienna: Herold, 1978.

Rothschild, K.W. *Austria's Economic Development between the Two Wars.* London: Frederick Muller, 1947.

Rozenblit, Marsha L. *The Jews of Vienna, 1867–1914: Assimilation and Identity.* Albany: SUNY Press, 1983.

Spira, Leopold. *Feindbild "Jud'":* 100 Jahre politischer Antisemitismus in *Oesterreich.* Vienna: Löcker Verlag, 1981.

Wistrich, Robert S. *Socialism and the Jews: The Dilemmas of Assimilation in Germany and Austria-Hungary.* East Brunswick: Associated University Presses, 1982.

Articles

Barkai, A. "The Austrian Social Democrats and the Jews." *Wiener Library Bulletin,* XXIV (1970), no. 1, pp.32–40 and no. 2, pp.16–21.

Boyer, John W. "Karl Lueger and the Viennese Jews." *LBIYB,* XXVI (1981), pp.125–141.

Bunzl, John. "'Arbeiterbewegung,' 'Judenfrage' und Antisemitismus: Am Beispiel des Wiener Bezirks Leopoldstadt." In *Bewegung und Klasse: Studien zur österreichischen Arbeitergeschichte,* ed. G. Botz. Vienna, 1978, pp.743–763.

Freud, Arthur. "Um Gemeinde und Organisation: Zur Haltung der Juden in Oesterreich." *Bulletin des LBI,* 1960, no.10, pp.81–100.

Gelber, N.M. "Die Wiener Israelitische Allianz." *Bulletin des LBI,* 1960, no.11, pp.190–204.

Haag, John. "Blood on the Ringstrasse: Vienna's Students, 1918–33." *Wiener Library Bulletin,* 1976, no.29, pp.29–34.

Jacobs, Jack. "Austrian Social Democracy and the Jewish Question during the First Republic." In *Austrian Social Democracy 1918–34: The Socialist Experiment and Its Collapse.* Ed. Anson Rabinbach. Boulder: Westview Press, 1985, pp.157–168.

Karbach, Oscar. "The Liquidation of the Jewish Community of Vienna." *Jewish Social Studies,* II, no.3 (1940), pp.255–278.

Lafleur, Ingrun. "Five Socialist Women: Traditionalist Conflicts and Socialist Visions in Austria, 1893–1934." In *Socialist Women: European Socialist Feminism in the Nineteenth and Twentieth Centuries.* New York, 1978, pp.215–248.

Moser, Jonny. "Der Katastrophe der Juden in Oesterreich 1938–1945 —ihre Voraussetzungen und ihre Ueberwindung." In *Der Gelbe Stern in Oesterreich.* Vol. V. *Studia Judaica Austriaca.* Eisenstadt: Roetzer, 1977, pp.67–134.

Oxaal, Ivar and Weitzmann, Walter R. "The Jews of Pre-1914 Vienna: An Exploration of Basic Sociological Dimensions." *LBIYB,* XXX (1985), pp.394–432.

Pulzer, P.G.J. "The Austrian Liberals and the Jewish Question, 1867–1914." *Journal of Central European Affairs,* XXII (1963), no.2, pp.131–142.

Schorske, Carl E. "Politics in a New Key: An Austrian Triptych." *Journal of Modern History,* XXXIX (1967), no.4, pp.343–387.

Silberner, Edmund. "Austrian Social Democracy and the Jewish Problem." *Historia Judaica,* XIII (1951), no. 2, pp.121–140.

Simon, Walter B. "The Jewish Vote in Austria." *LBIYB,* XVI (1971), pp.97–121.

———. "The Jewish Vote in Vienna." *Jewish Social Studies,* XXIII (1961), no.1, pp.38–48.

Toury, Jacob. "Troubled Beginnings: The Emergence of the OIU." *LBIYB*, XXX (1985), pp.457–475.

_____ . "Years of Strife: The Contest of the OIU for the Leadership of Austrian Jewry." *LBIYB*, XXXIII (1988), pp.179–199.

Index

Achduth Israel, 132, 136, 138, 141, 142

Adas Jisroel, 116–117, 120, 121, 122, 129–137, 144, 161, 168, 179, 196; allied with Liberals, 135–136, 141; as separate community, 129, 163; criticism of, 133, 161–162; demands of, 130–132, 160; kosher slaughtering activities of, 121, 134, 137, 160, 161; leadership of, 123, 125, 131; rabbinate of, 131, 132, 134–135. *See also* Secession, Orthodox

Adler, Friedrich, 92

Adler, Max, 94

Adler, Viktor, 92

Agudah. *See* Agudat Israel

Agudas Hacharedim, 139

Agudat Israel, 75, 77, 81, 115, 116–118, 125, 127, 129, 139, 141, 144, 145, 150, 156, 157, 159, 179, 182, 196, 199, 205; allied with Liberals, 42, 43, 103, 135, 137; communal mandates of, 44, 46, 78, 80, 106, 122; leadership of, 122, 123, 131; policies of, 4, 118, 127–128, 135, 137, 158, 202; support for, 117, 129, 138

Alliance for Social Action, 100, 104

Alliance of Jewish War Veterans, 172, 198, 202; defense activities of, 181, 187, 191; patriotism of, 197, 200

Alliance of Jewish Workers, 100, 105–109, 112, 165, 207

Alliance Israélite Universelle, 24

Alsergrund (IX), 14, 70, 88; Orthodox prayer-houses in, 121, 138; support for Jewish list in, 63, 66, 68; support for Liberals in, 31, 33

Anninger, Walter, 31

Anschluss, 64, 154, 186, 204–206

Antisemitism, 2, 6–9, 16, 17, 24–26, 35, 53–54, 81, 93, 154, 157, 173, 180–195, 198–200, 204–207; at universities, 8, 26, 54, 64–65, 180–181, 183–185; defense against, 24–26, 29–30, 34, 37, 47, 53–54, 62, 63, 66–67, 69, 95, 103, 113, 172, 181–195, 197; effect on Jewish voting of, 1, 9–10, 32, 84, 88, 239n121; protests against, 182–186, 187, 189; Social Democratic Party and, 9, 88, 95, 113; varieties of, 25–26, 69–70, 180–181, 202. *See also* Christian Social Party; German Nationalists; National Socialists

Apolitical Electoral Alliance, 138, 144

Apolitical Orthodox, 122, 143–145, 164

Apostasy, 17–18, 20, 30, 74, 89, 92, 105, 143, 185, 188, 206, 240n21

Arbeiterzeitung, Die, 88, 92

Assimilation, 2, 89, 94, 118, 124, 155, 180, 209

Association for Progressive Religious Judaism, 150

Association of Jewish Physicians, 189, 198

Association of Radical Zionists, 80, 166

Association of Socialist Jews, 107, 108

Auschwitz, 206

Austerlitz, Friedrich, 92

Austria: as German-Christian state, 186, 193, 196

Austrian Antisemitic League, 8

Austrian Mizrachi Federation, 138–139, 142

Austrian Young People's Organization, 200, 202

Austrian Zionist Federation, 34, 55, 66–71, 80, 82, 85, 90–91, 93–94

Autonomy, communal, 73, 178, 205

Baptismal certificate: as job requirement, 26, 51, 189

Bar Mitzvah, 156

Bauer, Otto, 90, 92, 94

Bauminger, Viktor, 142–143

Betar, 200

Beth Israel, 116, 117, 120, 121–122, 132, 138–141, 144; communal mandates of, 122, 136, 144–145, 175; leadership of, 122, 143–144

Binyan Ha'arez, 110

Birnbaum, Nathan, 51

Birthrate, Jewish, 18, 155

Bloch, Josef Samuel (Rabbi), 24

B'nai B'rith, 28, 169, 172, 182, 205; Lodge "Wien," 28, 39–40, 148, 167, 193

Bohemian Jews, 5, 27, 31, 39, 111

Böhm, Adolf, 172

Braunthal, Julius, 94

Breitner, Hugo, 92, 102

Brigittenau (XX), 13–14, 57, 70, 157, 175; Orthodox in, 115, 121; Socialist vote in, 87–88, 89; support for Jewish list in, 44, 63, 68

Budget, communal. See Finances, communal

Bukovina, 5, 60

Bund, 86, 100, 113

Burgenland, 5, 27, 116, 163–164

Businessmen, Jewish, 12–13, 16, 28; as communal leaders, 38, 122; boycotts against, 26, 189, 190, 194

Cantors, 119, 120, 121
Catholic Center Party, 87, 115
Catholics, 20, 30, 184, 187, 199
Cemetery, 37, 132, 134–135, 151
Censorship, 186, 195
Central Welfare Bureau, 154
Centralverein, 24, 26, 30
Chajes Realgymnasium, 54, 97, 156, 157, 160, 199
Chajes, Hirsch Perez (Chief Rabbi), 56, 123–125, 131, 133–134, 145
Charitable organizations, 20, 153, 154
Choirs, 119, 120, 121
Christian Social Party, 6, 7, 15, 30, 32, 34, 36, 82, 90, 96–97, 128, 159, 165, 186, 196; antisemitism within, 7–8, 67, 69, 84, 88, 115, 184–188; Jewish support for, 9, 35, 195
Citizens' Council, 193
Citizenship, Austrian, 58, 94, 169, 175, 202; as requirement, 27, 40–41, 77, 138, 140, 171; eligibility for, 12, 26, 51, 53
Civil equality, 22, 42, 52, 126, 167, 186, 194, 196–198, 200; protection of, 4, 25, 51, 53–54, 63, 65, 67, 102, 149, 174, 181, 183, 187, 188
Civil servants: discrimination against Jews as, 12, 16, 30, 51, 53, 67, 69–70, 93, 95, 180, 188, 190, 194
Civil War, 96, 110, 164–166, 186, 189, 195, 196–197, 201
Committee of Jewish Workers, 95
Communist Party, 9, 84, 85, 207
Communities, provincial, 94, 163
Community, Jewish. See Kultusgemeinde
Confirmation: for girls, 155, 156
Constitution, Austrian, 78, 97, 186, 194, 196, 197, 200, 202
Constitutional Court, 184
Conversion to Christianity, 17–18, 20, 30, 31, 32. See also Apostasy
Conversion to Judaism, 17–18
Corporate state, 7, 16, 128, 158, 181, 186–202
Coudenhove-Kalergi, Richard, 191
Council of Elders, 206
Council of State: Jewish representation on, 193, 200, 201
Credit bureau, 26, 153
Creditanstalt, 16
Cultural Council, 193
Czech Jews, 5, 48; as Liberals, 23, 57; as Socialists, 85, 99. See also Bohemian Jews; Moravian Jews
Czechoslovakia, 5, 6, 49, 82, 152, 235n26

Czermak, Emmerich, 184, 188
Czernin, Ottokar, 33, 34, 66

Dachau, 204
Decorum, 2, 119
Defense force, Jewish. See Self-defense, Jewish
Democratic Center Party, 35
Democratic Middle Class Party, 63
Democratic Party, 22, 33, 35, 63, 87, 127
Democratic Zionists, 55, 70, 71, 80–81
Democratization, 46, 77, 149, 150, 205; opposition to, 19, 23, 40, 43; support for, 5, 38, 74, 98, 101, 102, 108, 142, 147, 174
Demographic decline, 2, 16–18
Depression, 16, 21, 45, 95, 148–149, 151, 154, 172, 181, 188, 190
Deutsch, Julius, 92
Discrimination, against Jews, 16–17, 26, 69–70, 95, 105, 181, 185–190, 194. See also Antisemitism
Doctors, Jewish. See Physicians, Jewish
Dollfuss, Engelbert (Chancellor), 96, 147, 159, 165, 186, 194, 196, 200, 201

Eastern Jews, 5, 8, 44, 116; as foreigners, 5, 27, 141; as Jewish Nationalists, 58, 82, 123. See also Galician Jews
Economic class: effect on voting of, 1–2, 9, 12–13, 22, 48, 68, 87
Economic crisis, 2, 14–16, 54, 76, 95, 103, 147, 149, 154–155. See also Finances, communal; Inflation; Depression
Education: adult, 24, 75; higher, 28, 39, 58, 70, 82, 99, 116, 122; Jewish, 51, 54, 64, 75, 94, 97, 141, 143, 146, 149, 155–158, 174, 177, 180, 199–200; religious, 19, 37, 42, 43, 89, 97, 126, 131–132, 134, 139, 141, 144, 151, 153, 155, 157, 160, 167, 199; vocational, 139, 157. See also Schools
Ehrlich, Jakob, 58, 66, 71, 72, 127, 193–194, 201, 204
Eichmann, Adolf, 205
Elections, communal, 2, 50, 72, 86, 98, 171; of 1912, 37; of 1920, 41, 76, 100, 130–131, 139–140; of 1924, 41, 77–78, 100, 103, 135, 139, 140–141; of 1928, 42, 44, 79, 105–106, 143; of 1932, 45, 80, 82, 108–109, 144, 145–146; of 1936, 110, 163, 172–175; results of, 42, 46, 75–80, 103–104, 110, 117
Elections, municipal, 2, 9, 87, 89; of 1912, 32; of 1919, 65–66, 67; of 1923, 42, 67–68, 102, 103; of 1927, 35, 70; of 1932, 35, 71, 91
Elections, national, 2, 7, 9, 71, 87, 89, 91; of 1907, 31, 60; of 1911, 32, 60, 62; of 1919, 33, 60, 63–64, 127; of 1920, 63,

90; of 1923, 34–35, 42, 90, 95, 102, 127; of 1927, 35, 95; of 1930, 35, 70
Electoral Alliance for Social Action, 102–105
Electoral Alliance of Jewish Workers, 99
Electoral curia: in Austrian politics, 6, 51, 60, 188; in Kultusgemeinde, 19, 37, 40, 72, 74
Electoral reform, Austrian: national, 70; municipal, 67
Electoral reform, communal, 19, 38, 40, 41, 46, 149–150; opposition to, 43, 73, 140; demand for, 52, 66, 72, 74, 76, 101. *See also* Suffrage
Electoral system: Austrian, 1, 62–63, 65; communal, 19
Ellenbogen, Wilhelm, 92
Emancipation, 6, 22
Emigration, 154, 205–206
Employees, communal: as Socialists, 90, 94–95, 102; conditions among, 15, 19, 20, 75; payment of, 20, 74, 77, 147; rights of, 40, 41, 72, 77, 102, 142, 150
Employees, salaried, 12–13, 16, 38, 91, 98–99, 122
Employment bureau, 149, 154
Endowments, 20, 37
Engel, Emil, 170
England, 206
Ethnic homogeneity, 5, 49, 82
Evian Conference, 205

Factionalism, 5, 209; among Jewish Nationalists, 56, 176–177; among Orthodox, 116–118, 132–133; among Socialists, 98, 107–109
Fatherland Front, 7, 96, 147, 186, 189, 190, 195–198
Federation of German Aryan Lawyers, 190
Federation of Jewish Women of German-Austria, 27
Federation, communal, 37, 163–164, 194; opposition to, 127, 158; support for, 52, 74, 149, 174
Feldsberg, Ernst, 47, 110, 123, 159, 208
Finances, communal, 20, 37, 44, 102, 143, 148–149, 151–158, 162; crisis in, 41–42, 47, 76, 149
Floridsdorf, 24
Foreign Jews: discrimination against, 64, 181, 184
France, 49
Frankfurter, Salomon, 193
Free Zionist Association, 60–61, 69, 91
Freud, Sigmund, 14
Friedmann, Desider, 58, 69, 76, 80, 106, 112, 123, 148, 167, 173, 192, 201, 204, 206; as president of Kultusgemeinde, 147, 148–149, 161, 165, 170, 177, 193, 194, 200, 202

Friedmann, Salomon (Rabbi), 160

Galician Jews, 2, 5, 13, 27, 48, 49, 60, 81, 86, 117, 155, 156, 160, 163, 173, 179; as foreigners, 5, 141, 171; as Jewish Nationalists, 48–49, 55, 58, 60, 82, 86, 111–112, 129; as leaders, 58, 123, 144, 169, 178; as Socialists, 86, 89, 99–100, 111–112; as war refugees, 25, 53; as voters, 19, 40, 41, 63, 73, 81, 136, 175; Orthodox among, 116, 118, 119, 121, 123, 135–136, 138–146, 159–160, 161; prejudice against, 5, 142, 169
Gegenwartsarbeit, 50, 55, 129
General Jewish Association, 192
General Zionists, 4, 55, 60, 70–71, 82, 112, 141, 149, 175, 192; A Group, 55, 80; B Group, 55–56, 66, 80–81; communal mandates of, 80, 164
Geneva Protocols, 15
Geographic origins, 57–58, 99, 116
German, 2, 5, 23, 48, 65, 116, 119, 126
German Nationalists, 6, 9, 32, 36; allied with Liberals, 22, 29, 34; antisemitism among, 8, 67, 84, 88, 181, 183–184, 187–188
German Progressive Party, 31
Germany, 1, 5, 6, 10, 26, 30, 49, 84, 87, 115, 116, 145, 152, 161, 172, 182, 186, 187, 195, 200, 202, 204
Gestapo, 204–205
Gföllner, Johannes Maria (Bishop), 187
Girls: education of, 155, 156, 157
Goldmann, Nahum, 201
Government, Austrian, 20, 51, 162, 164, 171, 178; and antisemitism, 30, 181–190, 208; lobbying with, 26, 181–182, 185, 194; relations with Kultusgemeinde, 185, 200, 204–205
Güdemann, Moritz (Chief Rabbi), 30, 123, 125

Hakoah, 191
Harand, Irene, 191
Hasidim, 2, 115, 117, 119, 120, 122, 129, 132, 135, 138, 145, 161
Hebrew, 51, 54, 75, 119, 124, 126, 142, 143, 156, 157, 199
Hebrew Teachers' Institute, 54, 169
Hebrew University, 78, 137
Heimwehr, 7, 8, 181, 186, 196; Jewish support for, 9, 35
Herzl, Theodor, 19, 50, 60, 100
Hitachdut, 4, 70, 71, 85–86, 91, 93, 109, 110, 165
Hitachdut Jereim, 144
Hitler, Adolf, 173, 180, 186, 187, 195, 201, 204
Hock (Baron), 31–32
Holocaust, 206–207

Hospitals, 37, 189; communal, 20, 76, 101, 136, 145, 153, 190, 194
Housing, 14–15, 16, 93
Hungarian Jews, 2, 5, 13, 37, 48, 99, 111, 117; as Liberals, 23, 27, 57; as Orthodox, 116, 119, 123, 125–133, 158–164, 178
Hungary, 5, 6, 49, 90, 145, 152, 184, 202

Inflation, 15, 102, 147, 151, 153
Inner City (I), 14, 36, 57, 92, 99; Liberal support in, 30–33, 35, 175; Socialist vote in, 87–88; support for Jewish list in, 44, 63, 68; synagogues in, 120, 121, 132, 208
Innitzer, Theodor (Archbishop), 187
Institute for Agriculture, 183, 184
Institute for World Trade, 183
Intellectuals: and Social Democratic Party, 92, 99, 112. See also Professionals, Jewish
Intermarriage, 17, 18
International Conference of Jewish Women, 59
Israel, State of, 2, 4, 5, 19, 207, 208
Israelite Theological Seminary, 124, 157
Israelitische Allianz, 24, 28, 37, 167, 182
Israelitische Kultusgemeinde Wien. See Kultusgemeinde

Jellinek, Adolf (Chief Rabbi), 124
Jewish Agency for Palestine, 56, 62, 148, 167
Jewish Electoral Partnership, 67–68
Jewish list, 34–35, 42, 63–71, 90–91, 103, 127
Jewish National Council for German-Austria, 38, 39, 52–55, 67, 72, 127
Jewish Nationalism: opposition to, 4–5, 43, 48, 85, 89, 94, 113, 117, 118, 129, 167, 171. See also Jewish Nationalists
Jewish Nationalist Association, 66
Jewish Nationalist Party, 51, 62–66, 89, 97, 127
Jewish Nationalists, 2, 4–5, 6, 10, 31, 48–83, 104, 111, 118, 147–150, 178, 239n121; achievements of, 154–158, 177; allied with Liberals, 34, 40, 41–42, 62, 67, 69, 77, 90, 103; allied with Orthodox, 117, 160; and Social Democratic Party, 67, 68, 70–71, 89–91, 201; as communal leaders, 45, 76, 78, 80, 147–148, 164, 169–170, 171, 176, 205; characteristics of, 56–59; communal mandates of, 76, 78, 80–81, 106, 164, 166, 170, 171, 175; communal program of, 19, 74–75, 78–79, 174; criticism of, 168–174, 200–201; defense activities of, 181, 182, 183, 186, 189, 190, 192, 195; factionalism among, 56,

168, 176–177; goals of, 48, 49, 51–52, 62, 140, 149, 157–158, 184, 198, 199; opposition to, 34, 45, 47, 90, 101, 126, 127, 130, 137, 158–164, 166–168, 178; role in Kultusgemeinde of, 36–37, 72–82, 147–158; support for, 52, 72, 75, 80, 82, 174–175
Jewish People's Alliance, 192
Jewish People's Association, 71
Jewish People's Group, 100
Jewish People's Party, 51, 71–72, 192, 197
Jewish State Party, 55, 56, 62, 175
Jewish Territorialist Organization (ITO), 129
Jewish Theological Seminary, 118
Jewish Youth Federation of Austria, 202
Jews: as nationality, 5, 7, 34, 38, 39, 48–49, 51, 52–54, 63, 65, 69, 81, 82, 94–95, 118, 126, 184; as religious group, 4, 19, 25, 26, 43, 53, 65, 85, 94, 135, 158, 167, 208
Joint Distribution Committee, 20, 77, 115, 153, 156, 205
Jüdische Korrespondenz, 125, 126, 127, 128
Jüdische Presse, 125, 128, 137
Jüdische Weg, Der, 56
Jüdische Wochenschrift, 139

Kadimah, 50, 60
Kashrut, 131, 134, 135, 136–137, 141, 145, 160. See also Kosher meat
Keren Hamizrachi, 137
Keren Hayessod, 78, 137, 139
Keren Hayishuv, 137
Knöpfmacher, Wilhelm, 172
Kohn, Gustav, 31
Kosher meat, 115, 121, 126, 129, 134, 137, 140, 158, 160, 161. See also Kashrut
Kreisky, Bruno, 207
Kresse (Deputy Mayor), 188, 190, 194
Kultusgemeinde, 18–21, 147–179, 204–208; defense activities of, 53, 181–186, 187, 189, 194–195; hiring practices of, 168–170; Jewish Nationalist involvement in, 72–82; Liberal involvement in, 28, 36–47; Orthodox involvement in, 116–125, 129–145; relations with government, 148, 162–164, 185, 200, 204–206; role of, 18–19, 23, 37, 40, 42, 43, 50, 101, 118, 137, 139, 141, 160, 167, 173, 181–182, 205, 207; Socialist involvement in, 97–111; structure of, 18–21, 74, 77; unity of, 118, 132, 142, 143, 149, 158–164. See also Education; Elections, communal; Finances, communal; Leadership, communal; Social welfare, communal; Subsidies, communal

Kunschak, Leopold, 8, 188
Kuranda, Kamillo, 31–32

Labor Zionists, 4, 81, 82, 85, 91, 94–95, 96, 98, 99, 100, 105–106, 108–113, 149, 165, 176, 178, 196; communal mandates of, 80, 81, 107, 109, 111, 164; support for, 81, 85–86, 109, 110, 111–112, 175
Landau, Leo, 122, 143–144, 175
Landau, Saul Raphael, 51, 100
Landespolitik, 47–54, 56, 58, 59–71, 82–83, 148, 192; abandonment of, 70–72, 91; opposition to, 60–61, 69, 86, 140
Latin America, 206
Lawyers, Jewish, 190; as communal leaders, 28, 31, 37, 66, 148, 167, 169
Leadership, communal, 80, 106, 159, 160, 164, 169–170, 207–208, 209; age of, 37, 38, 58–59; fate of, 204, 206; geographic origins of, 57–58, 82, 178; Liberals as, 28, 31, 36–40, 41, 42, 44–45, 166–167, 176; Jewish Nationalists as, 61, 66, 76, 78, 148, 193–195, 200, 205
League of Nations, 52, 64, 185
Leopoldstadt (II), 13–14, 57, 90, 92, 129, 156, 157, 159, 175, 191; Jewish Nationalists representing, 63, 66, 68, 70; Liberals representing, 30–33, 37, 60; Orthodox in, 115, 122, 138, 143; Socialist vote in, 88, 89, 99; synagogues in, 120–121, 243
Leopoldstadt temple, 101, 120, 150, 160
Liberalism, Austrian, 6, 8, 10, 22, 29, 33, 84, 87; and antisemitism, 7, 8–9, 22, 29–30, 31, 34, 62; Jewish support for, 10, 29–36
Liberals, Jewish, 2, 4, 5, 22–47, 75, 81, 101, 109, 147, 149, 150, 156, 157, 160, 172, 174–175, 196; allied with Jewish Nationalists, 41–42, 77, 103; allied with Orthodox, 23, 42, 43, 117; allied with Socialists, 23, 45, 89, 108, 196; as communal leaders, 28, 36–40, 41, 42, 44–45, 46, 76, 78, 80, 164, 166–168, 176; as opponents of Jewish Nationalists, 23, 147, 166, 168–171, 194; characteristics of, 2–4, 22–23, 37, 38–39, 57; communal mandates of, 42, 44, 46, 78, 80, 106, 164, 166, 170, 176; communal goals of, 19, 23, 40, 43–44, 172–173; role in Kultusgemeinde of, 36–47; policies of, 72–73, 153, 156, 158, 163, 184, 188, 199. See also Union of Austrian Jews
Librarian, communal, 168–169
Loan fund, 153, 154
Löwenherz, Josef, 45, 58, 78, 80, 108, 112, 164, 192, 204–207; as executive director, 168–171, 174, 175–177

Löwenherz, Sophie, 207
Löwy, Josef, 123
Lueger, Karl (Mayor), 6, 8, 180

Machsike Hadath, 132
Mannheimer, Isak Noa (Rabbi), 119
Mayer, Sigmund, 29–30
Migration, 5–6
Mikvah, 116, 137, 141, 145, 158, 160
Military: Jews in, 39, 51, 53, 126
Minority rights, 79, 82, 89, 94, 95; opposition to, 9, 23, 25, 36, 52–53, 171, 184; support for, 4–5, 52, 69, 74, 78, 86, 184–185, 192, 193–194, 198
Minyanim. See Prayer-houses, Orthodox
Mizrachi, 4, 42, 75, 116, 117, 118, 138–139, 140, 145, 149, 175; communal mandates of, 78, 80, 81, 122, 140, 143, 164; communal program of, 141–143; leadership of, 122, 123, 142, 160; support for, 80–81, 136, 144
Moravian Jews, 5, 13, 27, 111, 123; as communal leaders, 167–168, 178, 208; as Jewish Nationalists, 48, 55, 58, 61, 66, 148; as Liberals, 27, 28
Müller-Cohen, Anitta, 59, 64
Municipal council, 6, 51, 127; Jewish Liberals on, 30, 32–34, 37; Jewish Nationalists on, 60, 65–67, 68, 70, 83, 89–90, 97, 193–194; Social Democratic control of, 7, 67
Municipal government, 97, 102, 169, 171
Murmelstein, Benjamin (Rabbi), 206
Mussolini, Benito, 201

National autonomy, 49, 51, 52, 60, 62, 86, 94
Naturalization, 12, 88–89, 226n19
National Socialists (Nazis), 7, 8, 18, 81, 173, 181, 182, 186, 189, 191, 192, 201, 202, 204–206, 209
Neue Welt, Die, 56
New York, 86
Newspapers. See Press
Numerus clausus. See quotas

Oath of allegiance, 39, 53
Occupational distribution, 12–13, 38, 58, 98–99, 122
Oesterreichische Wochenschrift, 32
Ofner, Julius, 31–33, 34, 60
Old age home, communal, 20, 76, 101, 136, 153
Old Yishuv, 38, 126, 129
Oppenheim, Hermann, 28, 47, 166–167, 176, 200, 202, 204
Organ, 119
Organization of Zionist Women of Austria, 59

Ornstein, Jakob, 28, 42, 45, 47, 106, 164, 166, 168, 196
Orphans, Jewish, 101
Orthodox, 2, 4, 13, 23, 42, 46, 75, 115–146, 147–148, 149–150, 158–164, 178, 181, 196; allied with Jewish Nationalists, 116, 117, 160; allied with Liberals, 42, 117, 127, 135; as communal leaders, 45, 76, 131, 136, 142–144; attempts at secession by, 116, 119, 145, 158–163; attitudes of, 73, 125, 128, 196, 199; communal mandates of, 78, 80, 81, 106, 122, 131, 136, 140, 142, 144–145; communal program of, 19, 130–131, 139, 144; demands of, 42, 126, 131–132, 160, 173; differences among, 2, 116, 145–146; electoral choices of, 10, 115, 127–128; involvement in Kultusgemeinde of, 117, 118–125, 129–145; leadership of, 122–123; opposition to communal federation among, 163–164; religious standards of, 118, 126, 140; support for, 113, 117, 131, 136, 143, 144

Palestine, 38, 45, 58, 65, 86, 103, 112, 156, 173; communal subventions for, 78–79, 107, 137, 140, 142; emigration to, 54, 205, 206; Jewish homeland in, 4, 8, 10, 49–50, 52, 55, 113, 125, 174; Jewish state in, 49, 55, 61; non-Zionist view of, 25, 44; Orthodox support for, 126, 129, 138–139, 159; rebuilding of, 42, 69, 74, 78, 95, 137, 144, 149, 306
Palestine Liberation Organization, 208
Palestine Office, 54
Pan-German People's Party, 8
Pan-Germans. See German Nationalists
Pappenheim, Wolf, 122, 129, 131, 135–137, 141, 142
Parallel classes, 198–200
Paris, 86
Parliament, Austrian, 1, 6; dissolution of, 96, 147, 186, 193, 195; Jewish Liberals in, 31–34; Jewish representation in, 33, 51, 60, 62–65, 68, 69, 83
Patak, Erna, 59
Patriotism, Austrian, 39, 167, 171, 182, 183, 193, 196–198, 200, 202
Peace treaty. See St. Germain, Treaty of
Physicians, Jewish, 39; discrimination against, 16, 189–190, 194
Pick, Alois, 39–40, 41, 42, 44, 47, 106, 147
Plaschkes, Leopold, 58, 66, 68, 70, 71, 79, 80, 88, 90, 112, 127, 166, 206
Plebiscite (1938), 201, 202, 204
Poale Zion, 4, 55, 85–86, 91, 94–95, 99–100, 105, 107, 108–109, 110, 112, 165, 166
Poland, 1, 5, 6, 15, 49, 50, 53, 83, 86, 112,

113, 115, 116, 117, 127, 135, 139, 182, 235n26
Pollack von Parnau, Bruno, 66–67, 127
Polytechnical Institute, 183, 184
Population, Jewish: size of, 5, 6, 13, 17, 20, 206–207
Poverty, Jewish, 2, 13, 19, 20–21, 101, 115–116, 141–142, 153–155, 161–162, 205
Prayer-houses, Orthodox, 98, 122, 132–133, 139–140, 144, 161, 208; subsidies for, 42, 101, 118, 119, 121, 131, 133, 139, 143, 145, 158, 160, 173, 177; types of, 119–121, 132–133, 138, 141
Press, 104–105, 159, 186, 187, 188, 190, 202; Jewish Nationalist, 55–56, 194; Liberal, 25, 32, 194; Orthodox, 124, 125, 126, 136, 139, 160, 196
Pressburg, 116
Pro-Palestine Committee, 90, 187
Professionals, Jewish, 12, 16, 20, 58, 98–99; as communal leaders, 28, 38, 60, 82, 122. See also Lawyers, Jewish; Physicians, Jewish
Progressive Club, 29, 31–32
Progressive Party, 31, 37
Proportional representation: in Austrian politics, 6, 34, 51, 52, 60, 62, 65; in Kultusgemeinde, 19, 40, 72, 74, 76, 104, 130
Protestants, 20, 198
Provincial assembly, 31

Quadragesimo Anno, 128
Quotas, 8, 26, 34, 54, 67, 88, 181, 184–185, 188, 190

Rabbinate, communal, 123, 131, 133–135, 145, 158, 160, 161
Rabbis, 117, 120, 121, 126–127, 131, 136, 140, 161. See also Chajes, Hirsch Perez
Radical Zionists, 55–56, 62, 66, 71, 79, 91, 166, 175, 176
Rath, Moses, 168, 169
Reform, religious, 22–23, 118–119, 124, 145, 150–151, 160, 161
Refugees, Jewish, 13, 15, 20, 25, 33, 53, 54, 58, 67, 88, 138, 153, 154, 155, 205
Relief, communal, 20–21, 152–154, 165, 177
Religious affairs, 136, 150, 153, 158
Religious Bloc, 136, 141–142
Religious Zionists, 4, 42, 75, 78, 80, 82, 116, 118, 119, 129, 138, 140, 150, 176. See also Mizrachi
Residency rights, 12, 26
Residential distribution, 13–14, 57, 99, 122
Revisionist Zionists, 55, 56, 62, 70–71, 80, 91, 175, 200

Riehl, Walter, 173
Rohling, August, 24
Rothschild, Louis (Baron), 38–39

Sabbath rest, 51, 126, 160
Schalit, Isidor, 31, 60–61, 69
Schiffschul. *See* Adas Jisroel
Schober, Johann, 35
Schönerer, Georg von, 6, 180
Schools: elementary, 54–55, 79, 157, 177, 200, 205; Jewish, 54, 156–158, 194, 199–200; secondary, 54, 156, 157, 205; segregated, 26, 188, 198–199, 201; supplementary, 155–156, 177, 199. *See also* Chajes Realgymnasium; Education
Schuschnigg, Kurt von (Chancellor), 186, 194, 200, 202; Jewish support for, 196, 197, 201–202
Schutzbund, 92, 197
Schwarz-Hiller, Rudolf, 32–34, 38–39, 67, 73, 127
Secession, Orthodox, 116, 131–133, 144, 145, 147, 150, 158–163, 172, 178, 196
Seipel, Ignaz (Monsignor), 7–8
Seitenstettengasse: communal offices on, 18, 38; temple, 120, 208
Seitz, Karl (Mayor), 90
Self-defense, Jewish, 53, 181, 182, 183, 191
Sephardic community, 119, 132, 134, 244n14
Shanghai, 206
Shtadlanut, 26, 182, 185, 194
Slovakia, 5, 27, 116, 123, 129
Social Democratic Party, 7, 16, 30, 67; and antisemitism, 7, 9, 62, 68, 69, 88–89, 185; and Socialist Jews, 85–86, 95, 105–106, 107, 112–113, 165; and Zionism, 89–90, 107; dissolution of, 7, 96, 128, 165, 186, 189, 193, 195; Jewish Liberals and, 32, 35–36, 54, 81; policies of, 2, 65, 84–85, 96–98; reasons for joining, 84, 92–94, 112; relations with Jewish Nationalists, 71, 90–91; role of Jews in, 84, 91–93, 97, 128, 189, 207; support for, 10–11, 22, 35, 61, 83–88, 91, 96, 113, 127–128, 166, 195, 201, 208, 209
Social justice, 84, 90, 93
Social Political Party, 22, 30–31
Social welfare, communal, 20–21, 43, 115–116, 146, 147, 153–155, 162, 165, 170; funding for, 76, 94, 97, 107, 153; reform of, 75, 77, 98, 101, 110, 139, 142, 144, 149, 173, 174, 177
Socialist Alliance, 42
Socialists, Jewish, 2, 4, 10, 84–113, 148, 149–150, 175, 178, 181, 195–196; allied with Liberals, 45, 107–109; and Judaism, 25, 85, 89, 92, 98; as communal leaders, 45, 78, 98, 106, 109, 164, 207; attitude toward Jewish Nationalists of, 104, 106–107; characteristics of, 84–85, 98–100; communal goals of, 19, 100–103, 108, 149; communal mandates of, 46, 78, 79–80, 104, 106, 107, 109, 110–111, 164, 166; dissolution of mandates of, 110, 165, 178; persecution of, 110, 165–166, 183, 189; role in Kultusgemeinde of, 100–101, 104, 105, 106, 109, 111, 196, 207–208; support for in Kultusgemeinde, 103–104, 106, 113. *See also* Social Democratic Party
Sokolow, Nahum, 201
Soup kitchens, 20, 205
Soviet Union, 49, 208
Sports, 94, 160
St. Germain, Treaty of, 12, 26, 53, 70, 78, 79, 97, 185
Steinberg, Michael, 93–94, 110
Stern, Alfred, 37–38, 40, 52, 163, 182
Stimme, Die, 56
Streicher, Julius, 173
Stricker, Robert, 55–56, 58, 61–65, 93, 112, 173, 201, 204, 206; involvement in Landespolitik, 33, 34, 60, 61–65, 70–71, 127, 192; role in Kultusgemeinde of, 61, 72, 79, 80, 140, 141, 170, 176
Students, 27, 29, 50, 54, 58, 181, 183–184
Subsidies, communal, 20, 153, 155–156; for Orthodox prayer-houses, 42, 118, 121, 131, 133, 139, 143, 145, 158, 160, 173, 177; for Palestine, 78–79, 107, 137, 140, 141, 149
Subsidies, municipal, 70, 79, 94, 97, 101, 113
Subsidies, state, 20, 51, 70, 79, 149, 194
Suffrage, communal, 103, 115, 117, 177; for communal employees, 40, 102; for non-citizens, 19, 73–74, 140–141, 171; for women, 19, 40, 46, 59, 73, 80, 140, 150, 160. *See also* Suffrage, universal
Suffrage, universal, 6–7, 63, 77, 79, 111, 150, 166; opposition to, 19, 40, 43, 46, 108; support for, 31, 52, 66, 72, 80, 100, 110, 142, 149
Sulzer, Salomon, 119
Synagogues, 2, 4, 19, 37, 75, 119–122, 140, 144, 156, 208; funding for, 101, 119–120, 143, 149, 151, 156, 158, 173. *See also* Prayer-houses, Orthodox

Talmud Torah, 155, 157, 199
Taxation, communal, 20, 74, 77, 102, 132, 151, 152–153, 159, 162, 173; as voting requirement, 40, 43, 46
Taxation, municipal, 87, 102
Taxpayers, communal, 12–13, 20, 40–41, 46, 92, 103, 151, 174

Theresienstadt, 206, 208
Ticho, Josef, 47, 106, 123, 160, 166–168, 176
Turkish Israelites. *See* Sephardic community

Unemployment, 14, 15–16, 17, 95, 149, 154–155, 181, 188, 190
Union of Austrian Bar Associations, 190
Union of Austrian Jews, 23–35, 39, 47, 79, 91, 159, 161, 166, 196–197, 200, 202; defense activities of, 25–26, 181, 182, 184, 185–186, 187, 189, 191–192; leadership of, 28–29, 66–67, 166–167; membership in, 26–28; patriotism of, 27, 171, 196, 200; policies of, 23–26, 35, 43–44, 53, 159, 167, 191–192, 196–197; relations with Jewish Nationalists, 34, 67, 168–171, 175–176, 200; relations with Socialists, 45–46, 89, 165, 193
Union Women's Club, 27
Union Youth, 27, 29
United Jewish Parties, 42, 135
United Religious Jews of Vienna, 131
United States, 183, 206, 207
United Viennese Temple Associations, 139
University of Vienna, 14, 183–184, 187
Unser Wort, 128, 245n30

Violence against Jews, 8, 180–181, 182–183, 188, 191, 204, 206, 208
Vocational counseling, 149
Vocational training, 26, 64, 79, 154, 155, 157, 173, 205
Volksgemeinde, 19, 50, 52, 74, 79, 82, 174; opposition to, 23, 43, 135, 147, 158, 160
Voter eligibility, 12, 73; in communal elections, 19, 40–41, 46, 72, 77, 81, 174, 177. *See also* Suffrage, communal
Voter participation, 36, 41, 44, 174

Voting patterns, Jewish, 1–2, 9–10, 13

Wahrheit, Die, 24–25, 32, 34
Waldheim, Kurt, 207
Warsaw, 86
Weizmann, Chaim, 55, 112
Western Jews, 5–6, 27, 57, 82, 116, 140
Wiener Morgenzeitung, 34, 55, 66
Winter Relief Campaign, 21, 149, 154
Women, 73, 108, 119, 120, 142, 150; and Union of Austrian Jews, 27–28; as Jewish Nationalists, 59, 64; communal suffrage for, 19, 40, 46, 73, 81, 140, 149–150, 177
Workers, 9, 13–14, 16, 84, 86, 87, 91, 92, 95, 96, 99, 188
World Zionist Congress, 59, 90, 148; elections for, 56, 57, 60, 111, 139
World Zionist Organization, 19, 50, 55–56, 60, 62, 85, 107, 112, 138, 148, 201

Yiddish, 2, 5, 51, 86, 116, 126, 226n19
Youth, 27, 28–29, 58, 89, 149, 154; religious services for, 155, 156. *See also* Education; Schools
Yugoslavia, 49, 50, 82

Zionism, 4–5, 49–50, 59, 148; Social Democratic Party and, 9, 89–90, 93–94, 95, 103, 113; Christian support for, 8, 90, 187, 193, 201; opposition to, 38, 43–44, 45, 85, 86, 108, 118, 125, 129, 137, 144; support for, 5, 56–59, 85, 118, 139, 144
Zionist Electoral Committee, 58
Zionist National Committee for Austria, 59, 60, 69, 148, 170, 182
Zionist factions. *See* Democratic Zionists; General Zionists; Mizrachi; Poale Zion; Radical Zionists; Revisionist Zionists
Zionists. *See* Jewish Nationalists

HARRIET PASS FREIDENREICH, Associate Professor of History at Temple University, is the author of *The Jews of Yugoslavia* and has published numerous articles on twentieth-century Viennese and Yugoslav Jewries. She teaches modern Jewish history, East European history, and European women's history.